P9-BAU-858

1939
The Lost World of the Fair

DAVID GELERNTER

AVON BOOKS ◆ NEW YORK

Any resemblance between the characters in the fictional parts of this book and actual people, living or dead, is unintended and accidental.

AVON BOOKS
A division of
The Hearst Corporation
1350 Avenue of the Americas
New York, New York 10019

Copyright © 1995 by David Gelernter
Cover art by John Cruz based on a stamp from Culver Pictures, Inc.
Published by arrangement with The Free Press
Library of Congress Catalog Card Number: 95-4137
ISBN: 0-380-72748-X

The Free Press edition contains the following Library of Congress Cataloging in Publication Data:
Gelernter, David Hillel.
    1939, the lost world of the Fair/David Gelernter.
        p.   cm.
Includes index.
1. New York World's Fair (1939-1940)—History.   I. Title.
T785.B1G45   1995   95-4137
909.82'074'747243—dc20   CIP

First Avon Books Trade Printing: May 1996

Printed in the U.S.A.

OPM 10 9 8 7 6 5 4 3 2

For my Jane
and the
blessed memory
of our grandmothers

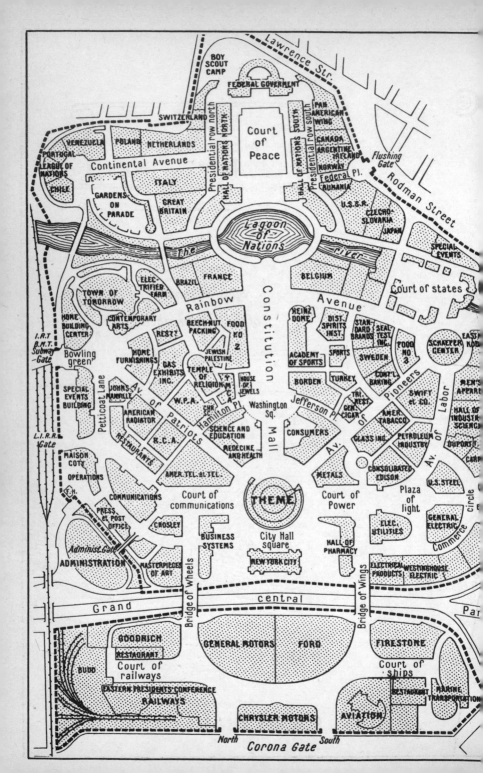

1939 NEW YORK WORLD'S FAIR

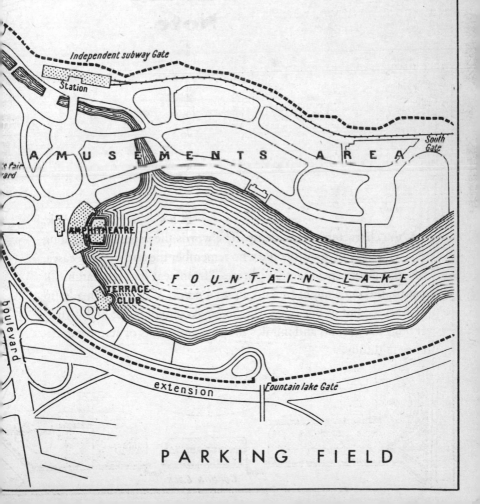

Independent subway Gate

Station

AMUSEMENTS AREA

South Gate

AMPHITHEATRE

FOUNTAIN LAKE

TERRACE CLUB

boulevard

extension

Fountain lake Gate

PARKING FIELD

Author's
Note

This is a history book, but the characters are made up. The words they speak reflect long discussions with many people who remember the fair; in some cases, my characters speak actual phrases "from real life" verbatim. Of course the same might be said, up to a point, of nearly all made-up characters; but in this book, the fictional content is not high-flying. It hugs the ground and mimics the dips and peaks of actual experience faithfully.

Contents

CONTENTS

CONTENTS

Preface

Although my book relies mainly on the literature of the fair's own age, I have benefited enormously from other modern books. The mandatory starting point for any study of the fair is the collection of essays edited by Helen Harrison, *Dawn of a New Day*. I find the pieces by Joseph Cukser, Eugene Santomasso and Helen Harrison herself particularly good, but the entire set is valuable. Next, three books largely devoted to photographs. My text doesn't cite them, but anyone who cares about the fair will want to look at all three: *The New York World's Fair 1939/40,* arranged, introduced and annotated by Stanley Appelbaum and published by Dover; Zim, Lerner and Rolfes' *The World of Tomorrow,* published by Harper and Row; and Cohen, Heller and Chwast's *Trylon and Perisphere,* published by Abrams.

Several other modern books are particularly important: the collection of essays on both New York fairs ('39 and '64), *Remembering the Future,* published by Rizzoli and the Queens Museum; Robert Caro's magisterial biography of Robert Moses, *The Power Broker;* Robert Rydell's *World of Fairs.* I confess to finding Rydell's book consistently tendentious (no doubt he'd think the same of mine), but I learned a lot from it. A collection of scholarly essays edited by Joseph Corn, *Imagining Tomorrow,* contains much of interest to fair enthusiasts, and Warren Susman's anthology *Culture and Commitment, 1929–1945* is an excellent starting point for any study of the fair's cultural context. Stern, Gilmartin and Mellins' *New York 1930* is an indispensable (if dryish) reference; it's a shame the book weighs as much as a grand piano, because it deserves to be read. (Suggestion: re-issue it in several volumes, or throw in a free winch.) My book cites only a tiny fraction of the vast and growing literature on twentieth-century American culture, but of the books I do cite, three are so useful and beautiful that they demand special mention and a round of applause: Martin Greif's *Depression Modern,* Stephen Whitfield's *American Space, Jewish Time,* and John Mueller's *Astaire Dancing.*

The extensive period literature on New York and its fair is for its part no mere mess of museum pieces. Books like Cecil Beaton's *Cecil Beaton's New York* (1938), E. Stewart Fay's *Londoner's New York* (1936), Marjorie Hillis's *New York, Fair or No Fair* (1939) and Riesenberg and Alland's *Portrait of New York* (1939) are consistently interesting, beautifully written and unjustly forgotten. A. J. Liebling, James Thurber and E. B. White are as fresh and compelling today as they were in 1939.

My goal in this book is to convey something of what the fair was like. Any reader would be justified in hypothesizing that a 300-page book about a (mere) world's fair must be *the* comprehensive, exhaustive account—but actually, I regret that I have had to leave a great deal out. I'm certain that some readers who were actually there will feel that "I can't believe he doesn't talk about *that*! That was the best part of the whole damned thing!" But today as in 1939 the fair presents any visitor with an embarrassment of riches, and he is forced to pick and choose. My discussion in the last chapter of the fair's origins and history up through opening day might easily (in fact) have expanded, had I let it, into a book in itself. The fair is fascinating, its cultural context and its history are fascinating, and moreover the whole story was chronicled in blow-by-blow detail by newspapers and magazines and the Fair Corporation itself. A book of this type *must* leave interesting things out; I only hope not too many readers will find their favorite bits missing.

Many people have contributed generously to this project.

I've talked with a great number of people about their memories of the fair, and some were willing to lend me photographs and memorabilia as well. A few have been particularly crucial to the whole production, and the book could never have been written without their help: Ernest Schwartz, Arthur Nowick, Richard Backus, Melvin Halbert, Walter Chestnut, Sona Ekizian and John Ekizian.

Chris Hatchell helped with every aspect of the book from start to finish, particularly with the constant far-flung research demands a book like this presents; I could never have done it without him. Judith Gelernter assisted with key aspects of the research as well.

Several people helped me improve the manuscript. My long-suffering editor Susan Arellano (the author happens not to be the easiest guy in the world to edit) and my friend and literary seer Barbara Harshav; Myron Magnet, who gave me valuable suggestions about the "Dynamite" chapter; Susan Llewellyn. Needless to say, the stubborn peculiarities that remain are not their fault.

The Yale Department of Computer Science in particular and the university in general, with its matchless libraries and archives, are ideal places for scientific and scholarly work. Whatever the quality of the finished product, the fact that a book like this could roll out of a computer science department seems to me to speak volumes about why a university is such a good idea in the first place.

I'm grateful, finally, to the small cast of characters that makes the whole enterprise possible. To the medical people who are continuing with superb painstaking skill to stitch me back together, particularly Marcia Dymarczyck and Doctors Spinelli, Caprioli and Glore; to Martin and Beverly Schultz; to Rabbi Benjamin Scolnic for his continuing friendship and support; to Lenore Zuck; to Nick Carriero, Soledad Morales and my family. And of course, none of it could ever work without my boys and Jane.

1

Prologue: The Center of Time

We remember our best citizens. We mourn their deaths and celebrate their achievements. I don't know why we should not mourn and celebrate our best eras the same way. Consider, then, the tail end of the 1930s in the nation's first city.

It was an era in which New York City reveled in the beauty of the brand-new things it had made: New Yorkers would have mentioned the "towering shaft of the R.C.A. building" in Rockefeller Center first, I think, even before the Empire State Building. "If that doesn't make you catch your breath," says a charming and chatty 1939 guidebook, "you might as well go home." They might have mentioned Paul Manship's *Prometheus* at the foot of the RCA Building, or "the splendid example of the sheer beauty of form following function," as a 1937 picture book puts it, "the loveliness of naked steel and cable" that is the brand-new George Washington Bridge. The thirties produced an unprecedented and never-equaled explosion of color in the city: a skyscraper tiled in aquamarine, a lobby mosaicked in blues, golds and vermilions, the Rainbow Room atop the RCA building, where "a color organ throws shifting patterns on a reflecting dome," Radio City Music Hall, where concentric semicircles framing the huge stage may be lit up in any desired sequence of vivid colors by a "color orchestrator" behind a switchboard.

This New York was reputedly the best-governed city in the nation. Fiorello La Guardia had been elected on a Fusion ticket in 1933. New York's had been, said one unsentimental insider, a government of "dumb bunnies, playboys and crooks." La Guardia promised to close the book on all that. He did. "To the victor belongs the responsibility for good government" reads the epigraph he ordered for *New York Advancing,* the city's official self-portrait. La Guardia had a vision that bothered and possessed him—of a city absolutely honest and absolutely decent. "I shall not rest until my native city is the first not only in population but also in wholesome housing; not only in commerce but also in public health; until it is not only out of debt but abounding in happiness." He squashed corruption, ran the country's largest public-housing program, oversaw Parks Commissioner Robert Moses' gigantic public works enterprise. He pursued the nation's best experts relentlessly until they gave up and joined his administration. And he made New York the capital of the New Deal. "Our Mayor is the most appealing man I know," said President Roosevelt of La Guardia. "He comes to Washington and tells me a sad story. The tears run down my cheeks and the tears run down his cheeks and the first thing I know he's wangled another $50 million."

PROLOGUE: THE CENTER OF TIME

La Guardia, who was half Jewish, campaigned mainly in English, Italian, and Yiddish but was said to have four other languages in reserve should the need arise. His antics were famous. Robert Moses listed them in his memorial essay after La Guardia's death. Not all were harmless or endearing, but they show the mayor to be the rarest of political rarities, a man of principle and a passionate original. "Crucifying a market inspector for accepting a cheap necktie from a pushcart peddler, acting as a committing magistrate to pillory a welfare inspector who did a favor for somebody on relief . . . driving the gay hurdy-gurdies from the streets . . . directing traffic, laying out airports, acting as impresario of the City Center." He smashed confiscated slot machines with a sledgehammer. He rushed off to fires in a motorcycle sidecar—helped rescue a fireman, once, who was pinned under a fallen beam. He conducted the Sanitation Department Band at Carnegie Hall: No special treatment necessary, he told the stage manager, "just treat me like Toscanini." When a strike stopped delivery of the city's newspapers, he took to the airwaves to read the Sunday comics over WNYC, the city-owned radio station. Two generations later, New Yorkers of that era still vividly remember him doing it.

New York City worked, to its fingertips. "When she sees uncollected garbage on the street," A. J. Liebling reported of a "vast, scolding, chuckling mulatto woman" who lived in Harlem, "she calls up the Commissioner of Sanitation. 'Don't give me no underlin's or subordinates,' she says. 'Give me the Commissioner. This is Pearl Hankinson speaking.'" No, the city was not immaculate, but standards were high and the government was accountable. "New York City," a 1939 *Harper's* magazine smugly informed the nation, "happens to be one of the communities in the United States where good

government is measured by getting a great deal for your money.''
Even the terrace cafeteria in the Central Park Zoo was first-rate, and
you could count on the service and the food being excellent and the
prices reasonable, because the zoo was after all ''under the direction
of the Mr.-Moses-Managed Department of Parks'' (according to the
travel guide). Need we say more? Robert Moses and his New York
Parks Department were world famous. Not only had the parks commissioner built beaches, highways, the Triborough and Bronx–
Whitestone Bridges and dozens more engineering masterpieces,
he'd also seen to it that Battery Park in Lower Manhattan was ''kept
spick-and-span . . . with benches and a minute spotless cafeteria,''
no less, ''surrounded with parasols and tables in the summer.'' And
by the way, don't try any funny stuff, another guide book cautioned;
New York was the ''best policed city in the world.'' ''One may walk
the streets for years,'' an English visitor observed, ''without seeing
anything more criminal than the solicitation of alms or the manifes-
tations of inebriation.''

Transportation was much on people's minds. It was the Streamlined
Age. Manhattan had, in Grand Central and Pennsylvania Station,
the two most magnificent rail stations in America. It had crosstown
streetcars on Forty-second Street, three subway and two elevated
lines and a Downtown Skyport, where seaplanes debarked Wall
Street–bound commuters. New York's was the greatest port in the
world. ''A dark blotch appears, takes form—an anchored tramp:
coffee from Brazil, rubber from Sumatra, bananas from Costa Rica.''
One fine day in 1937 saw the *Europa, Rex, Normandie, Georgic* and
Berengaria, among them four of the world's six largest ships, drawn
up side by side along the Manhattan waterfront at a row of extralong
piers newly constructed by the Department of Docks. ''The City is

ever vigilant to retain and enhance the importance and the desirability of New York's natural harbor," *New York Advancing* explained. Ocean liners provided wonderful opportunities for seeing people off and meeting them. If it happened to be December 17, 1935, George Gershwin would be arriving home from Mexico, and not only reporters and photographers but the entire company of *Porgy and Bess* would be turned out at the dock.

New York was a city of ethnic neighborhoods and its citizens enjoyed them. They condescended to but unabashedly admired them. "Harlem," for example said the picture book, "a name that is world famous. . . . Here you will find an exuberant, an exultant, a frenzied gaiety as the merry dancers go 'Stompin' at the Savoy' or 'Lindy Hoppin' . . . White folks are frequent visitors—observing, admiring or dancing." ("Maybe real Communists steered clear of Webster Hall," Mary McCarthy mused, "just as ordinary black people did not go to the Savoy on those Friday nights when so many white people came.") "Don't go to Harlem unless you have an escort," cautions the guidebook. "Not because it's dangerous, but because it will be dull."

"They feel that the white world is taking advantage of them," Liebling reported matter-of-factly about the residents of a certain overstuffed Harlem block. Birthrates in this "greatest Negro metropolis of the world" (as a newsreel called it) were among the city's lowest. This particular block happened to be, nonetheless, the most densely populated in the United States. In some cases half a dozen married couples shared one apartment and its single bathroom. And yet "people maintain the forms of politeness." Standards were high.

New York had the tallest building in the country, and also the second-, third-, fourth-, fifth- and sixth-tallest. It was by far the greatest manufacturing city in the United States. Fifty percent of all U.S. foreign trade passed through its port. Then as now New York was restaurant capital of the nation. New Yorkers ate roughly what they do now, with the occasional odd twist: a hearty tomato sandwich—spiked with frilly toothpicks—for lunch, or sliced eggs with mushroom sauce. Most Chinese restaurants were down-market, the chop suey joints of Edward Hopper's hard, lonely paintings. Chinatown bustled as it does today, but shop windows and doors were plastered with STOP JAPANESE AGGRESSION signs. (Japan was a source not of cars, certainly not of restaurants, but of delicate paper flowers that unfolded out of seashells dropped in water.) "Beigels" were confined to pushcarts on the Lower East Side, still home in that era to closely packed hordes of first-generation Jewish immigrants. The Lower East Side was a neighborhood much like Harlem, but less fashionable.

New York had three major league baseball teams, eight "major" daily newspapers and the largest theater in the world. The biggest of those eight newspapers, the *Daily News,* boasted better than twice the circulation of the second-largest U.S. paper. The top of the journalistic food chain was a matter of exquisite balance between the liberal *Times* and the conservative *Herald Tribune.* The well-informed gorged on both every morning. The *Times* was larger, but the *Trib,* discerning readers agreed, was better written and edited. And that theater, Radio City Music Hall, had in addition to its color orchestrator the world-famous precision-dancing Rockettes: "Their triumph at the Paris 1937 Exposition was deserved, inevitable," the picture book announces offhandedly, but you can hear the smirk.

PROLOGUE: THE CENTER OF TIME

Today's triumphs and distinctions are spread out, one might argue, more equitably around the country. But that is not the point. Today no such nation-dominating pinnacle as 1939 New York exists. It is not there for its residents, or, more important, for the country at large, as an irresistible lure for ambitious young people ("the literary genius of Aurora High School, the prettiest actress in the Burlington dramatic club, a farm boy hoping to start for Wall Street"), as a tourist destination, a model and an ideal. When you were talking about U.S. cities, New York was *it*.

New York in 1939 had its own style of life, and the nation as a whole admired, copied and enjoyed it. Once they experience The Great White Way, "visitors sometimes wonder if New Yorkers really begin to live only at dark, or if they work all day and play all night . . . The glamor of Broadway radiates across the country . . . Times Square has been called the center of the world." Broadway in this era meant not only the theater but Tin Pan Alley, the center of the popular music business in an age when business was good. The Broadway area at night looked like "an incredible scene in the movies," says the guidebook, "its streets packed with people and lighted by millions of twinkling lights." Movies of that era were not filmed in New York, but from *The Jazz Singer* (which officially inaugurated the talkie age) and *Forty-Second Street* (first "modern" musical) onward, they were often set there. New Yorkers went to the movies in droves, even the children of Harlem—who "attend neighborhood movie houses after school when they can assemble the price of admission—which is surprisingly often."

What of the *feel* of that city, though? Wasn't it, when all's said, basically the same as it is today?

Of course the *look* was different. Skyscrapers grew narrower in stages as they went higher. Thirties New York was a city of dingy white four-square upended telescopes, no plain boxes, no sheer walls of glass. There was an antique fussiness to the incidental details: the wrought-iron street-light standards, like candy canes with curlicue decorations. The one-way signs in the shape of arrows. Traffic lights came in green and red only, with a lights-off pause instead of yellow. A 1939 photo showed a small herd of cattle standing in steadfast glumness on an ordinary concrete sidewalk in midtown Manhattan, a few blocks east of the looming Chrysler Building. First Avenue in this part of the city was a long string of slaughterhouses; New Yorkers called it Blood Alley. No doubt horses traipsed past the beef. Delivery vans and milk trucks were horse-drawn. And so on: A catalog of physical differences between that city and today's would go on for pages.

But all the same. Then as now the shops had awnings for hot summer days "to spread the agreeable shade, the rectangles of relief sketched on the sidewalk," as E. B. White puts it. Out at the World's Fair grounds the breeze might be said to be "stirring the leaves' cool fragrance and blowing prisms in the mist over the fountains." Has anything *really* changed?

Yes.

Roger Starr, in *The Rise and Fall of New York City,* presents two intriguing pairs of incidents. The first centers on colossal disputes between the city and powerful labor unions. In 1946 New Yorkers united behind Mayor William O'Dwyer in his call for a bit of civic sacrifice, and the city got what it needed. In 1966 Mayor John Lindsay, under similar circumstances, was more-or-less ignored. In 1965 the whole city was blacked out, with no special consequences; a blackout in 1977 saw gangs of looters take to the streets. Starr plausibly chalks up the contrasting responses to a gradual collapse of the city's civic spirit. But I believe there was something broader and deeper at work at the same time, something that transcends the relationship between the city and its citizens.

Something that accounts not only for the modern city's inability to draw together when it needs to, but also for the unmistakable strangeness to our ears of 1939's way of expressing itself. I don't mean that it used phrases we have dropped, although of course it did—"It's the smartest hat," "those companionable young ladies," "over Brooklyn [not *the* Brooklyn] Bridge." I refer to something more like a tone of voice:

> We seek to present here an accurate picture of New York City's administration . . . The idea of politically selected or politically influential persons heading these important specialized departments has been discarded, and I believe the results warrant the assertion that the old system will never return.

This is Mayor La Guardia writing in *New York Advancing,* and the strange foreign note you hear is *authority.*

"No matter the year, no matter the field, if you start in business you need three things: a stout heart; an honest mind; the ability to add and subtract." An ad for Mimeograph Duplicators in *Life* magazine, but it strikes a pose that 1939 knew well, the authoritative pose. In October 1940 conscription cranked back into life, and the army exhibited the layout of its new processing centers. Draftees who flunked the physical got to change back into civvies, and in the army's plan, the rejects' changing room is labeled "Rejects' Changing Room." The army did not propitiate. It possessed, and spoke with, authority. At Robert Moses' wildly popular Jones Beach State Park on Long Island, the flag was lowered by uniformed staff to the strains of the National Anthem every evening, while "every bather, picnicker, stroller, game player, and onlooker within hearing stands at attention facing toward the flag as it slowly descends into the arms of the color guard." Even assuming that the June 1939 issue of *American Home* was overoptimistic by 100 percent—that actually only half of all beachgoers stood spontaneously to attention—what emerges is (to our eyes) a strange picture. But authority inhered in the flag.

The newsreels bristled with authority. "Throughout the land countless private organizations are attacking the youth problem on a scale greater than ever before; their object—to provide young people with the recreation, guidance and fellowship so necessary to the making of good citizens." "The peddling of obscene books—a furtive and despicable occupation—has become a lucrative sideline for shopkeepers."

The president bristled with authority. He addressed the left-leaning American Youth Congress on the White House lawn. "It has been said that some of you are Communists." Indulgent smile. "That is a *very unpopular* term today." Another indulgent smile. Not a "relating to" or "sharing with" but an *indulgent* smile. "As Americans you have a *right*—a *legal* and *constitutional right*—to call yourselves Communists, those of you who do. You have a right peacefully and openly to advocate certain ideals of *theoretical* communism. But as Americans you have not only a *right* but a *sacred duty* to confine your advocacy of changes in law to the methods prescribed by the *Constitution* of the *United States.*" Authority inhered not only in the president but in adulthood itself.

It is easy to assert that this physicist or that journalist speaks with authority today. Authority still lingers in small pockets here and there. But those are tidal pools; the grand sweep of ocean is far away. Power remains today just as it always has, but not authority. Authority has all but vanished. Its disappearance from American life is just as significant an event, I believe, as the closing of the frontier.

PROLOGUE: THE CENTER OF TIME

Authority in 1939 New York was vested, of course, in the country's powerful and popular president. It was vested in Mayor La Guardia, Parks Commissioner Moses, renowned pastor Dr. Harry Emerson Fosdick of Riverside Church, Columbia University's eminent president, Nicholas Murray Butler; and in teachers, priests, rabbis and ministers throughout the city, in the *Herald Tribune* and the *New York Times,* in mothers and in fathers. Authority was vested in the cop on the beat, even in the railway conductor on his rounds. In a novel of the 1930s, the young train-traveling female narrator anticipates no unwelcome advances, because conductors on this line were always so "strict." Authority was a free pass entitling the bearer within reasonable limits to be obeyed or believed, as the situation warranted. Among other things, the existence of those free passes allowed ordinarily skeptical, sophisticated people to suspend their native incredulity every once in a while and, within bounds of reason, to believe what they were told.

And that takes us to the World's Fair, an event that cannot be understood unless we reconstruct what "authority" was and what it meant. Because that fair was above all *authoritative.* It ran for two years. In 1940 fairgoers at the most popular exhibit on the grounds, General Motors' Futurama, were addressed from "the future" by a deep, portentous narrator's voice: "Man has forged ahead since 1940. New and better things have sprung from his industry and genius."

New and better things have sprung from his industry and genius. Fairgoers on the whole credited the deep, portentous voice, which turned out, after all, to be speaking truth; and they were pleased at what it had to say. Not because they were more innocent or more credulous or less sophisticated than we. They weren't.

Rather because the voice spoke with authority: The whole fair did. And authority, once upon a time, meant a great deal indeed.

The fair epitomized late-thirties New York. It thrilled and enthralled the city.

The interesting thing about Wanamaker's department store in Lower Manhattan was that you could see all the way out to the fair from its lunchroom. The great thing about the brand-new Triborough Bridge was that it connected Manhattan to Long Island and the fair. The title of the Manhattan picture book I have cited is *New York, the World's Fair City*. The guidebook is called *New York, Fair or No Fair. New York Advancing* was reprinted in a "World's Fair Edition." The fair's theme structures were a towering three-sided obelisk and a great sphere, side by side. Those structures, the Trylon and the Perisphere—"the somewhat too familiar Trylon and Perisphere," as the guidebook has it—appeared everywhere, all over the country, on advertisements and road maps, Remington portable typewriters and Bissell carpet sweepers, RCA radios and Kodak cameras, children's games, women's print dresses and untold thousands of souvenir doodads. "Building the World of Tomorrow" was the fair's theme. "All the World of Tomorrow's a stage," mused James Thurber moodily. "The World of Tomorrow is my oyster . . . The World of Tomorrow and Tomorrow and Tomorrow creeps in this petty pace from day to day." The fair was so ubiquitous, it drove grumpy people crazy.

The fairgrounds were in Queens, the easternmost borough of New York City, at the base of Long Island. Adequate provision had been made for getting there from downtown. You could drive if you really wanted to: There was parking space for 35,000 cars. The BMT, IRT and the new Independent subway line went to the fair.

PROLOGUE: THE CENTER OF TIME

Fifth Avenue buses ran to the fair. Special city buses left Fiftieth Street for the fair. Grayline tour buses and several private bus services ran to the fair. You could get there from Brooklyn on the Flushing-Ridgewood trolley. There were boat services from Manhattan. And, most of the day, Long Island Rail Road trains left every ten minutes for a new, specially constructed World's Fair station from Pennsylvania Station on Seventh Avenue. What a ride that must have been! Penn Station was a magnificent granite-and-marble building two city blocks long. You entered a monumental waiting room where the mere pedestals on which the columns stood were taller than you: a vast sculpted block of air crossed by sun shafts, barely stirred by the busy throngs buzzing round its floor. But that waiting room was just a warm-up for one of the most stupendous spaces ever conceived, the steel-and-glass concourse. It was roofed in intersecting rows of glass-paneled barrel vaults, like a stylized forest far overhead; open stairways led majestically down to the tracks. Charles Follen McKim's masterpiece was destroyed in 1963 in a last desperate act of violence by a railroad sinking inexorably into ruin. In 1939 trains for the fair cost ten cents and they got you there in ten minutes. What a ride!

As early as 1936, an out-of-towner's innocent remark that he was planning a visit to New York City made E. B. White suspect that his goal was the fair. The fair was *big*. People came from all over the world to see it. One man hitchhiked from Detroit in four days in a frenzy of anticipation. Two young Massachusetts girls struck out for the fairgrounds with $1.70 between them. (The police were asked to scrounge them up and send them home.) Romances blossomed there; ask any fair veteran to reminisce, and chances are you will hear about a couple who became engaged on the grounds. It happened all the time. "The New York World's Fair," the guidebook proclaims, "as everybody knows, by now, is so stupendous, gigantic, super-magnificent a greatest-show-on-earth that one could write a whole book about it, and a great many people have." Tongue in cheek, but just slightly.

What did this fair amount to? Why read a book about it, or write one? What *was* the New York World's Fair? Merely the "greatest show of all time." More than half a century later, that *Time* magazine boast still stands. The New York World's Fair was "the biggest, costliest, most ambitious undertaking ever attempted in the history of international exhibitions . . . A spectacle of surprising beauty and magnificence . . . The miracle wrought by Grover Whalen's armies" (the *New York Times*). (Whalen was president of the Fair Corporation, its chief spokesman and number one booster. He was fascinating and colorful in his own right—a former commie-hating, speakeasy-busting New York police commissioner who served for decades as the city's unpaid "official greeter," in which office he established the ticker-tape parade as a Manhattan institution.) New York's fair was "the most stupendous exposition the world has ever known," according to the newsreels, "the greatest peacetime project ever undertaken," and it was "revolutionary in its contrast to other Fairs" (*Harper's*). Furthermore, noted *Harper's,* "in a world swept by terror and hysteria and an unparalleled preparation for war, sixty nations have participated in the Fair . . . no other fair has ever had anywhere near so great an international participation."

The fair was the first ever "to attempt building itself on a constructive world concept"—it had a coherent world view to put across, in a series of official "focal exhibits" and the famous theme show inside the Perisphere. Buildings at the fair (according to an architecture journal) "reached an entirely new degree of fluidity." On a walk around the grounds you would discover "the liveliest, gayest, most spectacular adventure in pigments, lights, murals and plastics since man first began to mix paint." And "man," by the way, "in his efforts to awe himself, has never hit upon a thing so fantastic and yet beautiful as the great fountain which rises from the Lagoon of Nations." It's hardly surprising that half of all fairgoers who gave opinions to a group of survey takers "used superlatives for their appreciation—'wonderful,' 'perfect,' etc." It had to be that way; "New York cannot get away with a second-rate world fair," La Guardia had explained while planning was still at the early stages. "This fair must be something perfect, something no other city has. So much more is expected of us than other cities." ("His Italian vigour tends to deprive him of his dignity sometimes," wrote the foreign visitor who noted down his words on this occasion, "but that is not so important as it would be in London.") The fair's was "a fabulous history" that was destined to "become a part of American folk legend." (The *New York Times* again, on closing day).

I have talked to people who went to the fair only once but were struck by the experience and still vividly remember some of the details. I have met people who visited nearly forty times. I have encountered people who were inspired to make their careers by what they saw there, and others who keep extensive, lovingly preserved collections of the brochures and souvenirs they took home. "There was never another fair like it," one of them says simply. I have heard of people who acquired "a new view of the world" at the fair, and people who, decades later, thought of their visits there as the most exciting days they had ever spent; people who visited when they were young but referred to the fair constantly all their lives. New York dominated the country in 1939; New York was accustomed to the biggest, newest and best, and it was enchanted by the fair. The fair mesmerized New York the way New York mesmerized the nation. To understand the United States of America in the late 1930s, you have no choice. You must see the fair.

In that small slice of time and space, the city and its vast visiting crowds enjoyed what might be the best gift of all—to glimpse and yet not possess the promised land.

Mrs. Hattie Levine is representative of the many people with whom I have talked who remember the fair. She is seventy-five and has young-adult memories of the event. She lives alone in a large, sunny apartment on a corner of Fifth Avenue in the sixties: She was born wealthy and is still wealthy. She has gray hair streaked with white, and her face is lined. She projects authority. Her life has something to do with the fair in a personal sense—is somehow intertwined with it—but that is important for my purposes only because it has served to fix the fair itself with special vividness in her memories.

"Indeed it was remarkable," she tells me. "First, it was huge. And the grounds were dominated by the great sphere and the obelisk at the center, the Trylon, so-called, and the Perisphere. My clearest memory of the place is the blazing white Trylon and Perisphere—you had to squint at them, it hurt your eyes to look at them when you were up close on a bright day—against a brilliant cloudless sky." The Trylon was a slender three-sided pylon 610 feet tall (a good 50 feet higher than the Washington Monument), and the Perisphere was 180 feet across. Picture an eighteen-story building, some actual, particular building, if you will; that is the Perisphere's height, and it was essentially an empty shell. As you can imagine, it was big inside: twice the size of Radio City Music Hall. The two theme structures side by side in their poised, perfectly balanced monumental whiteness—the Perisphere seeming as if a gentle push might set it rolling away—look like nothing else that ever was. "The fair had a remarkable mood and feel to it. At least for us. It was an air of . . . how should I say . . . ?" She pauses. "I don't want to lapse into rosy romanticism. I'm skeptical of it. But what I *want* to say is, acute hope."

PROLOGUE: THE CENTER OF TIME

It opened on April 30, 1939, and ran through October. The first season was a critical and popular success: a late-August survey of fairgoers found that 83 percent liked it "very much" and 84 percent wanted to go again. Of Americans who stayed away, most wanted to go—less than 10 percent didn't—but couldn't afford to. A different survey suggests that most visitors liked the fair a lot, some loved it, some were outright fanatic about it. In October 1939 over three-quarters of fairgoers had come before, and nearly a third were on their fifth visit at least. Among this last group were "many who had made from 20 to 100 visits."

But times were tough. The fair was an expensive day out, not even counting the costs of reaching New York and putting up there. Attendance never came close to expectations. It cost seventy-five cents just to get in. One sixteen-year-old, who was inspired to become a mechanical engineer by what he saw at the fair, searched for bottles in the Bronx and paid his admission with the accumulated deposits. (Years later "he could still describe the rivet points" that had been used in the construction of some of the buildings.) Of course you would have paid eighty-seven cents just to get into Roseland in Manhattan and dance for a few hours—but the fair was expensive all through, not only at the gate. "The nickel is a coin no one recognizes at the Fair," *Harper's* complained. "Even bus rides round the Fair cost a dime. . . . Hot dogs and hamburgers are all a dime." The complaint wasn't strictly true; the fair's eight-page daily newspaper cost a nickel. But that was two cents more than the *New York Times*. Admission went down to fifty cents in October, and the board decided on a less expensive and, into the deal, less-high-minded approach for the 1940 season. The official theme became "For Peace and Freedom" instead of "Building the World of Tomorrow," and there were many other small changes. The gates reopened again in May and closed forever on October 27, 1940. The fair died bankrupt.

The Nazis invaded Poland on September 1, 1939. The Russians invaded Finland in November 1939. In June 1940 Paris fell. The Battle of Britain raged throughout the late summer. When the fair opened, Winston Churchill was an eccentric, "a flagrant opportunist" (according to *Life* magazine) well past his prime. When it closed, his promise "not to flag or fail"—"we shall fight on the beaches, we shall fight on the landing grounds, we shall fight in the fields and in the streets, we shall fight in the hills; we shall never surrender"— these most memorable and defining words of the twentieth century were famous all over the world.

The fair *was* huge. "Three and a half miles long, and, in many places, a mile wide," says a Greyhound advertising brochure, also noting that the fairgrounds cover 1,216½ acres. The thirties are mesmerized by numbers. The site had been a particularly foul garbage dump—"a miserable meandering tidal backwater," says the 1940 *Official Guide Book,* mincing no words, "a pestilential eyesore"— before the summer day in 1936 when work began. The tidal backwater bred mosquitoes, and the rest of the place had been covered with the leavings of the Brooklyn Ash Removal Company, heaped into towering, grotesque ash mountains. At the groundbreaking a succession of officials—La Guardia and Moses included —delivered grand speeches about the wonders in the making, after which the Queens borough president politely noted that if the Fair Corporation merely cleaned out the mosquitoes, it would be all right with him. Then La Guardia hopped onto a steam shovel, scooped a big, enthusiastic load of dirt and praised the delicacy of the controls.

PROLOGUE: THE CENTER OF TIME

Was the fair full of hope? The thirties were, for most Americans, the worst years of the century. By 1939 the economy was back on its feet, though just barely; but few Americans were so naive as not to feel threatened by the approach of another world war, even if they believed the U.S. could stay out of it. Only a few years back, long shuffling lines of unemployed men and women had been an everyday sight at local relief stations. In 1939 Americans believed, according to a Gallup poll, that staying out of war was the nation's most urgent need. At Princeton a tongue-in-cheek student organization called Veterans of Future Wars caught on and spread quickly to colleges all over the country. The past was grim and the future uncertain at best. The brilliance of New York at the decade's close was a temporary thing and people knew it, as if the whole city had bustled momentarily into a shaft of sunlight on the floor of Penn Station's monumental waiting room, and knew implicitly that it would be bustling right back out again soon. Ephemerality may have intensified the era's beauty, as it does autumn's.

I ask Mrs. Levine what she means by "acute hope."

When I put a question, her gaze abstracts and her head tilts away as she ponders before answering.

"I'll give you an example. The General Motors building was, as I recall, close to one of the entrances. The Futurama ride was in the General Motors building. It was a big building, and you filed in through a tall, narrow slit. Like a cleft in a cliff. I think the cleft was bright red. The rest of the facade was silver. Two serpentine ramps led up to the slit—it was always mobbed, and you waited in line on one of the ramps."

An aerial photograph shows a long facade—low at one end, high and curled forward at the other. The letters *GM* flank the cleft and the ramps enter between them. Each waiting line is hundreds of yards long. "At General Motors the crowd was decoratively the making of the building," according to a 1940 issue of *Architectural*

Record, "giving life, brilliant color, and motion to the snaked ramps against the blank cliff-like wall."

"I remember the GM, those flanking letters." She breaks off and looks out the window at the gray tangle of branches rimming Central Park across the street. "You know, it would have been in the fifties. Mid-fifties. I was visiting the Bronx Zoo. The tractor-drawn trains of carts that took visitors around the fair had been given to the zoo. I hadn't realized it. I came up a slope and at the top, suddenly, it was passing right in front of me—unmistakable. In orange and blue. And the horn played a snatch of the 'Sidewalks of New York.' I was so startled. . . . The person accompanying me asked in his kindly, clinical way if anything was wrong."

She is silent a moment.

"The letters on the General Motors building, yes; they were stylish and understated. Silver on silver. The first time, you couldn't wait to get in. The excitement built as you approached that tall dramatic cleft. You see: As you inch closer and make your way up the gentle slope of the ramp, here is this huge red-and-silver facade towering over you, and the line behind is a sea of bobbing hats—a happy crowd. The future at that point had none of the ominous crazy-robot overtones it does today. You could see the Trylon and Perisphere as you waited on line, and your eyes were drawn there again and again. They were already such well-known forms—as if a famous movie star were behind you on line. And you inched forward." She pauses. "I guess I'm just blathering and not telling you much."

No—I can find the details in books, but the look of the place, the taste and smell of it, are what I want most to grasp.

"Exhaust," she says. "It smelled of exhaust. I have the impression that GM was quite close to the Grand Central Parkway."

Yes it was.

She nods with a slight smile. "Cars were smellier then. And sea air; and you were never far from the smell of hot dogs." (Roughly sixteen million were consumed on the grounds during the fair's two seasons.) "You heard music everywhere. Musicians were stationed in small groups around the grounds. Popular music: swing music. Wail of the clarinet." She stops, evidently imagining it, and smiles. "And the drone of airplanes, it was near the new airport. Planes flew lower then and made a heavy drone like a buzz saw. I can see the traffic on the new Grand Central Parkway extension that went past the fair, those roly-poly hunched-up cars. You moved more slowly then and higher off the ground, you didn't zoom so much as sail along. Looking out through those flat, heavy plates of windshield glass, like crystal."

She pauses—"Mind if I smoke?"—but she is already lighting up. Gazes out the window. Her hands are tan and worn, marked in brown, with prominent knuckles; a shade darker than her face. "I've given up apologizing ages ago." Then murmuring almost under her breath: "Filthy habit. Took it up again the month my husband died.

"Inside"—she clears her throat—"was the Futurama. You stepped first onto a moving platform, then plopped down in a tall, cushioned moving seat, very comfortable—it seemed terribly comfortable in part because your feet ached so from standing on line—and you had the sensation of flying over a diorama of the world of the future." Fairgoers arriving finally at the door to the exhibit shuffled down a switchback ramp—their faces in one photo look more exhausted than eager—into a darkened room. They saw a large map of the United States on the far wall, and the narrator gave a talk about the country's overburdened road network. Then: "General Motors invites you on a tour of future America. The moving chairs below the map will transport you into 1960."

"Specifically," she continues, "the world of 1960. Your chair had its own piped-in sound track with music and narration." The Futurama was one virtuoso piece of thirties engineering. The train of chairs was more than fifteen hundred feet long. Each chair had to travel smoothly and keep level over the twisting and turning, rising, falling track, which was twenty-three feet off the ground at its highest point. But the train's mechanicals were child's play next to the sound system. Proper narration had to be delivered to each passenger, in sync with the passing scenery. No computers, of course, and you needed to maintain physical contact between the central sound source and each continuously moving chair. (How would *you* do it? The Futurama solution is revealed in a later chapter.) The sound track features the emphatic, richly inflected, meticulously e-nun-ci-a-ted, deep-voiced narration popular at the time, with corny organ accompaniment. The sound has the characteristic stale, pickled flavor of the pre-hi-fi age, with high and low frequencies removed and a hissy background.

"The ride just tickled you," she continues. "I was on it, I think, three times despite the enormous waits. You snuggled into the seats. They were partitioned, two seats, then a partition, like a box at the opera, your own private show—and then you got the lovely feeling of eavesdropping from your box seat as you winged it over the futuristic landscape. It tingled your insides and you wanted it not to end. Of course you didn't credit the details, we weren't fools; whether fruit trees would really grow under giant bell jars, whether the highways would be seven lanes each direction—who knew? What mattered was the luminous feeling you got that, come what may, the future had good things in store for you if you persevered.

"The end was enormously clever. The last you saw of the diorama was a particular street intersection of the future, up close. Then the chairs curved round and you got off, the Futurama ride was over—and there you were at that precise intersection, life-sized. It occupied the heart of the GM complex. 'All eyes to the future,' the narrator said."

All eyes to the future. That strange, obsolete tone of voice again, the voice of authority. It dominated the fair.

PROLOGUE: THE CENTER OF TIME

This particular future was designed by Norman Bel Geddes—all the top industrial designers in the country were represented at the fair. It was an age when industrial designers were heroes. Raymond Loewy's dramatic, racy designs for cars, ships, appliances and whatnot, up to and including steam locomotives, were famous. The flamboyant Loewy himself—with his slicked-back hair, tailored mustache, elegant suit and disdainful-imperious smile, he looked like a Spanish nobleman or conceivably a very rich and successful gangster—was a well-known public figure. Loewy was represented at the fair, along with fellow design stars Donald Deskey, Russel Wright, Walter Dorwin Teague and Henry Dreyfuss—Dreyfuss, like Loewy, contributed startlingly streamlined steam locomotives to the design world.

Geddes's Futurama took you on an imaginary flight across America from coast to coast. The landscape in soft greens and browns wasn't based on any actual coast-to-coast slice of the country, but each feature was modeled on a real locale. There were frequent changes of scale, to give you the sensation of swooping down closer or riding higher in your cross-country flight. "You somehow get an almost perfect illusion of flying," *The New Yorker* observed. You encountered cities of the future along the way: Their skyscrapers were thrusting tall boxes with rounded edges and wraparound glass walls, vaguely Miesian. You would call them distinctly "modern" today. A photograph shows several unidentified children—the son and daughter of a GM executive?—wandering around on the set, and the largest skyscrapers are a head taller than a five- or six-year-old. Another photograph shows the customers in their traveling chairs, leaning forward eagerly to peer down through the angled glass window into the futuristic microworld below. (The ladies cross their legs; their skirts just cover the knee.)

You pass fantastic and imaginative details along the way. A suspension bridge hanging from one graceful, central tower. A blimp hangar on a round floating platform that can be pointed in any direction. In an apple orchard "the fruit trees bear abundantly," says the narrator, "under individual glass housings." ("How will the little boy climb it?" asks E. B. White of a glassed-in tree, not getting into the spirit. "Where will the little bird build its nest?" There were a vast number of trees on the Futurama set, only a tiny fraction enclosed in glass. But White's skeptical conservatism is a counterpoint worth hearing.) In the cities, cars and pedestrians circulate separately—cars on the ground, sidewalks one level up; a neat idea that originated with Leonardo da Vinci. "Atomic energy," according to the narrator, "is being used cautiously."

The Futurama's was a gentle utopia, not a perfect but a *comfortable* one. There were big green parks and big amusement parks—"But, what's this just ahead?" the narrator asks. "An amusement park in full swing.... Here's fun and merriment in this world of tomorrow!" One thing the world of tomorrow *didn't* have was churches, and their absence was noted with disapproval. For the 1940 season hundreds were added, and a university. The United States then as now was regarded by its fellow nations as a notably religious place. *"Les Américains, d'esprit profondement réligieux...,"* as a French commentary on the fair had it. But high-tech roads were the Futurama's favorite topic. Superhighways crisscrossed the country and thousands of tiny cars moved along them.

"The effect at the end of the ride," Mrs. Levine continues, "was startling, as if you really had landed in the future, while the illusion lasted—a few seconds, no more; but here is my point. From 1939, 1960 seemed like a brilliant, glittering dream. And looking back, 1960 *was* a brilliant glittering dream. The fair kept its promises. So many of its predictions came true."

We're facing each other in armchairs across a small table by the window. Her voice is crisp bordering on stern, but the eyes are smiling—or almost.

The Futurama was the fair's most popular exhibit by far—"the number 1 hit of the Fair," as a General Motors brochure modestly notes. There were long lines at all hours outside the Futurama, and a fair attendance survey alludes compassionately to the "four-fifths of the people who had come to the Fair and had tried to see it but failed to get in." As the fair's biggest draw, the Futurama was discussed at length in the popular press. The most striking thing about those accounts is what they omit, an aspect of the show so obvious we still barely see it: When Geddes and his people turned their minds to the future, what they saw was *good*. Technology in particular was good. The future in general was good. These themes are repeated over and over at the fair.

We might be tempted to guess that this optimism was a mere corporate come-on, not a true reflection of the mood of the time. That guess won't hold water. The Futurama was General Motors' show, but Geddes's vision lay behind it—and his vision, his career and his pet causes far transcended the profit interests of GM. Nonetheless, suppose we leave the corporate exhibits behind for a moment and go to the heart of the fair.

The fair was no mere anthology of corporate America and its foreign guests. The fair had its own vision, developed by a Theme Committee under Robert Kohn. Kohn had practiced architecture in New York for more than forty years; his specialty was bigness. He designed Manhattan landmarks R. H. Macy's ("World's Largest Store") and, together with Charles Butler and Clarence Stein, Temple Emanu-El on Fifth Avenue, which improbably enough seats more people than Saint Patrick's Cathedral. But he was an authority on low-cost housing and city planning also. Along with Lewis Mumford and others he was cofounder of the Regional Planning Association of America, and he had served as director of housing for the Public Works Administration during the first Roosevelt administration. His Theme Committee produced documents that inspired the Fair Corporation's exhibits—the huge Democracity diorama inside the Perisphere and seven others focused on Transport, Production and Distribution, Food, Communications, Medicine, Science and Community Interests. "The Fair designers could not divide it into such categories as science, art, agriculture, manufactures—the classic divisions of fairs for centuries," Kohn explained. The Theme Committee invented "functional" divisions instead, corresponding to "things with which the average man comes in contact in his everyday life." Like the Futurama and so many other corporate exhibits, the fair's own shows brimmed with optimism. "Peering through the haze of the present toward 1960 is a great adventure," Geddes wrote, and the crowds agreed. A survey discovered that the fair's two biggest, brightest utopian extravaganzas—GM's Futurama and the Theme Committee's Democracity—were fairgoers' first and second favorites.

The fair hired the best artists in the country to decorate its buildings and grounds. Their work brims with optimism; I will discuss it later. The *Times* and the *Trib* both published collections of authoritative essays about the Fair, and the authorities brim with optimism. "The promise of the future is still greater than all the glories of the past," writes David Sarnoff. "I am optimistic for the future," reports Secretary of Commerce Harry Hopkins. "There are big changes ahead for humanity," Charles Kettering argues. "I am a great believer in a wonderful future." If these are mere platitudes, the point is the same: Optimism is in the air. In September 1940 the fair and New York City chose a "typical American boy"—Alfred Roberts, age 12. The closing sentence of his prize-winning essay? "That is why America still has a future."

Is it possible that business leaders and intellectuals, New

Dealers, artists and the typical American boy were optimistic but the public was not? Even though it sought out and savored all that optimism? Possibly yes, probably no. More likely the fair's optimism reflected—maybe amplifying but not distorting and certainly not concocting—a deep strain of optimism among fairgoers themselves. The fair's science director, Gerald Wendt, actually *accuses* the public of being "optimistic"—it is not soberly thoughtful enough for his tastes. A public sour on the future would have found the fair's great ebullient outbursts annoying or even obnoxious, not compelling and exciting and irresistible. In actual fact "there have been hit shows and sporting events in the past which had waiting lines for a few days," Geddes wrote in 1940 of the Futurama, "but never had there been a line as long as this, renewing itself continuously, month after month, as there was every day at the Fair."

Most polls tell us little about deep aspects of the public mood. We learn from Gallup polls that in January 1938 a majority expected the economy to get better, that in August 1939 a still-larger majority agreed. Fine; but that kind of optimism doesn't go to the heart of the matter. Consider instead a Roper poll from the middle of the fair's second season, taken at a moment that ranks with the very darkest in history. During the summer of 1940, with France crushed and England hanging by a thread, this particular survey found more than half the U.S. population predicting an Axis victory in the war; more than two-thirds believed that if the Axis won, the United States would be in danger; almost three-quarters favored immediate reimposition of the draft; almost 90 percent thought that, in response to an Axis victory, the United States should "arm to the teeth at any expense." And a handsome plurality, 43 percent to 36, was optimistic about "the future of civilization"! (The remaining 20 percent didn't know whether it was optimistic or not.) What did that plurality see in those blackest of months that made it, against all odds, optimistic about the future?

Why were the fair and its public optimistic? That optimism is surprising. After all, we hold a much bleaker view today. Our pessimism about the future goes back at least to the early 1970s, when historian Sydney Ahlstrom wrote that "the mythic quality of the American saga has evaporated. The air seems less salubrious, the future more ominous." The tendency remains pronounced. "America today is not the same nation" it used to be, writes author and editor Ellis Cose. "Our confidence has been shaken in any number of spheres and our vulnerability is showing." Cose is reviewing a book called *Divided We Fall* by journalist Haynes Johnson. Johnson is left leaning, but gloom is not restricted to the Left. A recent book by one of the Right's most learned and distinguished scholars is called *On Looking into the Abyss.*

When our own view of the future is neutral or dark, how could the fair's have been so bright? Because today's world is just darker? But our world is incomparably better off than 1939's. The U.S. economy then was still staggering from a blow that makes our modern recessions seem trivial. New technologies then had killed hundreds of thousands in the World War and—immeasurably more terrifying—the Germans had just taken the brand-new technology of aerial bombardment out for a satisfying test drive in Spain. World affairs then were dominated by Hitler, Mussolini, Stalin and the Japanese, and had never seemed grimmer—although in the fair's first year, they were to draw still closer to pitch black with the Hitler-Stalin pact and the long-anticipated outbreak of war.

When the authorities of 1939 wrote about the fair, they did

PROLOGUE: THE CENTER OF TIME

so in full awareness of the world crisis and asserted their optimism in the teeth of it. "Pride and conscience have been profoundly shocked," declared H. G. Wells, "by the black horror produced by race mania, nationalism, economic dogmatism and financial dislocation in recent years." And yet "we are in the darkness before the dawn. . . . Steadily in the near Tomorrow a collective human intelligence will be appearing." "The immediate future of Europe is clouded by the electric storms of today," writes a *New York Times* foreign correspondent, "but of the more distant Tomorrow no one who has looked behind today's sputtering headlines can have much doubt." Her article is called "World of Undying Hope."

The chaotic violence of our cities is frightening and incomprehensible by any standards. But the tense and sometimes violent labor battles of the thirties hardly made for a peaceable decade domestically. And don't forget that in the meantime we have beaten polio (in 1939 the president was a paraplegic) and racked up countless other fundamental medical advances (there were no antibiotics in 1939), have outlawed racial discrimination, have accumulated gigantic, awe-inspiring wealth. If our view of the future is bleaker than 1939's, it cannot be because the world is worse off.

Maybe we just don't buy the pap, pablum and Pollyanification of the Futurama world view any longer because we are simply more sophisticated than the 1939ers. That's a hard proposition to assess. It is true that America, then, was more provincial than it is today. In 1939 the world was shrinking—"The World Grows Smaller" (not to put too fine a point upon it) is a chapter title in a book by Gerald Wendt—"it takes but a day to cross the Atlantic or the continent." Still, that "smaller world" was mammoth next to today's shrunken global community. It is unlikely that a senator would rise today and shout "To hell with Europe and the rest of those nations!" as Senator Schall of Minnesota did in 1935. It is unlikely that anyone today would feel it necessary to explain that "Wines made 'dry' (not sweet)" are called "*table* wines," as a Wines of California magazine ad did in 1939.

But my guess is that Americans today, as a whole, are no more sophisticated than they were then—more likely the opposite. It's true that roughly a fifth of today's public has a college education; in the thirties that figure was around 4 percent. ("Quiet backwaters of a troubled world," a newsreel called 1930s colleges.) On the other hand, our elementary and secondary schools seem to impart considerably less knowledge than the schools of two generations ago. For example, the 1940 sixth-grader evidently knew around 25,000 words, versus 10,000 for the 1990s edition. A large sign at the fair's Du Pont exhibit read, "From Miscellaneous Ores & Inorganic Raw Materials Chemistry Makes . . ." Would any modern exhibit inflict on the public such terms as "miscellaneous ores" or "inorganic raw materials"?

New York in the thirties supported—in addition to those eight major daily newspapers—thirty-five foreign-language dailies (three in Italian and four in Yiddish), the Brooklyn *Daily Eagle* and the Bronx *Home News,* the *Jewish Daily Forward* and sundry others. Magazines thrived too. The population of that era was willing to read. ("*Yessir,* wha'd'ya read?" the newspaper man asked as you walked up.) Radio reached gigantic audiences, and it was a "literary" medium—you listened and imagined. Literacy itself meant more than it does today. A late-thirties movie trailer communicated the fact that its score was full of hit songs by displaying a pile of sheet music. A bit of musicianship was no extraordinary attainment. (To get a bargain on sheet music you went to Union Square, where hawkers peddled it on the sidewalks.)

Consider the intellectual stance of the labor movement at that time. Radio station WEVD—after socialist leader Eugene V. Debs, and still in business today—was New York's "Voice of Labor." One of its most popular offerings was the "University of the Air": "A distinguished volunteer faculty conducts four nightly periods a week." The success of the university was such that transcripts of the on-air lectures were in demand all over the country.

Educated doesn't mean sophisticated, of course. How can we gauge sophistication? "We shall eat the Sandwich of Tomorrow," *The New Yorker* gamely announces, tuning up for the fair. "Sentence of Tomorrow, compiled from the official bulletins: 'The exit from Democracity in the Perisphere is a Helicline.'" Of course *The New Yorker* was no magazine of the people in 1939, any more than it is today. Let's turn instead to the sort of information product that found a mass audience. *Life* is a good example. The way to describe its late-thirties tone is "wry." "Because most pictures of starlets in bathing suits are for the simple but serious business of getting publicity, starlets seldom have to go near the water. Exceptional then is this week's cover picture of . . ." "What Congress most wanted last week was to go home, but several people stood in the way . . . President Roosevelt popped another federal lending program . . ." The tone might be too wiseguy genial for our tastes, but it is no less sophisticated than those we prefer.

We might glance at the era's favorite movies. The wildly popular Rogers-and-Astaire series epitomizes thirties taste and style. Dance films have been big hits in our own epoch—*Saturday Night Fever, Flashdance, Dirty Dancing* and so on. Whatever their merits, you would hardly call them more sophisticated than Rogers and Astaire. *Top Hat* of 1935 was the biggest box-office hit of the series. It parodies the wildly artificial conventions of the dance-film genre: I suffer from an "affliction," Fred tells Ginger; "every once in a while I suddenly find myself dancing." It spoofs studio-lot productions with "Venice" sets that are swirly, deco takeoffs on Venice. Irving Berlin's songs are memorable ("Cheek to Cheek" and four others became hits), and the dances are perfect. In his natural state Fred is massless and infinitely flexible; he assumes precisely the degree of weight and rigidity that each dance requires, no more. Of all technically brilliant woman dancers, Ginger is the most feminine. Astaire-and-Rogers's best dances are the ones in which they seem, superficially, to be making the same moves—but the space between his masculine and her feminine gestures is electric. Summing up the dance, music and the witty, enchanting deco stage sets, these movies are the crown jewels of American popular culture.

Top Hat opened in Radio City Music Hall and stayed six weeks—most films stayed only one. Imagine the crowds at that elegant movie in its elegant theater. Are you quite sure, as you lean back and relax at the local multiplex, that you are part of a more sophisticated audience? When Irving Berlin escorted his little girl to Top Hat, it was her first movie—"deliciously adult," she writes in a memoir; "Technicolor would never be so grown up." The songwriters and musicians who dominated thirties pop music—Berlin, Cole Porter, Duke Ellington, Benny Goodman, the incomparable Gershwin—also hold their own rather nicely, so far as sophistication goes, against their modern pop counterparts.

Consider finally the fact that, according to the 1940 *Official Guide,* the fair's popular parachute ride "packs more thrills in ninety seconds than any wings-in-sky interlude since Icarus—with landing a lot safer." 1939 had been judged an excessively high-brow season at the fair, and the 1940 guide was a dumbed-down version. But the "common man" of 1940 knew all about Icarus. It is hard to imagine a new Disneyland attraction described in comparable terms. Today, of course, such a ride probably wouldn't be described at all. Videos and high-quality color printing are cheap, and increasingly we needn't strain to interpret word pictures of any kind, because there aren't any.

PROLOGUE: THE CENTER OF TIME

In short, I don't believe we are a whit more sophisticated than the generation that built and loved the fair. We might be uneasy with that conclusion. Picture a late-thirties newsreel: The image is spattered with white flecks and the sound is hoarse. The music is hoarse. The narration marches double time, expresses itself in its own strange "no *and*s, adjectives first!" idiom.("Bright are the prospects for . . . ," "Ever increasing are the profits of . . . ," "Emphasized is the fact that . . .") Our verdict is *unsophisticated,* and it is easy to imagine the entire era in those terms and to forget the half-smiling young woman in the corner of the theater whose relationship to the stagey newsreel is the same as yours to this afternoon's TV soap operas. But how is it possible that the late thirties reveled at the fair in the sort of production that we would be likely to dismiss, with our characteristic cynical detachment, as hokey nonsense? Aren't we *forced* to assume that we are more sophisticated than those people? We ought not to confuse cynicism with sophistication, of course, but in any case I think the answer is no. It *is* possible that other factors allowed a sophisticated audience to accept what we would not. That authority still flourished in late-thirties America is one such factor. It is easier to be optimistic when authorities tell you to be, harder when there are no authorities (or virtually none) to tell you anything, one way or another. There are other factors too, important ones.

It is of course crucial not to flatten the complexity of 1939's world view. It was not uniformly optimistic any more than we are invariably pessimistic. But we would be idiots not to notice a big difference in characteristic attitudes, and having done so we must inevitably wonder about the difference and attempt, however haltingly, to account for it. Why was 1939's future so much brighter than ours? It is an intriguing and important question. Authority supplies part of the answer. But there is much more to this story. We will have to search deeper, and elsewhere, for the rest.

"The superhighways didn't exist at the time," Mrs. Levine continues, "but by 1960, they did. It came true. And the layout of the diorama had exactly the spread-out, sprawling feel of the modern built-up suburbs." The Futurama made whopping big mistakes, but you don't predict the future if you lack courage to look foolish in retrospect, and the astonishing thing is, unquestionably, how often the fair was right.

"It is astonishing. So much retrospective on the fair focused on those big errors, and made the whole thing out to be quaint and silly. It always annoyed me." She looks out the window. "You got a button at the end of the ride, that said 'I have seen the future.' "

Since 1939 we have traveled deep into the utopian future as the World's Fair saw it. The Futurama's predictions are a prime example; we have achieved many of them, not in detail but in the large picture.

This is another fact we need to understand in order to grasp the fair, its world and our own: the fair made promises that came true. It expressed hopes that have largely been fulfilled.

The Futurama was obsessed with cars. It made some spectacular errors. You would be able to buy a 1960 automobile for $200. It would be teardrop shaped. It would be diesel-powered and rear-engined; now we are getting warmer, but diesel-powered and rear-engined cars are not ubiquitous, as they were supposed to be. On the other hand, "cars will be smaller but roomier," Geddes wrote in 1940. "Interiors will be more flexible as to use." Was he thinking of the minivan? "They will be air conditioned. Cars will be more comfortable to ride in, more economical to run, and capable of higher speeds. But none of these improvements will mean a thing," he adds presciently, "if there is not a corresponding advance in safety."

PROLOGUE: THE CENTER OF TIME

The Futurama cared most about roads. Again, it made spectacular mistakes. It imagined an elaborate infrastructure of control, modeled on the railways: Along highways there would be lookout towers at five-mile intervals. Speeds would be maintained and entrances, exits and merges carried out automatically by a collaborative partnership between the car and the highway. The goal was nothing less than "to make automobile collisions impossible and to eliminate completely traffic congestion."

But there was another message more basic than all that. Geddes puts the case plainly: "It costs too much—in time, money and energy—to do a long-distance automobile run in the country today." In 1939 the age of the bypass highway had barely started. The Futurama's most important and deeply held belief was that "superhighways" (a 1930s word) would eventually be everywhere, would run sheer across the country, would let you work, shop and play miles from home, would make it possible for urban workers to live out in the green countryside, would allow the whole nation to *spread out*—and it was right.

That's what you call the glittering future? we demand incredulously. Just *highways?* So what!

Yes, 1939 replies evenly. Travel is important to us, and automobile travel that is faster, easier and safer is a big part of our utopian future. To get to the fair from New England in 1939 we have to travel the Boston Post Road, you see, crawling through every small town along the way, and it's the same all over the country. Good roads are lacking—and for that matter, so are cars. (In 1927 44 percent of American families owned no car. By 1950 the figure had dropped only to 41 percent.) And so, yes, cars and roads are a big part of our utopian vision. Because, when we picture utopia, it isn't perfect; it's just *better*. It's comfortable. It is a world where, for vast numbers of people, life all in all is pretty good. In 1939 life is not, but that is our goal. And you have achieved it. Although you may be too spoiled or self-absorbed to realize that you have.

Of course, once postwar America built the superhighways, it stopped. We did not bother with the elaborate control infrastructure Geddes imagined. Many of his ideas were fantastic, but many were reasonable and far more practicable in our computer age than they were in his. Why did we stop? Once the interstate highway program was under way, powerful lobbies like the American Road Builders Association were satisfied. But a control infrastructure would have benefited another set of interests and industries, and they could have formed their own lobby. The real reason it never happened is that technologists and visionaries had long since lost interest in problems like making automobile travel a bit faster, safer and more convenient. They'd discovered goals more momentous than merely making people's lives easier in modest ways.

Mrs. Levine continues remembering. "In the RCA exhibit, the big thing was television. It was brand new, of course, but they predicted a big future for it."

Regular American commercial TV broadcasts began in New York on April 30, 1939, the fair's opening day. The president spoke, and his speech was carried live by NBC. "The pictures are unreeled and flashed into space from aerials atop the Empire State Building," the *Times* explained. The president stood facing the Trylon and Perisphere from the far end of an immensely long vista. Built into his podium, hidden from the audience by the decorative surround, were two handles he gripped firmly to steady himself. He gestured as always not with his hands but with his head, throwing it backward, thrusting forward with the chin. "I hereby dedicate the *World's Fair,* the *New York* World's Fair [*Fair* as he pronounces it does not end with *r*—the word is *Fai-ah*], of *1939* [each syllable ringing out as a distinct utterance: *nine-teen-thirty-nine!*], and I declare it *open* to *all mankind!*" A couple of top hats rested brim up on the table beside him. The press corps clustered in front.

RCA's featured TV set was housed in a huge wooden case, its little seven-inch picture tube pointing straight up. The image bounced off a tilted mirror hinged to the top of the case. To watch TV you looked in the mirror. TV was all over the fair: It was featured in the Westinghouse, General Electric and Ford displays as well as at RCA in 1939; during the fair's second season, DuMont televisions showed up in the Crosley Appliance building as well. The picture on those early sets was called black and white but was actually black and pale green.

"First you recall isolated scenes," she says. "In time the memories start growing together. But I still have these detached brightly lit scenes in mind, complete with all sorts of improbable details. It's foggy, and I'm admiring a tall post with a bright ribbon of aluminum spiraling upward like a vine, and bundles of fluorescent tubes tacked to the post, rising between the tracery of the shiny ribbon, and the Perisphere is a ghostly white thing in the background. I'm in a restaurant with a friend getting coffee and doughnuts—the bill is maybe twenty cents each—of course you know the coins were different then, so many of the little texture-making things were different—and I've grabbed his tie across the table and I'm holding it taut, and we're both laughing and he's trying to tell me something about the coffee but he's laughing too hard. I'm there with another girl, this is odd, and I'm crouching as demurely as I can on a big lawn—I think maybe she'd dropped a brochure, or something, and it was windy and the thing had gone skittering off, and I was grabbing it for her—and for some reason I dip my head and shyly, maybe the word is "gingerly," take a deep sniff of the bright sunny grass; and I look up and there are the Trylon and Perisphere, and I stand

and there's a fair policeman checking on what I'm doing there, and I smile nicely at him and we walk on and I'm thinking, you could be mistaken for a tolerably charming girl, Miss Glassman, so long as you don't open your mouth—" She rises abruptly. "I need some pills. I'll be back in a minute or two.

She pauses on her way out at the sound of the front door opening; calls something to the maid just entering; notices that I am eyeing the photographs on the table beside her. Props herself with one arm on the back of a chair and touches the first. "My father and me. We were very close." In the photo she is twentyish and strikingly pretty. She has a pipe in her mouth, and he looks at her sidelong with a startled scowl. Touches the next: "My late husband and me, on our wedding day. Everett Levine. He was a cardiologist.

"The color photo." She takes it, holds it at a distance and studies it, like a jeweler with a loupe. "It's relevant to your current project. It was taken at the fair, right in front of the Perisphere." She is twentyish again, and her yellow dress ripples in a stiff breeze before fountains. Her hair is auburn. It is a tall, narrow picture, and a bit blurry. I can just make out the upsweep of the huge ball behind her. "It will sound odd, but I think of this as a photograph not of me, but of the man who took it. In the sense of a fossil impression, so to speak. To say he captured or epitomized the age is to diminish him. But he did do that. The impression he made on people is so palpable that you can see it, I'm sure, fifty years later in a blurry image of a perfectly unimportant twenty-one-year-old girl."

She hands me the photo, rests her finger on the next and pauses for several long moments. Whether her musing is occasioned by this photograph or something else entirely, I have no idea. "Miss Sarah Abbot." A photo from roughly the same period as the earlier ones of herself, I would have guessed, showing a girl roughly the same age. She waves abstractly at the other three. "Cousins, uncles, aunts . . . Step out on the terrace if you'd like. It's stuffy in here."

PROLOGUE: THE CENTER OF TIME

I spend a few minutes studying the color photo. She smiles serenely, her eyes are almost shut, her right hand steadies her hat and the left is clenched in a fist at her side. Odd pose, as if she were just about to dive off a high board, or take some sort of gay, reckless plunge; or burst into song? But I can't say, to be honest, that I discerned anything at all about the man who took it, aside from the fact that he pleased her.

"In the AT&T building the featured technology was long-distance phone calls, which were terribly exotic." We're seated again, with coffee supplied by the maid. "I remember the large room, a sort of auditorium, in which they allowed visitors chosen by lot to place free long-distance calls from glass booths—and then everyone listened in! They gave you special earphones just for eavesdropping. I wouldn't have dreamed of entering. I would have died of embarrassment." Her voice is warming. "But of course it was a very exciting thing in those days to receive a long-distance phone call." "Wow idea of the Fair is American Telephone & Telegraph's Co.'s stunt," *Time* magazine reported. "Sample embarrassments: a man, thinking the telephone company is calling him, apologizes for not having paid his bill; another, roused from sleep, curses; a kid brother greets his sister (whose beau is listening in) with: 'Hi, screwball, have you hooked him yet?' " "Perhaps no other display on the grounds made a service seem so immediate and so human," said *Architectural Record.*

The auditorium in the AT&T building had a low stage to which three French-curvy steps led up. In place of the movie screen was a gigantic map of the United States, with pinpoint lights marking long-distance switching stations. In the spare, architectural fonts of the 1930s, raised lettering beside the map announced "Demonstration TELEPHONE CALLS to any one of the 16,000,000 telephones of the BELL SYSTEM and to any of the 4,200,000 telephones of the other companies in the UNITED STATES." The thirties loved numbers. In smaller letters below, "visitors who wish to assist in this demonstration" of Bell's leading-edge technology "will please register at the desk."

The simple dignity of the age's architecture matched, in a sense, the formality of its rhetoric.

"Yes, there was a dignified formality to public discourse, unquestionably, though it was an inheritance from earlier decades. At the same time though, there was more of a gap between educated and upper-class speech, and working-class, than exists today."

The world in general was more partitioned, no?

She smiles outright, for the first time. "I'll have to think about that. In any case. FM radio was demonstrated as a new technique at the fair. Fluorescent lighting. Fax machines." (At the RCA Building, the "radio living room of tomorrow" was equipped with a fax machine. Newspapers were faxed in at a rate of eighteen minutes per eight-by-twelve-inch page.) "The Westinghouse building had a big robot." Her voice tends to go gravelly when the volume drops. But at any volume it has a presence that compels you to look at her, as she pauses behind a blue curl of cigarette smoke. "One thing the fair absolutely missed was computers, though I think of that hulking silly robot as a sort of premonition of computers. But I'm not talking only about technology."

Technology is one of my central themes, and the fair was remarkable for the way art and technology were blended and balanced there. Technology and art faced each other eye to eye at the fair. Art is no longer in a position to look anything in the eye; since 1939 it has spiraled listlessly ever downward in public esteem. If you stop an average college graduate on the street this afternoon and solicit the names of a distinguished living painter, a poet and a classical composer—please don't hold your breath awaiting an answer. In the thirties you might have been told "Picasso, Yeats and Stravinsky," or maybe "Diego Rivera, Eliot, Gershwin." (New Yorkers paced Lewisohn Stadium to hear Gershwin's classical music.) La Guardia conceived New York's four greatest problems to be "finance, housing, transit and art." One of the incoming mayor's first proposals was a new public high school for students who showed promise in art and music. And by the way, La Guardia was "a virtuoso, a political Heifetz, an administrative Gershwin."

More surprising, since the late thirties science and technology too have withdrawn from the public mind. We depend on computers, of course, and rush out eagerly to snag the latest models. Still: contemplate a song by George and Ira Gershwin that Ginger Rogers sings in *Shall We Dance?* of 1937. The theme is, everyone laughs at visionaries; but the visionaries have the last laugh in the end. One verse gives four examples: Columbus, Edison, Wilbur and his brother, Marconi (rhymes with "phony"). Edison died in 1931, Marconi the same year as the film came out, Orville Wright in 1948. Wilbur died prematurely in 1912. It is not characteristic in contemporary pop lyrics to discuss the achievements of living or recently-deceased technologists. Merely naming three, much less writing a song about them, would pose a challenge. No technologist commands the authority of an Edison, Wright or Marconi today.

In 1939 art was good enough, technology revolutionary enough to compel public attention. When the public turned to the wide world it found a rich and varied menu of topics for contemplation. We are just as hungry today for famous people and spectacular achievements, but we satisfy our craving with junk food. Granted, 1939's public was better educated and arguably more sophisticated than we, but *the public* didn't force art and technology from office; art and technology abdicated. We have celebrities. 1939 had authorities.

I tell Mrs. Levine that at some point I would like to hear more about technology.

"I know nothing about it. Mr. Mark Handler was an engineer, though. The man who took my picture at the Perisphere. An intensely idealistic engineer. That concept, an idealistic engineer, made sense in 1939 as it never had before and never has since. Does that idea mean anything to you? Oh well, at any rate."

She looks out the window and speaks with her face turned away. "Here we are in the future. Just as we were promised. Just." And turns back to face me. "One of the things that troubles me most about the present age is the utter ignorance of you younger people, some of you, respecting how far we've come. I don't mean you personally. Don't know a thing about your politics. Don't know if you're a whiner or not. But in 1939, poor didn't mean you had a TV set and a car and clothing and were deprived of, Lord knows, a VCR. It meant you were hungry. The fair promised us a future in which life in this country for the great majority would be vastly richer and easier, and it was absolutely right. But needless to say, we are no happier and the amazing thing is, the fair said that, too—somewhere—somehow—I can't quite put my finger on where and how it conveyed that message, but I'm absolutely certain that it did. You see," and she stops.

The window is closed, but the muffled gasps of buses come through, and the screech of cabs as they stop at the corner traffic light. The room creates the same impression she does: crisp and austere.

She continues. "The fair was so uniquely earnest. It could only have happened just at that moment, in that narrow, narrow gap between the depression and the catastrophic war, which utterly rewrote the world."

The gap was narrow indeed. It closed before the fair did, and the results were haunting and bizarre. On the very eve of the fall of Paris, you could dine in elegant splendor at the French Pavilion in Queens. France's restaurant was an especially chic eating spot at the fair. The food was world-class and the large windows overlooked the Lagoon of Nations, where spectacular fountain, firework and flaming gas-jet displays were staged every evening. Hitler and Stalin collaborated on the destruction of Poland in time for the close of the 1939 season. The Poland Pavilion's staff did not go home that winter. Home was no longer on the map. They opened a Polish restaurant on Fifty-seventh Street. A successful Polish businessman struck out for New York in the summer of 1939. He was well aware of the precarious international situation, but had planned for years to visit the fair. He never saw his wife or homeland again. "Every evening at dusk," says the 1940 *Official Guide,* "a horn call sounds out loud and clear above the tumult of the Fair . . . This is the 'Hejnal,' blown from the top of Poland's golden Pavilion tower, commemorating the death of a Polish watchman who, centuries ago, saved the city of Krakow from invaders. He fell dead with an arrow in his throat, the unfinished warning ending on a broken, jarred note."

Which is how the fair itself ended. Hitler destroyed Czechoslovakia even before its pavilion was complete. The building was finished with funds collected in the United States. "The Pavilion appears under the flag of the independent Czecho-Slovak republic," the fair's official *Book of Nations* quietly notes, "such as existed prior to the events of last September and March." For an edgy and anguished American Jewish community that contributed decisively to the fair's character and its success, the Jewish Palestine Pavilion was a big draw throughout the fair's run. When it opened several weeks late on May 28, 22,000 chairs were set out for the crowds—but hours before the ceremony began every chair was taken, and some 50,000 people attended in all. Albert Einstein spoke: "I am here entrusted with the high privilege of officially dedicating the building which my Palestine brethren have erected." Only eleven days earlier the British government had issued the infamous White Paper announcing a ban on Jewish immigration to Palestine; that was one reason the crowd was so enormous. "First at Munich and now again in this White Paper," Senator William King of Utah declared, Britain "seems to be surrendering to a policy of appeasement where expediency is the sole measure and barometer of her conscience." When the fair opened, Europe was more or less at peace. "R.A.F. HITS REICH," the newspapers reported on the day it closed. "LIVERPOOL AND MIDLANDS UNDER ATTACK—LONDON DEFENSE EFFECTIVE." "BALKAN WAR BEGINS AS 200,000 ITALIANS INVADE GREECE" was the banner headline in the *Herald Tribune.*

"One attractive feature of the League Pavilion," says the *Book of Nations,* describing the League of Nations building, "is that in the large rotunda ample space is provided where the visitor may rest and reflect."

"The fair," Mrs. Levine continues, "did not come at you with the arch smirk of the twenties. Or the ragged desperation of most of the thirties. Or the brash razzle-dazzle of the forties, or the glitzy commercialism of the fifties—it came at you absolutely on the level . . . And in retrospect—"

She gazes past me and sighs.

She rose and left the room and returned with a bundle that she set down before me: Three notebooks of the classic black-and-white marbled "composition" type, grayish-yellow with age, bound in rough twine. The twine looked as if it had not been disturbed for a long time. "I wasn't certain I was going to show you this, but I find

PROLOGUE: THE CENTER OF TIME

I am more than willing to, if you'd like to see it. Actually, the whole story, I put off looking for it until an hour before you came. I was sure I'd have to turn the place upside down to find it and probably wouldn't, even then. But in fact it was right there in the first place I looked. It's the diary I kept in 1938 and '39 and sporadically for a few years after that, and my longest entry describes one particular day I spent at the fair—one of many, I was there over a dozen times in 1939 and maybe five or six in 1940—but this one day was, in personal terms, the most significant . . . That part doesn't matter. The upshot is, there is a fair amount of detail in there on the fair itself. I'm not positive where the entry is. Toward the beginning, I'd guess."

I thank her. She nods abstractedly. Thinking about something else. "You know my sharpest fair memory of all? I'm sitting on a bench in the early morning in the sun in spring. I'd barely slept the night before, and my head is resting on the shoulder of the friend who sits beside me. There is a warm-sounding sleepy buzz of bees, and across the walk is a grass field full of bright red tulips. Did you know the fair was full of flowers? And the sound of fountains. There were fountains everywhere. Could I be confusing the sound of fountains with the sound of bees? *Were* there bees?" She bites her lip in thought, and draws with a finger on the table: "The bench. The walkway. The tulips. Let's say there were. Behind me, I believe, are the General Electric and the U.S. Steel buildings. U.S. Steel looked like a big blue helmet, a steel hemisphere with ribs of some sort running along the outside. General Electric had a big zag-zaggy lightning bolt out front, and inside they demonstrated artificial lightning, which astonishingly did *not* disrupt the FM broadcast signal they were also demonstrating. Inside the Perisphere you'd seen the big utopian diorama called Democracity. The fair was filled with big utopian dioramas. With flowers and fountains and utopian dioramas. And somehow it all just filled you up with acute hope. Passionate hope. Yearning hope. Just plain yearning. I don't know how to put it, really.

"And then I fell asleep. Right there on the bench."

I summarize for her the modern academic view of the fair: that it was a successful entertainment but fraught with "contradictions" between the idealism of its social message and the blatant consumerism of most of the exhibits. That judgment accords with the decidedly nonacademic view of E. B. White at the time: "Suddenly you see the first intimation of the future, of man's dream—the white ball and spire . . . I might have been approaching the lists of Camelot, for I felt that perhaps here would be the tournament all men wait for . . . A closer inspection, however, on the other side of the turnstile, revealed that it was merely Heinz jousting with Beech-Nut—the same old contest on a somewhat larger field."

"No, that is wrong," she says. "It utterly misses the point.

"You see: This fair was our greatest public exposition because it took place at the direst of times. Throughout the thirties, you know, people despaired of the American form of government. Thoughtful people. Throughout those years there was a significant—at least among intellectuals, who are reliably the stupidest element—communist presence in this country. People made jokes about 'Comes the revolution . . .' Nervous jokes. And overseas it was a nightmare full of creatures who actively scared you, and those mammoth, hideous crowds egging them on. Hitler yes, but also Stalin and Mussolini and the Japanese warlords. And our great friends in Western Europe wrung their hands and did nothing, and there was a sort of odious, fretting-and-smirking—something, I want to say *stench*, about the whole of France and England in those years; oh I'm sure that's unfair, but, that's the way it seemed.

PROLOGUE: THE CENTER OF TIME

It was a nasty time when the fair opened. People *were* optimistic and yet they were also afraid. Can you blame them? They were afraid of the fascists and the communists and just *upset*, nervous, jumpy, at loose ends. So you see the fair was a *cri de coeur*. Just under the surface it had a terrible, compelling intensity because in a manner of speaking, it was an emotional summation to the jury. In those thousand acres, whatever, of marshland, it laid out in hugely compressed *pressurized* form exactly what this country was, just what we'd managed to accomplish, just what we had to show for ourselves after all. Of course there was a big commercial element because in this country, Beech-Nut is more important than ideology, because that's what people want, and that's what it's all about. Particularly in 1939—the mood in 1940 was different, it was all grim resolution and building tanks—people saw *America* in those thousand acres, crying into the wind."

"So you agree with me," I ask her after a moment, "that the New York World's Fair had a certain urgent importance, and still does?"

"Yes."

And I make off with the notebooks. "I want them back," she says. "But keep them as long as you like."

How to understand the fair? In the light, I think, of these verses. They are the end of Deuteronomy, the last verses of the Pentateuch:

So Moses went up from the plains of Moab onto Mount N'vo, top of the Pisgah, facing Jericho. And the Lord showed him the whole land—from the Gil'ad to Dan; and all of Naphtali and the land of Ephraim and M'nasseh; and the whole land of Judah, right up to the Sea beyond. And the South, and the Plain, the valley of Jericho, city of palms, as far as Tsoar.

And the Lord said to him: this is the land that I promised to Abraham, to Isaac and to Jacob in these words: I will give it to your descendants. I have allowed you with your own eyes to see it; but you will not pass into it.

And Moses the Lord's servant died right there, in the land of Moab, as the Lord had decreed.

He was buried in the valley in the land of Moab, across from Beit Pe'or; and no man to this very day knows the location of his grave.

Moses was one hundred and twenty years old at his death; his eyes had not weakened and his natural powers were unabated. The Israelis mourned his death for thirty days on the plains of Moab; and with that, the weeping-days of Moses' mourning were over. Joshua bin-Nun was inspired with wisdom, because Moses had vested authority in him. The Israelis obeyed him, and did as the Lord had commanded Moses.

No prophet ever rose again in Israel like Moses, whom the Lord had known face to face—throughout all the signs and wonders that the Lord sent him to make manifest in the land of Egypt, to Pharaoh and to all his servants and to his entire country; throughout all the mighty deeds and grand terrors that Moses wrought in the sight of all Israel.

What did the fair mean, and how did we lose the future? There is no pat answer. The question itself is too pat, in a way; obviously, as I have said, the fair's generation wasn't monolithic in its views and did harbor doubts; nor are we ourselves unanimous on the future, or wholly without optimism. Any intelligent reader understands the qualifications, of-courses and bear-in-minds that *must* inhere in any generalization about history. But we ought not to allow those qualifications to destroy our ability to struggle off the ground and see such patterns as there may be.

In studying and listening to late-thirties America, we will find, I think, that it was a deeply religious society. Ours is an irreligious one, and that makes all the difference.

By religious I don't mean Jewish or Christian. I refer to the American religion, the "civic religion" which has always been characteristic of this country, what Franklin Roosevelt called "our creed of liberty and democracy." In the late thirties it was an intense and heartfelt faith. The civic religion emerged in modern form in the second half of the nineteenth century, with the nationwide spread of nonsectarian public schools. If Christianity were not to supply the ethical and spiritual basis of the child's daily schooling, *something* had to. The "American way of life" was an attractive candidate. That civic religion was reinforced in the late nineteenth and early twentieth centuries by the obvious need for a good healthy fire under the "melting pot" in which millions of new immigrants simmered.

Like virtually all other Judaeo-Christian religions, the American civic religion made eschatological predictions: It promised a utopian future to believers, in the end of days. And then an amazing thing happened—a thing without parallel, so far as I know, in the whole history of religion: In the years following the Second World War, those utopian promises came true.

A society is religious when its typical member subscribes to certain beliefs on emotional, not rational, grounds, accepts certain obligations, expects certain rewards and feels himself to be a member of a community of believers. The central tenet of the American religion was, of course, that American democracy is good and right, for America and for the whole world, and is destined ultimately to supersede tyranny everywhere. Look around you at the World's Fair, New York's Governor Herbert Lehman declares. "On every hand there is symbolized something far more precious than material progress—our faith in our destiny and our confidence in our future." "It is a young nation," he says of America, "that has had only thirty-two rulers. It is virile and imaginative; capable and resourceful. Free men everywhere look to our land for leadership and guidance." La Guardia affirms the belief. The New York World's Fair will be dedicated, he says, "to the future of the American people and the glory of the country."

An American of this era freely accepts certain obligations, as befits a member of a religious community. He lives by the rules. We tend to believe that people live by rules because they are forced to, or because they have analyzed the rules and decided they pass muster. But in a religious community neither holds. People live by the rules because they are the rules—because they give the community shape, coherence and a shared viewpoint and make the faithful feel worthy of the rewards they are promised. Thirties America is a rules-following society, an "ought culture" versus our own culture of desire, not obligation. The American who believes in the democratic creed and lives by the rules is rewarded with a profound sense of *control,* mastery, ownership of the American landscape. Above all, he is promised the American utopia. A utopia not perfect but *better:* a land where the middle and working classes and not just their bosses are rich and comfortable.

Events conspired to bring American religion in the late thirties to an intense pitch. Throughout the 1930s there seems to have been a special fascination with the "American Way of Life" (a term that evidently originated in this period); "few, if any, decades in our history could claim the production of such a vast literature—to say nothing of a vast body of films, recordings, and paintings—that described and defined every aspect of American life," historian Warren Susman writes. As American ideals came under hostile attack in Soviet Russia and the fascist tyrannies of Europe, the creed grew more passionate. A central idea is on display at the fair, La Guardia proclaims: "We are most unselfish about it, and pray and hope that other countries may copy." That idea is "to let every man and woman have a say in their own government." Nineteen-thirties America is a religious community whose citizens (not all but most) believe deeply in the rightness and goodness of American democracy. Also, the depression dogged the nation throughout the thirties; after years of improvement, the economy took another turn for the worse in 1937. The depression made the utopian future an urgent and compelling belief. In the late thirties, technology and the future were firmly linked, as they had been for years; and in the thirties, art made a powerful alliance with technology as well. Machine art had been gathering steam for several decades, but it reached maturity in the thirties; Jane Heap's 1927 *Machine Age Exposition* was a milestone. Engineering emerged with a spiritual glow that made it comfortable inside a community of faith. In 1940 Walter Dorwin Teague displayed pictures of the George Washington Bridge and the nave of Chartres side by side. In most ages technology is a big part of the American scene, but in the thirties technology wasn't merely useful, it was profoundly beautiful; and so the future was beautiful too.

The religion that emerged was worlds apart from mere patriotic fervor of the sort sweeping 1930s Germany, for example; the American religion was evangelical and bore a utopian message to the whole world. Although 1930s America was an orderly, rules-following society, it was the farthest thing from a *mere* rules-following society because of the ebullient future that was foretold. The future in 1939 was ever present. Like the Trylon and Perisphere—merely raise your eyes and you couldn't miss the future.

The promised land was attained. We have reached the promised land in the Biblical sense, not where *everyone* but where vast numbers of "ordinary" people have the means to be happy. We sometimes forget what an astonishing historical anomaly that is.

There are poor and suffering people in our utopia. The poor, says Deuteronomy, will never cease out of the land. It says so not complacently but with resignation. And yet if we allow the sufferings of the poor (as large and important as they are) to blind us to what the great mass of Americans has achieved since 1939, we overlook a deeply significant story.

And even our poor are materially better off than 1939's. In 1939 you could hold a full-time secretarial job and have no money for breakfast aside from a cup of coffee, no money to buy dinner more than a few days a week (other times you scrounged off friends); and you might feel obliged to devote sixty-five cents a week of your hard-earned wages to cigarettes because they made you feel less hungry. Or you might be out of a job and live in an ancient tenement with no bathtubs or fire escapes and a toilet down the hall. Or you might be a factory worker and rear your children in a slum where rickets, tuberculosis and polio were real and constant threats. Or you might be a farmer and, like three-quarters of 1939 farmers, have no electricity or running water—your wife cooks at a coal stove, you grind your tools by foot power, you do your evening chores and watch your children tackle their homework by flickering oil lamp.

It turns out that, unfortunately, utopia is a costly thing to achieve—not materially but spiritually; the poor suffer with the rest of us, and probably suffer more. Because a religion that has seen its promises realized is bound to crack apart. It has served its purpose. And today the American religion—in the passionate intensity of its

PROLOGUE: THE CENTER OF TIME

heyday—is dead, is a mere memory. America exists today in a post-utopian twilight.

The American religion paraded its eschatological predictions and deep utopian faith most memorably and definitively at the 1939 New York World's Fair. The fair was a credo in stucco and steel. Behind the fair and its theme stood "a group of forward-looking young architects, city planners, industrial designers, sociologists and young visionaries from many walks of life." They shared "a fundamental conviction"—that the fair ought to deliver a "powerful," a "prophetic" message. *Fundamental convictions, powerful prophetic messages* are words that came naturally to the New York World's Fair. It was the mountaintop: Fairgoers ascended and looked out at the promised land.

As such that World's Fair is important to any credible effort at deciphering modern America. There is near-universal agreement that ever since 1970 or so, we have been economically and spiritually adrift. But attempts to explain *why* invariably founder when they neglect a central fact: In 1970 or so we entered the American utopia. To insist on this point is not to undermine or contradict all the other theories about what has happened to us since the late sixties; they may all be right. But they need to be rooted securely in this fact— that once upon a time we envisioned utopia and then, at length, we came to live there. And to understand why that is true, how it could *possibly* be, we need to study the fair—because it was the Daniel, Ezekiel, Isaiah, Revelations of the American religion. Not the basic meat-and-potatoes but the ecstatic closing vision. The fair laid out the end of days. And having studied the fair, I think we will see that we are adrift, at least in part, because we are no longer marching toward utopia: We no longer can, because we are *in* it. And we will understand, too, that the fair ought to be approached today with the respect for its fundamental strangeness accorded by all civilized people to the shrine of a dead faith.

The end of Deuteronomy teaches us something important about the fair, and vice versa. The fair is a commentary on the Bible; the Bible is a sort of commentary on the fair. The lesson is: gazing at utopia is a finer thing than entering it. Achieving utopia turns out to be a logical impossibility in the end, because utopia achieved means no world of tomorrow.

Why return to the fair? Why climb back to the mountaintop?

I have outlined an argument about why 1939's America was so different from ours. I have outlined an argument about why the future that accompanied us so faithfully, our pillar of cloud by day and fire by night, should now in the end have left us. Yet in the end those arguments are secondary, and whether you buy some, all or none of them matters little. My most important goal is not to make an argument but to lead a tour.

The best of all reasons to return to the fair is that travel is broadening, and time travel most of all. My tour aims to make it possible, however dimly, to see the sights, smell the smells, hear the sounds, eavesdrop on the conversations, try on the anxieties and exultations; buy a hot dog in a roll wrapped in a paper napkin from a white-jacketed someone, hand over your dime, look hard at the man's translucent root-beer eyes until he turns away. Notice the wry facial crinkles that make him seem older. Draw mustard with a spoon onto your hot dog. (Where does he live? What is his wife fixing for dinner? When were his grandparents born?) Turn around and take a bite slowly, facing the Trylon and Perisphere at the far end of a thronged avenue. Then, as the sun burns through and pulls the shadows back into focus and you find that you are standing right at the tip of the Trylon's, smile. Have another slow bite. Reflect that the Perisphere looks to you the way a distant golf ball must look to a very small ant. Hear someone speak your name. (If you would add to this scene the imagined sound of your name, the author would be grateful.) Turn round again and smile wide. The 1939 New York World's Fair is one amazing show. It still stands undisturbed on Flushing Meadow, just over the edge of time; it would be an unforgivable shame to miss it.

2

Into
the Fair

On Thursday, May 18, 1939, a young woman in a blue dress and white sweater stirs and awakens on a bench at the New York World's Fair.

She had been asleep cradled in the right arm of Mr. Mark Handler, her head resting on his shoulder. Handler was a slim, tallish man in a blue tie and tan poplin suit, a year older than she. He had brown hair verging on red and a boyish face that was often thoughtful (evidently she thought him "cute" at such times). His smile is "comforting & kind beyond his years." In his left hand he holds a copy of the fair's daily newspaper folded in half; he'd read everything visible and then stopped because he hadn't wanted to wake her by rattling the pages. (*"Tallulah Reads Ode to Tree.* Tallulah Bankhead, famous Broadway dramatic actress, will recite an original ode at the planting of an authentic Royal Oak . . . *Fair Gardens a Fairyland of Colors . . . Official Program of Today's Special Events . . . Bloomingdale's speaks 27 languages. A staff of interpreters at our World's Fair Service Center . . .*")

A pigeon breaks its descent with outstretched wings and lands near his left foot, pecks casually at the asphalt walk and takes off again. ("The pedestrian finds it pleasant to stroll at the Fair," says the 1939 guide, "where the walks are of bituminous asphalt, which has been found much 'easier' on feet than either concrete, wood or other hard surfaces.") The odor of cigar smoke passes before him with a stately, solitary gentleman.

For the last twenty minutes he'd been looking around, affably watching the procession of fairgoers, turning frequently to his left to take in the Trylon and Perisphere, which fill up the middle third of his visual field. In an age in which abstract painting is still a relatively new and debatable proposition ("voices had risen in lively controversy," says a novel of the 1930s, "over the new play, the new strike, the new Moscow trials, the new abstract show at the Modern Museum"), the Trylon and Perisphere are the closest we have ever come to a major piece of abstract architecture.

What did he see? In 1939 one didn't dress quite as one does today, and although this is not news and everybody knows, generally speaking, how things used to be different, I think we would find the actual sight of it startling. In 1939 men wore suits or occasionally sport jackets to a fair. Women wore dresses or sometimes a blouse and skirt. Most adults wore a hat. In warm weather the men's hats are often straw boaters, and jackets may be removed, but ties stay on no matter what. Children are dressed like miniature adults, in jackets and ties or dresses or skirts, except that the boys might be wearing shorts or knickers. We know all this; but I think we would find the procession passing before

Handler that Thursday morning as strange as we would a tie-and-jacketed, dress-or-skirted entourage frolicking on a beach.

I can't say precisely where Handler was sitting. But I do know that he had a clear view of the Trylon and Perisphere, and I conjecture that he was sitting somewhere to the south of them. "After half an hour or so," we learn, Hattie "stirred and stretched and stood up & Mark gave me a squeeze & then, though he'd wanted to see General Electric, we spontaneously walk off in the opposite direction toward the Trylon and Perisphere. They draw one like rubber bands." We also learn that he calls her Laurie, from her middle name (Hortense Laura Glassman), and that "on the way I first raised the topic of children, which he & I both understood as an invitation to the effect that he might now ask to marry me. When I do he stops dead—turns to me & rests both hands on the side of my arms, such a turbulent face—but then says not a word! & we walk on."

His features were average, and I assume he blended into a crowd. She was striking, with wavy short hair cutting south across her forehead—sort of a flapper style that I associate more with the twenties—and pronounced cheeks, a slightly too-prominent chin, parted lips and soft wide eyes. Earlier, on their way to the bench, she writes that they had

> walked down the mall away from the theme center—fountains everywhere which mist you as you walk past, & with the bright sun on the water & flags snapping & the whole place so gleaming, colorful & gay, it just makes one thoroughly happy, exhausted as I was. The Fair is a place where wonderful things are all around, buildings with tall aquamarine waterfalls rushing down their faces, with automobiles driving round their rooftops, with lush purple-lit scenery that you fly over in gliding easy-chairs; you have read & heard &

seen so much about these buildings beforehand—Italy's waterfall, Ford's Road of Tomorrow & now, you turn a corner & there it is!—it is like the morning in '36 when we saw the President. At first as we hurried forward I saw nothing but orange leaves, long dark automobiles & a sea of faces, and then my father pointed—& it was *his* face. It is exciting just to be on the grounds.

After she reports on her nap, the account cuts back to their arrival an hour earlier:

Upon disembarking Mark buys a map & a *Today at the Fair* at a small umbrella'd stand near the station. He has borrowed a *Guide.* The instant you leave the station the blare of color hits you like the wall of sweet summer air outside an air-conditioned movie theater. This is a golden-yellow zone and the yellows are vivid. (Even the inside of the station was colorful, an unusual purplish.) My plan for our Official Entrance is *not* to cut away from the station forty-five degrees to the right & make straight for the Trylon & Perisphere, but rather to stride off in the opposite direction & then, when we hit Rainbow Avenue, to make for the enormous long mall, stubbornly *not looking* to my right—Mark does likewise, teasing & obliging me simultaneously as usual. We make straight for the bridge over the long blue pool that runs up the mall's middle—& then we wheel round triumphantly & *there*, at the climax-point of the double-ranks of green trees rushing forward like a drum roll, over the long pool stretching before us, through the mist of the fountains, beyond the cheerful white statuary & to the other side of the huge George Washington *there* is the Trylon and there is the Perisphere. It is a *beautiful* vista. Having brought Mark to just this spot I accept full personal credit for the view. Mark concedes he is deeply impressed.

"At certain rare moments," the diary continues,

> one has a feeling of being exalted, physically lifted for a moment without effort as if you are afloat with eyes closed & a wave swells up beneath you—& then rolls away again; you feel directly linked to the Fair as if it were intended just for you; the future *does* seem lovely & you are quite sure that everything will be all right in the end. And I felt just that way as we gazed together down the beautiful mall.

The Perisphere was set in a shallow pool and propped up by a ring of square columns only thirty feet or so out from its bottom. It sat in its ring of columns like a basketball in an egg cup, further steadied only by the walkway joining it, a quarter of the way up, to the Trylon. The Perisphere had been intended to seem as if it were floating on jets of water. Postcards printed in advance show a water dome of arching fountain sprays, with the Perisphere nestled in a hollow on top. But the great sphere proved insufficiently watertight. The fountains had to be scaled back, and you could see the mirrored supporting columns plainly.

> So after my little nap here we are approaching T&P down Pioneers Avenue. From this angle the Trylon stands to the left & in front of the Perisphere. You inevitably grow excited as you draw closer to this huge looming structure amidst crowds all streaming T&Pward. It is unclear till you get close

how you actually get into the thing. But it turns out that there is a ticket booth (the long line moves pretty fast), then you enter a chrome door in the front face of the Trylon & step onto one of two side-by-side escalators. The escalators are enormous and of stainless steel, the longest in the world (naturally!)—they rear up before you like roller coasters, proposing to carry you upward from the floor of the Trylon across the narrow space separating it from the Perisphere, then into hatches halfway, roughly, between the Perisphere's equator and the ground. You catch your breath as you step on—and then they are eerily silent—which inspires the crowd, too, to fall reverently silent, & you have the sensation of being some sort of minor tidbit that has been scooped up & is being conveyed into the heart of a top-secret electro-something in the Saturday serials; you have a real sense of drama. But the getting-inside process is nothing next to *being* inside.

(The typical escalator of this period had wooden treads and emitted a steady clickety-clack and the occasional clonk.)

Inside the Perisphere you step off the escalator onto one of two balcony-rings rotating slowly in opposite directions, one directly above the other. As you step onto the balcony you are inside a short tunnellike section, but you soon rotate out of the tunnel into the great awesome space of the Perisphere itself. There is a several-foot gap between the sphere's inner wall & the edge of the balconies—evidently they are supported from below, but they seem to float. You sail slowly into orbit. Below you the model is like a vast round pool, with immeasurable great echoing spherical vastness when you look up. The bigness of this space is such that you feel it in your stomach. The huge dome lit with blue. I know it is absurd to compare it to a medieval cathedral, but that great, shivery-vast feeling of enclosed space . . . It almost makes you dizzy to look up. That falling-backwards feeling . . . As I take it all in I experience again that upswelling moment of exaltation.

Down below is Henry Dreyfuss's Democracity, a representative American city and surrounding suburbs of 2039. Spectators on the balconies have the impression of viewing the landscape from the lordly height of seven thousand feet. On the banks of a river, the model city radiates outward in widening concentric half circles round a single towering skyscraper in the center. Power is generated by a great hydroelectric plant on the riverbank, inspired by FDR's much-admired Tennessee Valley Authority. The rolling countryside is full of towns and parks. It is the definitive high-thirties utopia.

By "high thirties" I mean, roughly speaking, the period beginning in 1936—the year the electorate turned to Roosevelt not in desperation, as in 1932, but in breathless wild approval. The day after FDR pulverized Republican Alf Landon in an unprecedented landslide, there were parties all over the country. "If he were to say a kind word for the man-eating shark," the *New York Times* opined of Roosevelt soon after that event, "people would look thoughtful and say perhaps there *are* two sides to the question." The Republicans stormed back in 1938, but Roosevelt's personal popularity remained high.

In 1936 John L. Lewis's newly formed Congress of Industrial Organizations sparked a nationwide revival of labor unionism. In October 1935 at the annual American Federation of Labor (AF of L, as it was invariably called) convention, Lewis had punched Bill

Hutcheson in the face. That was a significant punch, as punches go. Hutcheson was head of the Carpenters Union and an old-line crafts union man. Lewis wanted industrial and not crafts unions: not a union of all and only carpenters, but an "auto workers" or "steel workers" union. He quit the AF of L and founded the CIO.

In 1936 an English graduate student in mathematics named Alan Turing completed work on a paper, "On Computable Numbers, with an Application to the *Entscheidungsproblem,*" that laid the basis for the theoretical study of computers—thus in a sense for the postwar world. This technical paper is also, in its way, part of the thirties fabric. Turing had left Cambridge for Princeton to study with a great mathematician, arguably the greatest of the century. John von Neumann was a Hungarian Jew by birth. He had been teaching in Germany and had left for the United States in 1933. "If these boys continue for only two more years," von Neumann had said of the Nazis, "they will ruin German science for a generation—at least." And so they did. The mass escape to the United States during the 1930s of European scientists, including Einstein as well as such non-Jews as the great physicist Erwin Schrödinger, decided the war. Many of the émigré scientists played key roles in developing the atomic bomb for the United States. More important, they did *not* develop the atomic bomb for Germany. Their absence doomed the German bomb project. After the war von Neumann went on to lay the practical basis, as Turing had the theoretical, for the computer age.

In 1936 Joseph Paxton's Crystal Palace burned to the ground. Elderly visitors at the 1939 fair might in principle have seen every one of history's greatest world's fairs, except for the very first—the London Exposition of 1851, housed in the famous glass-and-iron palace. They might have visited Philadelphia in 1876 and seen the American Centennial exhibit, Paris in 1889 to view the brand-new Eiffel Tower—the only world's fair centerpiece more celebrated than the Trylon and Perisphere. (Eavesdropping on the high thirties is one of my goals. When that era looked at the Eiffel Tower it saw the archetypal "skyscraper skeleton"; alternatively, "Paris's ugliest landmark.") A hypothetical elderly globetrotting visitor at the 1939 fair might have seen the famed "White City" in 1893—the World's Columbian Exposition in Chicago—and the Saint Louis Exposition in 1904, the San Francisco and San Diego Fairs in 1915, Chicago's Century of Progress in 1933. He might even have seen the Crystal Palace on Sydenham Hill, where it stood after its removal from Hyde Park until 1936. (There had been a previous World's Fair in New York, as a matter of fact, in 1853 and '54, but hardly a great one. It had been housed in a leaky building at Fifth Avenue and Forty-second Street.)

Nineteen thirty-six was the year the big bands arrived, under the auspices of Benny Goodman, "the man who started it all." Goodman had been attracting crowds since the summer of 1935. But it was October 1936 when the Goodman band made its New York debut in the Manhattan Room at the Pennsylvania Hotel on Seventh Avenue. For the next ten years (until they abdicated in favor of their own vocalists) the big bands dominated popular music.

In 1936 a group of army officers posted to Spanish Morocco rebelled against the Popular Front government in Madrid. Officers all over Spain joined them, and the Spanish Civil War was on. Italy and Germany jumped at the chance to aid the right-wing rebel forces. After some hesitation Stalin poured the resources of the U.S.S.R into the fight on the Loyalist side, helpfully including secret police operatives to give the Spaniards tips on organizing things. The Spanish Civil War—were you for the republic and what were you *doing* about it?—became *the* moral touchstone of the thirties.

Nineteen thirty-six was the year *Life* magazine was born, and ground was broken at the fair. "High thirties" is a culture centered on New York City. As such it leaves out a great deal but sets the tone for much of the rest of the country. In 1939 New York City's population of seven-and-a-half million exceeded the population of any state in the Union, including the rest of New York State itself. A conventional witticism referred to the city as "the forty-ninth state." After London it was the largest city in the world. New York was hardly the apple of every eye; it was no object of undivided admiration from coast to coast. "New York is accused of being parochial as well as un-American," Robert Moses wrote in 1943. "There is something in this observation." And yet "it's curious," said a novel of the thirties. "After the war New York . . . Nobody can keep away from it . . . New York's the capital now."

"Mark whispers 'the architecture in the model is blasé, but the *drama of this place!*'" The buildings generally resemble those in the Futurama and, for that matter, the real buildings of the fair itself. They are streamlined modern. Handler had recently completed a B.S. in electrical engineering and had been admitted to the MIT doctoral program in civil engineering—though had deferred admission to work a year or two as an engineer for the Parks Department of the City of New York. His real love was architecture.

"The show has daytime & nighttime segments," the diary continues:

> A recorded narrator describes this amazing though idiotically-named "Democracity" (even "Futurama" is a less-stupid name, though not by much) & its surroundings. The center of the city is full of air & light . . . & no-one lives there! People pour into town & outwards to great parks in the countryside over fancy high-speed roads *à la* Futurama.

They live in beautiful green towns. Those who don't work in the city live in towns clustered round the factories where they do work. As night falls the domed sky grows dark & stars come out. It is gorgeous, uncannily like a real night sky. The lights in the model city come on & it sparkles like a dream-world.

(In the show's night-time segment, ultraviolet spotlights mounted beneath the revolving balconies picked out fluorescent paint in the model and made it glow.)

Then a choral song starts, softly at first & with the heavy sound of a very large choir. Groups of people appear in the dome, projected images—perhaps ten or a dozen separate groups spaced evenly around the perimeter. At first each group is tiny. But the images repeatedly dissolve and are replaced by larger & larger ones, so you can imagine each group growing closer or (if you prefer) getting pumped up like a balloon. The intent is for all these people to be converging on Democracity. Each group is a coherent set, teachers with books, farmers with tools, miners with lamps on their helmets, architects or engineers with blueprints and so on. When the groups have arrived (or at any rate, when they are as pumped up as they are going to get), shimmering light rises from the horizon to engulf the entire dome. Then it fades & the show is over. After a brief pause it starts again. It lasts just long enough to allow you to make one complete orbit. We came in nearly at the start, but that was by chance—people stream in continuously.

The climactic picture show is intended to illustrate a point that Theme Committee chairman Robert Kohn regards as central, "the interdependence of all people, trades and classes in the modern world." The choir has a thousand voices. The movie screen furnished by the dome is an acre and a quarter large.

Now Democracity itself: It is no "planless jumble of slum and chimney," says Kohn, but an exquisitely crafted instrument. Today we would—on balance—hardly want to live in such a place. Everything is sparkling new. There is no variety to the buildings and no history. But the high-thirties view is captured revealingly in that "planless jumble of slum and chimney." Nowadays we find old buildings quaint and edifying. We revamp them and turn them into shopping centers and office space. But in the thirties people *lived* in them, and there was nothing quaint about it. "Old-law tenements" were still standing in New York, buildings without central heat or hot water or bathtubs or (sometimes) fire escapes, where every apartment on the floor shared a bathroom. Cities then didn't boast about their old buildings. They condemned them and tore them down as fast as they could.

It is essential that we understand Democracity if we are to understand the fair. In the future you would no longer have to live in a city just because you *worked* in one. You would live in the countryside or in "garden apartments" around the city's rim. Factory workers would live in green towns just like everybody else. You would drive to work, or to sprawling green parks in the countryside, not on packed city streets but on landscaped highways.

In other words: Democracity's utopian World of Tomorrow amounts, in essence, to the modern suburbs.

But what is the big deal, we are forced to wonder, about mere *suburbia?* To put it another way, how could 1947 New Yorkers have been launched into ecstatic transports (as indeed they were) by Levittown? The typical lot in that archetypal modern suburb was sixty feet wide by a hundred deep. The typical Cape Cod had a living room, a kitchen and two bedrooms on a concrete slab, no basement, an unfinished attic upstairs. The floors were tiled in asphalt.

To understand the passion behind Democracity's utopia, it helps to look at a film called *The City,* which debuted at the fair. *The City* is a propaganda piece—"a hectoring documentary film," one modern study calls it—but it was very much a part of the fair's official world view. "It is believed that an ordinary exhibit of city planning," reports a publicity release, "with drawings and photographs and models of bad tenements, means very little to the average citizen who is not a technician." So a film seemed like a good idea instead. The goal was to show fairgoers the slums that made "decent living impossible for the under-privileged," the evils that "laissez-faire" (the opposite of planning) had inflicted on modern cities. And most important, to show them how to make things better.

The City was produced by the American City Planning Institute. The narration was composed by Lewis Mumford, the brash and sullen music by Aaron Copland. *The City* hates the city. The modern American city, according to this film, is full of noise and fumes and shouts and shrillness and ambulances, drunks, fire trucks stuck in traffic, angry cops. The city streets are hectic and dangerous. The city is a hateful place for children to grow up. The hovels that factory workers inhabit are worse—dark, dirty, primitive, ugly, disastrously unhealthy.

The future, by contrast, is a place where people live in suburban towns—where children romp in green fields, ride their bikes and play softball (softball is a nationwide craze in the thirties) far away from the grind of city traffic, the filth of city gutters, the danger of city railroad yards. In the future "the motor-parkways weave together city and countryside," and people drive to work or the beach on "townless highways" that "go around the town, not through it. Once started, nothing stops you till you're there." The narrator's tone has now assumed an odd bite-your-lip sort of cheerfulness, hope against hope.

A newspaper piece about Democracity, based on an interview with chairman Kohn, underlines the same anticity themes and their antidotes. Democracity is no "city of canyons and gasoline fumes, it is one of simple functional buildings—most of them low— all of them surrounded by green vegetation and clean air. A city where no streets actually intersect and, therefore, where no traffic accidents occur." Most important, a city where no one lives.

In 1939 Americans yearned for suburbia. After the Second World War they flooded out of the cities. It is true that many factors egged them on. During the war tax rates had risen, and the long-standing mortgage interest deduction had grown in value correspondingly. The Federal Housing Administration of 1934 and the Veterans Administration of 1944 insured mortgages and favored suburbs over cities for new construction. But it is also clear that the public longed for the suburban countryside: for a place where you could own a house, tend your plot, let your children ride their bikes in the streets and hear the jinging of crickets on a summer evening. Where you could live and yet still work in the city, commuting over crowded but decent highways. Where you could own a backyard and yet still find schools and shops that the 1930s would have described (intending a compliment) as more urban than small-town in character. Those austere 1947 Levittown houses had central heating and telephones, stoves, refrigerators and washing machines. They had front yards and backyards. People wanted them. Of course there were suburbs before the war, but after the war they exploded. People flocked from the cities in such a rush that in 1956, Robert Moses felt obliged to assert "I do not believe that the metropolis is obsolete."

Promise made, promise kept: We have largely achieved Democracity's utopia. We have suburbs that are not only for shopkeepers, professionals, businessmen and the wealthy, but also for factory workers and secretaries, Koreans, blacks and Jews. The 1970 census was the first in which suburbia was more populous than the nation's cities or rural areas. (Also around 1970, middle-class blacks began moving to the suburbs in significant numbers. Before then they had been excluded, informally or—as in Levittown before the mid-sixties, for example—by explicit contractual stipulation.)

Of course, there is much we have *not* achieved of Democracity's vision. Democracity was "a perfectly integrated garden city of tomorrow." In 1902 the Englishman Ebenezer Howard had published a book by that name, *Garden Cities of Tomorrow.* "Town and country must be married, and out of this union will spring a new hope, a new life, a new civilization." By 1939 several American towns directly embodied Howard's ideas. Radburn, New Jersey, was one. It was planned in the late 1920s. Its houses were grouped closely together, each bordering one street for vehicles and another just for foot traffic. "The motor highway surrounding the whole super-block sends its tributary streets inward toward, but not to, the park core . . . The central park core and its rimming footway send out arms to the boundary." Land was held in common. Radburn had its own school and library, year-round programs for children and an endless list of earnest discussion groups. *The City* illustrated its suburban ideal with pictures of another planned town—Greenbelt, Maryland—that was much like Radburn.

Planning was sacred to the Democracity world view, and few of our suburbs are planned (although planned towns are making a comeback). The city proper, in the Democracity view, was a place where no one lived. But our cities remain moderately robust living places; and obviously the slums are still with us (although nowadays the working class is rarely obliged to live in them). People commute today not only between the suburb and the city, but increasingly between one suburb and another. But that development would have come as no surprise: "The City of Tomorrow will be inspired by the automobile," the fair's literature explains. "Communities will spread outward in breadth, rather than grow upward in the congested fashion of the city of today."

Like the Futurama, Democracity makes many erroneous predictions. Suburban homes, for example, are built on hills or riverbanks "so as not to utilize the land designed to produce the fresh food for Democracity." "Intoxicated drivers will be rare because of the gradual education of the human race to the dangers of mixing alcohol and automobiles into a death cocktail." (Cocktails were big in 1939.) Robert Moses for one was skeptical about the whole city-of-the-future idea—the City of Tomorrow, he wrote, would be a spiffed-up City of Today, not some brand-new Democracity-style concoction.

Mulling over the many important aspects of Democracity's vision we have not achieved or have simply rejected, it is easy to forget that we *have* realized the heart of it. We take the "marriage of town and country" for granted, and when 1939 gets excited about it, we shrug our shoulders. It's not utopia, we point out, it's just suburbia.

It looks a lot like utopia to us, says 1939. Utopia is a place where, for vast numbers of people, life all in all is pretty good.

Many people still can't afford the suburbs; but please let's contemplate, just for a moment, the vast numbers who can. Their lives are not sheer heaven on earth. By and large they are merely comfortable.

But that is what we longed for, says 1939, and you have got it. Promise made, promise kept.

The 1939 public in orbit round Democracity is a community

of faith circling a shrine. All that faith and fervor paid off, and the
community of the faithful emerged, after the war, into the promised
land that had been foretold. But in the promised land there were no
more shrines to circle, and no more pilgrimages. When you live in
utopia you can't yearn for utopia anymore, and the community of
faith is dead.

Democracity's central district is called "Centerton," and the
surrounding towns are either "Pleasantvilles" or "Millvilles," the
Pleasantvilles being entirely residential. The straightforward roll-up-
our-sleeves, solve-the-problem, make-it-work *seriousness* of the high
thirties echoes still in those artless names. The poetry is in their plain-
ness.

The Perisphere had a staff of more than a hundred people to
manage its complex machinery. Despite their best efforts it broke
down every once in a while. Naturally it broke down when E. B.
White visited—"when I finally presented myself there at the base of
the white phallus, face to face with the girl in the booth behind the
glass window with the small round hole." It turned out there would
be a wait of several minutes. "Just some minor difficulty in the Perisphere," the guard explained. "Is there anything in there to scare
you?" a lady asks. "No, Madam," the guard reassures her.

3

Color
Coded

" '**I**'m not sure I quite got all of that' says Mark of the sound and light show, 'But I suppose I see the general idea.' We walk out onto the Helicline." (The Helicline is a ramp spiraling downward from the Perisphere's exit to the surrounding plaza. It loops gracefully in a long arc, making three quarters of a turn round the sphere before reaching ground.)

Mark leans, propped on both arms, on the guard-rail, & surveys the grounds. "You wonder whether central planning might not produce a certain sterility, but *look* at this place. It's beautiful. That's the only word. It's *beautiful*. There's tremendous variety in the buildings, tremendous color & swagger, & the neat rational layout of blocks &

pathways & radial avenues—the wildness of the buildings fights the neatness of the layout, and the result is just vibrant & full of energy . . ." His voice has a child's candy-smeared radiance. "Don't believe it took me so long to make it out here. Thank you for dragging me here . . ." Leans over and administers quick kiss to the forehead. "I must say, however, the Steel building looks a bit too much like a Jello mold for my taste."

We can see it across the plaza. "Blueberry Jello. *Is* there such a thing? I can hear the newsreel now." Using his deep stentorian voice: "And here, out of the vast mucky plains of Queens, an army of workmen lay the foundations for what will be, upon its completion, the *greatest blue gelatin structure* known to man. Dumptruck upon dumptruck filled to the brim with sweet blue powder deposits its load in the huge mixing-bowl specially constructed at the site . . ." "Mark," I say. Face him. Cross arms over my chest & draw the sweater closer round me, for no reason. "What about children?"

We start down the Helicline. "Laurie, it comes down to this." Big excited voice suddenly collapsing. "Can you answer this question for me, because no-one else can." He stops slightly above me on the ramp. "When the U.S. is in a war with Hitler, head-to-head, because that's what it will come down to in the end—just how exactly do you know we'll win? And have you ever considered the consequences of losing?"

Suddenly the whole place seems to me engulfed in dead silence.

"We are a stronger country I know, true, but we have a sense of honor. He is a lunatic." I just stand there looking at him with my hand on the cold railing. I have a vision, don't

know why, of the Trylon's needle soaring ominously upwards through a suffocating blanket of clouds. Am I just
imagining it, or do passers-by cast dark looks?

"How can you bring children into the world? . . ."
Now I'm looking down & can't look up. He moves forward
and takes my hand & we stroll on. Takes my hand in both his
like a baby chick. His tone entirely changes. "Sorry. It sounds
pompous to be agonizing like this." Looks over at me un-
happily. "Of course when I see this place," weak smile, "it
seems expressly designed to make pessimists feel dumb. Did
you have 'em build this place just to convince me that I'm
stupid to be pessimistic?" That's right, I say, I had it built
just for that purpose. I look up & I guess he sees wet eyes.
"Isn't it perfect?" I say. He sighs & says "It really is." He
pulls me closer and tucks my arm under his. Here we are at
the bottom—"Let's walk around," he says, "and let me figure this out, OK? You have the advantage—after all—we're
doing it at the Fair."

As you come off the Helicline you are looking at one
of the most interesting sculptures on the grounds, & it suits
my mood—a tall narrow piece on a tall narrow pedestal
called the Astronomer—a male nude modelled in a strong
simple way, gazing upward away from the Perisphere—the
whole piece carries you soaring upward; the man is gazing
with a look that is thoughtful & troubled & poignant. Most
everything at the Fair is planted symmetrically—in the center, at the four corners, to the left & the right—but this piece
is simply plopped down, & it is very effective that way. It
seems perpetually surrounded by people with cameras.

(I have one such picture, kindly given to me by the photographer. As
a teenager he went often to the fair with camera and tripod, and he

spent an hour around the Perisphere carefully composing the shot.
The Astronomer was by the Swede Carl Milles.)

"They say I am cold," Miss Glassman continues.

> But when Mark made this pronouncement about children &
> the threat of war—I had assumed he wasn't serious, that he
> would just drop the whole thing—I'm sure the blood went to
> my face—& so on. He can defeat anything but his own better
> judgment, whether it makes sense or not. His stubbornness
> is positively incandescent. Don't mean he is inflexible—usu-
> ally he is not in the least. But when you arrive at—*certain
> issues*—you could as soon push a hundred-foot maple out of
> the way as push him, because of the roots, which you cannot
> argue about because you cannot see them. It is a matter of his
> family & particularly his father. Did Chopin, I think, describe
> *rubato* as the graceful swayings of a tree that remains firmly
> rooted nonetheless? And I know I also thought at the time,
> it's not just the fact that he is stubborn—his parents are no
> doubt responsible *somehow* yet again for the substance of
> this particular dreadful worry . . .

This last sentence is hard to make out because it is overwritten—
same hand, slightly different ink—with the words *"Fool* fool fool!"

The Fair's Flushing Meadow site ran alongside the Grand Central
Parkway, which connects Manhattan via the Triborough Bridge to
the counties of Long Island, east of the city. The bridge and the
parkway were built by Robert Moses, and the site itself was cleared
under his auspices: Robert Moses, Mayor Fiorello La Guardia and
President Franklin Delano Roosevelt are the power triumvirate that

molded the character of New York City in this era. And they are three of the most explosively vivid big shots in American history, three quintessentials who inspired raw hatred or, more frequently, admiration to the brink of awe or even love. They *look* like quintessentials. Many years after the fact they retain an uncanny ability to reach out through the frames of the old photos and grab you by the lapels and make you remember: the stocky pint-size La Guardia, eyes burning with energy so fierce you can feel the blast right off the page; Moses, with his sour, stony grandeur; FDR, whose smile is otherworldly. It transcends politics and seems imbued with a sort of saving power. You cannot possibly understand the fair or the thirties without a sense of these men.

Moses and La Guardia were two of a kind. Each had an overarching vision, pursued it ruthlessly and achieved it. In 1939 Moses was New York City parks commissioner, New York State parks commissioner, chairman of the Triborough Bridge Authority, sole member of the New York City Parkway Authority and executive officer of the New York City World's Fair Commission. Among other things. His biographer Robert Caro notes that "during the 1930's, Robert Moses reshaped the face" of New York City:

> In a city in which there had been only 119 playgrounds, he built 255 new ones. In a city in which not a mile of new arterial highway had been built in fifteen years, he built fifty miles of arterial highway. In a city in which a new bridge had not been built in a quarter of a century he built not only the three new big bridges—Triborough, Henry Hudson and Marine Parkway—but 110 smaller ones.

His relationship with La Guardia had to be stormy at times. They fought with each other, screamed at each other and occasionally, La Guardia sicced the cops on Moses to make him stop doing what the mayor had explicitly ordered him not to do. All the same, there could be no doubt that "the most visible fruits of Fiorello La Guardia's service as mayor," as New Dealer, columnist and all-around pundit Raymond Moley wrote, "were the miracles wrought by Robert Moses." And when you got down to brass tacks, "the question which posterity will ask," wrote Moses of La Guardia, "is whether he has been a good Mayor, and the answer will be that he has been the best in our history."

Caro's thumbs-down on Moses—the "master builder," he argues, was a power-mad master destroyer also, of neighborhoods valuable in themselves and vital to the city's character—is gospel today. But the Moses phenomenon transcends even Caro's influential book. The fundamental divide between our world view and the high thirties' shows plainly in our respective canonical views of Robert Moses.

Caro is right, without question, about the man and his ruthlessness. His enemies (he had many) always knew it; his friends have known it for a long time too. Moley quotes Moses on Baron Georges-Eugène Haussmann, the creator of modern Paris: "Everything about him was on a grand scale, both good qualities and faults. His dictatorial talents enabled him to accomplish a vast amount of work in an incredibly short time." "It is no mere vagary of temperament," Moley notes, "that the name Haussmann appears so often in the abundant writings of Moses." Moses makes his "dictatorial" inclinations perfectly clear in his own writings. "We must employ ingenious means and a good deal of determination to do what needs to be done. When there is any sign of weakness—the minute a politician says we can move a highway over a bit or curve it around a group of apartments—that is when the trouble starts." Indeed.

But as Moses likes to say, for better or worse, "The critics build nothing." In 1940 Walter Dorwin Teague singles out Moses' projects for praise again and again in *Design This Day:* the Hudson

Parkway, the Astoria Municipal Pool, the Bronx-Whitestone Bridge. The Triborough Bridge: its Manhattan approach, the traffic distribution system on Randall's Island, an elbow in a cable anchorage, the awe-inspiring Harlem River lift-bridge segment. "He has vision," writes the famous journalist Herbert Bayard Swope, "and that is why he and his works will live." "The New York Parks Department," announces Teague, "plans and builds for human happiness."

It is tempting when we study history to mistake accidents of personality for big, abstract principles. In the thirties, Americans tolerated an enormous expansion of the federal government. The depression and Franklin Roosevelt's character were the main reasons they did, but in the 1930s Robert Moses was a fairly good argument for expanded government all by himself. An Englishman contemplates Moses' Jones Beach: "You know, I said to an official there, 'this is socialism.'

'Yes,' he said. 'That's what it is. Middle-class socialism!' "

Bathgate Park was another Moses accomplishment, its four golf courses centering on "the kind of club-house Hollywood assigns to millionaires . . . But this is not for millionaires; it is for whoever can afford six shillings for a day's golf." Moreover, the whole thing was financed by a bond issue that is being repaid from golf receipts. "Middle-class socialism—and self-funding at that!"

The Right doesn't like to acknowledge that the power and authority of government can be a good thing, up to a point, in the hands of a genius. The Left doesn't like to acknowledge that geniuses are few and far between.

Finally, add Franklin Roosevelt to the volatile Moses-and-La Guardia mix. Between Roosevelt and La Guardia there was liking and respect; between Roosevelt and Moses, hatred. Yet it is one of the more striking facts of modern American history that, when Moses and FDR finally fought a pitched battle in Roosevelt's first term, the popular president attempting by dint of his vast powers to get Moses axed as head of the Triborough Bridge Authority—Moses won.

FDR was, of course, the leading quintessential of the age. Roosevelt was dismissed by Justice Oliver Wendell Holmes, in a famous pronouncement, as "a second-class intellect. But a first-class temperament!" He was dismissed by Walter Lippmann as "a pleasant man who, without any important qualifications for the office, would very much like to be President." But there was an ingredient in the complex FDR concoction that these distinguished commentators missed. They may not have attended the 1924 Democratic Convention and Roosevelt's first major speech after he got polio. They may not have seen him "moving slowly towards the podium alone, sweat beading his brow, jaw grimly set, eyes on the floor—left crutch forward and weight shifted to it, right crutch forward, left leg hitched forward, again and again . . ." He gave a powerful, tremendous nominating speech for Al Smith, and the crowd went wild. Herbert Swope, the same man who praised Moses, had advised FDR that his draft was lousy and he ought to deliver a different one, composed by one of Smith's aides. Which he did. Does that matter? The ingredient Holmes and Lippmann missed was ferocious will.

Moses and La Guardia were brilliant and were visionaries in a way FDR was not. They may have been in the strictest sense more talented than he. But the element all three shared, Roosevelt above all, was ferocious will. In an age of authority they were *the* authorities. They light up the high thirties like fireworks.

One final prerequisite to any attempt at understanding the fair: We need to know, briefly, where the nation's affairs stood in 1939.

By the spring of 1937 the economy had rebounded to the

predepression levels of 1929. The president took the strong economy as his opportunity to start cutting federal spending and the deficit, both of which had risen fast and furiously during his first term. Late in 1937 a stiff recession took hold. In April 1938, with the economy still bad, Roosevelt abandoned his short-lived budgetary conservatism and announced his intention to get back to serious federal spending. In 1939 the economy was coming back, slowly.

In 1935 and 1936 the Supreme Court had nullified a large collection of New Deal programs; stalwarts feared for the lives of the National Labor Relations law and the Social Security Act, two of their favorite achievements. In February 1937 Roosevelt proposed that the president be allowed to appoint a new justice for every sitting justice past seventy years of age. The plan was unpopular (it looked too much like a naked power grab), and it died in July. By that time, though, the Court had realigned itself and was voting to uphold New Deal legislation. That same year, Supreme Court retirements finally gave Roosevelt a chance to start putting his own people on the bench. As the fair opened, the New Deal, with its sweeping expansion of the federal government's prerogatives and responsibilities, was (judicially speaking) home free.

It was also a thing of the past. It was over. In the 1938 midterm elections, the Republicans had gained eighty-one seats in the House and eight in the Senate. Roosevelt's 1939 State of the Union address was the first in which he proposed no new programs.

Foreign affairs were starting to monopolize the president's and the country's attention. The Neutrality Act of 1937 had been motivated by the belief of Congress and the president that the United States ought not to choose sides in the Spanish Civil War. It is hard today, and for many people it was still harder then, not to sympathize with a government that was battling Hitler and Mussolini—as the Loyalists were doing in Spain. But the conduct of the war was beyond sickening on both sides, and in time the Loyalists managed to wear out the affections of some of their most devoted and determined friends (George Orwell, for example). "In this quarrel," wrote Winston Churchill, "I was neutral. Naturally, I was not in favor of the Communists. How could I be, when if I had been a Spaniard they would have murdered me and my family and friends?" By late March 1939, the Republic was beaten. As the fair opened, Francisco Franco ruled a united fascist Spain.

Roosevelt was well aware of the threat of fascism in Europe, of Japan in Asia. In October 1937 he made a speech suggesting that the dictatorships be "quarantined" as if they were infectious killer diseases. In March 1938 Hitler went into Austria; in September, France and Britain awarded him a prime, juicy slice of Czechoslovakia, and the following March he brought the rest under Nazi control. In mid-April 1939 Roosevelt sent a note to Hitler and Mussolini asking that they specifically renounce any plans to attack the small countries of Europe. They casually brushed him off, and his dedication speech at the fair was FDR's first occasion to answer them. "For those who had expected a more direct reference by President Roosevelt to the state of affairs in Europe," the *Times* reported, "there was disappointment." But some in the audience construed his words (said the *Herald Tribune*) "as a polite but pointed lecture to Chancellor Adolf Hitler on the advisability of peaceful cooperation among nations."

The fall of France in June 1940 was Roosevelt's opportunity to grab the initiative against the isolationist leanings of Congress and much of the nation. He requested and Congress approved huge sums for defense. He named two prominent Republicans, Henry Stimson and Frank Knox, his secretaries of war and the navy. In September he announced the massive Lend-Lease program—desperately pressed Great Britain got fifty First World War American destroyers, in return for granting the United States long leases on naval and air bases in the British West Indies. In October the draft was revived. (On October 16, the 5:30 P.M. presentation of "Railroads on Parade" in the Transportation Zone was canceled so that male employees could register.) On the fair's last day the 1940 presidential election campaign was in full swing, as the crisis-driven arms buildup continued apace. FDR was seeking an unprecedented third term. The surprise Republican nominee, Wendell Willkie, addressed the large closing-day crowd at the fairgrounds. "I have predicted," he said later that day, "that if the present administration is restored to power for a third term, our democratic system will not outlast another four years."

But the administration was and our democratic system did.

It goes without saying that, during the 1930s, Roosevelt faced massive disapproval from Republicans and conservatives to his right. We sometimes forget that he was disdained, also, by many intellectuals to his left. The literary critic Alfred Kazin (who ranks among the most effective chroniclers of 1930s New York) writes that, as a young man, "like all my friends, I distrusted Roosevelt as a wily politician and a professional charmer." Kazin was attracted to socialism, but the communists had "Silone, Malraux, Hemingway, Gide, Rolland, Gorky, Aragon, Picasso, Eluard, Auden, Spender, Barbusse, Dreiser, Farrell, while the Socialists seemed only to have their own virtue." Lionel Trilling neatly captures the high-thirties intelligentsia on the topic of mere socialists: " 'Mr. Folger is a socialist!' " says a lady in his novel. " 'Not that I think much of socialists as such, but it does mean something, doesn't it, for a farmer to have come even so far?' " Her tone will be strikingly familiar to any modern-day academic.

In a 1936 book review Dwight Macdonald observed, with the unfailing acuity of the New York intellectual, that most intelligent Americans could be expected to welcome fascism as "superior to liberal capitalism as a technique for running modern society." Contrast Franklin Roosevelt at work on his first radio "fireside chat." The banks were shut and the whole economy teetered on the brink of ruin that day in early March 1933. Roosevelt's task was to comfort and to reassure. He lay on a couch and dictated the speech as it came to him. He "looked at the blank wall, trying to visualize the individuals he was seeking to help: a mason at work on a new building, a girl behind a counter, a man repairing an automobile, a farmer in his field, all of them saying 'Our money is in a Poughkeepsie bank, and what is this all about?'" The president hailed from near Poughkeepsie. And here is the point. What Macdonald, what the New York intellectuals, what the whole world's supply of intellectuals lacked was not intelligence. It was not compassion. It was imagination.

Franklin Roosevelt had ferocious will, and Franklin Roosevelt had imagination.

Grand Central Parkway runs generally east-west, but alongside the fair it is more north-south. The fair's main axis leads out from the parkway to the east. The theme center with the Trylon and Perisphere is located along this main axis, separated by only one building from the parkway. Suppose you were to walk from the parkway right through this intervening building and right through the Perisphere, and then pause with your back to the T&P. The fair's layout was the responsibility of the seven-member Board of Design. In July 1936 the board settled on a plan presented by the architect William Orr Ludlow and the visionary designer and architectural illustrator Hugh Ferriss. Their plan centered on a half circle, with avenues radiating out from the Theme Center through the fan-shaped sweep that lies before you.

You are looking straight down Constitution Mall, which connects the Trylon and Perisphere with the large and boring United

States building—like two upright shoeboxes joined by a flat-lying shoebox—far in the distance.

The building behind the Theme Center is New York City's, so the host city, the Theme Center and the host country are all lined up on axis.

Pools with fountains, escorted by double rows of trees on either side, march down the center of the mall. The pool parade is interrupted a quarter of the way up by a gigantic George Washington: The official occasion for the fair was the 150th anniversary of George Washington's inauguration in New York City. Two-thirds of the way up is the oval Lagoon of Nations, big enough in itself to encompass all of circa-1939 Rockefeller Center. The pavilions of foreign countries congregate mainly around the U.S. building on the far side of the lagoon. To the right of the lagoon, the exhibits of thirty-three U.S. states cluster around another pool.

Between the Lagoon of Nations and the U.S. building is the Court of Peace, the fair's main ceremonial plaza. Roosevelt spoke there on opening day, Einstein when the Palestine Pavilion was dedicated, Willkie on the day the fair closed.

Most of the commercial exhibits lie on the near side of the lagoon. This area has the mall down its middle, the Avenue of Pioneers radiating off at forty-five degrees to the right and the Avenue of Patriots likewise to the left. The Court of Communications stretches out at ninety degrees to the mall on your left, the Court of Power on your right.

The buildings in this central fan-shaped area follow an elaborate and intriguing color code designed by William Ludlow, the muralist Elmer Garnsey and a "consultant on mural painting" named Ernest Peixotto. The key inspiration was evidently Peixotto's. The Trylon and Perisphere are painted pure white, immediately surrounding buildings off-white and buildings beyond those in colors that deepen with greater distance from the Theme Center. The Avenue of Patriots goes from pale to deep yellow, the mall from rose to burgundy, the Avenue of Pioneers from baby blue to ultramarine. The curving walkway that arcs from Patriots to Pioneers, crossing the mall on the near side of the lagoon, is (appropriately) Rainbow Avenue. The interior of the Long Island Rail Road's temporary fair station shows the design board's care. The station was rose-violet on the inside. Violet is yellow's complementary color, and the violet interior was supposed to make the golden yellow buildings right outside seem more brilliant.

The fair's elaborate color scheme was generally regarded as a beautiful idea—and a total failure. A building didn't have to be painted entirely in its theme color; a few were, but usually the official color appears only in accents, and other surfaces are predominantly beige or off-white. No one who had not been warned in advance seems to have noticed the overall color scheme, and even if you had been warned it was not easily detected except from the air, where few visitors were typically to be found. But if the scheme failed in the large, the bright colors made a big hit in themselves. "Great stretches of eye-filling hues, canary yellow, orange, blue, green, rose, carry the eye along unbroken wall surfaces," writes Gardner Harding in 1939. (Harding's essay remains one of the best short pieces on the fair. Harding was an author and journalist. Foreign trade was his specialty, but he published books, newspaper and magazine pieces on many topics.) "It appears that the Board of Design approached this problem in a cheerful mood," reports the *Herald Tribune,* "tossed its hat in the air and turned on the color faucets with zest and abandon." On top of all the color-schemed buildings, the fair's "official colors" were bright blue, orange and white. They appeared on banners, uniforms, shoulder patches and signs all over the grounds.

COLOR CODED

The design board promulgated many other rules besides the color scheme. Names of exhibitors could not appear more than fifteen feet off the ground. Every building had to be approved by the board; unpleasing shapes were exiled to the amusement area. Exile was the embarrassing fate of the cash-register-shaped National Cash Register Pavilion, which showed each day's attendance on its numerical display. Neon was prohibited; red lighting was banned.

Buildings fell into three main categories: those put up by private exhibitors, by foreign nations and by the fair itself. The fair's own buildings were "frankly enclosures for rentable space," Talbot Hamlin wrote. (Hamlin is one of the surest and most interesting of the fair's contemporaneous critics. He was a professor of architectural history at Columbia and a prolific writer.) "Whatever aesthetic effect they have must come from color treatment and applied mural painting and sculpture." But he liked some of them: Mines and Metallurgy, for example, and the Aviation building. The private exhibitors' buildings were better, he thought; many are "interesting and beautiful, and seem to have that combined quality of gaiety and open invitation which somehow means Fair." The foreign pavilions "form a group of great interest, quite different in character from the American buildings." They use more glass, for example. Hamlin's judgments can be harshly negative. The grand axis from the Theme Center to the United States building, to choose a key example, "was a magnificent conception"; but only those who "saw the mall before the statues were in place know its real greatness." At the finished fair, it was spoiled by the "characterless and gigantic Washington" and other statuary—the "frivolous filigree" of an enormous sun-dial, "ungainly" representations of the *Four Freedoms*. Yet for all his reservations, Hamlin praises the "daring and dynamic" fair in the end.

You are still standing (or maybe by now you are sitting) with your back to the Theme Center. Far off to your right is Fountain Lake, and wrapping around the shore closest to you and continuing on up is the Amusement Area, featuring the Parachute Jump and lots of other amusement-park attractions. You can see the towering parachute ride from where you stand, looking like an open umbrella on a huge steel-latticework traffic cone. Customers are hoisted aloft by wires hanging from the tips of the umbrella's ribs, then drop back down, with parachutes breaking their descents. "They drop you twenty floors," *The New Yorker* explains with characteristic cogency, "and once you start going up you can't change your mind."

Behind you the fairgrounds cross the parkway on two bridges, the Bridge of Wheels behind you to the left and the Bridge of Wings to your right. On the far side of the parkway lies the most popular zone of all, Transportation. This is, after all, the Streamlined Age.

4

The Necktie

It turns out that "they" who said Hortense Laura Glassman was cold are not so vague as first appears. In the yearbook of the private girls' high school she attended she was identified, as best I can reconstruct, as the "smartest girl in the class, and a famous cold beauty too," or some variant on basically those words. Clearly it hurt her and, several years later, there are at least four references to it in the diary: One says merely, at the end of an unpleasant date, "Neither cold nor beautiful!!" I hesitated to ask her whether I could look at the other entries in the notebooks, but as we talked it became clear that, however much she deprecated them, it wasn't merely that she was indifferently willing to let me read the entire diary; she *wanted* me to read it. That was the whole idea.

We stand at the base of the Helicline & Mark says "Laurie, I want to see the whole thing—you've been here before" (twice) "so you show me—& the way things are running who knows when I'll be back—let's see the whole shmear! And I want to take you dancing & we'll see the fireworks—let's stay until they kick us out. OK? Y'know—which way?—one summer when I was seven maybe or eight, my folks took me out to Connecticut for the day, along with my uncle and aunt and cousins, to visit my uncle's boss . . ." We're walking off down the mall, vigorously. He tells me about an occasion on which, although he didn't know how to swim, plunging into a pond turned out to be a great idea. He wants to plunge into the Fair.

Toward the end of the last notebook I discovered an occasion on which Miss Glassman spends hours awaiting Handler, not knowing where he is. It is early 1942. She waits in her father's small study in his cracked leather armchair, then rises to stand at the window and fiddle with the slats of the Venetian blinds. (Venetian blinds are stylishly avant-garde in the early forties.) She takes the cord and sends them clattering open and stares out at West End Avenue. Something important is to happen the next day. What? Not a wedding, but otherwise I don't know. Those particular hours evidently trouble her for the rest of her life—down to the moment at which she hands the notebooks over to me. She stared, it seems, at the faces of the large somber apartment buildings as they sank into their complex shadows and the sun went lower. She sat again, picked up and put aside again the book she was attempting to read. She went to the window again. The sky was lavender to the south, the round headlights coming uptown were yellow and questioning and she rested her forehead on the windowpane. Eventually he arrived.

After reading this passage I resolved to make no more raids into the latter parts of the diary, but to go in order and ask questions.

Off they go: If you are walking beside them, you might notice the uniformed fair policemen strolling or standing; you might be struck by the shiny stainless-steel underside of the Helicline. A flock of pigeons lands with emphatic beatings near your feet. On one of the wood-slat benches grouped round the Perisphere's pool, a little girl dangles her feet and eats a hot dog. You hear the fountains round the Perisphere, the mumble of the crowd and shrieks of children and, occasionally, the smooth rolling chatter of the "guide chairs" in which tired or lazy visitors take in the sights. The service is operated by American Express. The visitors sit; the guide stands behind and pushes the cart where they direct. There are several variants. You could rent a single-seater or a double. There are also guide-driven electric-powered chairs that seat three. They all rent by the hour. In the event of rain the guide immediately breaks out a cellophane cover that slips handily over the patrons. But "the perspiration from the encasement" wasn't much of an improvement over raindrops, one visitor complained.

On a warm May day the guide wears a pith helmet, a white shirt with a Trylon-and-Perisphere patch on the arm and, of course, a necktie. The fair is full of color, but the crowd itself, with its neatly suited male component, is darker than at a modern fair. Those suits and ties, and the women's dresses, play a role in a larger drama whose theme is the bigness of the chasm separating our world from 1939.

Nineteen thirty-nine America was a community of faith. One symptom of the fact is the vast number of distinctions it religiously maintained. Energy and effort are required in order to maintain a distinction—between, for example, clothes for home and clothes for a day out at the fair. We are apt to ask Why bother? But 1939 was less apt to ask that question. A religious community lives by the rules. It is defined and held together by the rules. Not because the rules are imposed by force, and not necessarily because they have any moral significance; of the countless distinctions 1939 observed, some were evil and some were meaningless. A few were good. They were upheld not because of their moral significance but because they were rules. By honoring the traditional distinctions—between sacred and profane, priest and layman, holy and ordinary day, kosher and *trayf,* saint and sinner—the faithful are made to feel part of one community, and worthy of the rewards they are promised.

In 1939 distinctions were maintained between the way children dressed at school and at home, the way they addressed an adult versus a friend, the way boys were treated versus girls, ladies versus gentlemen (a gentleman, for example, invariably stood as long as any lady in the room was on her feet), between those who were entitled to call you by your given name and those who were not, up staircases and down, Sunday and other days, blacks and whites, Jews and gentiles, Chevrolets and Pontiacs, misses and missuses, legitimate offspring versus bastards, married couples versus those living in sin, the behavior, demeanor and clothing of clergy versus those of laymen (Protestant clergymen for example wore "clerical waistcoats"), the manners and attitudes of "a *college* boy" (or girl) versus those of an ordinary specimen, the status of high culture versus low (the only virtue of a certain Gershwin concert in 1936, one critic wrote, was that it made "a certain class of people conscious of such a thing as symphonic ensemble"), loiterers versus law-abiding citizens, proper attire in New York versus the rest of the country (thus in New York, white shoes or sports clothes are simply not acceptable on well-dressed ladies), words you might speak versus words fit to print, the subjunctive mood versus the indicative ("even though he perform this office himself . . ."), behavior allowed in private versus what might appear in a picture magazine versus what might appear on screen; plus hundreds of others, nowadays lapsed or outright despised.

There is nothing to justify ambivalence about the steep decline of racial discrimination and anti-Semitism that has taken place in this country since 1939. It is the direct result of allowing distinctions once rigidly enforced to lapse. But, troubling though it may be to admit, that steep decline is part of a broader phenomenon with dangerous consequences.

Many people nowadays agree that the distinction in community standing between, for example, married and unmarried mothers was a valuable one to have had around.

In tonier suburbs today, children call adults by first name. What happens when more substantial adult-child distinctions dissolve? Lucinda Franks catalogs some of the consequences in a fascinating magazine article. "We have abrogated the moral authority our parents wore as easily as gloves," she writes. "In Westchester County in New York, for instance, where kids in their early teens come into the city to party until the early hours of the morning, some parents are afraid to give their children curfews for fear they will move out and live with a friend." A school administrator hears parents "all the time asking their kids 'Is that O.K.?' as though they needed their kids to approve every decision." A third-grader is asked to list questions that have occurred to her during a sex education course, and responds with a very reasonable one—"Why do we have to know about stuff like this?"

Meanwhile a local school board in Half Moon Bay, California, takes up a motion to ban homework—after all, "some students are simply in a better environment to succeed than others," the local newspaper editorializes, "and it is unfair to grade students on their home life." In the summer of 1994, news reports told of a mother who slapped her nine-year-old in a Winn-Dixie supermarket for picking on his sister. Out in the parking lot she was arrested on a felony charge (cruelty to children), and her husband had to cash in his pension fund to raise the $22,050 to bail her out. The next move, said the news reports, was up to local prosecutors.

Perhaps it *is* better for the experts to enforce their views of child rearing on pain of imprisonment. There are lots of rotten parents out there; of that I have no doubt. My point is not that these events are bad or good, rather that 1939 would have found them astonishing—but very much of a piece with a whole raft of other astonishing changes in postutopian America, all tending toward the indiscriminate abolition of distinctions that, like the one between adults and children, were once taken to be fundamental to civilized life.

Of course 1939 was five years after Cole Porter had announced that, heaven knows, "anything goes." Gerald Wendt commented on the mood of the late thirties: "The ambitions of women, the disintegration of the home, the liberalizing of education, the respectability of divorce, the unrestrained dreams of youth, the decline of the church, are all facts not accounted for in our inherited culture." The thirties themselves were years when long-established barriers seemed to be falling left and right. When Benny Goodman played jazz in Carnegie Hall, it was news. When FDR's Surgeon General Thomas Parran spoke the word "syphilis" on the radio, it was news. The process is ongoing, and it's interesting to speculate about the distinctions still in force that will be undone a generation hence.

An American Express cart pusher is not to be seen without his pith helmet, his shoulder patch and his tie. *Neckties:* merely one minor curlicue in the elaborate pattern of distinctions erased since the high thirties, but an interesting one. In F. Scott Fitzgerald's lovely unfinished novel of 1940, *The Last Tycoon,* the hero picks up his girl on a Sunday afternoon, takes her for a long drive to the coast where they inspect his unfinished house, drives her back home (stopping for dinner) and back out to the house again; they make love and stroll on the beach. ("I think I was a bit sex-starved," says Kathleen afterward, this creature of a more innocent, less sophisticated age.) He takes her home and returns home himself, and then works until 3 A.M.

Slightly after three, it seems he entered his bedroom. There "he took off his tie."

Either he had put the tie on again that evening in the beach house or he had never taken it off. So there he is at 3 A.M. finally removing it. The entire late twentieth century presses round this exhausted man to scream, almost beside itself, *Why bother?!* Couldn't you maybe (we scornfully ask) have loosened your collar and taken the thing off at *midnight,* at least? He does not deign to answer. There is a right way to dress, and rules are rules. But if we were thoughtful in the slightest, we would mobilize every spare historian and sociologist at our disposal to examine the question *Why bother?* How is it that, within the space of one lifetime, a question that was formerly too childish to ask has become impossible to answer?

Miss Glassman and Mr. Handler make off down the mall, but before we leave the Theme Center, let's glance at it one last time. The Theme Center commission was awarded to the firm of Wallace Harrison and André Fouilhoux in November 1936. Harrison reports that the Perisphere's shape was inspired by the domes of Saint

Mark's in Venice. The Trylon and Perisphere are gone, but if you have spent any time at all in New York City, you are familiar with Wallace Harrison's work. Not his best, unfortunately. He presided over the design of Lincoln Center, erected from 1962 to '68. He personally designed the goofily bombastic Metropolitan Opera House. It's curious that Edward Durrell Stone is probably best known to the general public today as the architect of a project that apes Lincoln Center, Washington's dumb gorilla of an arts complex, Kennedy Center. The two had collaborated in the 1930s, Harrison as head of the design team and Stone as senior draftsman, on Radio City Music Hall. And Radio City is a main feature of what is today widely regarded as the "greatest urban complex of the twentieth century," New York's Rockefeller Center. (Harrison is responsible for another of New York's highest-profile structures as well, the U.N. building. But once you have had your fill of bad or indifferent Harrison designs, it is only fair to look at a beautiful one: Harrison and Fouilhoux's Rockefeller Apartments of 1936, a block north of the Museum of Modern Art. It is one of the most elegant buildings in the city.)

André Fouilhoux was an engineer, and the firm was created in 1935. More than one thousand pilings were driven into the bogs to support the T&P's immense weight. Structurally it was an odd mix: The fantastically intricate steel framework (the Perisphere undressed recalls the dense twine tracery of a baseball with its cover off) is surfaced with gypsum board, the sort of stuff used to face interior walls of ordinary houses. The fair's buildings were temporary, and were moreover intended to *look* temporary. The fair's architectural scheme, says the 1939 guide, has the aim of "frankly expressing the temporary nature of the buildings." Modern architecture was never phony; it looked like what it was. A number of buildings carried that idea to the obvious extreme—the Marine Transportation building looks like ships, the Aviation building like an airport, the Railroads building like a roundhouse. The Trylon allegedly stood for "the finite" and the Perisphere for "the infinite" (or maybe it was the other way around—there are sources for both versions), but the impulse behind the structures was strictly aesthetic and the meanings were concocted after the fact.

The theme structures were supposed to have been even larger—the Trylon seven hundred feet and the Perisphere two hundred—but financial constraints forced a reduction. The Trylon and Perisphere occupied the position they did because that spot afforded the site's solidest underpinnings. The rest of the plan fell into place around them. It was mere coincidence that if you extended the fair's principal axis to the southwest, you would pierce the Statue of Liberty. But fair publicity played up the Statue of Liberty connection. A French magazine pointed out another, stranger coincidence: When a map of the fair is overlaid on the plan of the 1937 Universal Exposition in Paris, the one where New York's Rockettes triumphed—a series of remarkable similarities emerges. New York's main axis, from the Transportation Zone through the Theme Center to the United States building, is the same length as Paris's main axis, from the École Militaire to the Trocadéro. Constitution Mall is the same length as Paris's central promenade. The Lagoon of Nations crops up exactly where the Seine does when the plans are overlaid, and the Court of Peace coincides exactly with the central court of the Trocadéro Gardens. New York's fair was much larger, but the resemblances are odd and striking.

Despite the architect's intentions, the finished Perisphere was never perfectly sleek; it was supposed to have been finished in concrete, but the budget wouldn't allow for it. The stuccoed and "Tymstoned" gypsum-board surface would have reminded you less of a bowling ball (say) than of a very delicately ribbed-and-veined, stunningly round melon. "In many ways," Harrison reflected, "it was more beautiful when it was just steel." At night, colored spotlights projected cloud patterns onto the Perisphere, white on blue, making it appear to revolve. On patriotic evenings it was banded in red, white and blue, and to celebrate Halloween 1939, it was lit up like a jack o'lantern.

Four thousand tons of steel went into the Theme Center. The United States won the Second World War with weapons made, in part, from the scrap.

5

The Monkey Goddess

"We wander first into the Heinz building," Miss Glassman writes:

It is the second-to-last building on the right side of the mall before the Lagoon, as you make your way out from the T&P. It is a pale-pink dome the shape of Harpo Marx's hat with bright red trim. You enter between two smallish fin-like pylons (pylons are *everywhere* at this Fair), beneath a bold red '57'—the number of products in the Heinz canon, I think; 57 takes on a mystical significance at the Heinz building because it is such a prominent & meaningless decorative element, large 57's & small ones, outside and in. As if it were an ancient masonic mystery symbol. [Talbot Hamlin disliked all the pylons. "Particularly dangerous to human scale," he thought; they were scattered around the grounds "without much rhyme or reason."]

There is a wondrously strange space beneath this dome. It is so typical at this Fair to walk into a space that is simply *not like* anything you have ever seen before.

As you enter you hear cascading water & look immediately toward the middle: a tall narrow blue column, green leaves & golden figures attached, rises toward the center of the dome out of an oddly-shaped pool of water, a sort of round-pointed star. Way on top of the column the Goddess of Perfection (yes honestly) crouches like a monkey. She is a golden nude female & holds a crystal sphere. For *perfection*. Don't you see? Don't be obtuse. But that's not all. The column wears a huge glass saucer like a tutu fifteen feet up, & water streams from the saucer's edges toward the center. Just before reaching the column it cascades in a cylindrical waterfall (taking all this in?) into the pool below. Gold hoops & accent lines zoom off into space around the column. You can walk up to the pool & gaze heavenward through the glass water-saucer towards the monkey goddess. Everyone who enters the room makes straight for the pool as if in a trance, drawn by the rush of the water. Crowds of entranced pilgrims gaze upward at the goddess. And then you close your eyes & the sound makes you feel as if you are standing under the eaves in a downpour; your face is misted gently. And there is the distinct smell of vegetable soup. Unquestionably this building is best appreciated with your eyes closed. That's what the Guide Book ought to say.

"Huh," says Mark emphatically. *"Well—"*

(The fair loved water effects of all sorts. One of the most unusual was at the Men's Apparel Quality Guild, a building with exhibits by men's clothing makers—Hart Shaffner and Marx, Interwoven Socks, Botany Worsted Mills, the Frank H. Lee Hat Company. The ceiling was a vast aquarium full of goldfish.)

"As we stand there," the diary continues,

I find myself thinking of a late-summer day as I wait under a shop's awning during a sudden rainshower. I am a child, but can't say how old. The rain hisses & a steamy primeval mist rises off the hot pavement with an oily-summer smell, & I remember the cars parked at the curb, two groups of square black Fords & a lower modern car between them. The rain thrumming the curved hollow enclosure round its front wheel. The tense waterdrops that break & reform & break again reflecting like a crazy mirror the blinking red neon of a sign—the sign belonging to the shop I stand in front of, I suppose. Is it a pharmacy, with those hanging glass urns filled with red liquid & blue liquid, silent & witching, that used to fascinate & scare me? I have a child's sense of the city as infinite. Going on like this block after block, right to infinity. I seem to be alone. I like being alone & watching the storm unseen. The neon blinks. Where was I? Where was my father?

Well. After paying homage to perfection, most people move away quickly because this is, of course, the *Heinz* pavilion. Aside from the Westinghouse time capsule, the most widely noted Fair fact on the streets of Manhattan is that you can get free food at Heinz. You can also get a little pickle pin. [Heinz had been handing out pickle-shaped souvenir pins at world's fairs since 1893 in Chicago.] The free food is distributed by pretty girls behind a long counter. There is soup of different kinds, baked beans, spaghetti, macaroni, pickles, tomato juice—all lovely things I suppose, but not what I feel like eating before lunch, nor Mark either. But there are lots of other exhibits round the dome's outer wall. We stroll off to examine them.

My sweater is hanging cape-like & my arms are folded & I'm leaning against Mark & sort of bumping him with my shoulders from time to time in a friendly way as we look around, with the rush of water at our backs. "Is it that, you're sure we *will* beat Hitler," he says, "or is it that, you want to have children even if we lose?" "Well, no" I say in a way that sounds more friendly & teasing than is probably appropriate—"It must be one or the other," he continues, "& would you please tell me your reasoning? After all, you're—" "the philosopher"—I finish the sentence along with him. He's always saying that. "It's neither," I say, "I just feel that the question of children is on a different plane somehow . . ." He puts his arm around me. "Why?"

She had majored in philosophy and was toying with the idea, evidently, of continuing for an advanced degree.

"It's not a matter of analysis," I tell him, "to have children at a time like this. It's a matter of *overcoming* analysis. It's a matter of hope. The hope drive. The triumph of the hope drive. Like the hunger drive, or reproductive drive . . ." "The *Hoffnungstreib,*" he announces, professorially. Deep voice. "Did you just make that up? This hope drive?" "Yes." We wander out of the building because he is impatient to see the Rotolactor, and suspects it must be nearby . . .

When we emerge from Heinz we are on the great,

wide bridge running across the mall's blue pool—the bridge where we came first this morning. It is actually one segment of Rainbow Avenue, which sweeps a shallow arc between the two avenues departing the Theme Center at 10:30 and 1:30 if the mall is noon. Gazing down Rainbow Ave is like gazing down an arc of seats in a football bowl. Its gentle curviness makes you think about the T&P at the focus of it all, even when you are not actually looking that way. We walk out onto the bridge again, stop at the center & turn our backs to the T&P. Across the great rippling reach of the oval Lagoon, through the mist of fountains, at the head of a large plaza where it presides like the father at an extra-large dining table the United States building: foursquare, imposing, too earnest. But the flags decorating the plaza give it a comfortable & genial kind of magnificence. A bit like the President's. The building embraces its plaza with long arms stretching forward toward the Lagoon. Lesser nations without pavilions of their own are housed in the arms. Big nations with their own buildings have secondary display spaces in there as well. Why? Because it is some sort of rule of international exhibitions, I think.

(Italy's space in this Hall of Nations, for example, is "dedicated to the Duce" and contains "an imposing statue of the Italian leader.")

Then we turn round & gaze again down the alley-way of bright trees over the pool, through the fountains, past George Washington (who stands with his back turned) to the Trylon & Perisphere—the Trylon well over to the left; there is a large gap from this angle, at least a third the Perisphere's diameter, between it & the Perisphere. There are four sculptures at the bridge's corners. Mark discovers in the

Guide that they are the "Four Freedoms," speech, religion, press and assembly. "What is this, like the Marx brothers?" he ponders. "Speecho, Presso . . ." As a matter of fact they are awkward things, yet this is a beautiful spot.

(The sculptures are by Leo Friedlander.)

"I could take a photograph," says Mark as we gaze, "but what I wish I could do is fix it in memory & always be able to recall it." Often he says what we are both thinking. We pass to the other side & he unfolds a map & squints at it in the sunshine, then gestures the right way & we head back in the T&P's direction. Things that look pretty close on the map (to me anyway) turn out to be not so close at all when you are walking. Across from the Heinz building is a sprawling structure in *bright* red, one of the Fair's official buildings housing exhibits about food—it has a big drum-like thing in the corner where bridge & mall intersect—it is too covered with murals, a tattooed sailor of a building. Running along the mall you see a mural & then a great solid-red bay, & another mural & another bay, & a mural & a bay—the murals also predominantly red, with orange, brown & off-white patches. Too red for my tastes, the whole thing.

We head back down the mall, with two ranks of trees to our left & the pool with fountains to their left (the breeze stirring the leaves' cool fragrance & blowing prisms in the mist over the fountains), then more trees & finally a walkway matching ours on the other side. "But this place is no triumph of the hope drive," Mark says, gesturing round. "It's full of hope, but it makes *arguments*. It's full of *rational* hope." "Yes? Well." I'm uncertain.

To reach Borden we make a wide loop round the big

George Washington, swinging about so we are again heading away from the Perisphere, & there is Borden just beside us. The broad loop reminds me of the subway at South Ferry. Mark likes this axis—"beautifully done"—but strongly disapproves of Washington's location. "Here we just spent five minutes walking towards the *back* of the damned thing. Why did they *do* that? As if at the mall in Washington, some genius had installed a monumental Cupid at the foot of the Washington Monument with its rear end pointing at the Capitol." I see his point, though the Washington itself is dignified & stately. "Maybe I should do a sketch of that for the exhibition, by way of architectural commentary—" I give him the look he is expecting. He often teases me along these lines.

The figure is sixty feet tall, in off-white plaster. Washington gazes solemnly at the Theme Center, hat in his right hand and his left resting on the hilt of his sword. He was made to gaze at the Trylon and Perisphere on purpose—he was to seem occupied in calm contemplation of the future. Fairgoers developed the habit of writing their initials on the statue's base. The sculptor was James Earle Fraser, famous for designing the Buffalo nickel. The Jefferson nickel replaced it in 1938. The Washington quarter of 1932 was the second-newest arrival in the high-thirties coin kingdom. At the fair most nickels were buffalo, most quarters Washington; but there were still many "standing Liberty" quarters about, the occasional prebuffalo nickel and pre–standing Liberty quarter (both nineteenth-century designs featuring a sulking, mannish Liberty in profile) and the odd Indian-head penny.

"Borden is a funny building centering on a tall upright gold-colored cylinder," the diary continues.

> The cylinder's bottom third is glass, and it is surrounded halfway up by three broad flat rims, like purple hat brims, supported by red columns. As you approach, the building beckons you in under the brims like a carousel beckoning you under its tent. You find yourself wishing to get closer & find out what it is all about, and the colors and the mood are festive. They only need a calliope. Above the main entrance a sign says "Borden presents DAIRY WORLD of TOMORROW."
>
> There is a crowd several people deep peering in at the windows round the cylinder's bottom. As we stroll toward it Mark looks up at the top & says "What happened, was it Cow Season or something when they built this place?" Because—. Never mind.

(Around the upper band of the cylinder is a continuous frieze consisting of the word BORDEN alternating with sculpted cow heads, which might be taken for incongruous hunting trophies.)

> "The rotunda sits at the bottom of a shallow well of broad circular steps, like an amphitheater—those closest are at the level of the building's floor, with recent arrivals standing on higher steps and peering over hats & squirming hoisted children. Leaning on a fence at the back we finally get a clear view of the apparatus. Mark stares & then starts to laugh. (I love the way he laughs, deeply & with pure delight.) The cows are standing on a turntable enclosed in a sort of metal contraption, turning very slowly. They look bored. Perhaps cows always do. (?) "Hail, cows of the future!" Mark says. We watch for a while.

Borden's exhibit was one of the most charming and funniest at the fair. To the rear of the large building several dozen cows stand in stalls, in a "shiningly clean stable of white enamel." When a cow's turn comes, she is escorted to a long conveyor belt that delivers her to the threshold of the Rotolactor, which accommodates five cows at a time. She steps aboard. She is washed, and dried with an individual sterilized towel; milking cups are attached and she is electrically milked; the cups are removed and attendants massage her udder; an automatic gate swings open, her rear end is gently bopped by an automatic rear-end bopper, and in response she steps casually (as if this were just the most natural thing in the world for a cosmopolitan cow) off the Rotolactor onto the conveyor belt for her return trip to the stalls. The building also houses "Dairy World Restaurant," a milk bar and the "prize cow exhibit," where Elsie the Cow made her debut and rapidly became famous. In the restaurant you could get Mel-O-rols—highly engineered ice-cream cones, flat on the bottom, designed to accept a horizontal cylinder of vanilla, chocolate or strawberry ice cream on top.

(The fair was a serious undertaking, but a number of exhibits are whimsical or gently self-mocking. The focal exhibit in the Community Interests Zone, for example, features a scene called "Mrs. Modern orders a house." "Hello, the ready-made-house department, please. . . Send me that little number you had in this morning's paper. . . Now give me the grocery department. . . I am having a house sent up. Would you please have them deliver my dinner at the same time?")

In one important respect the Rotolactor read differently in 1939 than it would today. Contemplate the sign inside a 1930s White Tower hamburger restaurant: "CLEAN as a whistle. Just look at this White Tower. Notice how CLEANLINESS predominates. This is your assurance of being served with pure and wholesome food." White Towers were white because white meant clean. Whether store-bought food was sanitary or would make you sick was a more pressing issue then than it is today, and the Borden building's white stalls, its public washings and sanitized dryings, were intended to convey a reassuring and important message.

The bored cows ensconced in the shiny metal apparatus of the Rotolactor are (furthermore) a perfect thirties image. To the thirties eye it would have looked a tad less strange than it does to us, because in the thirties, technology *itself* was wholesome.

The diary continues:

"See," Mark says, "this place *is* full of hope. But not blind hope; it makes an argument. This building argues that in this country, we think milk for children is just as important as anything else, we lavish just as much engineering on milk as on war planes, and *furthermore,* we're not afraid to laugh a little. I mean, the cow heads on top. They're silly, but they were *meant* to be. And I can look at this thing and laugh. Could you picture Hitler saying to his thugs, 'You vill make a new buildink,'" broad comic German accent, "'and it vill be *fonny!'*" Smacking right fist in left hand. "If I tried the same stunt in Nazi Germany, a brownshirt would have put a knife in my back by now."

Someone smacks his shoulder and says "Right, right" gruffly—startling me; he had been standing behind us in the loose clutch of people awaiting their turns for a look. He smacks Mark's shoulder again & strides off. Mark turns (as he would!), follows him a step & calls out: "Where are you from?" He *would*—Mark being the man who politely challenges the assertions of strangers in elevators, arises in the absolute *last* row of huge auditoria to ask pointed questions, writes detailed letters to the secretary of state & is then as disappointed as a child writing to Mickey Mouse when no reply is forthcoming—such a man has obviously *got* to make a scene at the Fair. The quarry turns round but continues walking slowly away from us backwards, both hands thrust in the pockets of his ragged black sports jacket, cigarette dangling. "München!" he calls out.

I am afraid this is one of those moments I am doomed to remember forever. The sound of a passing band in a trailer being towed down the mall playing "I've Got Rhythm," a saxophone with the melody, and the music gradually dissolving in the breeze as the trailer moves away, into the background: leaves rustling. Fountains sprinkly-sparkling. People are listening in now & watching. Turning just their heads or not turning at all but frowning to hear better. "What did you see there?" Mark calls out ringingly. The German or whatever he is has stopped backing off & stands facing us, perhaps fifteen paces away. The well-dressed man beside us re-settles his glasses on his nose, folds his arms & studies his shoes intently. My heart's still bumping. I glance up to look, just a quick glimpse, at the German—his eyes are very bright, *too bright,* a person might have thought him slightly crazed. *"Look people in the face, Hattie Dearest,"* I hear my brooding velvet mother intoning with intense quietness at a younger me in one of those downtown ladies' restaurants where tables-full of over-perfumed women titter, "One can't walk about with one's eyes perpetually *downcast."* ". . . And the palm fronds bent and wheeling / Here I feel the ocean's feeling / Endless soft dissatisfaction." The fragment of poem that trails after my mother like the train of her gown in her regal progress through my mind. "Greater Germany!" the man calls, making a face as if the words tasted foul, spits on the ground & turns & walks away.

The shabby coat, urbane cigarette, crazy eyes: a figure

out of nightmares. I am returned suddenly to a freezing bright morning ten years ago in a crowded, overheated butcher shop with steamed-up windows on Seventh Avenue, where my father is introducing me to a Russian in a shabby black coat—whose family had been killed in a pogrom perhaps twenty years before—who spent the rest of his life in a daze. His close-cropped hair, bad teeth, bad breath & gentle eyes. And then: a long black limousine, old-fashioned with a squared-off back, and a woman, some woman I have seen in real life & my nightmares, with a sinister blank face, slowly emerging.

Such a relief to snap out of this black reverie & there is Mark, as serious & thoughtful as if the man had delivered a lengthy sermon & not a mere three words, & the Trylon & Perisphere which seem to me now so cheering. And then I hear another man several rows ahead of us say distinctly in a tremulous high voice suggestive (why?) of a bony face & over-prominent Adam's apple, without looking back (not caring or not daring?) "Go peddle your papers." He did not add *Jew*. There is a flustered-pigeons stir around him. Another man turns & shows us his frowning profile, which is a gesture of sympathy for Mark. Mark ignores the whole thing & we set off in the same direction as the German, but slowly.

"At any rate," he says after a while, "this place, the whole Fair, doesn't merely say trust me—the future is bright. It attempts to *convince* you that the future is bright. Doesn't merely *assert*. Whether it succeeds, I don't know. But don't you at least have to *try*?"

I don't know what to tell him at this point because I think he is wrong, that it is a matter of pure faith & nothing more, but I still don't know how to say it to him.

He wants a cup of coffee & has determined that there

is a doughnut shop in the Science & Education building, more or less across the mall from where we are. We head back towards the T&P & he plants himself facing it. "I love it," he says. "It's beautiful. Not such a great surface, though. Should be smoother. It's finished in Tymstone." "What's that?" "A magnesite compound, magnesium carbonate." Ah yes, of course, thank you thank you. *"But—"* he is hurrying on & does not stop for explanations—"I'd have done it differently. I would have covered the Perisphere with steel lattice-work outside, & put lights in the lattice-work shining onto the smooth wide globe underneath; and I'd make the Trylon cut *into* the globe, just slightly, instead of standing apart; and I'd have made its surface absolutely flat. Perhaps of glass. That's it. The Trylon glows from inside, the Perisphere is bright beneath the silhouetted lattice-work."

"You look so much like a pixie," I tell him, "when you've just gotten an idea. Truly, as if you'd just stolen a cookie and you're afraid to look *too* pleased with yourself—"

[I imagine her voice as a low rustling.]

He looks puzzled, which makes him still cuter. "In any case," I say, "that's the sort of thing I *would* put in the exhibition." "Maybe," he says, unconvinced—"so let's eat, but maybe we should stop at the Consumers building first. It's right next door."

6

Doughnuts

The Consumers building [the diary continues] is one of the sober structures ringing the T&P. George Washington is at 12:00, pointing straight back at the mall, Consumers is over at around 1:30. It's a sprawling three-sided building surrounding a courtyard.

The so-called Focal Exhibit of the Production & Distribution Zone is located in here. It has a large concave movie screen which shows you simple everyday activities at the center—a lady powdering her nose, or ordering food in a shop; & then all around it, scenes of the far-flung business upon which the simple act depends. Interesting, but more interesting is a display that makes you grasp how poor this country is. I feel somewhat defensive in there but I guess that is the point. The actual numbers & scenes are dismaying. There are boxes devoted to each of the main categories of spending—food, clothes, housing, health, & three or four others. The Government has decided on four official income levels.

"Subsistence" required a family income of $800 a year, "maintenance" $2,000, "the good life" $2,500 and "luxury" $5,000. In early 1990s dollars, those amounts would be roughly $7,200 (subsistence), $18,000 (maintenance), $22,500 (the good life) and $45,000 (luxury). Attendance surveys suggested that fairgoers tended to be wealthier and better educated than the average American. Nonetheless, the fraction of attendees per month who earned less than the $2,000 "maintenance" salary ranges around a quarter and is sometimes more.

You press buttons under the boxes & see how each level of family copes. The claim is that a third of the country makes less than subsistence and nine-tenths less than the "Good Life minimum." It strikes me that I have no idea what Mark earns, but it is almost certainly less than the "Good life" officially requires. But he never ever complains about money.

The exhibit was designed by Egmond Arens. It proposes the simplest, most basic of all the fair's utopian visions: In the future people will make a decent living. "One hundred and fifty years ago," the exhibit observed—at George Washington's inauguration, in other words—

the proposal to raise the incomes of the entire population to the Good Life Minimum would have been considered impossible. With modern technology and power production it is no longer physically impossible. We have the techniques and the power to produce abundance; we need now to discover a workable formula for its distribution to "Three-Thirds of a Nation."

The language deliberately echoes Franklin Roosevelt's second inaugural address, which was cited again and again during the high thirties: "I see one-third of a nation ill-housed, ill-clad, ill-nourished."

Of course we have *not* found a way to allow three-thirds of the nation to live the good life. But in 1935 the typical middle-class family lived in a four-and-a-half-room apartment or a rented six-and-a-half-room house. Food, clothing and shelter accounted for almost eighty percent of the average 1935 income. Roughly three percent of the nation's families owned their own homes. (Today, almost two-thirds do.)

The average 1939 income was $1,266 a year; that would come to roughly $11,400 in modern terms. The comparable modern figure is twice that, around $22,500—a figure that has fluctuated only modestly since the great settling-down of around 1970. Other measures, for example of average hourly wages then and now, tell similar stories. Direct comparisons across decades can only be approximate, but this much is clear: We are a vastly richer nation than we were in 1939.

Arens's exhibit closes with a series of questions. Today's "network of communications systems makes for speedy exchange of ideas . . . Can we improve the spiritual side of life as we did the physical apparatus? Can serious breakdowns be avoided in such a complex system? Will increased leisure bring political and cultural renaissance?"

The fair's Theme Center and its focal exhibits were crucial to its character and dear to the hearts of its planners. The focal exhibits were housed in fair-built structures that usually housed smaller private exhibits as well. "In the New York Fair the theme permeates the chief features of the Fair," writes the Fair's research director, Yale history professor Frank Monaghan. "It has determined much of the physical lay-out and the arrangement of exhibits." Fair officials are decided that the theme "shall be the determining, dominating fact of the Exposition."

Gilbert Rhode's Community Interests Focal Exhibit was designed to make a point that was central to the fair's world view—that nowadays people depend on each other to an extent unheard of in the past. Modern versus bygone America represents "a change from relative independence to greater interdependence." There is a huge room with a semicircular wall and a series of scenes arranged before it; one by one the tableaux are lit up and the narrator propounds. (The "entire timing is controlled by electric phonograph," Rhode's typescript notes.) Scene one, 1789: "No leisure. No time to play. Eight hours to sleep and sixteen to work." The final scene: 1939. Eight hours' work, eight hours' rest, eight hours' leisure. "At last man is freed . . . Freed in time and space." The lights fade and a spotlight picks out the words "For What?" It was Rhode's intention to introduce "a feeling of uplift, expansion and mysticism" with this ending.

So 1939 has utopian visions and is keenly aware, too, of having come a long way and accomplished great things. And after all, one part of having a future is simple momentum. When things have been getting better, it is not too hard to believe that they will continue that way.

Russel Wright's Food Zone show was, by general agreement, the most entertaining of the focal exhibits. Would a modern world's fair even *have* such a thing as a "food zone"? Here and everywhere the fair stands much closer to the sheer wonderment of modern times than we do. The 1939 guide asks us (waxing rhapsodic) to picture "the amazement of great-great-grandmother could she but return to earth to find our tables veritable magic carpets upon which may be set at any season (and all at one time, if we will), food from any part of the world." The climax of the exhibit is a sixty-foot egg. Inside are an avocado with five glowing jewels in its skin, a flock of lobsters flying inland from the sea, an aqueduct spilling roses in the desert, an eye blinking within a cave, a can holding a clock racing backward. "This is the kind of world your great-great-grandmother would imagine we lived in if she were told of our countless achievements in food." The jewels in the avocado symbolize carbohydrates, proteins, fats, vitamins and minerals. The lobsters signify that inlanders can eat fresh seafood. The blinking eye reminds us of "man's victory over night-blindness through Vitamin A foods." The aqueduct means that irrigation has made wastelands flower, the backward-running clock that "canning has perpetuated harvest times." Surrealism was no sterile academic plaything; it mattered to popular designers when they communicated with their publics.

The Consumers building also holds a bunch of small exhibits including 'Dr. Scholl's Foot Comfort Service' & a glass column in which water-resistant Kem Playing Cards get drenched & buffeted & yet (praise the Lord!) triumphantly *survive!* [Gardner Harding calls the Consumers building a "nearly empty shell" aside from the focal exhibit, with "playing cards, artificial flowers, footease, a private loan company, and the only bank exhibiting at the Fair ... Happily, the consumer himself is there in the person of the Consumers Union."]

"The Consumers building," the diary continues,

> has a courtyard giving out on the pool running between Washington & the T&P. The pool holds four white sculptural groups arranged in a diamond, each sitting on a tubby little cloud and the cloud on a box like an upright orange crate, with misty fountains playing round the crates. There is a principal unclothed person in each group, two men two ladies, each sprawling and straining (*Emote!* yells the sculptor at his models, *EMOTE!*), and each surrounded by a cloud of smaller odds and ends, such as a horse, a crescent moon, little men gliding through the air, et cetera. As if they had been posing in the lounge on a train and the brakes had been slammed on and they had all gone flying. I find them funny rather than beautiful, and yet the modelling has a certain gristly Look-At-Me! toughness that I admire despite myself.

(The sculptures are by Paul Manship. They depict "the moods of time." The misty fountains around the pedestals are intended to simulate clouds.)

> At the end of the pool, right before T&P, is a giant sundial— yes, *the biggest sundial in the world.* It can only be described as bizarre. There is a tree growing up the underside of the huge pointer. A lady stands upright beneath it &, in front of her, beneath the pointer's tip, another lady stands on another tough, tubby little cloud (I take it the same artist who made the ones in the pool did this also)—the second lady leans forward like a ship's figurehead & holds a tall pointy spool of

yarn, or maybe it is cotton candy. There is a third huddled-up lady facing in the other direction, holding what looks like poultry shears. The loose classical dress of the upright woman is slipping down her shoulders, & the leaning-forward woman is naked to the waist, which perhaps accounts for their terribly somber frowns.

(Manship's sundial is called "Time and the Fates of Man." "The Future, holding her distaff, passes the thread of life to the Present; she in turn moves it along to the Past, where it is snipped off.")

Mark studies it thoughtfully & then, giving me his *deepest* most fraught-with-meaning look announces, "the Spirit of Constipation." We walk down towards T&P, hook round the sundial, I notice once again my *Astronomer* at the foot of the Helicline, we gaze all the way down the mall past Washington into the distance—one is always gazing down or up the mall, one can't help it . . .

The Fair's buildings are mostly one story or one-and-a-half, & the few taller structures show clearly from a distance. Far away & to the left you see the top of the League of Nations building—a squat cylinder, as wide as it is tall, made of rectangular columns linked by a round platform on top. Through the circular colonnade you see flags displayed on a stepped wedding-cake platform at the center. Moving your gaze right you see the very top of the Polish pavilion's striking tower. Its walls are a lacy grid in which the overlapped strips form diamonds—like a garden trellis folded back on itself into a square tower, but instead of roses there are gold plaques within each diamond, and the tower is a shimmering golden haze. Scan right again & you see Italy, from the side. It is a strange building & I find it unlovely, but do look forward to seeing it head-on. From here you see the profile of a giant staircase terminating at a tower, & on top of the tower a giant Italia, stern, uncomfortable, bellicose & ridiculous, sits enthroned. But a waterfall flows from beneath her throne all the way down the staircase to the ground, so the facade must be remarkable. Scanning now to the right of the U.S. building, the view is dominated by the narrow tall tower of the Soviet pavilion. It is faced in rust-red stone [it was red porphyry] and has a steel statue on top—renowned Big Joe, he is called—a heroic striding-forward worker with one arm thrown back and the other clasping a red star high overhead.

("Bronx Express Straphanger" is another name bestowed by fair visitors on this statue, which was the highest thing on the grounds after the Trylon.)

We sweep round counter-clockwise to 10:30 where the Avenue of Somebodies leads outwards from the Theme Center, head up it a little ways & enter the Science & Education building & the doughnut shop.

It has square tables placed two abreast making rectangles that seat four. It's crowded & we sit beside another couple. The menu is doughnut-shaped & has a map showing that you can get this kind of doughnut at both World's Fairs—there is one this year in San Francisco too, a much smaller affair.

("The doughnut apparently is becoming increasingly popular as a 'typical American' food," the *New York Times* reported in 1940.)

So we each order a doughnut, & coffee. Mark takes out his pen & starts sketching on the paper napkin, but of course the line drools all over (for an engineer he is so *crazily* innocent about all things physical!—but he is typical in no respect whatever), so he takes the sketchpad out of his pocket and draws, & swings it round to show me. The Capitol, the Washington Monument. At the base of the Washington Monument a large Cupid with little wings & its rear end conspicuously pointed at the Capitol. Underneath, in the wide squat arty letters that you see on drawings by Frank Lloyd Wright, he has written with a flourish "Tuches," with an arrow showing the indicated part. [The word means "rear end" in Yiddish.] Something about it strikes me as awfully funny & I start to giggle—he's studying me straight-faced, with a bare smile. "About kids," he says—

I swallow the giggles & look down & gather my dignity (such as it is) & say—"I understand being uneasy about the world today. But suppose it keeps up for ten years with no resolution? How long should a person wait?"

"It won't. Look at the pattern. In March of '36 Hitler reoccupied the Rhineland . . ."

(The Treaty of Versailles that ended the First World War had ordered German troops to stay off the Rhine's left bank, and out of a fifty-kilometer band along the right—in other words, to keep the hell away from France.)

"I remember the date because it was during spring break & I had a girl on my lap—" "Sarah Abbot?" Slightly accusing, but I thought I sounded friendly—"Yes, Sarah," so sharply that I feel reprimanded & blush & look down. And then he reaches his hand out & cups it over mine; he does *not* brook pain, no matter what.

"I remember hearing it on the radio. One of those

things you sort of hear but you don't. We were discussing whether it was true that her legs were prettier than Eleanor Powell's, & we were getting to the point where we'd need to get down to brass tacks & have a serious appraisal of the evidence, & I was faced with this crisis, whether to turn my attention to foreign affairs or stay focussed on domestic issues." "And?" "Her legs *were* prettier than Eleanor Powell's." I kick him gently under the table. "Last March, he goes into Austria. Last September, the sell-out in Munich. In March he grabs the rest of Czechoslovakia. In the last few weeks he renounces the naval treaty with England & makes a new deal with Mussolini. So you see, the pace is picking up. You have a gap of two years, then six months," slicing ever-finer gaps with the side of his hand on the table-top, "then another six months, then one month, and here we are."

I have a shuddery brief vision of the Fair's beautiful mall decked with red, black, white swastikas.

"You know—" he rubs a fingertip on a thumb in a thoughtful remote way, as if trying to feel something he can't quite reach. 'I am sorry for Neville Chamberlain & I understand him. It's hard to believe. You want this guy to *like* you. Hitler. You look at him & say—how can this guy hate you? He doesn't even *know* you. It's pathetic. You want him to like you. And it's painful, I feel for Chamberlain, to grasp the fact that the man hates you profoundly & would just as soon see you dead in a ditch. Maybe that's what maturity consists of." It makes me uneasy that his eyes have stopped moving. "Finally laying hold of the fact that there are people out there who really & truly want to kill you. And your only choice in the matter"—his voice ever more abstract—"is to have the courage, whether you feel courageous or not, to face them down . . ."

Our coffee & doughnuts have arrived. And I say "Would they take over the Fair?" Stupid question. I meant—but who cares.

"I'm not expecting them imminently." Recaptures his drifting thoughts & sounds more himself. "But if it's still standing & God forbid the Germans arrive, I assume they will take it over, & scoop out all the Jewish and modernistic & American patriotic influences, like scooping the flesh out of a melon, & they leave the rind. That's their philosophy. Their view of civilization. Rind on Rhine." "So what *will* happen now?" I ask between bites. "Before the end of the summer," sipping coffee, "he's arranged for Poland to be signed over to him, in return for a promise to be *absolutely* on his best behavior for the next ten minutes. Then he attacks Russia. Or maybe France. It won't be long before the whole situation comes clear." "But a war could last years," I say, eating, "one can't wait forever. Having children is *always* just a leap of faith. If you truly *must* make an intellectual issue of having children, it seems to me that one would treat it as an occasion for defiance. *Defiance.* Though I don't mean one does it grimly. One should do it"—here I am being shamelessly direct, & looking right at him—"*courageously—gallantly—joyfully.*"

He is thinking about it & set to answer, but then the couple next to us stands & leaves, & it's my chance to grab his tie taut across the table like a leash & tell him, speaking *very* softly & distinctly, "my legs are prettier than Ginger Rogers'." I hadn't counted on this striking him quite as hilariously as it did, but I guess I had an intensely mock-serious expression. He's laughing so hard he has to put the coffee cup down because he's sloshing coffee out—"Shhhhhh!" I say sternly, wanting to giggle—

So after making a perfect spectacle of ourselves he takes the guidebook from his pocket. "Let's see what to do now." He thumbs through pages and then in a drawling mumble, as if he's reading, "Emily Post says—for a gentleman adequately to evaluate a young lady's legs, *um* . . . she needs to be sitting on his lap . . . Listen to this. For real." He reads from the Guide, words to the effect that "the true poets of the twentieth century are the designers, architects and engineers. They see visions, and translate those visions into reality . . ." He grins at me & makes a muscle like a prize fighter, & we walk out & head for the Transportation Zone.

7

Haven't
We Met
Somewhere
Before?

Handler sometimes appears to toy with the limits on acceptable public behavior but never quite oversteps them. What exactly is permissible in 1939? In *Follow the Fleet* of 1936, Fred is repeatedly put off his attempts to kiss Ginger goodnight on her doorstep by the reappearances of a nosy policeman. "At every corner" a pair of lovers in a 1936 novel "stopped and kissed." But that was after midnight, on "black empty streets."

Of course it would be a mistake to confuse the publicly done thing with the otherwise done. I have already noted that the 1939ers give every indication of being at least as sophisticated as we. If you are concerned that their sophistication might possibly not have extended to sex, don't be: Have a look at Thurber and White's 1929 classic *Is Sex Necessary?* All the same, 1939 adopts what might conceivably be described as a quirky position on sex. Public kissing is a matter to be approached with caution, yet soft-core pornography is arguably more acceptable than it is today. In fact pornography was a mainstay of the World's Fair. The Amusement Area was loaded with it, and some of the fair's best talents devoted themselves earnestly to the very finest in girlie shows.

One of my sources recently mentioned this fact to his sister, who refused to believe it. She had never been to the fair, but it was widely understood to be an elevated, sanctified place. It *was* a sanctified place—apropos of which, an attendance survey finds that most fairgoers had come to the fair before, but two-thirds had never visited the Amusement Area or had done so only once. Some modern accounts claim that the wild and raunchy Amusement Area was the hit of the fair, but that isn't so. "The Amusement Area was eclipsed by the showmanship of the exhibits in the main area," the survey notes. The amusements were found to be especially unappealing to enthusiasts who had been to the fair five times or more. Still they *were* popular, no question about that, and they give us an interesting glimpse of 1939 public taste.

Norman Bel Geddes designed the "Crystal Lassies" show. "The Loveliest Dancing Girls at the Fair," claimed the ticket booth. A nude manikin stood on a pedestal outside; behind her, the words "Inside she's real. 15¢." A dancer gyrated within an octagonal structure whose inner surfaces were completely mirrored. Two spectators could stand at each facet of the octagon and peep through narrow one-way mirrors at the many, many dancers evidently cavorting within. The dancer's costume varied at different shows. At times she was (in effect) naked. On another occasion a dancer was sighted topless but sporting a G-string labeled AMUSEMENT AREA.

Salvador Dalí designed the "Dream of Venus" concession. Inside are diving tanks in which four separate dreams are enacted.

One tank holds a fireplace, rubber telephones and a rubber woman painted to resemble a piano keyboard, among other odds and ends. "Whatever this may mean as art," *Time* magazine observes, "the exhibitors did not dilly-Dali over it. Into the tank they plunged living girls, nude to the waist and wearing little Gay Nineties girdles and fish-net stockings." Another dream entails exploding giraffes, a couch in the shape of Garbo's lips and Dalí's signature soft watches. In short, "The Dream of Venus," *Time* concludes, "should win more converts to surrealism than a dozen high-brow exhibitions." (Dalí was one of the *Dream's* investors as well as its designer, but wound up on the outs with the fair administration because it forbade him to exhibit a fish-headed woman on the sidewalk out front; also with the actual builders of his pavilion: "They did 'approximately' what I ordered, but so badly and with such bad faith that the pavilion turned out to be a lamentable caricature of my ideas." He stalked off to Europe without ever visiting the finished product. Not long before the fair opened, he had smashed a display window at Bonwit Teller on Fifth Avenue to protest the management's tampering with a Dalí-designed display. His judgments tended to the clear-cut, and he was not a shy man.)

There were many other soft-porn exhibits. Living Magazine Covers, for example, where topless women posed within a frame simulating a cover of *Romantic Life Magazine* dated 1949 (there was still the future to think about). One of my (male) sources remembers three things concretely about the fair; he visited only once, at age sixteen. One is an Amusement Area show in which a topless woman struck poses, holding each for fifteen seconds perhaps. Spectators wisecracked in an attempt to make her giggle and succeeded often, with consequences that they regarded—the nasty brutes—as aesthetically appealing.

It all sounds a little sleazy, doesn't it? But if we hope to un-

derstand the high thirties, there are a couple of points we should
consider while attempting to make sense of it all.

One is that actual, particular people and not abstractions performed
in the girlie shows. They were not imbeciles, and they did what they
did because they felt like it. We tend sometimes to view porno performers as witless victims. In 1939 people were less apt to make that
mistake. *Life* magazine commented on the Salvador Dalí show and
one of the players:

> Americans today consider the display of feminine beauty,
> however irrelevant to the matter at hand, essential in their
> industrial and public life . . . Betty's costume consists of a
> pair of brief trunks which leave her breasts bare. This semi-
> nudity, however, raises in her mind no serious question of
> her innate modesty. She rationalizes it something like this:
> the audience is in the dark, so you can't see them from the
> tank, so it doesn't make any difference and besides you
> wouldn't show yourself like that out of water where anyone
> can see you.

Betty Kuzmeck is "18, pretty and Polish." She lives with her sister in
a tiny Manhattan apartment in a "respectable but dingy part of West
90th Street." She regards her present living arrangements "as purely
temporary and not distasteful"—"like many New Yorkers," the
magazine notes. She makes forty dollars a week and is delighted with
the job and the pay. She had worked previously as a hatcheck girl for
fifteen dollars a week, and had to turn in her tips at that.

The spectators were individuals too. My source for the giggling model story is a distinguished scientist of impeccably progressive opinions (plus a sense of humor). He wasn't the "typical" spectator, but the typical spectator was no ignorant slob either.

Another point to consider, as we eavesdrop on the thirties and struggle to understand what we are overhearing: So many of its attitudes are so similar to so many of ours. Now I believe that the high thirties were *less* and not *more* similar to our own age than they seem to be at first. But sometimes the actual resemblances are greatest where we least expect them.

To start with, that age and our own are each divided into two camps on pornography. Some of us and some of them see it as harmless, others of us and them as evil. A minister from Brooklyn inveighed against the threat to "the laws of common decency" and the "menace to morals" posed by the Amusement Area at the fair. Disapproval by public and police was sufficiently vigorous to induce fair administrators to impose a Mandatory Bras and Net Coverings order on concessionaires—who then advertised the fact that they were flouting it. The Amusements were raided regularly. (On one occasion, the admirably straightforward charge against the performers was "insufficient clothing.") They were denounced regularly. "Does the city want this to go on?" a State Supreme Court Justice demanded. "Do the Mayor, the Police Commissioner and the Corporation Counsel want naked performances?" The answer was no— but as soon as they were rooted out they sprang up again, like dandelions on your front lawn. The demand was considerable and there was no shortage of aspiring performers. Today's social commentators denounce the fair's girlie shows for "dramatizing women as sexual commodities" and reproducing the "dominant power relations between men and women." Maybe they are right. If they are, so is the minister from Brooklyn: Perhaps the porno shows *were* morally obnoxious. We are divided on the point just as 1939 was. Between then and now the language and precise nature of the alleged threat has changed, but the seething outrage underneath has not. Different words, same tune.

If we are lazy, high-thirties culture will catch us off balance. When we see a society whose behavior is radically different from ours, we are apt to guess that its underlying assumptions must be very different too—but then again, they might not be. When we see familiar behavior, we guess that it reflects assumptions that are just like ours. Once again we might easily be wrong.

On the topic of married women, for example: In the 1930s they were expected to stay home and care for the household and children. In 1938, a thumping 78 percent of a Gallup survey disapprove of a married woman's working for pay outside the home "if she has a husband capable of supporting her."

But this consensus doesn't reflect indifference to "women's issues" (at least as the thirties defined them). "Women's participation was a first thought in the planning of the New York World's Fair of 1939": This according to an official fair publication of 1938. The role of women was to be "a key element" of the whole undertaking. "There will be no specified 'Women's Section' or 'Women's Building' at this Fair." Instead, women's interests and influence are to be manifest throughout. In 1934 La Guardia ordered that a certain female medical assistant be appointed to the surgical staff at a city hospital. No woman had ever served on the surgical staff before—but I fail to see, said the mayor, "why a woman cannot be a good surgeon." The mayor's intervention was "good sense, good politics," comments a 1937 biography, and also "good feminism."

We are apt to believe that, if true equality holds between women and men, then men and women will be indistinguishable in the degree and quality of their participation in the work force. It is *this* belief, not the inherent equality of women and men, that progressive high-thirties opinion rejects. Progressive high-thirties opinion might have been all wet; but my goal is not to judge, merely to report.

And by the way, "in this modern day," writes Emily Post in her famous *Etiquette,* "when women are competing with men in politics, in business and in every profession, it is really senseless" to insist that the man must always pick up the check. This is the 1937 edition, which also includes extensive advice on clothes for the businesswoman. ("Many a man has asked to have a girl transferred who was inclined to dress in transparencies.") In 1926 *House Beautiful* published a series called "The Handy Woman About the House"— the January installment was "Be Your Own Electrician." In 1994 the *Wall Street Journal* carried a piece about the toy companies' numerous failed attempts to interest girls in a broader range of their offerings: "Girls' Favorite Play Things: Dolls, Dolls and Dolls." We are too apt to classify as our own inventions attitudes that are in fact of long standing; too eager to believe that we are quite unlike the poor unsophisticates of an earlier day.

La Guardia was famous all over the country as a crusading, compassionate liberal. In a 1939 survey 64 percent hold that La Guardia is a liberal; 28 percent call him a radical. But if we picture him as a liberal in the modern mold, we are making a big mistake. "Liberal" had a very different meaning in 1939. Toward pornography, for example, modern liberals (though not feminists) are apt to strike a pose of sophisticated toleration. Pornography infuriated La Guardia. Out at the fair in June 1939, the Amusement Area's Cuban Village advertised a "Miss Nude of 1939" beauty pageant. Police raided it. ("Let the show go on!" irate customers shouted.) The manager and two publicity agents were charged with disorderly conduct, two women with indecent exposure. The mayor had the three men hauled before him in the summer city hall he'd set up in the

Arrowbrook Golf Club, on the eastern fringes of the World's Fair. New York mayors were empowered to sit as magistrates by an old rule that had long been disregarded; La Guardia revived it with a vengeance. On this occasion he found the accused guilty and imposed fines and suspended sentences. "I hope this will be a lesson for you," said the mayor.

La Guardia the crusading and compassionate liberal was also in the habit, when he witnessed city workers great or small behaving incompetently, of firing them on the spot. (Sample story: He finds a group of park workers lounging during working hours. He fires sixty of them for "loitering.") The city is to be run tautly, seriously, and whining drives La Guardia the crusading liberal crazy. I pay no attention, he declares, to "political whiners." *Merit* is a sacred idea to La Guardia the compassionate liberal. The modern policy of "open admissions" to the city's universities would likely have struck him as absurd. The high school graduate ought to go out and find a job, writes University of Chicago president Robert Hutchins in 1939, "unless he has the interest and ability that advanced study requires. If he has this interest and ability he should go on to the university, and he should go, if necessary, at public expense." That balanced declaration is vintage 1939 liberalism. The public bears a responsibility—specifically, to all talented students who are serious.

In a fall 1994 election Democrats and liberals were thrown out of office en masse. The head of a moderate Democratic policy organization was understandably upset and tried to explain. "The New Deal era is over," he said. "The nails are in the coffin of New Deal liberalism, and it is dead and buried." And yet the differences between modern liberalism and the New Deal variety are just as significant as the similarities. It is true that FDR played the class warfare card effectively on occasion, and enormously expanded the federal government. But in Roosevelt's mind that huge expansion was the right response to a very special emergency. When the economy improved, his first instinct was "cut spending." More important, Roosevelt's fundamental beliefs (like La Guardia's) about authority and personal responsibility are profoundly at odds with modern orthodox liberalism. La Guardia asserted in a 1938 speech that "Government relief payments could no more continue indefinitely than they could stop suddenly." The government dole, said Franklin Roosevelt, is "a narcotic, a subtle destroyer of the human spirit." At a time when the working and middle classes ought to be fighting to regain the economy of rising wages and growing hopes they once enjoyed, they have been thrown back in confusion instead, to defined their ideas of authority, dignity and responsibility. Territory that had never been threatened in the U.S. before; territory that a Roosevelt or La Guardia could never conceivably have forced them to fight for.

Modern Americans are apt to tote around a strikingly sophisticated, highly polished set of attitudes on topics like women and sex and the poor. If high-thirties people had similar attitudes, maybe they were dazzlingly sophisticated too? A few years back it was regarded as an innovation when welfare officials referred to the poor as their "clients." WPA officials used exactly the same word in the same circumstances more than fifty years ago. Vice President John Nance Garner was not amused. He complained to WPA head Harry Hopkins, evidently without effect. "Underprivileged" is a *thirties* term for the poor. The contribution of black people to American history began "when Western Europe moved to the 'discovery' of the New World," notes the fair's "Negro Week" program, deploying a set of quotation marks with which modern America is thoroughly at home. The idea that society and not the criminal is to blame, that (as a character in a novel of the 1930s puts it) "social causes, environment, education or lack of education, economic pressure, the character-pattern imposed by society" account for a criminal's criminality—that too is a 1930s idea. "Political correctness is not an innovation of recent decades," writes Diana Trilling, the liberal intellectual. "It is the natural successor to cultural Stalinism"—a phenomenon of the thirties and forties.

And by the way, "in the World of Tomorrow," according to the *Times* world's fair supplement, "the Federal Government may conceivably enter even more intimately into the lives of the citizens: with health insurance, furtherance of group medicine, conservation of natural resources, extension of benefits to domestic groups not now included." We are a very different society from 1930s America—but not necessarily in the ways we suppose.

8

Party

The next segment of the diary takes Mark and Hattie into the Transportation Zone. But I wanted to find out where Mark Handler had come from. I phoned Mrs. Levine.

"First," she tells me, "I feel badly about misrepresenting things. Or I mean—what? Conveying merely the bald facts. Let me take a moment to set things straight. All right? You already know the facts. Seem well informed enough. But you won't know the feelings. 1939 was a time of gigantic world events. You read the newspapers and listened to the evening news on the radio not out of casual interest or habit or duty, but with *thirst*. You gulped it down. There were Manhattan movie theaters in that era that gave up showing anything but newsreels, round the clock. It was frightening and riveting."

I am sitting at a plain wooden table spread with remnants of the fair: the *Book of Nations,* a map prepared by General Motors, the Sealtest recipe collection with a microscope on the cover, an elegantly produced description of the Polish exhibit. Watching absently the grays and dull greens of the bristling-stiff winter forest outside my window.

"Some high Victorian," she continues, "I think it was Sabine Baring-Gould—what a name! He reminisced about the swish of the scythe when men mowed the field, and the musical ringing of the curved blade as it was sharpened. It was a pleasant childhood memory for him but for me, it represents that era of the late thirties: The wolves were laying for us, and the United States was a powerful nation, but not the invulnerable superpower you younger people have always lived with. I don't believe there was any such word as 'superpower' at the time. And if there had been, it wouldn't have applied to us. Britain had a greater fleet. France was said to have a greater army. Saint-Cyr, and all that. Valorous young Frenchmen fencing in their white gloves. Seems ridiculous today. The French army was 'the greatest army in the world'—people were always saying that. Who knew what the Japanese and the Germans had? One heard everywhere, throughout the world, the ringing of whetstone on steel."

Disembodied and set down in the suburban forest, with hemlocks moving in the breeze and squirrels stopped still in brilliant blue shadows on the snow, her voice has a strange acuity; as if this were a worried ghost or the forest or the past confiding in me directly.

"I saw a news picture—late, it must have been, in 1939—of the liner *America* entering New York Harbor. On her sides AMERICA spelled out in huge capital letters, and beneath that UNITED STATES LINES, and giant American flags emblazoned left and right. The war was on, but we were still a noncombatant nation, you see, and the idea was to avoid having the Germans mistake you for a French or British ship and torpedo you. The image absolutely gripped me at the time. Gripped me. I remember staring at it, as if it were one of those photographs you used to see in the dry anthropology texts of naked people and bizarre primitive rituals. The image grips me still, it captures the pride and *vulnerability* of that era. I wish young people today could memorize that picture, somehow, though apparently they no longer memorize anything. Damn it, I so wish that I could convey to you the *feel* of that time: there was nothing foreordained about our absolute victory; America seemed a fragile, brilliant, precious thing."

The trees make shuffling blue shadows on the snow.

"You're an educator. How can you justify the disgrace of American education? You give your students nothing to memorize—well, maybe it doesn't matter, or maybe it's better that way. I don't know. What I do know is, more high school students, by a *huge* margin, were able to identify one Harriet Tubman than Winston Churchill in a survey of some kind. A huge margin.

"How can you justify imposing that kind of ignorance on your students? Can't teachers grasp that not every child has parents like theirs to clean up the mess when you feed children nonsense in school? You're in the process of eradicating a whole era. The most important era of modern times. Never heard of Winston Churchill. Unbelievable!"

I point out that I am only a college teacher.

"I realize that, but who takes responsibility for education in this country *as a whole?* I'll grant that the people immediately involved, the high school history teachers who are teaching this stuff—they're fools, all right, fine. And then everyone else washes his hands and says, Don't look at me, it's not *my* fault."

She sighs. "And when you academics use these crazy terms you've got, like 'Native American' for Indian—my Lord, I want to

retch. You parade your contempt for language so plainly it's painful—like watching a child be humiliated in a school play; you only
want it to end. But the thought that you are *teaching this to children* . . . Shame. Do you still understand that word, 'shame'? The
word you want isn't '*native.*' The word you want is '*aboriginal.*' I am
a native American. You are a native American. What are you, an
Albanian? It's beyond me how academics sleep nights, looking at
the educational devastation you people have wrought. Or perhaps
you're proud of it? Or perhaps you simply don't care. What a tragedy, when educators hate language and parade their hatred in front
of children.

"I suppose I don't get enough opportunities to sound off
these days. I'm not blaming you personally. I don't think." Pause.

"Anyway, I was saying. What? The politicians of that era,
particularly Mayor La Guardia and the president, were present in
your life. You lived with them. They seemed powerful forces for
good. You thought of them as protectors and defenders. There is
nothing comparable today. . . . And most important: the fair itself."

She sounds not merely willing but suddenly eager to communicate. Torn between a guarded confidence in my interest and a
fear that what she needs to say cannot be said. The wind picks up
and draws a hollow ringing from the trees.

"You went, you came home, then you thought about it constantly. You read every line of every brochure, then you badly, *rest-
lessly,* wanted to go back. You wanted your own very special
connection to it—wanted to be able to say, I've been to the fair more
often than you have, or I understand this or that better or, best of all,
that you knew some actual person who was involved in the thing. I
had been introduced by my father to the members of the Theme
Committee at a formal dinner in Manhattan. My father had all sorts
of high-flying connections. Not surprising, given he was a reason-
ably high-ranking journalist. It meant little to me at the time, but

once the fair opened I was mighty proud of the fact, and I told everyone. You craved the fair. It made you happy.

"It made you want to *do* things. Go home and be a scientist, or engineer, or wise statesman—a leader of men. It left you buzzing and aglow. You wanted to *live up* to it, not disappoint it; because it addressed you with authority. I don't mean condescendingly; with authority. Like an idealized father whom you wished to please. And again, there is no parallel today. I want to paint a picture, and the appropriate colors no longer exist."

A silence. "Am I making myself at all clear?"

I tell her yes.

"Well," with a sigh. She seems unconvinced.

"Mark Handler and how we met. I should start with Sarah Abbot: I was puzzled by her relationship to Mark the evening I met him, and I've remained puzzled ever since. Was she enthralled—head-over-heels in love? Or was she captivated in the way you might be by an exotic parrot? In either case she stared at him devotedly. To some extent she seemed to patronize him. On the other hand, he was far more physical with her than was at all customary at the time. Not that he manhandled her in the fashion that's common nowadays. But. Well, I'll leave it at that.

"I am glad, by the way, that you asked me about this. I would have volunteered it eventually if you hadn't. The day you're reading about just can't make sense without some awareness of the part that came before and the part after. That day was so important to us. It was the thing we held before us, the talisman as we went through hell. Whether it worked or not, you'll have to judge. But that day is a keystone and it only makes sense if you can see the parts of the arch that lead up to and down from it. Not that my life is worth understanding, you know, but that moment of history surely is. And Mark is, as a person not only exceptional but in a certain way also typical.

"He had come with Sarah Abbot to a small party in Brooklyn

Heights, and I was there too with someone or other. It was late 1937. I must have been an insufferable date. I hardly said a word and I expected the boy to entertain me as I evaluated him critically. But I'd heard about Mark Handler and wanted to meet him. Everyone knew about him—he was known as being—" Pauses. "More than charming. Captivating. And an unconventional thinker. Wherever he worked or studied he would attract with no effort a group of devotees. So anyway, Mark was the star of the party, Sarah Abbot sitting beside him.

"Of course she was a gentile. That won't strike you as being of revolutionary importance, and even then a Jewish boy with a Christian girl was unlikely to make the papers. But it wasn't the usual thing. I doubt whether there were any other non-Jews in the room. Certainly not, for my part, because I avoided gentiles. Nothing of the kind. It was the social pattern, that's all. In my case as a matter of fact my parents had told me, marry whom you please, just so long as you love him and he loves you. In that respect they would have been impeccable liberals even today. In their own time they were exceptional." The voice seems touched, somehow, with a faint grim smile.

It's been a longer phone conversation than I expected. I ask if she's tired. "I can go on a little ways," she says.

"My family was comfortable, but Sarah Abbot's was wealthy. And she was friends with the former Anna Roosevelt, the president's daughter. Everyone found that out immediately. She went to Vassar. She came from around there.

"She had long black hair that she flaunted to great effect, she'd tip her head and it would spill like a waterfall, and lovely hazel eyes. She was a show-off and mightily pleased with herself, which I don't blame her for one bit; I did blame Mark for not conceding what a show-off she was. People used to tell me I was pretty. I always thought they were teasing me. Not until many years later did I look at some old pictures and decide that, yes, once I had been pretty. But it never crossed my mind to think so at the time. Sarah Abbot, however, was beautiful.

"Mark was talking about the Spanish Civil War, I think. He'd heard André Malraux give a talk downtown. That led him to Mies van der Rohe's Barcelona pavilion—the political led always to the aesthetic with Mark—and *that* led him to take a pen from his jacket pocket and make a beautiful quick sketch of the building from memory, and that led to a series of other things. He was passionate about architecture and believed it to be—how would he have put it?—the defining artistic medium of modern times. The remarkable thing was the *way* he talked. He'd be looking at the far corner of the room, his eyes liquid with intensity—as if he were describing a dream he'd forgotten and all he remembered was how wonderful it had been. And he'd make funny comments—not hilarious, rather droll. Very entertaining. He made an unusual impression: gentle and passionate at the same time."

Are you certain that isn't *you* you are describing? I ask.

"Me, well . . . To a point, perhaps. Gentle and passionate. [Pauses as if tasting the words.] But you'd never have confused us. Mark was perfectly serene. I was full of self-doubt, and bitterly confused."

What did it feel like, I wanted to know. What was the atmosphere at the party?

"Brown and yellow. This was in the home of a married couple slightly older than we. For some reason I see Mark in a brown sports jacket and a dark tie. Lots of books, and piles of the old black albums that the shellac 78s came in. It's rather dark with a pool of yellow light over the coffee table where Mark is holding forth. He might have been wearing a small FDR button on his lapel.

"Sarah Abbot, with her shoes slipped off and legs folded under her on the sofa, facing Mark, her fine pale profile and swept-back long hair; she was formidably intelligent, and there was something steely about her—her eyes smiling and her fancy bag at her feet and her impeccably lipsticked lips poised in the manner of an adult regarding a delightful child who makes her proud. And my shoes also slipped off and my legs drawn up and clasped before me and the side of my head resting on my knees, looking with resigned hunger at a candy shop I never expect to be permitted to enter. And Mark leaning back, contemplating, with eyes closed and a serene happy smile . . .

"I saw him several more times in the months after. Once we double-dated—I was seeing an acolyte of his—nice boy, but I was interested only because of Mark. Merely using him, shamelessly. The boys took us, Sarah Abbot and me, to a very fancy restaurant that was called, I think, Café Latino. It was ridiculous, but it was sweet— they couldn't afford it, we could have; I remember the round peach-colored mirrors, and how beautiful she looked, and how fine Mark looked, and the glamorous lobby paneled in that black glass you saw all over at the time. What did they call it? Vitrolite. Vitrolite . . . All the shininess—glamour was shiny in 1938, the men's shiny shoes and lapels and slicked-down hair, the ladies' gowns, the floor, the chromium tubing of the easy chairs in the ladies' lounge. Maybe it's an odd thing to say, but the world was a bit heavier and plainer then as well. Even Bakelite was heavy."

("These materials are known as 'plastics,' " writes Gerald Wendt. "A good example is 'Bakelite' phenolic resin. The raw material from which it is made is coal . . . The black of the telephone instrument is due to the inclusion of carbon black. The attractive colors of fountain pens, lighting fixtures, radio cabinets and costume jewelry are due to added dyes.")

"A radio, a phonograph record, a desk lamp, a lady's shoe, a book—they were all heavier items than they are today. Food was heavier. Men brought ice for the icebox; they carried the heavy blocks with tongs at their sides. They'd come every other day. When you had your own place, men delivered coal too. When they painted a building they mixed oil into the paint carefully and laid it on with heavy wooden-handled brushes. What does it all matter?—well, life's texture was different. Anyway, we danced. An evening of strictly vicarious pleasure.

"Early that summer he asked me to meet him for lunch at a place near campus. The City College of New York. I went to Hunter. A delicatessen, with a high ceiling of ornate stamped tin panels, ceiling fans, a counter near the front and small tables; in warm weather the door was always propped open and the flies would circulate. Mark held court there. He and his friends, or I should say disciples, would have dinner every Tuesday night and then sit around and argue until the place closed. They'd talk about Corbusier, Wright, who was just coming back into fashion—Mark had always admired him; Raymond Hood, Eric Mendelsohn, Ely Jacques Kahn. Mark's own work."

There is a paragraph in her diary that (she says) dates from a later period, but conveys the character of the Tuesday-evening discussions:

The topic: Mark's new design for worker housing, each unit is a square with its own square central courtyard, all windows giving onto this private courtyard except for ones too high to see out of—so no-one but you can see into your court-yard—& the units are set out in a row & then stacked staircase-wise, each unit brought forward to the rear wall of the courtyard of the one beneath—actual outdoor stairs running up between units, walkways running the length of the structure at each level, screened by glass-block walls, the blocks stained pale blue and green—lit from behind at night, so it looks like a glowing glass sculpture; & the argument is, to the rear in the dark under-staircase area Mark runs road for buses & track for trolleys, so you hop on at your back door—& are cars needed too? He says no but the others yes, & then they are on about cars, workers & towns when Benny's friend Charlotte appears & informs all that Benny has promised to take her dancing (dance for Spain). This here, says Mark, is a Nosh for Spain! & they return to arguing. *The automobile could only be transient as it is currently conceived,* etc. etc. etc. Charlotte prettily holding her skirts does a little tap-dance step & actually she is quite graceful!—though she is what would be called a "large-boned" girl (but has a sweet face)—I like her dress, violet with a deep-purple sash looped round the neck, crossing below the bust, then round the back & tied at the side. Benny is ignoring her so I grab Mark's pipe & tell him I won't return it till Benny is dismissed. Charlotte curtsies by way of thanking me. I like her very much. Benny too. They all repeatedly drink half their coffee & leave the rest to get cold & then order another.

She takes up the story. "Mark was sitting by himself and rose to greet me when I came in, and—it was so *damned* typical of him; he had the newspaper on the table, but had gradually covered the whole page with pen drawings. He would sit down to read the paper, and wind up not being able to read a word . . .

"I asked how Sarah was and he said he hadn't seen her, and they were through; I didn't press, and assumed they'd had a fight. He had a problem. The youngish former wife—they were separated, I think, not divorced—if they were even separated—of a City College professor had taken to coming to his Tuesday evenings, and had fallen for him, and she wanted him to accompany her for a few days to a house her sister owned on the Jersey shore—and the problem wasn't exactly that Mark didn't want to; he *did* want to, and found the lady attractive; but he didn't *want* to want to. I'm not sure if he explained all this at the time, probably not. But he asked me in his charmingly diffident way, clearing his throat and eyes downcast— there was absolutely no swagger about him, and that's part of the reason why he so effortlessly accumulated followers, admirers, fans—whether I'd go to a lecture with him at the New School later in the week; and after that, we were pretty much of a couple.

"I learned afterwards that he *did* go with this woman to the beach house for a couple of days later that summer. Once he had *me*, he explained, he was no longer in danger of falling in love with her, and why waste the opportunity? He was very open and a bit inno- cent, and it obviously troubled him to tell me this, but he felt he had to; and I was less hurt than one might have supposed. She wanted him to entertain her with intense intellectual jabber, and it abso- lutely destroyed her to learn that he was not a Stalinist—was not even a Trotskyite; was not even a *socialist,* he was merely a *Democrat,* and slightly to the right of FDR on certain issues. He tremendously admired Brandeis and Frankfurter, and above all Robert Moses, who happened to be a right-wing Republican. He was far to *my* right—I considered myself a socialist but I had a lot of respect for the com- munists, when I first met Mark. In those days, intellectual life was intensely politicized, in a very naive leftist way." Pause. "*In those days.* Of course I mean, on an ongoing basis. . . .

"They'd driven down in her fancy car—she came from some rich old New York family. A bit like Sarah Abbot herself. He in- sisted on listening to a certain Yiddish news program he never missed on WEVD on the way down, on the car radio. He translated for her. She would have been driving. Mark was a terrible driver.

"But anyway, we were a couple.

"And that reminds me, it's odd. Two more vivid pictures of Sarah Abbot. History is just pictures, isn't it? In one she and Mark are embracing and he's kissing her energetically. They would have been in some private niche, and I'd have been passing by. Ordinarily you did that sort of thing in hallways. Every evening, the hallways of New York apartment buildings were full of lovers. The other is confusing. I don't see why or where or how I could have seen it, but it's such a vivid picture—she's alone and sobbing. Sitting, in a sheath skirt and lacy white blouse, with one leg folded beneath her and the skirt pulling up a bit so you can see her elegant knees, and her head pressed flat to the back of the chair; I'm looking at her from the wrong side, and I can see the ribbon in her hair and the seams of her stockings but not her face. Both hands limp in her lap, making not a sound. I know she is sobbing only because of the rhythmic slow heaving of her shoulders. And then somehow I've passed to the other side and now I see her face, staring as if at some point a million miles away in disbelief, and weeping. It's such a vivid picture and yet, though it haunts me—I can't tell you how it haunts me—I'm fairly sure I just imagined it. Simply made it up.

"Is it possible?" Almost to herself.

I tell her I don't know.

"And that brings us more or less to the day you are reading about. It happened in spring the following year. Marriage was on my mind, and also Mark's exhibition—does the diary say anything about that? The exhibition at that point was like a catapult getting all tightened down. Mark wasn't fated for an ordinary career."

I tell her the diary does mention the exhibition, and ask her to explain. "Next time. I'm all talked out."

With some hesitation I quote to her the peculiar first mention of Mark Handler in her diary. "With Mark dancing at Leon & Eddie's. Lovely, lovely time. There is something predatory about him that scares me."

"I wrote that? My first entry?" The voice sounds as if she is smiling. She is silent a long time.

"Well." Another long pause. "He was an intensely creative

man. He'd reach out and seize a problem and crush it and fling it away and go on to the next. There was something overbearing about his creativity. I knew it from the start. That's what I would have meant, I guess.

"We often went to Jascha Heifetz's recitals. After one of them he said, 'Heifetz *dominates* the violin. Nobody can dominate the piano the way he does the violin—it isn't possible.' And he had a sort of conspiratorial smile. Like a junior criminal pondering a very great one. Such childlike pleasure at the prospect of artistic domination. He was a sweet and noble man, and a kind and gentle man." Her tone is now utterly weary. "I mean it from the heart: You'll have to puzzle it out for yourself."

9

Choosing Ford

"As we leave the restaurant and the Sciences building," the diary takes up,

I am uneasy for reasons I can't quite grasp. Wherever I look they are just outside my field of vision. It's not that I am worried about whether or not I will be engaged at the end of the day, of course I will be. I can see now that it was the German with the cigarette and black jacket who was upsetting me. For some reason I imagined we would run into him again, which scared me. Though it made no sense, that's how I felt. But the Fair makes it awfully hard to sustain bad feelings. The Fair is joyous. If I had to pick one word for it, *joyous* would be the word.

We've decided to head for the Transportation Zone, across the highway from the main area. As we emerge from the Sciences building we are on the avenue that shoots off at forty-five degrees from the Trylon & Perisphere. This vista is very different from the mall. Actually it's a non-vista, much narrower than the Mall & thronged & with no big structure terminating it, so that all you see when you gaze outward is a great buzzing crowd. There are flags running up each side— you can almost picture it as a parade, with the crowd carrying the banners.

(Five thousand different flags and banners are said to be up and flying at the fair, including the flags of exhibitor nations and their colonial possessions, of exhibitor states and private companies, and specially designed theme banners marking out zones, courts and exhibits.)

We return to the T&P & then resolutely stride by the Telephone building, which Mark has determined we don't have time to visit. The Telephone building goes from 9 till 10 on a clock face round the Perisphere. Actually it is less a building than a huge gate facing the T&P. There is a massive stiff sculptural group decorating the gate, looking vaguely in its blank inarticulateness as if it were made of beaten eggwhites. The gate leads into a cool blue-green beckoning pine grove.

(The grove was a popular cooling-off spot during the summer. One of my sources, who visited the fair many times as a child of ten and eleven, remembers the grove "for its sweet smell and soft carpet of fallen needles beneath the trees; it was probably my first experience in anything resembling a forest.")

Aside from the free-phone-call stunt, the AT&T building

was famous for a machine called "Pedro the Voder." A large wall shows a man's face sketched in a few minimal, abstract strokes. A female operator sits at a control station below and a male announcer stands beside her. They are both on a low triangular stage thrusting out into the throng of visitors. Others watch from a surrounding balcony. People crowded in to listen, because "the Voder," as *The New Yorker* explains, "the machine with the human voice, is creepy and wonderful." (Either that, or because of the pretty girl operators: That was *Business Week's* theory.) "Voder" stands for "Voice Operation Demonstrator." The operator's console had keys like a piano's to produce the different component sounds of a human voice, and foot pedals to control inflection. "No listener can resist being profoundly moved by the ghostly human quality of this synthetic speech," writes Gerald Wendt. It is an odd choice of phrase, *profoundly moved*. Technology was a less capable yet far more wonderful thing in 1939 than it is today.

It took considerable skill to operate the Voder. Intelligible speech didn't just happen; it had to be coaxed out by the operator at the keyboard. But some operators had learned by the second season to make the contraption not only talk but sing. On the fair's last day, it sang *Auld Lang Syne*.

Leading at 9 o'clock straight away from the Perisphere (the Trylon is on the opposite side) is the Court of Communications. A white horse barrelling, rearing & leaping toward you, poised at the head of a pool that stretches out like a rippling mirror behind, with razor-sharp hedges running up the flanks. To either side of the pool at the rear, two towering red pylons with gold stripes up their centers. They frame a mural on the face of the Communications building. An Atlas struggles with the globe, a nude man fans a fire, a nude woman gestures in astonishment—reds, ochres, blues & golds. In shape & proportions the mural between those pylons is like a picture on a movie screen. The Fair's landscape is packed with energy, as if each building were a spring-loaded jack-in-the-box set to pounce.

The sculpted horse at the front of the pool is striking. It is a winged horse with head thrown back. A girl sits astride with her right hand thrust forward & legs hooked back, the wings zig-zag like lightning & neat, abstract rolling-forward waves bear the horse up. Maybe it is too obvious, but it says *speed* forcibly & memorably. [The horse is by Joseph Renier. Its name is *Speed*.]

"You could imagine a grouping like this in Washington," Mark says—"the lawn & pool terminating at one of those *nebbech* white buildings. But here it feels completely different, because of the towering pylons & the colors. Y'know yesterday—oh, actually we have to head down this way, that's great, the walkway leading to the bridge is partway down." Folding the map and putting it away, and we plunge into the Court of Communications. When you look back toward the Theme Center, you get the best view of the T&P there is. Trylon to the left & behind, the Helicline cutting across the Perisphere like a gunbelt slung low around a cowboy's hips—the whole composition is just *tight*.

"Yesterday," Mark continues, "I had to meet Marty in Union Square. At the movie house that only shows Soviet movies. Ever been there?" Union Square is so ugly, & the whole place smells like whisky on the breath & dust. Why does a city have to be like that? Why can't it be like *this*? Cool & beautiful. And gathered *round* something—ideally, a place of last resort. A place of comfort, where you could always go for a meal or a place to spend the night. I like that idea. A city hall & relief station combined: the mayor & the poor walk together through the same door. [La Guardia did as a matter of fact drop in routinely at the city's relief stations, unannounced, to find out how the poor were being treated.] "Have you ever been to Klein's?" Turning on me with sudden curiosity. He is interested in my family's comparative wealth the way he might be in an exotic vegetable that had suddenly appeared on his fork. Curious but wary. I shake my head no.

Mid-way through the Court we turn left and trot past Crosley & Masterpieces of Art to our right, Business Systems & Insurance (does anybody *anybody* feel the need to view an exhibit *on insurance*—except just out of sheer perversity??) to our left, making straight for the bridge.

Crosley was a radio company, but it also produced and exhibited at the fair an odd little car looking something like a Volkswagen Beetle wearing a pince-nez and a benign, quizzical expression. (The Volkswagen, of course, hailed from this period as well.) The Crosley had a twelve-horse-power, two-cylinder engine and a selling price of $350, $25 less for the coupé. Economic conditions "make it essential that we give some attention to mileage per gallon," the sales brochure explained to a not-wildly-enthusiastic public. "There's nothing fancy about it," *The New Yorker* reported of the Crosley. "There is no upholstery on its steel sides or anywhere else, except, to be sure, on the seats." It survived until 1952. The 1930s were decisive years for U.S. automobile history. In 1930 the car industry had been a free-for-all with dozens of competing firms, but in 1939 the only independent makers in good shape were Packard, Studebaker, Hudson and Nash, and the brand-new Crosley. GM, Ford and Chrysler defined the industry. Chrysler was the second-biggest firm; it dominated Ford until the early fifties.

Masterpieces of Art across the way housed a substantial on-loan collection, a show that would have done any museum proud: Vermeer's *Milkmaid* and lesser masterpieces from the Rijksmuseum in Amsterdam, works of Fragonard, David, Poussin from the Louvre, bunches of Dürers, Titians, Goyas, Rembrandts (or paintings believed at the time to be Rembrandts, in some cases since defrocked) lent by private collectors. "In the entire history of art exhibitions in New York nothing of such importance and so wide a scope has ever been attempted." Loan exhibitions were themselves a relatively new idea in America. The first spectacular of the type had been in 1909 at the Metropolitan Museum in New York, a show of seventeenth-century Dutch paintings.

Harrison and Fouilhoux's building was restrained bordering on elegant—four narrow, low-slung boxes around a rectangular court. The court was decorated with a pool, fountains and a wraparound mural by Lyonel Feininger.

Like the university and churches in the Futurama, this exhibit was an afterthought. It was financed by a consortium of private citizens and the Solomon Guggenheim Foundation. The exhibition's *Official Guide* tenders apologies. "It cannot be denied that the present exhibition is more concerned with the past than any other at the Fair."

The "insurance" exhibit was actually a building called Business Systems and Insurance. On the side facing away from the pathway where Miss Glassman and Handler approach the highway overpass is a striking sundial, in the form of long slinky silvery ribbons strung over the facade of a formal colonnade. A female nude in pink bas-relief wafts upward amid clouds from a rising pink sun. A hodgepodge of companies maintained separate exhibits inside. Underwood exhibited the "world's largest typewriter," a working fourteen-ton machine that typed letters three inches high. One exhibit explained how credit was analyzed and another promoted life insurance.

CHOOSING FORD

We pass over the highway on a broad bridge decked with flags, the poles sloped outwards; the closeness of the other highway bridge makes it feel a bit like Paris, a tiny bit. And so we arrive in the Transportation Zone. It is a sort of miniature Fair in itself—strike that, it is not miniature at all; but one has a sense of there being a finite rather than unlimited number of exhibits here.

There are nine exhibitors in the transportation zone: General Motors, Ford and Chrysler; Railroads, Aviation and Marine Transportation; Goodrich, Budd (maker of coach and locomotive bodies) and Firestone. And there was a Transportation Focal Exhibit, sharing a building with Chrysler.

A huge semi-circular road with a broad sidewalk leads from the bridge we just crossed round a gentle curve and back to the bridge on the T&P's other side. The road is travelled by buses and tractor-pulled cart-trains. The blue & orange tractors are blunt-nosed & seem to smile. We stroll down the sidewalk & get the lay of the land. First we pass General Motors to the left and Goodrich to the right—General Motors with a silvery facade like a long, low triangle, and a red portal in the center that ingests the slowly-shuffling lines. I've already seen the Futurama, & Mark reluctantly concludes that it would kill too much time. Goodrich has a tall facade that loops round on itself like a candy-cane. Evidently there is an exhibition track where they do stunt-driving behind it, something that doesn't interest either of us. Railways is the biggest building at the Fair—monumental structure in pinkish-creams with vermilion accents & a smoothly-rounded facade, with a pool & fountains out front. So many pools! So many fountains! So many immaculate acres of flower beds, all just a little like over-scrubbed, excessively-well-behaved children behind their neat razor-shape hedges. But that is unfair. It is all colorful & pretty, & the smart snap of the flags makes it gay. "I once planted marigold seeds," Mark is moved to remark, "on the small, flinty, weedy, packed-mud patch behind my parents' building in Brooklyn. Whether I was legally entitled to, I don't know. But it doesn't matter, because they never came up. Unless they did," he adds, "& took one look, & went back down again."

The Railroads building "presents a pageant of railroading," *The New Yorker* concisely reports, "with real puffing trains plus girls and Kurt Weill music."

"Midway round the long curving walk," the diary continues,

if we look back at the T&P—P at dead center & T to its right—General Motors is to our left, Ford to our right & Chrysler behind us. Lots of people in this vicinity are sporting the "I have seen the future" buttons that you get at the Futurama. When Mark notices them he is entranced & wants one. I have to promise to come back with him another day & head to the F. first thing. Chrysler's is a white building with outward-swelling chest, bold vermilion letters (Chrysler Motors) on top, a mural of glass showing streamlined automobiles & peculiar "modernistic" towers to either side. We take it in, turn back round & Mark suggests we go into Ford, which we do. "Children . . . I don't see how I can do it," he says gently as we head down the curved path.

The "modernistic" (a word that seems to shriek for quotation marks) Chrysler pavilion was designed by James Gamble Rogers, best known for conjuring the quintessence of collegiate Gothic out of honey-golden sandstone at Yale. Chrysler's was not a beautiful building, but in its broad-browed facade and formal approach it has at least a hint of the poise and dignity of the best college building in the country, Yale's Sterling Library. Chrysler's building also housed the Transportation Zone Focal Exhibit, which featured Raymond Loewy's Rocketport display. The rocket took passengers to London. It was going to be shot to London by a giant gun. The First World War, recall, included history's only pitched battle between dreadnoughts and their huge booming cannons. Naval artillery reached a pinnacle of sorts in the Great War; in the Second World War, the important naval battles were conducted by aircraft carriers. But in 1939 it seemed natural enough, if you wanted to get a rocket to London, to imagine it as a projectile heaved by a great battleship. ("Rocket flight is at present impossible," the Fair's science director writes in 1939, "but the problem is almost wholly limited to the invention of a proper fuel.")

From midway down the curved walk you would have seen not the Futurama entrance, which was set into the side of the large complex, but the front of the General Motors building. The facade is long and low, with GENERAL MOTORS zooming forward in bold capital letters seemingly extruded by the building and intent on meeting you halfway down the entrance walk.

"The Ford building is striking," continues the diary,

& very hard to describe. We are approaching from the left. Ahead of us is a spiral roadway, like a coil of rope, wider coils towards the bottom; cars zooming up & down; this is one part of the "roadway of tomorrow." Then the walk swoops around parallel to the building, leading us away from the spiral, towards the entrance. The entrance is in a doughnut attached at its rear to the main building, walled in glass block, with a tower & a charging-forward sculpture on the roof.

(The sculpture, of shaped stainless steel panels, is called *Mercury*. Then as now Ford sold a line of cars by that name. *Mercury* was the work of a certain Robert Foster and one of the most interesting sculptures at the fair, with a fluid, high-watt grace.)

"I don't see how I can do it," he says again. "I have a suggestion. Couldn't we just get married & put off the decision?"

"Is that a *proposal?*" I feel radiant & archly amused simultaneously—which adds up to giddy—but before he can answer I say, "No we couldn't." "Why not?" "Because it's cowardly." "I'm not accustomed to being called a coward," he says genially while fiddling with my hair & then kissing my neck. "Then don't *act* cowardly"—glancing beyond his left shoulder at the neatly-outfitted Fair policewoman & then kissing him one short peck on the mouth. "Is it true," he says, "that women just don't grasp, concretely, the objective reality of the world they read about in the newspapers? Or is it a natural compulsion to have children no matter what?" I put my arms round him. He takes me round the waist. Here we are intimate, face-to-face right in the middle of traffic streaming round us toward the Ford pavilion entrance. Smiles outnumbering harrumphs, I think, but I didn't count. *My* but this is little Miss Glassman's day to make a spectacle of herself at the Fair, yes indeed! I could see a children's story beginning just that way. I would be a bunny rabbit. "Listen," I say fondly, lean my forehead on his chin, then unhand him & disengage his fingers & we walk on. "Well you *did* just, in effect, agree to marry me," he says. & I say, "No I didn't."

We move into the entrance hall. "Well but you did," he says, "assuming we can work out this business about children?" He looks at me anxiously in an adorable way & I lean my head on his shoulder. It is a big round room. I ought to be distraught & distracted but the fact is, suddenly I feel *especially* fascinated by the vast wall-filling mural in oranges, yellows & blues before us jumping & whirling with activity— silvery pistons that move up & down, a bunch of other moving parts I can't identify—some sort of valves hopping in & out; silvery speed-lines streaming downward from above. A row of meshed gears frame pictures that show sunshine being transformed by stages into an engine's power. A looming three-dimensional spark-plug, painted factory production lines, cranes; on top, the criss-crossing conveyor belts & smoke stacks of the Ford Plant. [Ford's huge River Rouge factory was an instantaneously-recognizable thirties icon.] And a pale blue "F = MA" floating in the upper left corner. I am floating too, drinking it in with heightened effortless attention. "Is that some sort of special engine?" I ask him. "V shaped," he says, & demonstrates with his hands. "You probably know more about engines than I do." I beckon to one of the attendants who stand around waiting hopefully, & ask about the engine. A long earnest explanation tumbles out which I confess to ignoring completely (although I do come away with the fact that this engine is used in a kind of Ford that was highly praised by a certain bank robber.)

Would a modern Fair rely on Newton's Second Law as a decorative element? It's hardly reasonable to conclude that the average 1939 fairgoer would have recognized and understood the equation, but that's not the point. To that average fairgoer, the equation would have seemed incomprehensible (if it did) not in an off-putting but in a comfortable and vaguely inspiring way.

"Why do I have this floating euphoric feeling?" Miss Glassman's account continues;

We seem to have reached a profound disagreement. But it is just not every day that a girl is asked for her hand i.m., & by so remarkable & so wonderful a man, & the odd thing is, too, that . . . *I* seem to be in charge. Not that I wish to lord it over my dear Mark but, it is a sort of unexpected reversal. There is a great booming crowd-chattering noise in here, as if sound were being broadcast by the ceiling. We wander over to "Henry Ford's First Car" in a display case. It is a spindly black & yellow thing. It makes me recall travelling to the far Bronx as a six-year-old & understanding for the first time that one could actually *own* a car—had thought they were like trolleys or trains—but this person, the something night editor, had a tall rickety one in his garage, of 1910ish vintage . . . "Surely," I say to Mark, as we mosey over to "Henry Ford's First Engine," on a pleated green baize table as if it were *important,* "you wouldn't allow a thing like Hitler to ruin my marriage plans?" "Well it's," he says. "It's—" & he is so uncomfortable, & so seemingly stuck, that I just smile at him soothingly & suggest with a tilt of my head that we move on into the next hall. You are always being pulled onward at this Fair by the lure of something even *more* interesting than the interesting things you are already looking at.

So we wander into the next room, & there before us is an *immense* wedding-cake turntable, slowly revolving . . . & I look at it . . . & Mark looks at it . . . & we stand side-by-side at the railing looking together . . . & Mark says, "We

appear to have reached an impasse." I nod, & again rest my
head on his shoulder, & now there is tragic star-crossed lover
music welling up in my head, & I am feeling deeply *nobly
sad*—but I could not possibly have been enjoying myself in
this way had I not been absolutely positive that he *would
come around.*

The "Ford Cycle of Production" display is often described as the
most impressive at the fair. (The Ford exhibit as a whole ranked
fourth best with fairgoers, behind General Motors, the Theme Center and AT&T; ahead of the Soviet, British and Railroad exhibits.) A
round white turntable with stepped sides, like an uncommonly neat
volcano, is topped by a platform on which three bulbous blue Fords
are mounted in a triangle, nose to tail, canted slightly outward toward the viewers. The slopes of the turntable are covered with small,
colorful moving models. Smooth-surfaced men, in appearance halfway between realistic and abstractly Henry Moore–ish, perform all
the jobs that contribute ultimately to the magnificent finished product on top. They mine and harvest raw materials, refine and finish
them, make parts and assemble cars. The raw materials occupy the
bottom ring, with subsequent jobs stepping higher toward the pinnacle. The turntable is thirty feet high and a hundred in diameter. It
weighs 150 tons and floats on pontoons in a huge pool that is largely
invisible. Small motors crank it slowly around. "It shows how the
Ford Motor Company," a promotional brochure explains, "pioneer-
ing the idea of a low-priced car that millions could afford to buy, has
stimulated employment in every corner of the earth."

There are more displays in a ring around the turntable; spectators circulate between the turntable and the outer ring. The lettering is boxy upright sans-serif: "From the earth come the materials to

be transformed for human service by Ford men, management and machines." This message is repeated twice, on either side of the apse behind the rotating display. It seems imbued with an almost-biblical gravity.

"We watch the turntable in silence for several minutes," the diary takes up:

> As I watch & think my gaze unfocusses, & the display turns into a monumental overwrought ant-hill swarming with activity—& I hear a child nearby saying "that one is just like ours!" as his father struggles to lift him while insisting vociferously, "no *no,* ours is a"—something. "Isn't it beautifully done?" I venture finally. "Architecturally?" Mark says nothing, nods, small smile. Then I try, "I read, recently, that Detroit just became the fourth-largest city in the country. Can you imagine?" "That is pretty remarkable," he says. We watch for another minute or two, & are on our way.
>
> As we push out into the courtyard the fresh air & sun & play of fountains & snap of flags is especially nice after the enclosed and artificially-lighted display hall. There are American flags & Ford & Mercury flags—which are also red, white & blue (lest, perish the thought, anyone be familiar with the National Colors of Ford, Zephyr, Lincoln & Mercury); you sit at round tables under blue umbrellas. People are breaking out picnic lunches, but they don't appear to be selling food here and I am happy just to sit. The rows of tables curving gently round a bandshell are separated by rows of lawn & shrubbery, & you hear the crowd and the automobiles which circle constantly on the ramparts over the "road of tomorrow." They are real Ford cars—you get in & take a ride & emerge convinced, no doubt, that you ought to go out & buy a Ford at once. We sit for a while. Long lines of people slowly

mount three staircases cantilevered out into the courtyard; all three lead to the loading point for the "road" ride. We are content (unless I should say discontent) to rest our feet & listen to the crowds & cars & fountains—more fountains! I *love fountains*—& watch the endless procession of red, blue, pale-yellow circling Fords. The up-high automobiles give the place a slightly unnerving feel, as if one were trapped in some kind of mammoth sunken traffic island, yet it is pleasant anyway. I enjoy the sun's warmth on my face. Lean my head yet again on my Mark's stalwart shoulder. He glances through *Today at the Fair*. "They give 'Novachord' concerts in the bandshell," he says. "Don't ask me what a Novachord is." His voice is dry. "Anyway they don't start until 2:25. Looks like we'll never know." "Doesn't matter," say I. Triumphant. Perfectly comfortable.

10

Technology: Gorgeous

The "Novachord" that was featured in Ford's courtyard was a Hammond keyboard instrument, in effect an electronic synthesizer built with vacuum tubes. "What particularly baffled the pianists, composers and critics who examined the strange invention," *Time* magazine reported, "was this: the keyboard, exactly like that of a piano, yielded not only piano tones but harpsichord tones and simulated effects of many other instruments, such as trumpet, guitar and violin."

The Ford Novachord ensemble was directed by the composer and arranger Ferde Grofé. When schoolchildren in decades past used to be treated to music appreciation classes, Grofé's *Grand Canyon Suite* was a perennial favorite—possibly because it was program music of the broadest sort (simulated mule-clopping courtesy of percussion woodboxes, and so on) and possibly because it was so mediocre. But Grofé lives indeed in the annals of music history because he supplied several nicely turned-out orchestrations of Gershwin's *Rhapsody in Blue*. And the *Rhapsody* happens to be, as conductor and pianist Andrew Litton observes, "one of the most popular compositions of all time." George Gershwin is a quintessential.

He has more of a twenties than a thirties air about him, but he lived until 1937, and his 1930s music is, bar none, the best that decade produced. Gershwin was born in 1898 to Russian Jewish immigrants on the Lower East Side. He was athletic and handsome, with a just-shy-of-excessive Judeo-aquiline nose. When he died of a brain tumor he was unmarried, but his affairs with Hollywood actresses had rendered him one of the most gossiped-about bachelors in the country. His funeral at Manhattan's gigantic and (appropriately) funereal Temple Emanu-El was attended by thirty-five hundred people. George M. Cohan, Mayor La Guardia and former mayor "Beau James" Walker were honorary pallbearers.

When he composed the *Rhapsody* in 1924, Gershwin was a piano player who hadn't yet learned how to orchestrate. He learned fast, and did the bulk of his later scores by himself. Gershwin epitomizes the exquisite balance and poise of 1930s culture. A fair number of pop musicians have in our own time attempted to write or perform classical music, none with any real success. The fault is not wholly their own. Popular and serious music are divided today by a chasm. In the thirties they were merely adjacent countries. Gershwin's best classical music—the *Rhapsody in Blue,* the *Concerto,* parts of *Porgy and Bess* and some of the solo piano pieces—is luminous and superb. His best popular music is luminous and superb.

The public admired him and classical musicians admired him. He even "earned the unspoken tribute of the hot musicians," says an account published the year after his death; hot musicians being the ones who played in hot spots, naturally. "His *I Got Rhythm* was the number played most frequently at a jam session held in 1937 at New York City. In one set Artie Shaw (clarinet), Chick Webb (traps) and Duke Ellington (piano) improvised for ten minutes on this composition."

As a classical composer Gershwin has scant sense of shape or plot—but the careering, caroming, rocketing-onward of his sheer rhythmic inventiveness (not for nothing is he the composer of a song called "Fascinatin' Rhythm") drives the music forward by main force. His best compositions glow with the satiny black flame of polished ebony, jet, marble, granite, Vitrolite, top hats, grand pianos, the lapels of dinner and tailcoats: Deep and smoky blackness is the essence of thirties style.

His life as well as his music shows the mark of the master. He was no monomaniac. Only second-raters are monomaniacs. He was a devoted painter. Fred Astaire recalls that, when Gershwin showed up at rehearsal for the Broadway hits they worked on together, he would "often jump up from the piano and demonstrate an idea for a step, or an extra twist to something I was already experimenting with." Gershwin choreography would occasionally find its way into the finished product.

There is a photograph of Fred Astaire and Ginger Rogers seated beside him as he plays, with an easy smile, a tune he has written for them to dance to. His brother and lyricist Ira peers over his shoulder. It is a picture that shows us something worth knowing about thirties culture, about a self-possessed lyrical beauty that never lectured or talked down to us, devoted itself heart and soul to entertaining us and was never too proud to smile at itself. Gershwin, inevitably, was responsible for the fair's theme song, *Dawn of a New Day*. Ira assembled it after George's death out of material in his sketchbooks.

TECHNOLOGY: GORGEOUS

On the Road of Tomorrow visitors rose in late-model Fords on the tight loops of a coiled spiral ramp, zoomed under a succession of squared-off flying buttresses around a wide half-circle on the outer edge of the Industrial Hall that housed the turntable, tunneled straight through the Entrance Hall and looped back down the spiral again. The road promoted Ford cars, and was also supposed to give good views of the fair; the Ford building occupied the highest rise on the grounds. But it had a didactic purpose as well, as virtually everything did. It was surfaced with a rubber- and cork-containing compound and was accordingly "unusually quiet, and with excellent non-skid properties." The spiral ramp "shows how traffic can be lifted to the express level in the heart of a city without wasting space"—the City of the Future would be crisscrossed by elevated highways. The mere fact that there were no intersecting streets and no traffic lights was meant to be suggestive; the bypass highway was a new idea in 1939. There were only a few in service. Of course there was not much occasion for intersecting streets or stoplights on a demonstration roadway around the top of a building, but regardless, the point was made.

On the inside of the road's spiral was *Chassis Fountain,* by the eventually famous sculptor and designer Isamu Noguchi. A smooth shaft protrudes from an abstract engine block, another from a wheel, and the two are joined at right angles by an abstract differential. The assemblage is balanced on the wheel, with the engine block high in the air, so one gets the impression of a Ford having crashed to earth tail first and landed on its left rear wheel, then having experienced a strange process of decay that eliminated most of its parts while bleaching and fossilizing the few I have mentioned.

Sticking up through the center is a tall thin screw with water running down the threads. For the benefit of any reader who hasn't yet gotten the picture firmly in mind, perhaps I should spell it out: This thing is *ugly*. Noguchi has improved with age.

Noguchi's sculpture underlines a fact that is nearly as fundamental to the fair as optimism itself. At the fair, technology and art went hand in hand. The American religion is reflected in the way 1939 treated its technology.

Not that technology was approached with reverence—nothing of the sort. High-thirties society often seems to be more relaxed and sophisticated around technology than we are. It evaluated technology critically. Praised the good, damned the bad, reserved judgment when it was too early to tell.

This sort of comfortable sophistication shows up clearly in 1939's reaction to television (for example), versus ours to the "information highway."

Life magazine showed three RCA executives watching the company's latest-model 1939 TV. They know that the TV images are clear and that the sets will work decently, *Life* reports; "beyond that they know nothing."

In the same year Gerald Wendt presents a remarkably prescient evaluation. TV might change the country's impressions of war. "If the censors permit, can war itself be brought within the actual experience of those who stay at home, complete with cannon, screams and horror?" So far as education is concerned, TV looks like a mixed blessing. It is likely to make "passive learning" widespread. If it does, TV's "educational effects will be slight and perhaps illusory."

TV is apt to change, not necessarily for the better, the way public figures are evaluated. Its "greater intimacy" of presentation will give the audience "a more vivid presentation of personality." So don't be surprised if TV should "still further enhance the value of what is called personality in public figures." Because of TV "the cultivation of a personal 'public' will itself be a valuable art." Financial and political rewards may accrue "quite out of proportion to the actual value of the performer in his real job, whether it be President or statesman, labor leader or minister of God. In short, democracy, under the influence of television, is likely to pay inordinate attention to the performer and interpreter rather than to the planner and thinker."

In its first issue after the fair opened, *The New Yorker* reports that "last week, of course, witnessed the official birth of television, the first of a series of semiweekly broadcasts from the Empire State Building." After which it goes on to examine the "characters of the week" and doesn't have another word to say about the fabulous new technology. A month later a calm discussion appears:

> If you want to be one of the pioneer owners of home television receivers, you'll find at least four manufacturers ready to supply you with instruments. Most of the television receivers look like radio sets, except for a convex "viewing" device inserted in the top of the cabinet—the kinescope, a huge vacuum tube that reproduces the scene . . . The kinescope is the thing to worry about, if you must do any worrying.

A week before the fair opened, David Sarnoff dedicated the RCA building. His speech was the first news event to be carried on television. (Roosevelt's marked the start of regular TV broadcasts.) "It is with a feeling of humbleness," says Sarnoff, "that I come to this moment of announcing the birth in this country of a new art so important in its implications that . . ." *That?* It will change the world? Revolutionize civilization? ". . . it is bound to affect all society." RCA ran an ad a week later: "Television will contribute to the enjoyment of millions. When it becomes a nationwide service it should provide new opportunities for workers."

Contrast modern journalism's fevered reaction to new technologies like the "Information Highway." According to the *Economist* magazine, "It's the end of the world as we know it." Is that all? The *Times* quotes an industry executive: "This is going to forever change our lives." "A revolution in home entertainment and information," *Business Week* proclaims.

Generalizing is dangerous, as usual. Of course there was a certain amount of frothing-at-the-mouth over TV in 1939. Of course you can find thoughtful, rational analyses of technology nowadays, not least in the *Economist* and the *New York Times*. And of course our own view of technology can as easily be depressed as manic. Part of the difference between then and now can be accounted for, perhaps, by the simple fact that 1939's way of expressing itself is calmer and more nuanced that ours. But the change of mood overall is too dramatic to miss. A superficial conclusion is that we are more excited about the latest technology than 1939 used to be. On second glance, my guess is that we are naive where 1939 was sophisticated. We treat technology as an alien phenomenon; too often we are overawed by it; too often we seem incapable of evaluating it critically.

Nonetheless 1939 was a profoundly religious age, and its religiosity shows in the way it treated technology. It was not reverent. Rather it was spiritual; art made technology beautiful, made technology speak to the public not only pragmatically but emotionally. Art ministered to technology. Artists in the 1930s (not all but many) were technology's priesthood. As a consequence art found itself embroiled along-side technology in the future.

Here is a remarkable text masquerading as a commonplace one. It comes from the 1939 *Guide:* "The true poets of the twentieth century are the designers, the architects and the engineers who glimpse some inner vision, create some beautiful figment of the imagination and then translate it into valid actuality for the world to enjoy."

"Inner vision, beautiful figment, true poets"—that is the language of spirituality. But what does it mean exactly to call designers, architects and engineers "true poets"? And why precisely *these* professions?

First: A designer is an applied artist of sorts. It's unfair to call engineers mere "applied scientists," but any good engineer has solid training in physics and mathematics. An architect is part designer, part engineer. But designers *and* architects *and* engineers are allegedly the age's true poets. This one statement bridges the gap between art and science and fervently hugs the two together.

Then, too, technology in the 1930s inspired art which in turn glamorized technology. "Building the world of tomorrow" seemed inspiring because technology did, because art made it seem that way.

Roughly half the fifty-eight major murals on the fairgrounds have technology themes. They celebrate "Man and the machine," "the incandescent lamp, telephone, the discovery of electricity," wireless communication in the shape of "two muses diving into radio tubes" or "a lineman climbing about in a maze of wires and telephone poles" or "the resources of modern medicine symbolized by a sterilizer, retorts, beakers, test tubes." Heroic sculpture on the grounds depicts "the octet theory of the atom"; "the breathtaking speed of modern means of communication."

The topics may sound naive, but the art was sophisticated.

The best artists in the United States helped decorate the fair, including younger men who were largely unknown at the time but destined for big careers.

Stuart Davis's work for the Hall of Communications shows a vacuum tube, a microphone and telegraph wires. Fernand Léger's for the Consolidated Edison Building centers on power-line towers. Willem de Kooning shows a chemist with test tube and beaker. Philip Guston, Arshile Gorky, Rockwell Kent, Lyonel Feininger, Salvador Dalí painted murals at the fair. Paul Manship, William Zorach, Isamu Noguchi contributed sculpture. Technology-inspired art at the fair is louder and brasher, taken for all and all, than we might favor, and occasionally it blusters a bit. But more often it is strong and graceful. Almost always it radiates confidence, in the technological subject and the artist's means of depicting it. As such it is confidence-inspiring, and sometimes ebullient.

Art is important at the fair, and not only in its role as a friend of technology. You could no more go to the fair and miss the art than you could contemplate a wedding cake and miss the icing. The fair was encrusted with art. You could not have missed surrealism, in the focal exhibits and even the Amusement Area. You could not have missed the synthetic cubism or the bold chunky primitivism of the fair's heroic murals. You could not have missed neoclassical semi-abstraction at Ford, behind Pedro the Voder and in sculpture all over the grounds.

The murals at the WPA building were particularly important to the fair and to the high-thirties mood. Roosevelt's Work Progress Administration offered jobs to the unemployed. The WPA built or improved thousands of hospitals, schools, airports and playgrounds and conducted a grab-bag of other programs—prominently includ-

ing the Federal Art, Music, Writers and Theater Projects. Federal
Art Project murals at the WPA building were intended to show off
the program to the public, and they were painted with passion. The
muralist Anton Refregier described in his diary the studio where
they were made:

> The workshop is the closest to the Renaissance of anything, I
> am sure, that has ever happened before in the United
> States . . . Every person here is dedicated to the Project. Ev-
> eryone feels and knows that we must do our utmost. We
> know that there are a bunch of commercial mural painters
> preparing murals for the different buildings of the Fair
> Hildreth Miere and others. [Miere was responsible, among
> other things, for the slinky pink nude wafting heavenward in
> the elegant bas-relief on the Business Systems colonnade.]
> They are making at least ten times more money than we are.
> But they can have it. Theirs will be the usual commercial
> crap. They are not moved as we are by content—by our
> search for creative and contemporary design—by our con-
> cern for people . . . We will show what mural painting can
> be!!

The Fair Administration gave out prizes, and two of the top mural
prizes went to works turned out by the Federal Art Project for the
WPA building.

High thirties artists made images that glamorized technology. Designers took in scruffy, ugly, hostile-looking machines off the streets
and fitted them for polite society, changing commercial history in
the process. Artists were big at the fair. Designers were even bigger.

In 1929 Raymond Loewy began his spectacular career by converting an awkward, forbidding contraption called the Gestetner Duplicating Machine into a sleek piece of office furniture—with legs no longer thrust out as if expressly designed to trip up innocent passersby. In 1934 the Sears Coldspot refrigerator was an old-fashioned icebox lookalike. Loewy transformed it and sales took off, from 15,000 a year before the redesign to 65,000 after and, following more Loewy design work, to 275,000. Sears was convinced that Loewy's redesign had something to do with the sales explosion—convinced enough, anyway, to raise his fee from $2,500 for the first design to $7,500 for a second and $25,000 for the third. Henry Dreyfuss made similar magic with General Electric refrigerators. In 1934 he converted GE's aggressively odd "Monitor top" look (an icebox with the condenser in a sort of gun turret on top) into a clean modern design. Dreyfuss is responsible, too, for what might well be the most celebrated and significant of all thirties designs: In 1937 he developed the mother of all modern telephones. His design was produced until 1950, and doesn't differ much in basics from telephones we use today.

In the high thirties art, technology and design are so intertwined it is sometimes hard to pry them apart.

"Biggest" and "fastest" are words with tremendous appeal in the thirties. They tended to refer to technological achievements that were also artistic triumphs. When Othmar Amman's George Washington Bridge over the Hudson River opened in 1931, its suspended span more than doubled the length of the previous record holder. Its towers of riveted-steel X-trusses were designed for a masonry facade. But in New York there was general enthusiasm from the start for this "splendid example of the sheer beauty of form following function," for "the loveliness of naked steel and cable" that Amman's bridge embodied, and the masonry panels were never installed. The Golden Gate Bridge of 1937 was longer still, another high-technology triumph. Architect Irving Morrow was responsible for the famous deco towers and red-lead paint that made the Golden Gate an artistic achievement and national icon.

In thirties New York "biggest" referred to skyscrapers. When William Van Alen's midtown-Manhattan Chrysler Building opened in 1930 it was, at around a thousand feet, the tallest building in the world. When Shreve, Lamb and Harmon's Empire State Building opened a few blocks south in 1931, it became the tallest, at 1,250 feet to the top of its dirigible mast. Two more high-tech triumphs—and when American commercial TV was born in 1939, the signals were broadcast from the NBC antenna atop the Empire State Building. When CBS got into the act soon after, its antenna went up on the Chrysler Building. But the thirties cared about the bigness and technical sophistication of those buildings *and* about their beauty. "The New York skyline," the *New Republic* announced in 1932, "is the most stupendous monument ever erected by human aspiration."

"Biggest" referred to Radio City Music Hall. The Music Hall seated more than six thousand, its staff numbered six hundred, the movie screen at seventy by forty feet was the world's largest, the three-hundred-ton steel truss supporting the sixty-foot-high proscenium was the heaviest ever used in a theater. But Radio City wasn't merely a first-rate piece of structural engineering. It was first-rate art as well. It had Stuart Davis's 1932 mural *Men without Women* in its principal men's room. The main ladies' room had a green-on-gold, flowers-and-leaves mural by Yasuo Kuniyoshi, hung with round mirrors like portholes. The auditorium was exuberant. The gigantic stage is framed in concentric half circles, radiating outward. There are lights behind each fin, and their colors can be varied on command. When they are dialed to gold, the front of New York's largest auditorium glows like sunrise.

"Fastest" meant airplanes and locomotives. Airplanes largely inspired the streamlining that was so important to the thirties aesthetic. Locomotives were the occasion for the era's showiest, most brilliant design extravaganzas. The Pennsylvania Railroad and the New York Central competed head to head on the New York–and–Chicago route, the *Broadway Limited* versus the *20th Century Limited*. They competed on speed, but of course on style too. The steam locomotives that pulled those trains were designs, once again, of the presiding geniuses of the high-thirties industrial aesthetic, Loewy and Dreyfuss. Loewy contrived the sleek, forward-straining *Broadway Limited* engine, Dreyfuss the lovely lollipop-smooth *20th Century*. Samples of the two famous engines rolled out of the wings and met nose to nose at stage center in the climax of the fair's *Railroads on Parade* extravaganza. Art made technology beautiful. Technology made the future beautiful.

Since 1939 art and technology have broken apart, for many reasons. Architects still design skyscrapers, but they are rarely technological showpieces. We have stopped building bridges. Locomotives nowadays are not candidates for design competitions. Airplanes never were. Artists no longer paint heroic murals. Even if they did, one suspects that technology might not be a favorite subject. (Unless it were the villain?)

The art-and-technology divorce has been a disaster for both parties, and it has profoundly alienated us from the future. "The story of the reclamation of the site and the building of the Fair on it," says the 1939 *Guide,* "is a romantic saga of modern engineering." Yes, once upon a time, engineering was romantic. Ours is a generation, writes Norman Bel Geddes in 1940, "which has replaced the plodding horse and buggy with the swift-moving automobile, which has grown wings and spanned the world with them, which has built skyscrapers a thousand feet high. Modern engineering is capable of magnificent accomplishments." His language has spiritual fervor. His was an age of religious feeling. "When engineers are given a free rein the result may be almost anything"—thus an admiring reporter, describing the fair's spectacular fountain and fireworks show. La Guardia was entranced by engineers ("engineers fascinated him . . . engineers were his *gods*"); in 1932 the great literary critic Edmund Wilson made the amazing assertion that "it should be possible to convince Marxist critics of the importance of a work like 'Ulysses' by telling them that it is a great piece of engineering—as it is." Today we respect technology, spend heavily on it and can't live without it. But the spiritual glow is long gone. Art has lost its grip on technology, we have lost our grip on the future; and the American religion, in which skyscrapers and steam engines were beautiful and inspiring and numinous sacred objects, is dead.

The fair celebrated engineering. It also incorporated some engineering masterpieces. The Futurama's "Polyrhetor" is a good example.

Polyrhetor is a made-up word meaning "many orators." The Futurama's engineers, recall, were faced with the problem of delivering the right soundtrack to each chair in a continuously moving train. The words you heard had to describe the scenery you were passing.

The Polyrhetor weighed twenty tons and centered on a vertical revolving drum—a column twelve feet high. The designers fixed on the goal of delivering a separate soundtrack to each pair of cars. Each car carried two chairs. The pair-of-cars rule meant that the Polyrhetor had to deliver about 150 separate soundtracks simultaneously—which is quite a lot for any Polyrhetor to handle, even a deluxe twenty-ton model.

Seven parallel "trolley rails" ran beneath the cars. Each pair of cars picked up its soundtrack from a trolley sliding along one of the seven rails. The rails were broken into sixty-eight-foot segments.

As the lead pair of cars glided into a new segment, its trolley made contact with the first rail and slid along forward. A few seconds later the second pair of cars would glide into the segment, make contact with the second trolley rail, and so on.

Meanwhile, back at the Polyrhetor: Twenty-two bands of movie film are looped around the drum, stacked up like rings on a post. There are no images on the film loops, only soundtracks. (Magnetic-tape recording has yet to be invented. Phonograph records and movie film are the only practical alternatives for recorded sound.) Each ring of film supplies narration to a single seven-rail, sixty-eight-foot segment of track. There are thirty-nine seconds of narration per film loop, which is exactly the amount of time a chair-car requires to travel one segment. Each film loop is scanned by seven different light beams at once, equally spaced around the drum. Wires connect the Polyrhetor to the trolley tracks. As the lead pair of cars slips (say) into segment five, the audio signal it sucks out of the first trolley rail is provided by light beam 1 on the fifth film loop down. When the second pair of cars arrives, its signal comes from light beam 2 on film loop 5—and so on.

The system was supplied by Westinghouse and designed by James Dunlop. "For sheer originality of invention," said the *New York Times*, "it is the outstanding contribution of technology to the Fair."

11

Flight
in Space

The Ford and General Motors buildings were designed by the same architectural firm, Albert Kahn's. They differed in architectural feel, Ford elegant and urbane, GM bold and dramatic. "Mysteriously the crowd moved into the blank 'future' through a deep narrow cleft," *Architectural Record* reported of Kahn's General Motors building. "The conception was one of immense power." But they were distinguished most strikingly by their chief designers, Norman Bel Geddes at General Motors and Walter Dorwin Teague at Ford. In both cases the fit was perfect: Geddes was dramatic, Teague elegant.

Geddes was a main popularizer of the streamlined style. The Douglas DC-1 was launched in 1931; in 1932 Geddes's influential book *Horizons* touted and illustrated the streamlined aesthetic. Geddes carried out with distinction ordinary industrial design commissions—a 1932 stove, for example, today seeming merely clean and bland but startling at the time in its classy simplicity. But he was at his inventive best playing make-believe with a minimum of practical constraints, designing "airplanes of the future" (for example) consisting of single swept-back wings and little else, or the Futurama itself. Teague's private lounges at the Ford building were widely described as the most elegant interiors at the fair. Teague went on in the fifties to design the Boeing 707's cabin, and his low-key vocabulary of flush, smooth surfaces remains standard today.

The diary takes up.

> We leave the Ford complex through an underpass beneath the elevated Road in front. "Where to?" I say. Then I suggest that we should tour the rest of this Zone, then cross the other bridge to the power & electric company exhibits that lie just to the other side. Mark agrees. Lunch is beginning to loom large, but on the strength of the doughnut I can hold out a bit longer.
>
> Catty-corner across from Ford is the aviation building, with a plane parked on its front lawn. Mark pronounces its architecture mildly interesting. Then he says, "I'll try to see the thing from your point of view. Whether I can succeed is something I just don't know." I tell him "Thank you" & take his arm; I want him to tell me about the buildings. This is his natural mode, spilling over with energy, & I have temporarily stolen it from him. He tries to get himself started again but the engine is not turning over. But I can fix that. No question about it.

FLIGHT IN SPACE

The Aviation building is like a dome set on the ground & sliced in half—then throw out the forward half, & a sort of wedge-shaped thing with the snout-end in front backs into the dome. I guess it is aviation-like in a general way but the imagery escapes me.

(The Aviation building is supposed to suggest an airport. One account describes it as "one of the oddest buildings in the entire fair, embodying architect William Lescaze's idea of 'Flight in Space.'")

We decide to step inside just briefly. The moment you do, you hear the loud beating drone of propellers, lights are flashing in your face & airplanes are headed *right at* you!—it is unnerving. The far end of the building is a half-domed wall, and suspended inside the cup are four planes all coming in for a landing *right on top* of you. There is a real-looking sky-at-sunset projected into the dome as a backdrop. For several minutes we just stand & stare, transfixed, & then (neither of us being much interested in airplanes) we are on our way.

(The background scene varied—sometimes it was a sunny sky, sometimes a moonlit night.)

The aviation world itself hung suspended in 1939 between its rough-and-ready past, which helped make engineering romantic, and its businesslike future. The unclear state of the art emerges between the lines in the 1939 *Guide.*

A wide range of private aircraft are on exhibit, from "popular-priced 'flivvers' all the way to luxury ships." Just what *was* an airplane, more of a car or more of a boat? For all anyone knew, the Henry Ford of aircraft was even then hard at work on the plane-for-the-masses that would convert every driver into a pilot.

One exhibit at Chicago's 1933 "Century of Progress" Exposition had been a home with a built-in hangar. The two-plane garage would be an obvious next step. Once the airplane's safety problems are ironed out, writes Gerald Wendt,

> there will then be no reason why it should not be manufactured by the mass production methods of the automobile industry and sold in huge numbers at a low price . . . Suburban homes can lie 40 to 50 miles from the city or factory and still be within half an hour's flying distance. They will, of course, occupy enough land, an acre perhaps, to use the lawn as a landing field.

In a 1939 poll roughly 40 percent of adults declare themselves interested in learning how to fly, if lessons were free—half of males and about a third of females. And it is more than a bit surprising to learn that, in 1939, slightly more than a third of all adults have already been up in an airplane, if they are being honest with the poll taker.

As for commercial flying, the ship analogy seemed like a good bet. The airplane of the future would be gigantic, with all the amenities of a luxury liner. Geddes's hypothetical *Airliner Number 4,* designed jointly between 1929 and 1932 with German engineer Otto Koller, carried 450 passengers and 150 crewmen on nine decks. Along with a full complement of staterooms it had a gymnasium and there was, of course, ample room for dancing after dinner. A row of twenty propeller engines powered the enormous craft. Supposedly. Jet propulsion was in its infancy; the first successful jet flight took place in 1940. But all this ocean-liner-of-the-air talk was by no means *strictly* hypothetical. When the Nazis' prize dirigible *Hindenburg* blew up and burned on approach to its

New Jersey mooring mast in 1937, an event that was the "Challenger disaster" of its day—the whole world stared transfixed at the ghastly pictures—the age of the passenger airship drew to an abrupt close. But Geddes himself had been retained by Pan American to spiff up the interiors of its long-range aircraft, and Pan Am Clipper service, with its lounges and Pullman bunks and white-gloved waiters, was far closer to luxury liner standards than anything you are likely to encounter aloft today.

When 1939 sought a niche for the airplane, it conjectured, in short, that planes would take up where cars, ships and trains left off. They would be faster, of course, but either just as convenient and affordable as your car, or just as comfortable as a train or a ship. Long-distance trains were specially distinguished by how well you slept in their Pullman cars, "listening to the rumble of the wheels over the rails, the clatter of crossings, the faraway spooky wails of the locomotive." It all added up to a sedative effect, evidently. Travel by steam railroad was no unadulterated pleasure; cinders might leak in the windows, for instance, which made your mouth gritty and dry. It wasn't perfect. It was merely a good deal better than what we are used to.

The reality of modern plane travel—somewhat faster than the fair anticipated, and vastly less comfortable—is unlikely to have struck 1939 as a very desirable outcome. By 1939 standards modern air travel is a mystery. "To go from New York to Chicago, say, your planes," in 1939's view, "are much faster than our trains; but they leave you miles from downtown, you drag your own baggage, the food is rotten, it's impossible to sleep and it is in general very uncomfortable and no fun. What did you *do* this for? Did vastly higher telegraph and long-distance phone rates, or maybe much shorter life expectancies, force on you this awful compulsion to sacrifice everything for speed? Suppose we could get you from New York to Chicago in *zero* time," 1939 asks cagily, "in *infinite* discomfort? No doubt you'd sign up immediately!"

"The next building over," the diary continues,

> goes some ways toward rousing Mark. It's at the end of a long tree & banner-lined walkway running alongside the Aviation Building's lot. Once more there are fountains in play, right in front of the Marine Transportation Building, & a huge colorful flag—an orange boat with white sails against a blue background.

(The flag was designed by twenty-five-year-old Emrich Nicholson. We learn something about him in a short *New Yorker* piece. He has green eyes and comes from Indiana. He'd graduated from Yale with a B.A. in Fine Arts and worked as a textile and interior designer. In June of '38 he'd applied for a job at the fair's Board of Design; the board just happened to be looking for a flag designer. Nicholson also designed flags for the Aviation building, the Court of Communication, the Public Health building, one of the Food buildings and the Amusement Area.)

> "Another wonderful vista," Mark says. "Ely Jacques Kahn designed the building. I've seen pictures of it, but I like it more in color." The facade is decorated by the matched protruding prows of two giant liners, to each side of the entrance. As if two great ships were sailing at you side-by-side right *through* the building. They are creamy blue with a crisp white nautical stripe on top. Mark is especially interested in E. J. Kahn & talks about him frequently, especially his beautiful colors. He took me into the lobby once, downtown, of Kahn's film center building & it was dazzling—pink marble disks in the floor imitating sprocket holes in film, lovely

FLIGHT IN SPACE

bronze radiator covers & mailbox & directory board, a stunning mosaic decoration in red, turquoise & gold. [The building still stands, on Ninth Avenue.] We walk down the promenade to admire the structure. There is a gangway leading over the fountained pool to the entrance. "If you need a building about boats," Mark says, "no question whatever, this is what it ought to look like." We hesitate over going in but finally decide not to, because it is lunchtime & we've seen almost nothing: none of the "Production & Distribution Zone" buildings with all the technology, no foreign countries . . .

The Marine building was striking outside, but the inside was a dud. Moore-McCormack was the only big shipping company to mount a display, and the building was half empty. A large map showed the current position of American liners on the high seas. Marine equipment was on display, and lots of model boats. "Educational lectures and graphic motion pictures afford additional interest," the guide dutifully reports. In 1940 the exhibit was moved to a corner of the Communications focal building, and fair administrators took over the Marine Transportation Pavilion.

"We emerge from the passageway that leads to the Boat Building," the diary continues,

& make our way back towards the bridge, past Firestone. Firestone is another round building, like a low stack of pancakes with a tall fin penetrating halfway and another fountain in front—a "singing color fountain" to be precise, although it is not singing at the moment." ["Jeweled plumes of spray shoot high into the air in perfect synchronization with the tonal variation of the music."] There is an actual tiremaking operation inside & Mark feels strongly inclined to see it, so we decide to have just a quick look. In the entrance hall there is a diorama of a rubber plantation & another of Firestone factories. There are lots of tires on display with demonstrations of the kind of superior zig-zaggy tracks they make. Gripping. (Ha! I rarely make that sort of joke. Nor any other sort.) The "Factory of Tomorrow" (one naturally didn't expect them to show you a factory of *today*) is a huge *very very* long crowded room with the production line on a stage in front and stepped tiers for standing & watching. You can follow the process down the line by strolling from left to right along a tier. [Architecture critic Douglas Haskell wrote that "New York's most typical contribution to current architectural types" was "the 'ambulatory' stage or auditorium," a type illustrated by the Firestone factory. "The process is carried step by step across the stage, and the crowd moves laterally with it."]

The machines are streamlined & white, & the workers up on the long factory-stage area are in white: that's what makes the factory "of tomorrow," I guess, because their 150 tires a day are evidently ordinary ones that get sold by regular dealers. We stand towards the back: it's steamy, & the machines hiss & thunk, & the crowds chatter, & there is a powerful fresh-rubber-tire smell that evokes automobile dealerships & my father. We didn't spend too much time in there but it was interesting.

Tires are unexciting, but nothing better captures the industrial feel of this era than a tire and a tire plant. The very names of the production steps sound like a lost era: "mixing of crude rubber with sulphur and carbon black," "gum-dipping and calendaring," "ply-cutting," "building," "forming," "vulcanizing"; and the finished tire is wrapped in foil. The tires of this era are narrower than modern tires, designed for inner tubes, supplied with simple tread patterns—parallel wavy lines, in Firestone's case, the "famous gear-grip tread"—that look as if they are incised with a chisel. Technology in this era did not mean white-coated aliens fabbing wonder chips in silent clean rooms. Technology was the smell of new tires. There was science to the process but also raw labor, and the finished product bounced. Citizens at large were connected to technology as surely as their cars were connected to the road. There was a certain beauty to the homely finished product—it was fairly cheap, fairly durable, a big improvement over the previous decade's tire; and there is a certain beauty to those names even today.

"Out back is a farm with lots of rubber-tired vehicles," Miss Glassman continues.

The Trylon & Perisphere loom weirdly as a backdrop to a very ordinary-looking barnyard.

 We step behind some sort of metal shed & are relatively—only relatively—shielded from the rest of the spread. At which point Mark takes me hard round the waist & speaks into my hair, bearing down with his chin so I have to bend my head rather sharply to the side: "*I am not going to lose you.*" The position is uncomfortable or even painful for me, & he maintains it a few seconds for emphasis. "Good," I say, "Please don't lose me." "Her voice was ever soft, gentle & low, an excellent thing in woman." "You don't see me as Cordelia?" "No," he says, "you're stubborn but not that stubborn," & I have to laugh—"*Me, ha!* He hath ever but slenderly known himself." (He undertook Shakespeare on his own in high school because it was to him the epitome of everything "Anglo-Saxon" & he wanted to prove to himself that "it was really no big deal." Except, as it turns out . . . he has read & reread Shakespeare never-endingly ever since.

Nowadays it is almost the only thing, aside from architecture & the papers, that he *does* read. Except maybe also the Bible. Unless he knows it by heart?)

We make our way back out & across the bridge. Mark takes my hand but is not minding me. He has settled into an intensely thoughtful scowl, for evidently he is piloting a ship through uncharted waters. And thus we rejoin the main body of the Fair. When I left I was a mere spinster whereas *now* I am a mere spinster!—but at least my prospects are improving a bit. Of course, it wouldn't kill me if things just *worked as they are supposed to* once in a while.

12

Playgrounds

■ had another batch of questions for Mrs. Levine, and she invited me over. This time the photographs on the table drew me immediately. I studied the young Miss Glassman and Sarah Abbot. Then we sat as we had before, across a table before the window.

"The 'exhibition' in December of '39 was the culmination of a period beginning in the spring you are reading about. That period feels like a shot in a fireworks display—climbing and climbing, then exploding in a destructive dazzle. Mark worked at the Parks Department for Robert Moses, who was opening playgrounds like crazy all over the city. They had to be built of the cheapest stuff, because the WPA was paying for it, and they were all basically alike: swings, sandboxes, sometimes a wading pool. Mark and many others believed that better ones could be built just as cheaply. Mark made the point by designing some. Moses was sympathetic—his earlier work, Jones Beach and all, was creative and beautiful. But he was too busy to pay much attention to Mark's proposals or not interested or whatever.

"Mark worked closely at the Department with a certain Norman Ryerson, who shared his playgrounds interest. Ryerson was related to a trustee of the Brooklyn Museum. It happened as a result that a curator proposed a little exhibit on 'visionary playgrounds,' with drawings by Mark and Ryerson. The drawings would show exciting imaginary playgrounds that might in principle be built within the Department's budget.

"The exhibit was intended by the museum as a slap in the face to Moses. Progressives still admired the man, but they'd been upset for some time by his high-handedness. Mark didn't understand that aspect at all. He was a political imbecile. How a man that smart and wise could be so stupid about certain things was always beyond me. When you added on top the fact that he worshiped Moses, you had outright willful blindness. Not that the museum wasn't interested in Mark's work on the merits: It was. But attacking Moses was an attractive bonus.

"What a summer, and what a fall. We were engaged, of course—"

"You were?" A revelation that caught me by surprise.

"Well. Yes."

The simple declaration was remarkable, because of her confiding expression, as if temporarily I were a friend. The trace of an asymmetric shy smile, mock-serious eyes: I caught a startling glimpse of the twenty-one-year-old girl who had written the diary.

"I'd gotten a job . . ." She looks away, and the bass rumble to her voice and the precise, acid-etched syllables ruin the illusion like

pebbles fracturing a clear image in water. "I started early that summer, working at the New York Public Library on Fifth Avenue. I
was just a cataloger but it was a wonderful place to work. When the
weather was fine, I'd walk down in the morning from my parents'
apartment, and ride home on the upper deck of the Fifth Avenue
bus. Often I'd stop for breakfast at the terrace restaurant in the
Central Park Zoo. It was a hangout for intellectuals. Mornings it was
a wonderful place to sit and drink coffee and look at the newspapers
and watch the seals. Mark worked nearby in the Arsenal in Central
Park, at the Parks Department. I loved it that he was nearby. He
lived in a tiny apartment on Gay Street in the Village, but he was at
his desk before eight. For lunch there was an Automat right across
from the Library. Often Mark would meet me there. He'd allocate
fifteen cents for lunch—you could get a cup of coffee and a big
sandwich or a salad plate or something, but they had an endless
assortment of cakes and pies, and ordinarily he'd wind up with a
coffee and two cakes instead. They made a kind of raisin cake he was
specially fond of. That raisin cake. Raisin cake." She is silent for a
few moments.

"Often he'd have two slices of that. The food was good. Also,
the Automats were the only places in the city where you could sit for
hours over a cup of coffee.

"If you ask, by the way, why didn't he get the two cakes *and*
a sandwich? he wasn't on a diet; it's just, he wanted to spend fif
teen cents and not twenty-five. He didn't have the twenty-five to
spend on lunch.

"I got the job because of my former philosophy teacher at
Hunter. His sister was head of the department. He was a wonderful
man. Middle-aged, large and bulky and awkward, mostly bald, with
a big forehead and kindly smile—he would smile as he fought for
words, he was not articulate, and so easily flustered—and one suit,

hideous olive green worn shiny, and hairy knuckles and glasses slipping down his nose; he wanted me to go on for an advanced degree in philosophy. But there was a little more to it than that. His wife was a bitch. I use the term advisedly.

"She was a pediatrician—fairly rare thing, though by no means unheard of, for a woman in those days. Howard was unhappy in that marriage but you didn't just flick a marriage off, back then, as if it were a light switch, particularly if there were children. Howard had a crush on me . . .

"Mark also wanted me to continue for a degree in philosophy, so long as I did it at a school in the city—he was so funny on the topic, he had a very odd idea of why I should do it. There was never any question of a career. But Mark stood in awe of good writing. He thought himself to be a poor writer and me a very fine one—exaggerating, of course. I have no particular talent. But he'd get me to write him letters—honestly—almost every day, though we'd *see* each other nearly every day. After he got them, and they had to go through the mail, he'd lie on the sofa, in perfect thoughtful relaxation, and have me read them to him. He was so sweet about it.

"Right at the end of August—it's a period I vividly remember, for obvious reasons—I met Mark's parents. We'd gone to a recital at the Brooklyn Academy of Music. We went from the concert to his parents' apartment.

"His father was a shop teacher and his mother worked part time as a bookkeeper. They had come from Poland in their early twenties, and spoke Yiddish at home. We sat in the kitchen. Narrow with a high ceiling and a lingering sulfurish smell from the gas range. We had cherry soda and sponge cake and glasses of tea. There was always the 'Palestine box' on the kitchen table—small blue-and-white metal box distributed by the Jewish National Fund. One deposited one's spare change for the support of the Zionist settlement. This family had no spare change, but they deposited anyway. Mark was worldly and sophisticated and so were his friends, but there was nothing I admired in him more than his refusal to apologize in any way for his parents ever. I liked them. Except, I wondered whether they might not have a narrower world view than his.

"Or rather to be honest, I resented them from the very start. I resented them long before we met. They'd told Mark architecture was no field for a Jew. They were right, to a point. It was still an Ivy League gentleman's profession. That *was* changing, at least in New York. But they'd always told him, too, that engineering was just a more *substantial* thing to do than architecture, assuming he really didn't want to be a medical doctor; and so he dutifully became an engineer. They had their hearts set, too, on his getting a doctorate. It had to be Doctor Handler, one way or another. And so that was exactly his plan, he'd get a doctorate in engineering. Engineering wasn't much of a career for a Jew either, by the way. The big corpo rations, the ones at the Fair—AT&T, Du Pont—you never heard of a Jew at a place like that.

"Other things irritated me about his parents—and even at the time, I felt guilty about disapproving of them; I liked his mother very much—her quiet intelligent soft eyes with gentle mockery in them. But their stubborn accents, their stubborn Yiddish, their parochialism, the tiresome constant Zionism—a little was okay, but they overdid it. It just seemed like a lot of old-fashioned crankiness. It made me self conscious about being a Jew myself. The one thing his parents ever cared to see at the World's Fair was the Palestine pavilion.

"Mark once told me something about his father that came back to me when you described that cigar store on Broadway that was open every day except Yom Kippur . . ."

I had mentioned it to her in our last phone conversation: a shop on Broadway in the 1930s called the I & Y cigar store. It was open twenty-four hours every day of the year except Yom Kippur.

The proprietor, Izzy Yereshevsky ("I am the I. And I am the Y. Two initials sounds more responsible") owned a collection of fifty thousand dollars in bounced checks tendered by his friends over the years. "When the checks bounced, he was sorry because the friends often stayed away for as much as two weeks."

"The family was not religious," Mrs. Levine continues, "but they would go to the synagogue on the High Holidays. At age seven or eight Mark was standing next to his father in synagogue on Yom Kippur when he suddenly became aware that, with his eyes shut and a *tallis* over his head, his father, as Mark put it, *was actually praying.* It was a shock that stayed with him. And a puzzle, because he had relegated religion to so negligible a role in the household. But Mark always regarded his father as a sort of religious figure, almost a mystic, who would emerge butterfly-like from secular life on rare occasions and be transfigured . . .

"His mother once showed me some drawings Mark made as a child when he was eight, nine and ten. She kept them in her nightstand drawer. Some were in pencil and some in red conté chalk, with 'Mark E. Handler' written up the sides of each in a child's hand. Mainly skyscrapers. Also a palace with peacocks on the lawn, for his mother and father to move into someday. Clearly a child's work, and yet they were just so *bold* in the way they filled up the page, in the clear, clean lines—you knew at a glance that something out of the ordinary was going on. He also made balsawood models of his buildings. Boyhood couldn't have existed back then without balsa wood. His father kept them in his office at school. Promised he'd bring them home to show me, but he never did.

"On the first of September the war began. I stood with Mark, and I think also my friend Howard, clustered with a bunch of others round the open door of a taxi drawn up at the curb on Fifth. We were listening to the driver's radio. I remember that street scene so clearly. The driver's leather suspenders, the bobbing pigeons in front of the great gray library—Mark with a foot perched on the cab's running board; is there a pipe in his mouth? Sometimes he smoked a pipe. The taxi's yellow-orange bullet-shaped headlight mounts on either side of the radiator, the crowds moving round us, the odd Fifth Avenue traffic lights of that era—the two lenses mounted flush in a prim upright shoebox with a little statue on top. The news was horrible. It was horrible.

"The exhibition came to dominate our lives that fall, Mark's and mine, and the anxiety of the war constantly in the background. Mark drew and drew and drew, hundreds of playgrounds, no two alike. His inventiveness was supernatural. I had the satisfaction of playing a small role, helping him home in on the best ones. He had so many ideas he'd tend sometimes to go off in a million directions at once. He told me once that I was the coin on his tone arm."

She pauses with the cigarette cocked inches from her mouth. A breeze scatters the plume. Then she looks out the window in the same clipped, deliberate way in which she pulls a puff on the cigarette, fortifying herself on the view. And turns back to me.

"He'd work at the kitchen table in his apartment. The antithesis of the neat, meticulous draughtsman. The only tools he used were a triangle and T-square and pencils. He'd work with rolls of tracing paper and great big pads of newsprint. The clearest part of my recollection of those scenes is frantic activity. Hands and elbows moving fast and constantly as he draws, erases, traces, rips a page out, drops it on the floor and grabs another in a single motion— almost a blur of activity, is how I remember it. During weeks when he was hard at it, the kitchen floor would be just covered with a mass of discarded papers and eraser crumbs. You couldn't *see* the floor. I'd straighten up when I was down there, but it would stay neat for maybe half an hour at the outside.

"But there was more than architecture on our minds. We'd had dinner early on with Ryerson, and I'd sketched my view of the museum's anti-Moses agenda—it was Howard who'd put me onto it. Ryerson was no more of a politician than Mark, but he tended to believe what he was told, and got to brooding. Late in September he announced that Moses was likely to fire them both if they went through with the show, and proposed they reconsider. Mark talked soothingly, even suggested they go see Moses—but the bottom line was, Mark would not for anything even *consider* pulling out. He didn't believe it was remotely possible that Moses would fire them. And he wouldn't have pulled out anyway.

"Through October Ryerson got more and more agitated, and in November he told the museum he was withdrawing. The museum said fine, they'd go with Mark alone. Mark's work was incomparably finer . . . But Ryerson was mentally unbalanced. It's curious how an awareness of something like that can sneak up on you suddenly. We were sitting in the Automat on Fifth and he'd said something—he was a wiry small man—and we'd responded, I don't even recall what the topic was, but then he said . . ." Pauses, feeling for the exact words. " 'No I'm *not* kidding.' And there was something in the way he said it; Mark and I just looked at each other . . . It was late Sunday afternoon. Unseasonably warm. We sat by the window, as the shadows stretched out longer and longer on Fifth, and the gold sun surging up the avenue caught the traffic lights full in the face and made them glow strawberry and lime, like hard candy.

"I think I must have reached a hand out to Mark's arm. I can feel the weave of his jacket as we watch the smattering of cars and buses and nearer us, moving much more slowly toward each other, a horse pulling a cart and, on the sidewalk, a policeman, in the double-breasted blue jackets they used to wear with the too-far-apart columns of buttons. They move slowly, the policeman looks tired and thoughtful and I feel Mark's sleeve in my palm; at a table right behind us a lady makes an inaudible assertion and a man says,

President Roosevelt dedicates the fair, at three o'clock on a Sunday afternoon. In the charged political climate of 1939 some listeners construed this speech, said the *Herald Tribune*, "as a polite but pointed lecture to Chancellor Adolf Hitler on the advisability of peaceful co-operation among nations." The President faced the Trylon and Perisphere from the far end of the fair's magnificent main vista. Hidden by the podium's decorative surround are the handles he gripped firmly to steady himself. He gestured, as usual, not with his hands but with his head.
(UPI/BETTMANN NEWSPHOTO)

[*Above*] Laying the cornerstone of New York City's pavilion in January 1938 are (front row from the left) Queens Borough President George Harvey, Fair President Grover Whalen, Mayor Fiorello La Guardia and Parks Commissioner Robert Moses. When work began at the site two years earlier, Harvey had expressed the belief that if the fair's one accomplishment were to clean out the mosquitoes in the festering dump then occupying Flushing Meadow, it would be OK with him. The New York City building still stands today, home to the Queens Museum. At one point it briefly housed the United Nations. (ACME)

[*Below*] Italy's Pavilion is surmounted by "Roma" in a brick-red dress and naturalistic flesh tones, looking like a refugee from a waxworks. Behind the water cascade the facade is mainly pale aquamarine, elsewhere yellow buff. At the waterfall's base is a monument to Marconi. When Grover Whalen called on Mussolini to sell him on Italian participation in the fair, the Duce was sufficiently impressed to appropriate five million dollars on the spot, four for this building and one for "general expenses." The restaurant on the pavilion's second floor, modeled on the dining salon of a luxurious Italian Line steamship, was one of the most expensive and classiest at the fair. (THE BETTMANN ARCHIVE)

[*Below*] The fairgrounds from Manhattan. In any unobstructed view from Manhattan into Queens, it was hard to miss the Trylon and Perisphere. (It was a nice feature of Wanamaker's department store that you could see the Theme Center from its top-floor lunchroom.) The fairgrounds were ten minutes by Long Island Rail Road from midtown Manhattan. (THE NEW YORK POST)

[*Right*] The Four Freedoms decorate the plaza where Rainbow Avenue crosses the mall. In the distance George Washington is silhouetted from the rear against the lit-up Perisphere. The fair officially commemorated the 150th anniversary of Washington's inauguration in New York City. Some critics liked James Earle Frazier's *Washington*, others didn't—but on the ugliness of the *Four Freedoms* there was little disagreement. And yet their symbolic significance was large. (THE BETTMANN ARCHIVE)

[*Left*] Icarus Who? The parachute jump—bright red with a white top, decorated with Lifesavers in yellow, red and green. Each chute carried a pair of riders 250 feet high. It took forty-two seconds to reach the top (slack parachutes), ten seconds to come down (puffed-out chutes). The parachute jump, claimed the 1940 Official Guide, "packs more thrills... than any wings-in-sky interlude since Icarus." After the fair closed, the parachute jump was moved to Coney Island; it hasn't worked for years, but you can still see it there today. (THE BETTMANN ARCHIVE)

[*Below*] A waterfall pounds down the front of the Electric Utilities building. It was meant to suggest a hydroelectric dam. Dams are a powerful symbol of technological and social progress in 1939. Boulder (now Hoover) Dam opened in 1936, the Grand Coulee Dam in 1941. The power lines in the background mural are an eyesore today; in 1939 they stood for bold technological changes that made everyday life better. (THE BETTMANN ARCHIVE)

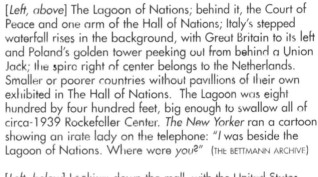

[*Left, above*] The Lagoon of Nations; behind it, the Court of Peace and one arm of the Hall of Nations; Italy's stepped waterfall rises in the background, with Great Britain to its left and Poland's golden tower peeking out from behind a Union Jack; the spire right of center belongs to the Netherlands. Smaller or poorer countries without pavillions of their own exhibited in The Hall of Nations. The Lagoon was eight hundred by four hundred feet, big enough to swallow all of circa-1939 Rockefeller Center. *The New Yorker* ran a cartoon showing an irate lady on the telephone: "*I* was beside the Lagoon of Nations. Where were *you?*" (THE BETTMANN ARCHIVE)

[*Left, below*] Looking down the mall, with the United States building in the distance. The fair's night-time lighting was an aesthetic and technological tour de force; "among scientific features introduced by the fair," Grover Whalen wrote, "perhaps the most revolutionary was the use of light." He was particularly proud of the tiny "capillary mercury tubes" that lit each tree on either side of the mall from underneath. The lit-up leaves had a rich blue-green tinge. (UPI/BETTMANN)

[*Right*] The Ford Cycle of Production is thirty feet high and floats on pontoons in a circular pool. It was cranked slowly round by electric motors. The animated model workers on the slopes were dressed in bright colors. On the pinnacle, three shiny blue Fords. The gigantic turntable was described by some people (not all of them Ford employees) as the most impressive exhibit at the fair. (MUSEUM OF THE CITY OF NEW YORK, THE GOTTSHO-SCHLEISNER COLLECTION)

[*Left*] A winter view of the Trylon and Perisphere, Ford and General Motors in the foreground. New York City's building stands between the Theme Center and the highway. The open square at the center of the General Motors complex (in the foreground to the left) is the life-size "intersection of the future" that Futurama customers previewed in miniature at the end of the ride. The GM building included late-model cars in a striking high-style display hall, a Pontiac with a see-through plexiglass body and a wonders-of-science show in a large auditorium as well as the famous Futurama. Ford, encircled by the "Road of Tomorrow," is immediately to GM's right. The GM and Ford buildings were designed by the same architect—Albert Kahn. (MUSEUM OF THE CITY OF NEW YORK)

[*Right*] The City of Light diorama, designed by Walter Dorwin Teague, in the Consolidated Edison building. The colors changed during the show but they were subtle, harmonious and beautiful throughout; in this photograph, the buildings range from off-white through various sand tones into soft rusty browns. The river and the sky are pale gray-blue.
(THE BETTMANN ARCHIVE)

[*Left*] The fairgrounds looking toward Manhattan. If the fair's main axis were extended down the mall toward and through Manhattan it would have pierced the Statue of Liberty—purely by accident, but fair publicity played it up. The fair looked like this (with statuary shrouded and the Lagoon drained) in early winter 1939-40; by opening day in 1940 the Soviet Pavilion (to the Lagoon's left) was gone and the goddess of perfection had been elevated from inside the Heinz dome (on the left side of the mall between Lagoon and Theme Center) to outside on top—among other changes. (THE BETTMANN ARCHIVE)

FUTURAMA

[*Left, above*] Inside the Futurama. "You somehow get an almost perfect illusion of flying," *The New Yorker* remarked. The landscape of 1960 was colored in soft greens and browns. (GENERAL MOTORS)

[*Left, below*] The front cover of General Motors' "Futurama" brochure. Long lines of people waited at all hours to get into the Futurama. "There have been hit shows and sporting events in the past which had waiting lines for a few days," wrote Norman Bel Geddes, "but never had there been a line as long as this, renewing itself continuously, month after month, as there was every day at the Fair." "Mysteriously the crowd moved into the blank 'future' through a narrow cleft," an architectural journal reported. "The conception was one of immense power." (GENERAL MOTORS)

[*Below*] Inside the Perisphere: Democracity at night. In the show's night-time segment, ultraviolet spotlights picked out fluorescent paint in the model and made it glow – a technique that was noteworthy enough to rate a "science note" in the *New York Times*.
(© 1939 NEW YORK WORLDS FAIR 1939 ACME)

Crowds entering and leaving the Perisphere on opening day.
Fairgoers entered by way of two long escalators (the longest in
the world in 1939), and left by the walkway that runs
parallel to the pool in the foreground. After passing through the
Trylon on the right, they strolled back to earth on the Helicline.
Note in the background Paul Manship's gigantic and distinctly
peculiar sundial (the largest sundial in the world, naturally).
(THE BETTMANN ARCHIVE)

Zatso? above the clattery din, which reminds me of the mayor, who used that phrase all the time. I'm probably conflating many separate memories, but it all seems so real and of a piece. The smell of coffee. The Automat had marble walls set with endless ranks of little chrome-framed windows. You'd put your nickels in the slot and the window popped open. There was a counter also, where you could get hot food. When you walked in, you traded a dollar for nickels. The nickel lady made change unbelievably fast. The coffee came out of a golden spout in the wall and it was first-rate. It was bright and very noisy in there. So there we sat, silently worrying together. The traffic lights glow strawberry and lime in the lengthening shadows and there is a sad, shabby sweetness—that is the thirties for you, if you're still looking for them.

I remember sitting there another time with Ryerson also, it must have been at lunch, because I remember thinking—Mark with his two plates of raisin cake, Ryerson with his chicken à la king and his little bowl of peas and diced carrots, or lima beans, or whatever—Mark can't help being unconventional, and Ryerson can't help being conventional. It's the way they're made.

"Anyway, Ryerson wanted in the worst way for Mark to pull out. He was sure he'd be blamed for instigating the thing whether or not his own pictures were on display, and would be fired just the same. I don't say there was anything crazy about *that*. He may have been right. But the way he talked got stranger and stranger, with violence in the background. I was scared and wanted to talk to the police, but Mark wouldn't hear of it. And then, three days before the show, Mark accepted Ryerson's offer of a ride to the museum from downtown.

"He drove a big, bronze Packard. On Eastern Parkway in Brooklyn he went wild—floored the gas pedal and sped out and around traffic. Informed Mark he was going to crash the car and kill them both. When he slowed down at a turn onto a side-street Mark opened the door and rolled out. But he decided instantaneously that he had to get back *in,* or Ryerson would kill himself and maybe other people too. He sprinted after the car, now on a side street, and there was a van blocking the way, so Ryerson had to slow down and thread his way round it—and Mark, unbelievably, leapt *back in.* Witnesses saw him do it, it was in the papers—needless to say; but then Ryerson swerved wildly and he fell out again. The door flapping open the whole time. One block later he rammed the car into the base of an apartment building and broke his neck, and nearly every other bone in his body. Four other people were hurt, not as badly.

"Well, it was some run-up to an art exhibit. The photo of the smashed-up Packard—a picture by Weegee, I think. The car's crumpled front climbing a wall, three detectives in black fedoras, one looking right at the camera—blank face; up above, at every last window there are people taking it all in, leaning over the sills. A terrible, terrible sight."

She sighs and puts out the cigarette.

"Three nights later, the show opened.

"It was nothing like what you might picture as a modern gallery opening. A short, serious evening. If there were refreshments, I've forgotten what they were. No liquor.

"There was a table up front and the audience sat on folding chairs. It was a large room hung with his drawings. Drawings filled two other small rooms besides.

"There would have been around a hundred people, from the Parks Department, from the newspapers—the papers often covered this sort of thing. I can tell you there was someone from the *Herald Tribune:* that was a thing I did not leave to chance. My father was assistant city editor at the *Tribune.* There weren't a lot of Jews at the *Tribune* at the time. When Herzberg became city editor after the war, that was the first really prominent Jewish appointment. Of course

Walter Lippmann was a Jew, and he was their leading columnist, the leading one in the country, but he was a very, *very*—" She stops. "Well, what difference does it make. My father, also, was a socially acceptable sort of a Jew, from a comfortable old-line German-Jewish family. Robert Moses was that kind of Jew. *Et cetera.*

"Mark's family and mine were there, of course, and Sarah Abbot. I hadn't seen her for quite some time. She came alone, and there was something so very regal about her appearance, I think I must have stopped and stared. I don't remember the dress or the hair, but I do the single strand of pearls. She was so beautiful and so elegant. And there was something about the way she carried herself. It raised a question in my mind that I didn't even know how to frame. Why had she come alone?—half New York was courting her. Well of course, one might have dropped by out of interest in the drawings, or friendly attachment to an old flame, but there was something—"

It is rare for her to pause and grope for words.

"*Not casual* about her appearance there."

She pauses again, inhales the view outside. We are across from Central Park. There is a low red-stone wall along the edge, with sycamore and beech crowding behind. Taxis and a delivery truck and a Mercedes pause at a red light.

"But I dismissed it from my mind because the topic of Sarah Abbot frightened me. She seemed a perfect creature. I was frightened that some day she would take Mark back again. She had it in her to do that."

"Speaking of Sarah Abbot," I put in, "do you recall what the occasion was when you and Mark met her at a dinner of some kind at the Waldorf-Astoria, just a few weeks before the exhibition?"

She is able to recall dinners at the Waldorf, but none right before the exhibition or having anything to do with Sarah Abbot. "I take it there's something in the diary to that effect?" There is, dated December 2, 1939. She asks me to read it to her.

To the Waldorf dinner finally, after prolonged struggle over clothing; finally Mark consented to have Dad's tailcoat refitted four days before the evening—a piece of heroic tailoring was required, but in the end he looked wonderful. I can't say it was a surprise to see Miss Abbot. Her escort was nearly a caricature of what one would expect, big broad blond stupid with a jutting chin—but she was a Romantic's vision of a Greek goddess—her long hair elegantly pinned up, flowing pink gown gathered under the bust, puffed "gay-nineties" sleeves, white skin whiter than usual but flushed a little & I have the distinct impression that she is not intoxicated, but has drunk enough to be *inspired*. Of course, she always seems that way.

She introduces the escort, in whom she appears to have utterly no interest. Then fixes Mark with her goddess eyes & announces in a voice that wants to laugh, "My Prometheus bound." Her eyes flash at him & her lips are pursed, in the way you would tug back on a kite that is about to break away. "We've been through all this before" he answers evenly. "But it's funny we should meet," she says. "I've just been mulling over the course of modern history—" "I'll bet you have" he says—but the unnerving thing is, the way he is swelling up into a big magisterial presence to match hers. The way his eyes, too, are taking on a subtle sheen of craziness, like the colors of a soap bubble. "May I?"—reaching a hand toward her hair, & he touches it delicately—I feel myself breathing; with arched fingers he supports her head in his fingertips as if it were a marble portrait bust he is appraising. Mr. Blond has his lips pressed grimly together to prevent his exploding. "Do you not understand what the twentieth century *is?*" she asks him, "That it means—" "We've been over all this before" he repeats, & she continues right through him—"crawling out of one's primeval box & blinking in the sunshine? Like a toad on a rock. Is it too much to hope for?"

He supports her head while his index finger traces a soft circle in her hair. "*May I?*" he says again. "Oh, by all means"—she turns her chin as if she is offering her cheek for a kiss, & he pulls a few black hairs out straight (a necklace to be examined before purchase?)—she leans away from him, the hair is stretched taut, she is tugging back, it is so obnoxious of her, & then—she shuts her eyes tight, pauses motionless—*tight*—Blond is a steam boiler with no valve that is about to start quaking forward across the floor—&—why is it that I conceive *so unmistakably* the idea that he is about to *rip the hairs out?*

"*What on earth are you doing?*" I say in hot urgent humiliation to my shoes. I would have sounded on the brink of tears. I glance up at Sarah Abbot. There are mad colors in her eyes brilliant & flashing.

Mark looks at me blankly. Withdraws his hand from the goddess's hair. Am I crazy? How could I even have entertained such an absurd idea? Yet it seemed so *clear*, what he was intending. And so preposterous, I must have been mistaken. I'm ashamed to have conceived such a thought. But I seem to have forced the skit to a premature ending; my relief is profound; we are allowed to walk off.

"What was all that about?" I ask him. He is frowning vaguely. "Oh—" as if an explanation were about to follow. None does.

"You're not still *seeing* her?" "No"—in a tentative way, as if once again there were more to follow. And again, there is nothing. But he is simmering down. The hectic noise-of-battle-hordes withdrawing, disappearing. He smiles at me in the regular way. "She's just a little bit of a nut," confidingly. And I am content, *quite* content to dance off with him & say no more about it.

She is so much like my mother, Sarah Abbot, in coloring, stature & elegant carriage—there is even a bare resemblance in facial features—that I almost think sometimes I must have conjured her up out of my own head. Except that she smiles, she *laughs* & my mother does not. With smiles & laughter a goddess grows all the more intimidating.

"That's the end of the entry," I tell her.

She looks with amusement at my folder of photocopied diary pages elaborately cross-indexed with Post-its. "Honestly, I draw a total blank. I don't remember a thing about it." She stops to contemplate. "It's easy enough to see why I forgot it.

"Anyway. After some introductions, it came his turn. He was nervous. His tie seemed too tight. But before long, he looked up from his notes and smiled his distinctive overflowing smile. That smile always mobilized warm memories. Of a childhood winter morning when the sun is dazzling on the snow, and it feels good to watch from your bed?

"The speech was well received. The exhibit was praised. The impression was unmistakable that here was a young man to watch. 'An uncommonly brilliant young man'—the *World-Telegram* said that. So—"

Her fingers tap rhythmically on the table.

"The next day Moses fired him. Evidently the man spoke one sentence in all, one half of which conveyed that Mark was fired, the other that Moses would be willing to write a favorable letter of reference. Mark chose to believe that the problem was not the exhibit at all but the hubbub surrounding the smashed Packard and Ryerson, who lay in awful condition in a Brooklyn hospital. Nobody blamed the incident on Mark, but the feeling was, it was the sort of thing one didn't want the Parks Department mixed up in. I don't know what the real story was. I do know that Mark left the department with his esteem for Moses still perfectly intact."

Smiling to herself.

"It was a strange situation. Mark went around looking as if he had just swallowed a goldfish. All of a sudden, first, he was out of a job—he'd loved that job, and his entire near-term future and mine too had been organized around it—and, second, he was a somebody. A definite somebody. Just like that. Well I mean, people weren't crowding round him in the street soliciting autographs. But people did read about his show, and a fair number came to see it.

"Well: My great find. Drum roll." She leaves the room—

And returns with a few typed pages. "During his talk at the opening he showed slides, lantern slides. I have here the first three pages of the comments he read at the lectern during the slide show. I guess there'd have been ten or fifteen pages in all. The rest are lost. I don't know what the dickens could have happened to them, why they are gone and these aren't, I wish I had them all. But these give the flavor, and they are so intensely *fragrant* with his character. Probably I'm the only one who could possibly see them that way. I lose myself in these pages."

13

His Own Words

The white pages have rounded corners and three holes for a looseleaf binder. There are occasional corrections and notes in brownish ink. I start to read.

"Would you read aloud?" she says.

Thank you . . . etc. I would like to discuss a sequence of twelve simple playgrounds.

1. Imagine an ordinary group of playground swings inside a large concrete half-cylinder, lying on its side, that mimics the arc of the swings themselves. I mean a large pipe, if you will, sliced in half. When a child sits on the swing at rest he is, let us assume, two and one-half feet off the ground. As he starts to swing he remains

always two and one-half feet off the ground, because the "ground"
follows him up and back as he swings. For he is swinging inside a
cylinder.

"Perhaps you would stand over there and read," she says.

A long shallow slope leads up to the lip of the cylinder on
either side. A child who is intrepid can grab a swing and swing Tarzan-
style from one slope to the opposite slope. The two slopes are edged in
concrete blocks. They are made of earth and planted with grass. They
are berms, in short. The grades are shallow enough to allow for easy
mowing. Despite their extreme simplicity these long gentle slopes are
important playground elements in themselves. Children may charge
up them, roll down them in wagons or slide down in the winter on
sleds—the concrete block edging makes a shallow parapet that pre-
vents wagons or sleds from straying over the edge—or just lie down
and look at the sky, which believe it or not is something which, in my
observation, children actually rather like to do. In elevation or profile,
the structure as a whole resembles the broken pediment atop an old
colonial highboy.

"You don't physically resemble Mark in the slightest," she
puts in. "Nor did Mark have any special interest in history. Nor did
Mark enjoy writing. And the gap of so many years makes a big difference that is harder to define. From the pipe in his jacket pocket,
to the way he spent his living in petty sums week to week on food and
rent—thirty cents here and two dollars there; a quarter for half a
dozen roses for me, when he arrived at my parents' to take me to
dinner—he had to budget for that quarter . . ."

The country was so much poorer in those days that everyday
life was qualitatively different.

Hunger, for example. It was a reality in 1939: That is the
plainest way to convey the difference. It was a fact. Not that large

numbers of people went to bed hungry—although more did, by far, than do today. The difference lies rather in hunger's sheer *familiarity* in those days. In the depression's wake it was not unusual for working- or even middle-class people to recall periods of hunger, or have friends or relatives who could. In 1934 William Saroyan published a short story that made him famous. The hero of his *Daring Young Man on the Flying Trapeze* is a writer dying of hunger. The story was shocking but not unbelievable. In the 1937 movie *Stage Door,* a struggling actress keels over from hunger. Not your everyday event; not incredible either. Everyone in New York knew how to assemble free meals in the Automats, and it seems that occasionally people actually did it. You poured ketchup in a bowl and added hot water for tomato soup. You squeezed lemon slices—they were laid out near the tea tap—and added water and sugar for lemonade.

Daniel Patrick Moynihan wrote in 1989, and it has since been widely accepted, that poverty today follows mainly in the wake of fatherless families; historically it had been the consequence of low wages or no work. We let that "historically" slip by, but it deserves careful pondering. It is too easily forgotten that, not many decades ago, you could hold down a full-time job and go hungry. A 1939 account quotes a letter from an officer of a social welfare agency to the *New York Sun*: "A girl whom I have in mind was earning $8.50 a week, a full time job. Out of this she paid $4. a week for a furnished room. The remaining $4.50 was all she had left for food, carfare, clothing and incidentals. This was her diet with costs for an average day:

Coffee in the morning	.05
Luncheon	.15
Dinner occasionally	.40
Total daily expenditure	.60

Most of the time she had dinner at a girlfriend's home. The friend was married, and the couple shared their dinner—"spaghetti, vegetables, etc." She spends sixty-five cents a week on cigarettes, and explains why: "It keeps me from being hungry when I smoke before a meal."

Another letter to a New York newspaper begins "I am a girl in my late twenties earning $10 per week." She lists her expenses for rent, meals and carfare. She has ninety cents left over. "A total of 90 cents can hardly pay for medical, dentist and clothes bills." The *Ladies Home Journal* publishes a menu submitted by a typically frugal middle-class housewife: "Dinner: An inexpensive main dish, such as macaroni and cheese or tomatoes and frankfurters . . . a Sunday pot roast or chicken, but not every Sunday."

"There are endless details of presentation," Mrs. Levine continues, "that strongly distinguish you two. His gait, the look in his eyes, the way he carried a newspaper. But there is also some resemblance, somewhere. I can't quite put my finger on it."

She nods that I should continue reading.

2. *This is a cube twenty feet on a side. The cube as you see is made of chain link fencing. It is a kind of three-dimensional labyrinth or maze. From the entrance at ground level in the middle of the forward face of the cube, the object is to crawl through the various passageways until you reach the elevated platform in the center—that central platform being a seven-by-seven-foot square dropped three feet below the level of the roof of the cube. But the roof over this central platform is cut out, so that when you reach it, you can stand upright.*

That is basically the whole story, except for some details. As you see, there are many other exits punched into the side walls of the cube. When children get lost in the maze we don't want them to feel trapped and claustrophobic. They can crawl out through the nearest exit. They can also crawl in through these "exits" and make their ways toward the center or some other goal. Some of the passageways are nearly vertical and have ladders in them. These are ladders from standard playground slides. As you will see from the next project, we might have some spares. There is ivy planted all around the cube, and it is meant to make the cube leafy and green but not wholly to cover the sides, because mothers and nurses will want to be able to see in, and anyway the idea of a big transparent cube all full of children at many levels simultaneously is just plain interesting.

"I mentioned he was stubborn," she puts in. "It's funny how you can see certain things yourself quite plainly, and then get to thinking they are just *obvious* when, of course, they can't be obvious if you don't know the basic facts. Well, Mark got his stubbornness from his father. At the start of the First World War his father had been drafted, and had fought in the Austro-Hungarian Army until he was discharged with a bad wound to his left leg. He went home to the Austrian regions of Poland and married soon after. He always walked with a severe, hitching limp. Although it meant leaving his family, and giving up a military pension and annuity—which he didn't know at the time would turn out to be worthless—he was determined that his children should be born in the United States. His wife was already several months pregnant when he succeeded in having them, I think the story was, smuggled over the Italian lines— the war was still on; and eventually they made it to New York without much time to spare.

"He was a stubborn man. Mark was the same."

She motions that I should continue.

3. *This is a large reinforced-concrete platform, let's say thirty feet by seventy-five, the exact dimensions are not too critical, propped up on one side so that it is an inclined plane. The propped-up side is*

roughly twenty-five feet in the air. There are ten holes punched in the plane at different levels. Mounted on the underside of the plane beneath each hole is a playground slide. Some are of standard length, others are a slide-and-a-half, others are two slides fastened together and the longest is three slides long. As you see there is a bar mounted atop each hole for grasping with the hands, as on many playground slides. So, a child charges up the slope, picks a hole, grasps the bar and throws himself down the chute. From the slope itself you only see the very top of the slide, and the whole contraption is designed to change the feel of sliding and make it seem more like bailing out of an airplane.

4. We start with a large, square wading pool. Towards the middle there is a construction of concrete cubes, two feet on a side, massed together so that in general the structure is low towards the edges and grows higher as you approach the center. There are three fountains mounted on the three highest cubes, and their waters flow down the structure into the pool. So a child can wade in the pool and then climb the structure, sitting or standing on the cubes.

On the southern side of the structure there are glass blocks set into the walls, stained blue. That gives it some variety, the water flowing sometimes over rough concrete and sometimes smooth glass. But it also indicates that the structure has an inside too, with several small, almost hidden entryways on the north side. Inside there are stepping stones and it is a little bit like a series of caves with streams flowing through them. When you reach the south side there is a grotto-like room lit with blue which should be beautiful and I hope not too crowded. But some children do appreciate a bit of serenity.

In the winter, the wading pool of course is drained, but—

And it breaks off.

I turn back to the first page. What are the initials *CGJ* underlined on top, I ask.

"Courageously, gallantly, joyfully."

After a while she says, "I guess it's the voice. The resemblance. I suppose it must be the voice."

I ask her if she will lend me a period photograph of herself. She hands me the color photo from the living room table; thinks again, takes it back, retreats to some other room and returns with the formal portrait in which her short, low-slung hair makes her look like a flapper.

She sits again and addresses me one more time across the table. "You respect the past. That's unusual. I give you credit for that. But," and she pauses. A cool dry hand on mine. "Don't live in the past. That is morally repugnant."

I wanted to know what happened to Handler and Hattie once he was out of work and a "somebody." But she was tired, and so I left with the three typed pages and the flapper portrait, wrapped in a newspaper to protect the glass in the frame.

14

Dynamite, Manhattan, 1939

A few months after the World's Fair opened, *Life* ran a "Portrait of America 1939" as a two-page spread, a cheerful, stylized map in ugly shades of red and gray. As we study and contemplate the late-thirties United States, it comes to resemble our own country less and less. But the differences that count are not, it seems to me, the ones we notice first. They are not the ones on which most history books dwell. They are not the ones that strike us immediately when we look at *Life*'s "Portrait." Those obvious differences are real and worth knowing about, but there is more to this story.

Let's glance briefly at the "Portrait." We see the forty-eight states festooned with cities and factories, roadways and farms and forests and fields. The country depicted is obviously not ours. It's easy to make out New York, Chicago, L.A. and San Francisco, but there is no city of any size in Texas or anywhere else in the South. Smoke-belching factories are rendered exuberantly. Long-distance passenger trains ply the heartlands, ocean liners converge on New York City; New England is represented by a textile mill, a church, a farm and a lighthouse.

Other differences are a tad more subtle but right there for the reading. The city of Washington is rendered iconically as a slice of the Capitol. In bulk and sheer graphic prominence it is dwarfed by Detroit. Hollywood is a high-kicking chorus line (plus spotlights, camera and director's chair). The movie business was important but not to be taken seriously; the idea of a screen actress trailing issues advisers and making political pronouncements would have seemed absurd.

All these differences become clear to varying degrees on the map. They are real differences, but ultimately they are not the point. We are separated from the world of 1939 by a phenomenon far deeper than any of these.

Question: What is wrong with this picture?

It appeared in a 1939 survey of New York City: a construction site with pedestrians walking past in front, leafy trees and apartment buildings to the rear. Painted on a fence around part of the work site are the words DYNAMITE STORED HERE—DANGER EXPLOSIVES DANGER. It is a tall, solid board fence. But there is no barbed wire, no policeman; "Women and children trip by fenced off magazine of high explosives," the caption reads. What on earth made 1939ers believe—correctly, it seems—that they could trust their fellow citizens to the extent of leaving an unprotected cache of dynamite in the heart of New York City?

Here is one aspect of the answer. In 1939 people lived in an "ought" culture. We inhabit more of a "want" culture, a desire-not-obligation culture. One of the most obvious and important consequences of the death of American civic religion is the sweeping aside of "oughts."

The ought culture made itself felt in many ways. For example: 1939's daily experience was assembled to a far greater extent than ours out of countless small rituals. A ritual is a piece of formulaic behavior that you enact not because you feel like it, necessarily, but because it is expected of you. Because it is the proper thing and you ought to do it.

A middle-class dinner or even breakfast of the 1930s might involve an entire family seated at table with the males in ties and the maid scurrying about. The ritual of each child's planting a breakfast kiss on seated Mama's cheek was sufficiently well-known to have been included in movie scenes not evidently intended to be farcical. There are rules about hats: a gentleman of course removes his when speaking to a lady on the street, removes it when a lady enters an elevator (unless the elevator is located in an office building or a store); replaces it when he steps off. He lifts his hat as a gesture of politeness to strangers, and executes a maneuver halfway between lifting and removing when he performs an outdoor informal (versus an indoor ceremonial) bow. (Hats play many roles in 1939. Reporters wear press cards in their hatbands. Nurses sport the distinctive caps of the hospitals where they trained. President John Kennedy dealt the American hat its deathblow, conventional wisdom holds, by not wearing one. Now and then hats seem poised for a comeback; but our general feeling seems to be, Why bother?)

The polite conversation of 1939 is scripted and therefore ritualized to a greater extent than ours. "Under all possible circumstances, the reply to an introduction is "How do you do?" ("The tabu of tabus is 'pleased to meet you.' ") When the need arises, one says, "I beg your pardon"—never *ever* "Pardon me," which is a barbarism. It goes without saying that first names are to be used only under the proper, restricted circumstances (never among strangers), and that "sir," "madam" or "miss" are not infrequently appropriate forms of address.

The rituals governing a gentleman's behavior toward ladies are best developed of all. A gentleman in a private home stands, of course, so long as any lady is on her feet. A gentleman is always introduced or presented to a lady, never the other way around, even if "he is an old gentleman of great distinction and the lady a mere slip of a girl."

I do not want to convey the impression that my principal source for these intelligences, Emily Post's 1937 *Etiquette*, is a prissy book. Not at all. It is breezy, amusing and wry (wry being a favorite thirties flavor). Nonetheless, rules are rules.

All this etiquette hardly made high-thirties New York a flawlessly civilized place. During his thirties building campaign, Robert Moses installed playgrounds around the edges of Central Park. At first they were charming, with the standard swings and slides but also sandboxes, crawling tunnels and striped, turreted "guardhouses"; they were fenced only with hedges. But dogs spoiled the sandboxes, drunks slept in the tunnels, perverts spied from the guardhouses and in the end, the playgrounds lost all their special toys and were surrounded by lockable chain-link fences. It is a story worth remembering when nostalgia threatens to get out of hand. In preparation for the World's Fair and the mass of tourists it would draw, New York's police, cab drivers and subway workers were provided with special courses in politeness—suggesting that proper behavior was valued but not always to be taken for granted.

But it is not the case, either, that manners mattered only to the rich. Visiting New York from London in 1938, Cecil Beaton noted that "the general rules of behavior are rigidly adhered to, and Mrs. Post's book on etiquette is as strictly interpreted in Gotham as the Koran in Mecca . . . Competitions are held whereat children from all parts of New York vie with each other to become the politest child in Manhattan, and demonstrate their courtesy before judges." The winner on one occasion was a thirteen-year-old girl from the Lower East Side. Courtesy wasn't only decorative either. It was a terse and pregnant form of communication. A small gesture might speak volumes. At a Lower East Side relief station, La Guardia dropped in unannounced. He was enraged by the lackadaisical bureaucrats he discovered. A supervisor wandered over to see what the fuss was, and mistook the visitor for another out-of-work troublemaker. The Mayor knocked the hat off his head. *"Take off your hat when you speak to a citizen."* After supervising an on-the-spot reorganization, the Mayor stomped off; on his way out, he pointed to the man with the knocked-off-hat: "There's another S. of a B. who has no job."

Many of the official rules would have been of utterly no concern to the typical member of an industrial union (let's say). But the general concepts would indeed have been, from hat management through a certain sort of courtesy—now largely though not wholly obsolete—to ladies and older people. Once again the movies are helpful. When Charlie Chaplin's factory worker in *Modern Times* (1936) leaps to his feet in a paddy wagon to offer his place to Paulette Goddard, when Danny Kaye's milkman in *The Kid from Brooklyn* (1946) pops off the sofa like a jack-in-the-box when he notices that Eve Arden is standing, they aim to seem innocent and lovable and even childlike, but not ridiculous. A factory worker or milkman with impeccable manners is a premise that this era is willing to live with. Even a lowlife gambler like Fred Astaire's companion Victor Moore in *Swing Time* (1936) can't help himself: He rises from his seat at a nightclub, admittedly for the merest fraction of a second, when Ginger joins the party.

The ought culture expressed itself also in clothing, which was more complicated and rule-bound than it is today. Why bother? Because you ought.

Ladies wear hats and gloves (and girdles). Men still wear detachable starched collars, though attached soft ones are becoming more acceptable. They wear hats of course, waistcoats (not "vests"—standing with your fingers in the armholes is a standard part of the gesture vocabulary, conveying that you are down-home and folksy), and a broad spectrum of formal clothing. There are tails and white tie ("Your stick should be of plain Malacca"), worn to formal events in the evening. Spats are still part of this outfit—although admittedly, they are on the way out. For restaurants, informal dinners, informal parties and the theater there is of course the dinner coat. ("Tuxedo" is a nickname stylish people do not use.) You wear a cutaway and striped trousers to church (but only in the city) and to formal or ceremonial daytime events. And then there are variants like the frock coat, black sack coat, double-breasted dinner coat (the waistcoat may be omitted), white dinner coat and silk house suit, each with its own special rules and occasions that might be spelled out in detail—but, never mind.

Naturally for a certain segment of the population, getting all dolled up in fancy, formal clothing would have been a pleasure and not a duty. But that segment can't have been *too* awfully large or we would never have abandoned the practice. We are more apt to shed duties than pleasures. And white tie, according to the 1992 *Emily Post,* "is almost never required today," in case you were wondering. Why bother? "For maybe ten years I have been devoted to the soft collar or sport model, the polo shirt, and other informal modes in collarings," Robert Benchley writes in 1927. "They have not been particularly adapted to playing up my good points in personal appearance, but they are easy to slip into in the morning." For Benchley and vast numbers of others, formal styles were a pain. When you wore them, you did because you ought.

Once again the formal range of the spectrum is of practical significance only to the upper and middle classes. Recall, on the other hand, that almost every man at the 1939 fair wears a tie. Nearly every woman wears a dress or a skirt. In 1940 the World's Fair Corporation concocted a character to exemplify the "jolly, average, every-day American" in a nationwide advertising campaign. The idea was to tone down the fair's image. The character they settled on was a fiftyish man in a gray hat and suit, brown shoes, blue socks with garters, white shirt, blue bow tie and a small American flag in his lapel. The antithesis of top-hat clothing wasn't a sweatshirt. It was a bow tie and a gray suit.

In 1939, just under two-thirds of the population hold it to be indecent for a woman to appear on the street in shorts. A third holds that "topless bathing suits"—on *men,* needless to say—are indecent. Late thirties styles of dress are more formal than today's across the board, and the population at large has sterner, more exacting attitudes toward the topic. And virtually everyone in 1930s society is familiar with the different styles of formal dress, just as any Englishman can tell a duke from an earl whether or not he frequently dines with either. After all, the plot of *Swing Time,* the greatest of all Rogers-and-Astaire movies, hinges on the distinction between a cutaway and a dinner coat. Astaire would appear to the untrained eye to be dressed to the nines when he sweeps Ginger off her feet in the film's first (and incomparably best . . . the best of all time) dance scene. He is wearing spats, a waistcoat and an outer coat that executes a deep, tailslike swoop in the rear. But of course, it is only a cutaway. He is sent off to fetch "dinner clothing" in preparation for a dance contest, and gets in deep trouble with Ginger when he can't come up with a tuxedo. The rules of the ought culture are recognizable at once to any 1930s movie goer.

Etiquette is attacked sometimes as an upper-class toy, not just irrelevant to the rest of society but actively bad. During the class- and ideology-infatuated 1930s it was bound to be vulnerable, particularly in Europe. ("Take off that collar and tie," a Frenchman tells George Orwell en route to loyalist Spain during the Civil War. "They'll tear them off you in Barcelona.") But at least in the United States, etiquette was as likely to equalize classes as to separate them. If the bank president had any manners, he removed his hat when the ditch digger's wife stepped into the elevator. If the ranking bureaucrat had any manners, he removed his hat when addressing the unemployed laborer.

Thirties America is a country in which service is rendered and expected. You could stop at a tailor's and wait behind a curtain while your suit was pressed. On a train you maintained an ongoing relationship with the porter: he carried your luggage but also served you in transit—making up your bed and waking you in the morning, alerting you to interesting views up ahead, delivering telegrams, brushing off your clothes. Filling-station attendants washed your windows and checked the "oil, water and battery." Perhaps workers were simply more servile than they are today. But it is also possible that they were not so much more servile as more obliging. Doctors were not servile, but they made housecalls. In a 1941 survey of people who happened to have colds, a quarter had consulted a doctor, and a third of those consultations entailed housecalls. So around eight percent of mere *colds* rated a private call. The filling station man waited attentively on the busy doctor, but the doctor wasn't above visiting the sick filling station man. *Doing as you ought* was not the only virtue and does not, all by itself, explain all those housecalls or train porters. But it offers one clue to the workings of a society that seems, in certain ways, to have worked more humanely than ours.

One last aspect of the *ought* society has to do with the power of those *oughts* to rally like Greek demigods to your side if you were pressed against your wishes to do what society said you ought not to.

Sex between unmarried people was not exactly a novelty in the 1930s. Recall unmarried Kathleen's post-coital announcement

("I think I was a bit sex-starved") in a 1940 novel; it is easy to pile up similar examples. And yet there was obviously much less of it going around than there is today. Philip Larkin declares in a famous poem (albeit an English and not an American one) that "Sexual inter-course began/in nineteen sixty-three." Of course a girl could sleep with her boyfriend (just who exactly was going to stop her?), but if she didn't want to, bully for her, because she *ought* not to. The *oughts* stood ready to fly to her defense.

In late-thirties America a divorce was hard to obtain almost everywhere. It had to be established that exactly one spouse was guilty of at least one moral outrage (desertion, cruelty, adultery . . .) chosen from an official list. (If they were both guilty, no deal.) Yet an uncontested divorce was easy. You simply caught a train for Reno. (The divorce-bound, train-traveling narrator of a 1930s novel tries to decide how to answer her male fellow-passengers when they ask where she is going. "To say 'Reno' straight out would be vulgar; it would smack of confidences too cheaply given. . . .") If you were willing to grant your unhappy husband or wife an uncontested di-vorce, fine, but if you chose not to—the *oughts* would rally to your side.

Contraceptives were widely available, in pharmacies, gas-station restrooms and the Sears, Roebuck catalog, among other places. But the distribution of information about contraceptives was closely regulated by law, and guidance was not always easy to come by. Yes, you can get contraceptives, but no (1930s society seems to reason), we are under no obligation to make the process easy for young, unmarried people.

In the late thirties (and in many other periods), the practical possibilities were *supposed* to be tinted by oughts, in the sense that tinting a black-and-white photo can change the impression it makes without altering the bare facts. Recently certain colleges have been jeered for their silly attempts to impose official rules on the making of passes, to insure that the woman is not taken advantage of. (As a logical next step, perhaps all attempted seductions should be refereed? And take place on regulation courts in the gym?) The proposed solution is absurd, yet the problem is not. Having spent decades methodically abolishing *oughts* because they constrain us, we are just noticing that we no longer have *oughts* to defend us either.

The oughts that covered big social issues like sex and divorce are important, but I am myself most interested, to sum up, in the little oughts that cropped up constantly in late-thirties daily life. I claim that the continual practice of proper behavior on an endless succession of trivial, meaningless occasions makes a person at least a *bit* more apt to act properly when the chips are down. I claim that all the little oughts late-thirties society treasured are one cause of the huge divide in social character between that era and this. That tipping your hat, rising under the right circumstances (ladies rise, too, for older ladies), not abusing first names, saying "how do you do" when you are introduced—that all of this penny-ante stuff helps build a society in which dynamite can be cached unprotected in the middle of big cities. Obviously those little oughts cannot be the *whole* story, and obviously, too, we all know people who are slovenly of behavior yet morally impeccable. Nonetheless the ought culture as an integrated whole has a significance we tend to miss.

How can I prove my claim? It's true that "family values" and civility and other desirable social properties thrived in the thirties ought culture, and that they are on the rocks today, but perhaps that is a mere coincidence and there is no causal relation. My claim is just a guess, and it is unprovable. But here are two far-afield pieces of information that seem to me to help make it plausible.

Teddy Roosevelt makes a fascinating claim in his *Autobiography*: He says that courage can be acquired "by sheer dint of practicing fearlessness." We often think of courage as a quality you are born with, or as a matter of sound moral instruction taken to heart.

But in TR's view (and it is a view that commands respect: He was a brave man), it is more of a skill, like wok cookery or playing the tuba. In this particular case proper behavior is held to require not merely thorough and correct instruction but dogged practice.

My other datum has to do with Judaism. Traditional Judaism is the ought culture par excellence, full of rigorously detailed injunctions to be carried out scrupulously despite their lack of any inherent moral significance. (The ongoing relentless attempt in some quarters to assign rational bases to the rules serves only to diminish them. If you observe them because they are sensible, you cannot do so because they are sacred.) Proper behavior is held, again, to depend not merely on knowledge but on constant practice. "Studying is not the essential thing, rather *practice*" according to the much-loved Talmudic tractate *Avot* (1:17). When you are practicing, *what* you practice is secondary; acquiring the habit of doing as you ought is the main thing.

Across the political spectrum we hear nowadays about family values. But to 1930s society, my guess is, the campaign as currently constituted would make no sense, anymore than it would make sense to install seedlings, harangue them constantly with sunlight, water and fertilizer and expect them to grow and thrive if you have planted them in gravel. The ground must be prepared. "Civility" has become another popular cause. But civility in the lost, late-thirties sense was one *effect* of the ought culture, not a cause of its own. That culture's motivating ambition was not to nicen people up but to prevent them from making fools of themselves. At base it was entirely selfish. Unfortunately, human nature being what it is, the exhortation "If you do this, people will think you're polite" is just not as effective as "If you do this, people won't think you are a lowlife boor."

We have newly minted oughts of our own, of course. We cannot let our search for patterns blind us to the complexity of social processes. But it does seem clear that we have destroyed more oughts than we have created, and that the oughts we treasure most are mainly negative: *Don't* smoke, or drink too much. (Thirties sophisticates were constantly getting tight, which for some reason did not count as acting like a lowlife boor.) *Don't* flirt or say anything that might be construed as offensive by a theoretical construct representing the most sanctimonious, ignorant and litigious member of any officially-sanctioned group. Because our own vestigial ought culture is built on a sort of second half of the Ten Commandments without the first, we aren't left with many occasions for doing what is proper as opposed to avoiding what is not.

Today's approach to the whole issue is captured perfectly on a recent *New York Times* front page. "They sweat into their summer suits," a reporter writes of New Yorkers at business in the summer, "and walk inside unbending shoes, ignoring comfort and common sense because convention, and their employers, expect them to dress up at work." The fools.* In our modern view, a series of 1939 tableaux on (let us a say) a fine spring day—the gentleman buttoning his waistcoat and choosing a hat, the lady pulling on gloves, the day laborer who tips his cap to a priest or removes it after stopping still when the flag happens to pass by, the businessman arriving home hot and tired who nonetheless presides over the family dinner with his tie still lashed to his neck—these are so many petty, pointless crimes against common sense.

If you were a nineteen-thirties man, woman or child, Henry Ford or a resident of the tightest-packed block in Harlem, society's *ought* was an all-day, everyday hand on your shoulder. It checked your freedom and cramped your style. You would have been more comfortable without it. But in the end, like the man's stiff collar and tie or the woman's girdle, it was something you got used to; it was

---

* Lest anyone misunderstand, the author is one of the worst-dressed men in the country.

DYNAMITE, MANHATTAN, 1939

tolerable; it was even—maybe—not as bad as it looked. We rebel in our very souls nowadays against the idea that mere conventional behavior, dress and manners could possibly matter. We abolished all those rules with the best of intentions—or rather, with the end of the American religious community, they simply fell apart. But there is no getting around the fact that in the 1930s, people got more practice in acting as they ought than we do. I can't say what all that dogged practice was worth when push came to shove. I do know that in 1939, you could leave a pile of dynamite unguarded in the middle of New York City.

15

Technology: Frightening

The diary continues:

Rejoining the main Fairgrounds we are face-to-face with a big sculpture that stands in the center of another long vista, stretching left to the Trylon and Perisphere & right to the Plaza of Light. The sculpture stands on a tall pedestal in the center of a circle of grass. Four warrior-like figures facing away from each other to the four points of a square, backs together. From directly beneath you don't get a very clear impression of them. They seem majestic & expressionless.

(The group by John Gregory represents *The Victories of Peace*—Wheels, Wings, Wheat, Wisdom.)

TECHNOLOGY: FRIGHTENING

We circle to the left & gaze T&Pward: a beautiful broad walkway, the "Court of Power," with lawns on either sides planted with thousands of red & yellow tulips in undulating beds, trees bounding the vista to left & right, the Perisphere dead ahead and the Trylon on its right & the Helicline starting its long graceful swoop downward. The crowds in silhouette up high, streaming down the Helicline. A tractor-train drives past & toots its *Sidewalks of New York* horn & children lean out & wave to no-one in particular. The casual happiness makes it feel like a beach.

(In 1940 *Architectural Record* asked rhetorically, "Was not the finest element in the World's Fair 'theme center' the 'Helicline,' with its long line of *people* held confidently against the sky?")

And yet as we stand beside a flower bed & gaze, the softness of the tulips & their shy brightness throws me off balance. The T&P seem grave & sad. At the climax of the Mall the Trylon and Perisphere are an exclamation point, they *are* the future dead ahead; here they are a question mark, a mysterious sculpture set down in a park. They look so natural. Why does this strange combination-of-shapes you have never seen before &, after the Fair, never will again—why does it seem so natural & so right?

We are supposed to be heading in this direction towards the New York City building, which stands between the Perisphere and the highway. But first we circle round to the other side of the Four Warriors and gaze away from the T&P into another lovely vista. Near us are four huge freestanding pylons, white with golden medallions, that suggest a gateway. Beyond the gateway is the Plaza of Light. It has a great round pool in its center with a ring of tall fountains, & the group of buildings clustered around the pool are almost, again, a self-contained Fair in themselves. Some have concave, scooped-out facades echoing the lines of the pool in the center. Beyond the pool to the left is the Blue Jello building and beyond to the right, the towering lightning-bolt zig-zag of General Electric. Far in the distance beyond a jumble of towers & weird rooftops is the great red Parachute ride. As you venture a few steps toward the pylons you hear *much* more water than you can account for—two of the Fair's most amazingly befountained buildings stand with their backs turned, on the near side of the Plaza. There is nothing that draws a person like the rush of hidden water. Nonetheless we circle back round as planned & march forward past the Pharmacy Building between the lovely soft tulip beds towards the T&P, on our way to New York City. But I stop midway down and announce that we *must* have lunch.

There is a Brass Rail restaurant in the Metals building which is, providentially, almost exactly where we are now. Pharmacy runs down one side of the Court of Power, Metals down the other side. It is past one, mobbed, noisy. We have sandwiches and coffee. Mark flips through *Today at the Fair*. "My boss was here getting a medal." Robert Moses, that is. "We missed him."

(Moses was awarded a horticultural society medal. At the ceremony, Whalen congratulated him: despite some experts' predictions that no plants would ever grow on this former ash heap, "We now see 10,000 trees and hundreds of thousands of bushes flourishing here.")

TECHNOLOGY: FRIGHTENING

"Hoover got a 21-gun salute on the Court of Peace. We missed him too. Just as well. I kind of *did* hear a booming when we were over at Firestone, though, didn't you?"

May eighteenth was an ordinary day at the fair. But there were enough "special" days and weeks to keep a wide-ranging constituency happy. The *Times* recited "just a sprinkling": "Bronx Week, Brooklyn Week, National Gastroentological Association Day, Holstein-Fresian Association Day, Grandma's Nite Out Day, Charlie McCarthy Day, Our Town Day, Kalamazoo Day, Crude Rubber Credit Association Day, Brite Idea Club Day, National Accordion Day, Uncle Don Day, Baptist Day for the Aged, Hay Fever Day, Brooklyn Poetry Circle Day and Brotherhood of Sleeping Car Porters Day."

Mark is broadcasting blackness like a radio station, & I am tuned in (my, what heroic similes for modern times this girl is capable of!) & yet as we head toward the T&P en route to New York City I feel glorious again. The air is freshened by all the fountains & you seem to feel the spray faintly on your face & lips &, as I say, it is hard not to feel joyful at the Fair. I suppose I should not be dwelling so on the fountains and ambiance, but one has the feeling of being in a unique place. And I do love the fountains. We pass Pharmacy on the left, then on to New York.

Pharmacy Hall had a monumental aqua-toned mural on the curved facade facing the highway. The exhibits included a huge medicine cabinet backed by a fifteen-by-twenty-foot half-silvered mirror. At intervals lights came on behind the mirror, and you could see through to a puppet show on the other side.

Also, the inevitable Drug Store of Tomorrow. "It will be highly compartmentalized," the 1939 *Guide* explains, "and none of the confusion so apparent in many drug stores today will be present." Naturally, the Drug Store of Tomorrow houses the Soda Fountain of the Future. "There will be no foods displayed," the *Guide* lays down with somewhat unanticipated sternness, "nor will there be any preparation of foods other than ice-cream mixtures."

Among the companies exhibiting are Tampax Incorporated ("a registered nurse is in attendance") and Ex-Lax: "The company engaged an internationally known designer and artist, Oscar Stonorov, to create a dignified theme."

New York's is a staid, foursquare building—unlike the others, it is intended to be permanent, and looks it—it is unfanciful and unwhimsical. Mark says, "I just can't see the future with us not married. But I also can't see the immediate future with children, because the image that comes right to mind is . . . I don't want to be morbid, but have to be frank about it . . . bombs dropping, & I see the two of us together making do, but I see the two of us with children, as the bombs fall & the neighboring houses explode and burn & more planes come on—I see myself utterly at a loss. *How do you explain what's happening to the child?* The child who'd been playing with a shovel in the sandbox five minutes ago? How do you protect the child?" His eyes on the ground ten feet in front of him, with the intensest frown.

Well, what can I say? But I have to rally my troops immediately & say something *right now* lest I lose the whole war in an instant—"but it's always, life is always, it's not as if—there are no guarantees, you're talking as if—for every child, there were a smooth life ahead . . ." I'm just blathering, thinking as I speak. "But, there are so many curses in the world." I guess this is the point. "A building could burn down. A father could lose his job. Or be hit by a truck. Or a child could get polio, God forbid. That's the world, is all. It's an evil world, but that doesn't give us the right to deny it to our children."

"Yes . . . And I wouldn't for anything," grabbing my hand, "deny my son or daughter the sort of happiness I get just by walking beside you." He springs on me out of thin air emotional propositions that make me want to cry, then strides on forward leaving me slightly lost; in a way it's not fair. "But my point is," he continues, "this time is not like others. Unfortunately, & there's no way you can possibly deny it, the powers that be are intensifying the natural evils of the universe more fanatically at this point than ever before in all history. It's just plain simple *prudence* to pause & see where this hellish world is going."

We're at the door. "I want you to look at the Fair & enjoy it," I tell him. "We'll continue later—all right?" He's still frowning intensely. I smile my sweet shy smile at him, smile number 10-A, with a slight tilt of the head—& there is nothing that he can deny me when I am smiling 10-A. He smiles ever so slightly & we walk into the building.

But we do not stay long, because there is such a big crowd inside. And anyway, we want to see the fountain buildings. They put on a show in here called "Murder at Midnight," about how the police solve crimes. Mark consults *Today at the Fair*. We missed it.

Crime was a big issue in the 1930s. In the early thirties, the nation was plunged into what felt like an out-of-control crime wave. The sensation is familiar enough. Kidnappings and bank robberies were the high-profile crimes of choice. The kidnap-murder of Charles Lindbergh's infant son in 1932 was the crime of the decade. J. Edgar Hoover—John Edgar, as he was sometimes called back then—had taken charge of the FBI in 1929, but it wasn't until 1934 that congressional action empowered agents to carry guns and make arrests, and reclassified kidnapping and most bank robberies as federal crimes.

The reincarnated FBI seems to have had a swift and decisive effect on thirties crime. Hoover's men gunned down "public enemy number one," bank-robbing murderer John Dillinger, in July 1934, and went on to retire a string of other charmingly nicknamed desperadoes: Baby Face Nelson, Pretty Boy Floyd, Machine Gun Kelly . . . (Melvin Purvis was the G-man who led the attack on Dillinger. He quit the FBI and went to work for Post Toasties promoting the "Junior G-men" club. For a quarter and some box tops you got a fingerprint set, a magnifying glass and a badge.) One sometimes gets the discouraging feeling that in the thirties, people were able to lavish more time, care and individual attention on their criminals than we can provide ours, because there were so few of them. A typical New York City statistic of this period is forty people a year dead of gunshot wounds, versus forty every ten days in the modern city.

Late-thirties society seems to have seen crime as a continuing threat that was, nonetheless, pretty much under control. Relatively swift punishment must have contributed to that feeling. Bruno Hauptmann was brought to trial for the Lindbergh kidnapping in January 1935. His conviction was duly appealed all the way to the Supreme Court. He was executed in April 1936. Next! In New York, Mayor La Guardia took a special interest in crime and the police. A young policeman had the effrontery to ticket a personal acquaintance of the mayor's. The acquaintance appealed straight to City

Hall. As a result of which the policeman got a box of cigars—La Guardia had them delivered in his official car.

"Along the New York Building's walls," the diary continues,

> are large display panels about, for example, the Department of Investigation, which shows a very large & strange-looking eye with the words "The Eye of the Mayor" above; a display on elections comparing "yesterday—ballots" versus "to-day—voting machines"; a display about the Fire Department, a *great big* one about Robert Moses and the Parks Department . . . Mark smiles his proprietary smile (the one that also applies to me). Large balconies overhang the display hall at each end, one of them housing a WNYC broadcast studio. [WNYC had a reporter on assignment wandering the fairgrounds, looking for angles.] You could call the whole thing a trifle show-offy, but it does give you (the New York native) a smug feeling, & you look with condescending pity at the overwhelmed tourists from Ohio and places like that . . . South Dakota . . . etc. And then we leave & walk between the tulips, past the Four Warriors through the Pylons into the Plaza of Light.

Handler is reluctant to father children. In the late thirties aerial bombardment was no small issue. People were bomb-minded. The idea that war could enmesh even civilians far from the front, that people would die as a result of dangerous objects dropped from airplanes into a sea of women and children—it's second nature to us, but in the 1930s that idea took a little getting used to. Gerald Wendt devotes a paragraph to the great speed modern man has attained; his very first example of a speedy modern phenomenon is, "Quick! The bombers are coming—may be here in an hour." In 1932 the Japanese had bombed Shanghai, and they continued to bomb the Chinese occasionally. The civilized world reacted with outrage and disgust. But the Nazi bombing of Spanish cities between 1936 and 1939 was the world's proper introduction to the sustained, indiscriminate slaughter of civilians from the air.

Bombing raids against Loyalist Spanish cities were an important activity of the German forces. The goal was not so much to advance the rebel cause or to kill Spaniards (who were of scant interest to the Germans one way or the other) as to conduct experiments. The results would come in handy in the large-scale war that Germany was itching to launch. How could planes and tanks be coordinated? What exactly *were* the effects of bombing raids on undefended civilian targets? The only way to find out, the Germans figured, was to give the thing a try. Germany "used her air power," Winston Churchill notes, "to commit such experimental horrors as the bombing of the defenceless little township of Guernica." Junkers and Heinkel bombers unloaded for three hours, while Heinkel fighters swooped low to kill with machine-gun fire the men, women and children who sought refuge in open fields.

The destruction of this ancient Basque town became the most famous of German atrocities in Spain in part because of Picasso's celebrated mural. Of course Picasso, too, is a vital part of the thirties climate. Early in 1937 the Loyalist government had commissioned him to paint a mural for Spain's pavilion at the 1937 Paris Exposition. In late April 1937 Picasso saw news photos of Guernica in ruins; the next day he started work on his painting. In June it was finished, and it was duly installed in Paris.

It is a picture of an air raid, of course. Man, woman and horse shriek. A mother holding a dead child looks at the sky, where an electric bulb explodes with light. The whole brittle image appears to have fractured like glass and been reassembled out of jagged shards that would draw blood if you touched them. It is in white, black and shades of gray—like contemporary news photos, it is often pointed out; but recall also how frequently Picasso retreats into monochrome: blue, rose, cubism's dead sepias, the black line and wash of the neoclassical ink drawings and engravings that are his least contrived, most beautiful and characteristic creations.

From Paris the picture went to Norway and London, and in the spring of 1939 it was shown at a gallery in New York. It was widely seen and discussed. Loyalists and art critics disliked it from the start. The Loyalists found the picture not inspiring but horrific and defeatist. As for the critics, Clement Greenberg issued after the war his famous pronouncement that *Guernica* looks like "a battle scene from a pediment that has been flattened under a defective steam-roller." Anti-*Guernica* critics often miss what the mural *is*: merely the greatest, most effective political cartoon of all time. Picasso had been immersed in the engraving of a bitter cartoon strip, "Franco's Dream and Lie," in the period just before he painted the famous mural.

In 1939 *Guernica* captured and symbolized the terror of aerial bombing as the clock ticked down to the next world war. There was nothing unusual about Handler's preoccupation. We veterans of the Cold War think we are accustomed to living with the danger of bombs. But the situation was very different in the late 1930s. At the 1939 fair there were airplanes overhead all the time, and when you looked up, it was easy to imagine that they were German planes loaded with real bombs that could casually be dropped from a rack and kill you.

16

When Life Turns Out to Be a Sand Castle

"**M**ark getting fired meant a great deal to our lives." Mrs. Levine and I were meeting again only a week and a half after last time. "We'd been planning for him to attend graduate school after we'd been married a few years. He'd have worked for awhile, and we would have accumulated a bit of savings. He'd have made contacts that would ensure him some steady part-time income while he went to school. But now he decided that he ought to plunge intensively into graduate school and emerge with his doctorate in maybe two and a half years. 'Plunging' was something he liked to do. And he thought it unreasonable to marry before the degree was granted and he could go back to earning a living. That was a standard attitude at the time. We made all these decisions together. We'd planned to marry that spring, and I

WHEN LIFE TURNS OUT TO BE A SAND CASTLE

wasn't happy with the long postponement, and neither was he. I'm not saying it *had* to be that way, don't misunderstand, it didn't *have* to be, there were alternatives, but this is the one we chose. The one *we* chose. Mark always wanted to do the proper thing. He wanted to do things right. That's the way he was. And I wanted to support him.

"And yet it was a triumphal moment, despite his getting fired and all. Friends from Parks organized a dinner." Pauses. "Janet of France. Near Broadway. It was a raucous place with a piano; I don't know why on earth we wound up there. Mark picked me up, and we had to drop off some papers at a fancy building somewhere way on the East Side. Then we got on the crosstown trolley to go to the restaurant. A block before we arrived Mark told me he wanted a newspaper, and he'd meet me at the next corner. So he got off and dashed ahead. [*Yessir,* wha'd'ya read?] And I remember seeing him on the corner a block later just before I got off—studying some building with a puzzled expression, then he saw me, and smiled his big smile and waved a big wave with the newspaper as though we hadn't seen each other in years. The trolleys had horns like cars. They blended into traffic. That view of him through the narrow tall window of the trolley as it glides to a stop— it's so perfect and so characteristic, his intense absorption in some building or other and then the big, big smile. Forty-second Street in the evening had rows of first-run movie houses with tiny lightbulbs under the marquee and barkers out front hailing you in. Like a carnival midway. It was fun.

"Several people came to the restaurant with reviews of his show and asked that he autograph them. A Professor Obermayer who'd taught him architecture at CCNY was also invited. He was an authority on urbanism and said to be friends with various cultural movers and shakers, and he was Mark's great favorite. Commanding air, prematurely gray hair, longer than one wore hair at the time—a striking person. Obermayer came late, which I think was a deliberate gesture, so everyone would be sure to hear. Before the assembled company all on their feet he shook hands with Mark, and we all heard him say loud and clear: 'I want you to know how much I admire your work.'

"A wonderful evening—you can tell for sure from the fact that, before it was over, every architect had his pen out. They were discussing Mark's ideas. Obermayer and everyone. I sat quietly, simmering with pride. Is that the word? No . . ." A flash of smile: There it is again, the twenty-one-year-old girl. "Oh, Mark had designed some apartment towers for public housing. One had, instead of balconies or terraces, a continuous spiral that wrapped round the building from top to bottom, so you could step out of your fifteenth-floor apartment, say, and go for a walk—a few spins around the building, or walk all the way to the bottom; he wanted there to be neighborhoods outside your front door, even though it was a high-rise. Another tall building, wide but not deep, a conventional apartment-house slab, but it had a big rectangular hole six stories high cut out in the middle. See-through building. There was a park on the base of the cutout. Another was a joke—the same sort of tall apartment building, with a cutout in the shape of a gigantic human profile. 'How wonderful if they would build it,' Obermayer said.

"He'd been admitted earlier to MIT, but he decided now that he wanted to go to Yale. The civil engineering program at Yale. New Haven was a lot closer to the city, so we'd see each other often. Yale also had the great distinction of being Robert Moses' alma mater. MIT had one advantage—there were a lot more Jews there; at least, that was Mark's impression. Maybe it seems odd that Mark was so sensitive on this topic, but he very definitely was. Of course, pretty gentile *girls* never bothered him in the least—yes, he did call them shiksas. I can see him wince when I use that phrase 'gentile girls'—he would have thought it pandering to avoid the obvious Yiddish word. It was also unusual, by the way, that he was so proud of Yiddish and so insistent on speaking it whenever the opportunity arose. In that age, I can tell you, most younger people kept their distance. But ... What was I saying ... He was self-assured and cosmopolitan, but he knew where his boundaries were. *Despite* that, he decided for Yale.

"I struggled with him one last time over architecture. I pleaded with him to apply to the architecture school. The fact that Harrison, who had designed the Trylon and Perisphere, was teaching at the Yale Architecture School was a point in its favor. Raymond Hood had taught there also. But it wasn't enough. He never made any histrionic speeches. He merely said, 'I owe this to my parents, and I'm going to design buildings in any case. It barely matters what my degree is in. And this way—' " She stops. Inhales the view outside her window and turns back. " 'When the time comes, I can help with the war.' And I'd say, 'You can respect your parents but not allow them to dictate the course of your whole life.' I would say it again and again. I even got *my* parents to say it to him. But he was a stubborn man, Mark."

She studies the spiral of cigarette smoke. Her eyes now big, dark and oblivious of me.

"He got himself admitted in short order to the Yale engineering program, in midyear. Largely on the strength of the Moses letter, he told me. Who knows. He believed it, anyway. And there we were.

"At the start of 1940, he threw himself full blast into the coursework at Yale. Lord, did he work hard! All the courses in that graduate program were a full year. He just plunged into the middle. He worked like a dog. *Statically Indeterminate Structures.* That was one of them. I have no idea what it was about.

"Yet for both of us, I think, it was the most serene period of our lives. He'd come down Friday evenings to my parents' house. My mother would have eaten already, and my father got home late, so Mark and I would eat together. He'd always insist on saying *kid-dush* first, because it was Friday night. I had to provide him with a glass of Manischewitz wine for that purpose. I marveled at it. He was not religious, exactly, but he was so damned stubborn. I argued with him at first—I was a fool about religion. Ignorant."

Her apartment has a *mezuzah* in every doorway, and other signs of punctilious Jewish religious observance. I ask about them. "Yes, the day came when my own view changed," she says, and continues: "I thought Mark and I should aspire, as a couple, to a cultivated citizen-of-the-world status, and religion seemed to me to be a fine thing—for people who were far less cultured and intelligent than we.

"But Mark refused even to defend what he was doing. He just chose to do it, period. He would fix on me his amused, teasing smile and say in Yiddish, 'A Jew should be a Jew.' *A Yid soll seyn a Yid,* and that was the end of it. Often when he wanted to tease me he would talk Yiddish. He knew I understood it though I made faces and professed not to. I knew German because of my mother and her parents, and so I understood Yiddish too, to some extent. 'The future is worth a lot,' he once said, 'but not everything. Not everything.' In any case; the meal was always very much as if we were a married couple. We'd have baked chicken, usually, and mashed potatoes, and tons of white bread and apple pie. I loved serving him dinner." She stops abruptly, then continues in a soft, smoldering monotone: "That's a thing someone like you, of your generation, could never conceivably understand."

I protest. "Yes, yes," waving me off, "I don't mean you personally. But the smugness of you people. Your generation. You expect me to watch this deliberate dismantling of a way of life and praise your marvelous principles—when I'm perfectly clear that, nine times out of ten, it's greed on the man's part and a pathetic desire to please on the woman's—*that* is what has created this marvelous egalitarian Eden. You tell a man, What'll you have? More money? Or better care for your children? And he chooses the money. *My goodness gracious,* what a shock! And then you pat him on the head for his liberalism. *Feminism,* my eye! The woman's capitulation, you mean, to the man's greedy universe." She glares at me. "I picture friends of my youth and I tell myself, *Such* a pity, had they only grown up today and not in the benighted past, this one could have been a lawyer, and that one a stockbroker, and that one— what?—a TV reporter? Such a pity! Such a waste! Just one thing though. What is it exactly this country needs, more lawyers, more stockbrokers, more TV reporters? Is *that* what it all comes down to? Or more mothers? What a masterpiece this world is, that all you smug people have made." She turns to look out the window.

I observe mildly that in my circle, many women would love to be full-time mothers but can't afford it. "Rubbish," she says. "Plain rubbish. You're intelligent enough to realize, I would have thought, that a woman's life reflects her own choices. She's not the slave of fashion *or* her husband. I wish you could've seen how my dear friend Charlotte Halpern lived in the years right after the war. They had three kids and they lived in Brooklyn. She could've used a car, but they didn't have one. She could've used a washing machine. It all depends on the woman's own choices.

"Maybe that's just crotchety old age speaking." Silence. "But I choose to be executed, if that is allowed, without blindfold. Saying the truth.

"Sorry. I didn't mean to get off on that. Had an unpleasant visit to the doctor this morning and am acting like a child." Silence.

"Well, the mood by early summer of 1940 was like a thunderstorm when you are cozy inside. Europe was going all to hell and we were frightened, anybody would be. It seemed as if Britain would be wiped out just like France had been. Then, our turn. People talked about 'the emergency.' I remember ads saying you should do this or that for the 'duration of the present emergency.' But our life, mine and Mark's together, was purposeful and serene.

"Late weekend evenings, Mark and my father and I would sit in the living room, them smoking pipes, me leaning on Mark's shoulder. Stretching a foot out from time to time to touch my father's foot on the ottoman of his easy chair. And I might look out the window, if the curtains weren't drawn, at dozens of yellow-glowing windows across West End Avenue. Where old women who'd been born when Lincoln was president were looking at their sleeping grandchildren. We'd be talking about the war, over the peaceful thrum of the black Sunbeam fan on top of the radio. The fan would swivel back and forth contentedly. At ten-thirty, I think it was, we'd turn on the radio and listen to the news. It made you feel important, waiting for the news to come on."

I ask whether Mark and her father would still at that hour have been wearing their neckties. "Yes. I suppose so." After a moment: "Doesn't kill a person, you know."

It occurs to me that the only document she'd taped into her diary might come from around this time. It was the last page of a handwritten letter, lacking a date. She couldn't recall the circumstances, but agreed it might belong to this period. The letter was from her aunt to the aunt's brother, Hattie's father: "And what has happened to my Hattie? My favorite niece my lovely brooding girl seems full of charm almost dare one say extroverted and I love to see her smile! Is it the young man?"

She continues. "He worked terribly hard. He'd set up shop on my parents' dining table, with piles of books and a gooseneck lamp and his slide rule and a box of Mallomars and work for hours, barely looking up. Yes, we had Mallomars then. He'd make himself comfortable. My parents didn't mind. One afternoon I remember nagging him to come out for a walk with me. I felt especially strong because, earlier, he'd taken off an hour or two to go see his college buddies. I told him something to the effect that, here he made this big production number about the Sabbath, and in fact you were supposed to *rest* on the Sabbath. He got furious. I remember him pulling his page of figures out of the notebook and crunching it in his fist and hurling it at the wastepaper basket and stalking out of the apartment and slamming the door. He did have a temper.

"But I loved how things were going—and then late that spring, *boom!* Another mammoth, exciting development." A diary entry a year after her big day at the fair comes to mind. She confirms that it describes the event she means.

"The most remarkable phone conversation," the entry begins:

Mark calling from New Haven. "This man in Manhattan. Arthur Tierney. Rich. Wants to start a new private school. Progressive school." Standing in the corner of my father's study, he's home early & at his desk, & I am admiring the profile of my slim waist in the glass of the large framed wedding photo of his sour Victorian parents—yes OK, a rich man, a school—"he wants to hire me as the architect; wants me to meet him at nine tomorrow morning. So I should come in tonight." I am making no sense of this, like when you walk into a movie in the middle. "He wants your advice about the architect?" My mother has the radio going in the living room, voices & then loud laughter & applause. I start to get the idea. "You? He wants *you?* To *hire* you? For *money?* To design *this school?*" Now I am sitting on the arm of my father's chair & then I tumble into his lap side-saddle. "You're meeting him *tomorrow?*" (From the living room: mumble-mumble-mumble laugh-laugh.) *"You? Design the school?"*

"Talent will out," says my father too confidently after I hang up—as I point my feet straight ahead, lean back & let my hair tumble to the ground as if I am swinging.

Soon after I am making up his bed in the guest room & towards ten, I spy him striding fast, threading past the sidewalk trash cans into the lobby. He is reserved, I am the one gushing & frizzling excitement—he is nervous, it might still not come off. If it does, how will he pack it in around his school work? But it won't, no no no no no etc. Evidently there have been discussions for weeks but he kept them secret because he was sure they would come to nothing. We dance for an hour to the radio in a weak attempt to calm us both. When I lie in bed the vastness of the possibilities are like a string of stars from one hand to the other, encompassing the universe on the way.

(You heard the radio constantly in 1939—at home, in a cab, in a hotel lobby; as you filed into the brand-new Hayden Planetarium and took your seat and waited for the sky show to start. A 1938 survey of New York City laments "the decline of the sheet music and phonograph record industry, and the rise of radio." "It furnishes a jazz undertone to the rumble of the city," one visitor writes. "Of course," writes another of the high-thirties New Yorker, "he never remembers to switch off the radio.")

"Next morning," the diary account continues,

I oversee the combing of hair, etc., & swap his hat for one of my father's (they match only in hat size). Mark is more himself. He insists on lipsticking me in retaliation. I put us in a taxi to Tierney's office, in the Empire State Building, no less, then continue to work myself, worried sick but grinning like an idiot. By lunchtime it is all over & he has the job! The school is to be along "advanced," progressive lines. School-children to be exposed to art. (An infectious disease?) We lunch at a drugstore facing out at Forty-second, & the surge of the crowd, the yellow taxi-whales swerving to curbside then plunging back into traffic, the trolleys' serene glide are all beautiful & even my "tuna fish, sliced egg" is delicious. Mark back to Grand Central & thence New Haven. Now *he* is grinning like an idiot too! I would call it a miracle, chalk it up to divine intervention, except that Tierney has a connection to the Brooklyn Museum evidently, & visited Mark's show a dozen times.

There is one related entry, shortly after:

Dinner at Brevoort with Tierney & his lawyer Bass. Tierney is not in the least bit like I expected. He is a smiling lofty red-head with a smug little nose. Slightly too smug altogether for my taste. Somewhat Omaha-ish. But he seems *very* well informed about Mark & admires Mark inordinately & I like him very much. Bass a big, loud clean-cut lawyer. The two of them together take up an awful lot of room. *Excellent* discussion though, Mark expounding at his ease in the haze of smoke. "I've got it!" he announces at one point as he tamps tobacco into his pipe. "The philosophical foundation of western civilization. I smoke, therefore I am." Turning to me: "You're the philosopher. Why didn't you think of that?" Then, lest they think I'm a bad philosopher, he launches into his story of how I am the best philosophy student ever to be seen at Hunter College. I rue the day Howard told him. I knew it was a mistake before the words were out of his mouth. Mark is not a man to keep pride to himself. (Or much of anything to himself.) In the taxi home he tells me "You know why I love to tell everyone about what a brilliant philosopher you are? Because you're so gorgeous when you blush." Then adds immediately "That's not the real reason." Then—"Well, maybe it is just a *small* factor!"

She enjoys hearing me read aloud from the diary. But the entry is over, and she takes up the narrative herself.

"Mark had been working hard, but now he worked even harder. He had to spend four weeks somewhere in Connecticut at the start of that summer, to learn surveying. At a camp they had, with Yale undergraduates—that was something of an experience in itself, evidently. Then he started to design the school.

"You know, La Guardia would talk about public housing for the poor. Mark and I would sometimes go hear him speak on weekends. I picture him speechifying at a dedication behind a forest of those big boxy microphones—you could barely see him; and the new buildings would stretch out behind him. He'd talk about cleanliness and disease, fighting crime, moral uplift—all riding on those new buildings. La Guardia was building a new *moral landscape*—do you understand?—and Mark was such a perfect man to embody those ideas.

"It was at one of those speeches that I saw Sarah Abbot for the first time since Mark's show. So far as I remember, at any rate. It was late summer, 1940. It is execrable that I remember so clearly how she looked, the brown culottes she was wearing, the sunglasses she did not wear but rather used as a prop, holding them to her lips, hailing a cab with them. We walked over to her. She gave Mark her hand and looked straight at me: '*How is Mark doing?*' I wanted to say, '*And where is your boyfriend, sweetheart?*'

"Why didn't I confront Mark and argue with him and dig out the truth? Because my way is to brood. Always has been. It is the one field in which I excel."

Silence.

"Mark worked hard on the school, and what an amazing building he designed!—I thought it was; Tierney and his people were thrilled with it.

"Picture a classical amphitheater, a half-circle of curved, steeply rising benches with stairways at intervals, and a stage in the well at the bottom. The classrooms were ranged around the back of the amphitheater. Each classroom led directly into the amphitheater through a wide doorway. Three stories of classrooms, the lower story with five, the second with seven and the top with nine—or something like that. Each floor's classrooms bent round into a half-circle so the classrooms could nestle right in behind the theater.

"The whole school could file into the theater in a couple of minutes; you'd simply walk out the door and sit down. Children would arrive in the morning, walk up one flight—the theater space started on the second floor—and emerge in the theater's well, and stream up to their classrooms. For Tierney, it was important that the school could see a lot of concerts and drama, so he loved the amphitheater. For Mark the theater served as a dramatic circulation space for the whole school. Students would eat lunch there, they would assemble there at the beginning and end of every day to hear announcements and pep talks . . .

"The facade is of glass except at the ground-floor level, where there is a one-story colonnade with Tuscan columns, I think he called them—essentially Doric without fluting or pediments; but he had them faced in copper, which would weather to a soft green, of course. The framing of the facade's glass panels was also copper, and there were two small and one bigger decorative half circles traced in copper, thrown up on the facade—their flat, open bottoms aligned with the top of the colonnade.

"It had other wonderful aspects. I could go on but I won't. Well, the front facade, for example, in the lower corner of each glass panel was a tiny stained-glass triangle. He made a beautiful drawing that specified the color of each. He had never poured himself like this into a single project before—the building simply got more and more beautiful, developed swirls and whorls and whirlpools and eddies—new details, new refinements, new simplifications; I loved the whole thing because it was so perfectly Mark-like—clever and beautiful, but with a streak of playfulness that served no purpose whatever except to make you happy. It was about that time that he had a stamp made up for his architectural drawings, with a Biblical quotation in Hebrew: CHOOSE LIFE. It suited him. It suited the school—its vibrancy.

"Well, by early 1941, the design was finished. Mark worked for Tierney again the following summer, on the detailed construction drawings. That fall Tierney had Mark come with him and address meetings up and down the East Coast, explaining the design, to help raise money. The drawings were published several times in the newspapers—I was accumulating a nice little scrapbook, which I've looked for of course. Without luck. 'His design for this school,' one newspaper wrote—or something like this—'forces a change in your idea of what a school *is*. It's not a collection of separate classes and classrooms. It's a single group of children united in . . . Something. The enterprise of learning . . .' Something like that. I wish I could find the scrapbook. And, 'the most truly *new,* modern and wholly original *classical* design we have ever seen.' " She smiles: "I made that one up myself. I told my father, and he passed it on to a friend who published a piece in *Pencil Points.* An architecture magazine Mark read. He read *every* architecture magazine.

"Mark didn't mind doing all the travel and speechifying, but it conflicted horribly with his schoolwork. Masonry, hydraulics, sanitation, soil mechanics, foundations, construction—all sorts of intensive courses. And he was at work also on his doctoral research, having to do with a steel framing technique for the school's roof and the cantilevers round the back. At best he might have finished by the end of the following summer—"

The phone rings and she is summoned by the maid. She returns several minutes later. "That was my aunt," she reports. "Ninety-two years old and still watching out for me."

I ask if they ever see each other, and she mentions a trip to Houston a few months ago. "I saw my Aunt Fran's great-grandchildren in a school play. Can you imagine?" Thinks it over. "You've made me more aware of the past then I used to be. At the elementary school I was introduced to a number of teachers. I'm afraid I struck them as a pretty formidable old thing. It wasn't my intention. But one of them introduced herself as Miss Volstead, I think it was, or something like that. Miss Volstead. I wanted to throw my arms around her. Have you any idea what *guts* it takes for a girl to call herself Miss Anything today? What *courage,* to throw it all back in their faces? This business about men not being able to see the woman's viewpoint, ordinarily it's plain nonsense. But I can't deny that I do feel drawn to wonder whether you as a man are able to grasp the terrific pressure a woman is under, nowadays, to knuckle under to the ideologues who are running the show. We suffered from all sorts of craziness in my time, but never this stark dread of breaking ranks."

And continues: "At any rate. If Mark remained a part of Tierney's group, it would be impossible for him to finish his Ph.D. when he had planned. And we agonized, and decided that he *had* to continue with Tierney—I was strongly for it, though it would put off his finishing, which would put off our marriage. Though—don't misunderstand—we were on fine terms with Tierney. He'd call at all hours, and Bass would call, and Olivia Harper would call—Tierney's education theorist—and Obermayer would call. And Mark would call them, and they'd all meet and conspire and it was all wonderful. Mark's friends from Parks and from college were in touch also, all the time. Benny, for example, Charlotte's beau and then fiancé and then husband. He was tall and thin, and pale—not absolutely the healthiest-looking specimen in the world, but a wonderful boy. He had dense curly hair and steel-rimmed glasses and a dry sort of humor that complemented Mark's. They were wonderful together. They'd been friends in college, and then Benny went to work for Ely Jacques Kahn, the architect. Benny would come over with drawings for Mark to criticize or sometimes just outright *change*—why don't we try this or this or this? Mark would generate more ideas in five minutes than the typical person in an entire lifetime.

"He'd say, '*Sholom aleichem,* Benny!'—he'd always greet his Yiddish-speaking friends in Yiddish. It used to be Benny would flinch. But Mark *acted* on a person, you see. And Mark changed also. Anyway, there came a time when Benny would say *Aleichem sholom!* back, and sometimes they'd even chat a few minutes in Yiddish.

"Mark confronted people. Always including himself. Always. I remember a time we went to a lecture at the New School. In an elegant, modern auditorium. A lecture by a reporter about the Moscow show trials."

She puts a finger to her lips and searches her memory intently.

"When it was over there were questions, and Mark asked the first one." Speaking slowly, hesitating between sentences to get it right. "We were in the very last row in back. He stood up with his hands in his jacket pockets and said—and there was nothing belligerent in his tone, just the purest curiosity—'You say these men risked their lives fighting for the revolution. And then they became the worst kind of louses, making secret deals with the fascists. And then they got so saintly again, they're willing to smear and humiliate themselves in public for the revolution. And now they deserve to be shot.

Listen, *do you actually believe this?"* And after a short, significant pause he smacked his forehead and said, more to the audience than the speaker, *'Meshugge!'*

"He sat down and the whole auditorium caught its breath. A few people clapped and more cat-called and everyone chattered— the quarter of the audience that didn't know the Yiddish word were all asking, simultaneously, what it meant. Years later, people were still talking to me about that lecture and what Mark had said.

"The fall of 1941 was lots of fun. We spent time with Mark's college friends, with Obermayer, with Tierney." I mention that there is an undated entry in her diary involving Benny and Charlotte on the Brooklyn Promenade. Does it date from this period? Yes, it must, she says, sounding pleased.

Charlotte, Benny, me & Mark [the entry reads] walked over Brooklyn Bridge & then traipsed all the way to the Promenade & there we sit resting our aching feet—Mark seated up on the back, feet on the bench proper. We watch the lower-Manhattan skyline & the bridges all lit up in the dark. A clear chilly evening. Ships & the dark profiles of lighters moving on the river. I taste the salt air coming in from the bay & Mark's pipe & the fall freshness—the straps of my shoes hurt from the long walk. Dry fallen leaves scatter on the walkway. I cuddle into Mark & he puffs—& all of a sudden he is in a tizzy & tells us "That's *it,* what an obvious idea!" I recall distinctly his saying *obvious,* & never was a word used so, as it were, *generously.* "I'll buy," says Charlotte—(I am too tired & comfortable to talk.)

"There ought to be an amusement park *on top of* Lower Manhattan!" So excited he's almost panting & one has *no idea* what he's talking about. "I mean, for example, put a Ferris Wheel right on top of one of those towers! A nice

tall tower with a flat top. That one." Points with his pipe
stem. "A different carnival ride on top of each building. With
walkways from rooftop to rooftop. And each walkway all lit
up by a million little lights, like Luna Park—the whole top of
the city is *garlanded*. The Ferris Wheel would be great.
Damn, can you imagine that? You take an elevator way to the
top & walk out on the roof & there above you in the stiff
breeze is this *immense* wheel reaching upwards into the
black—"

(Luna Park was the largest amusement park on Coney Island, the
beach-and-amusement district on the far side of Brooklyn. It "covers fifty acres with more than a million electric light bulbs. Dozens of
rides, including the ancient favorite, the 'Dragon's Gorge,' with its
blazing towers, the broad lagoon, and the spacious ballroom make
Luna Coney Island's most popular spot." Its pseudo-Moorish—or
are they Venetian? Byzantine?—domes and towers and arches are
amazing in the dark, their outlines picked out by the million lightbulbs. They are garish and beautiful and seem as though, like sky-
writing, they might dissipate into space at any moment. Luna Park
was intended not for children but for courting couples. That was
true of the rides in the fair's amusement area too: "Couples usually
went together.")

"Just the sound of it turns my stomach," Benny announces.
Mark looks somewhat crestfallen. Though it's hard not to
sympathize with Benny on this point. 'But it would be the
greatest tourist attraction in the world,' he says. "Honestly,
wouldn't it? The *Cojones Wheel*! You could see it for miles
around. I can picture the Germans saying, *'Vot iss diss nonsense? You haf shpent twenty million dollars to make a Ferris
Veel? You SHTUPID HORSES!'* And the Mayor would say,

'Don't get your bowels in an uproar, Adolf. In this country people are *allowed* to have fun!' " I love the way Mark plunges into an idea practically trembling in excitement. "Let's go to Roseland," says Charlotte—our original plan: what incredible stamina! "Why don't we go to Luna Park?" says Benny, "we could get the train at Montague Street." "No, it's a crime not to go on the boat & there isn't time"— for Charlotte it is Roseland or bust. Mark isn't sure Luna Park is open after Labor Day—Benny wants to go see—I say (old reliable), "I wish we could go to the Fair." Everyone looks to Mark as natural Decision Maker. "We said we'd take Charlotte to Roseland," the sage pronounces, & off we go. "I drove past the Fair site on my way to New Haven last week," Mark tells us as we set out. "It's raw & empty & covered with wreckage & garbage. It's very sad. It made me feel miserable."

(Roseland was and is a Manhattan dance hall. In those years it was "the downtown headquarters for hot music and such urban dance steps as the cake and collegiate, the Lindy and the Shag.")

"Roseland is such a noisy place," the diary continues.

It's so big but it seems to crowd in on you, it's too hot & dark & the ceiling is too low & the band is too loud. I hang in Mark's arms like a sack of laundry. The girls who come alone make me uneasy, chomping their gum *smack smack smack* like a rubber ball bouncing as they await a proposition. "Is it true"—Benny is debating the point with Charlotte—"that any girl nowadays who accepts a date for dinner and a play or something afterwards is outright *expecting* the guy to make a pass at her in the taxi home?" "Nonsense," says Charlotte and say I. "Yes," says Mark. Eventually I collapse at a table with Benny and watch Mark waltzing Charlotte around. In any crowd I see him instantly & exclusively. She adores him & he's so sweet about it, making it clear that he has the highest conceivable opinion of *her,* that she is his very particular favorite; are women fundamentally less jealous than men, or is it merely that we notice so much more, we have to operate on a different plane?

In the taxi home I am humming "Stairway to Paradise," & when Mark starts to speak, I keep humming. Sometimes a song just gets stuck that way, but I am listening nonetheless—"pondering the Manhattan skyline back in Brooklyn, I wished I were more articulate. I have an inkling of the deep significance of architecture. Somehow—the city as a living thing; the buildings like representations of ourselves—our noblest aspects; passion for beauty & truth—the *human* landscape; something like that. Something or other." Sounding tentative. He is stuck too. Very occasionally he arrives at a big question he cannot solve & he just tugs on it, as if it were a huge rock; he tugs & tugs. He has talked about this topic before, though never said even this many words about it. He tugs silently & I hum for a good fifteen blocks & then finally he speaks again: "Or am I just making excuses for doing the only thing I'm capable of doing? Over to Miss Laurie Glassman." His joke radio voice. "You're the philosopher. Take it, Laurie." But actually he is serious.

So I tell him that the purity of his devotion to architecture & his gift for it—that purity is *intrinsically* noble. And I understand the other thing he is trying to say too, but I don't know quite how to say it either. When we arrive he insists on kissing me for around three hours, with extreme tenderness; the cabdriver slams the door on us & fumes on the sidewalk. It will be three A.M. by the time Mark is back in

WHEN LIFE TURNS OUT TO BE A SAND CASTLE

New Haven. When I get home there is a note from my mother that Tierney has called & I am to call Mark—my mother conveys at least one message a week in this manner. Will Mark accompany him on the 5:55 to Albany on Wednesday evening? Meeting him at Penn Station at . . . Perhaps the point is, about architecture—that it is merely a technique for communicating emotions that can't be put in words, can only be shown, but are nonetheless the most important things a person can communicate; in Mark's case what he wants to show is a kind of nobility & joy; & a building unlike a poem or painting encompasses you, you literally live inside it. Or maybe I'm wrong. When I close my eyes at last I see couples dancing round & round as if on a carousel, & hallucinate the smell of double-mint.

(New Yorkers chewed gum at Roseland and at home, on streets, buses and the floor of the New York Stock Exchange. It was a gum-chewing age. Wrigley's had one of the splashiest signs in Times Square. Great fish drawn in little light bulbs blew bubbles and pushed Spearmint. At the fair "no meal was complete, it seems," according to the *New York Times,* "without the inevitable stick of chewing gum." Millions of sticks were mailed home from the Wrigley exhibit as souvenirs, and Beech-Nut gave millions away.)

That's the end of the entry. "I remember that crazy phrase 'Cojones Wheel,' " says Mrs. Levine. "Benny and Charlotte were married then, by the way. Charlotte was a dear. Such an awful life, her father was in an insane asylum. She was a nurse, and she was very good to me when I needed her help. We had fun on the Promenade and Roseland, and the whole bit. We had lots of fun that fall. Mark was thriving, and we were all so proud of him. And then in December the Japanese bombed Pearl Harbor.

"The damned Japanese. The goddamned Japanese. I'm

sorry, no doubt I shouldn't say such things. But for myself I can't help remembering how much was destroyed, *pointlessly, cruelly, evilly, despicably* destroyed."

Silence.

"It was Sunday. Mark did not go back to New Haven. On Monday we listened together to Mrs. Roosevelt on the radio. I still remember her exact words, or very nearly: I feel as if I am standing upon a rock and that rock is my faith in my fellow citizens. On Wednesday Mark enlisted. He tried on Tuesday, but the lines were so long he had to come back the next day.

"It was as if we were cartoon characters who suddenly realized we were suspended by nothing in midair, and down we went. We fell and fell and fell and fell.

"They were forming new engineering battalions. New everything, I guess. They told him to go home and expect a notice to report in a couple of months. So he went home. And we entered two months of such savage bleakness they're just plain *gone* from my mind, like the crater of a bomb. Like a crater. When you're my age you'll find out what an odd thing memory can be. But you have all the information, if you want it."

The diary's last entry is the story of those two months.

"I'm happy to have you read it if you want, but don't tell me about it. You know—it's not that I just haven't *happened* to open the diary over all these years. I've avoided it as if I were repelled somehow. Magnetically. Repelled. I was afraid of seeing that entry. And Beethoven's C-sharp minor quartet has dropped out of my life too. It's simply gone. Though I loved it more than any other piece of music. The one time I heard it accidentally in the years since, I didn't sleep for days.

"Well. Benny enlisted too. In the navy, of all things. He served in the Pacific. Bass enlisted. In the space of a few weeks Tierney's school project fell apart. We were assured it would be contin-

WHEN LIFE TURNS OUT TO BE A SAND CASTLE

ued after the war. Would have caused us despair a month earlier, but now it just made us shrug. The Manhattan skyline we had admired from Brooklyn Heights looked very different during the dimout. The idea was, to keep the German U-boats right offshore from spotting American coastal traffic in silhouette against the lit-up night sky. Lots of boats were sunk before it occurred to people that we ought to turn off the lights. You would see an occasional office lit, hanging by itself. The tall buildings all humbled—dark and quiet—waiting for the bombs. You could feel the darkness during the dimout, pressing on you as you walked. In turned out that the life you had been so carefully constructing was a sand castle, flattened that December by a few sweeps of the tide.

"Read the account of those months in the diary if you like. On one condition: Ask me nothing about it and tell me nothing about it. Agreed? What I've forgotten, I don't choose to remember."

17

Technology:
Good

"**T**he pylons at the entrance to the Plaza of Light are covered with large scales (I guess you would call them, like fish scales) & are decorated with medallions," the diary continues.

> With my famous obtuseness this was the *only* sculptural symbolism I deciphered at the whole Fair—I tell Mark they stand for the four Greek elements, & he checks in the book & I am right. One is covered with water-like medallions, Poseidons and sea-horses, one with fiery decorations and so on.

(The pylons and decorations were designed by the sculptor Carl Paul Jennewein.)

TECHNOLOGY: GOOD

This is a dramatic place even in the context of a dramatic Fair. [Some accounts refer to the axis from the Theme Center down the Court of Power into the Plaza of Light as the fair's "second main avenue," besides the mall.] Once you enter between the pylons there is the large round pool with fountains ahead of you. To the left, a lovely long curved wall of deep-blue glass fronted by a neat line of fountains with a rainbow hanging in the spray—that is the Con Ed building. [Consolidated Edison is—then as now—the local New York power company.] To the right the Electric Utilities building, put up by many companies banded together, is U-shaped & the courtyard wall facing away from T&P is gently sloped & has water *pounding* down it—a round glass tunnel pokes out through the waterfall & you walk in & out through the tunnel. On the far side of the plaza is the Blue Jello building, & across from it General Electric. If you walk to the center pool and peek out between Electric Utilities and G.E. towards the highway you see Westinghouse, with another crazy tower out front, in the shape of an ice-cream cone; & if you peek the other way between the curved blue wall of Con Ed and the Blue Jello helmet (this is evidently some kind of Blue Zone) you see the prow of a triangular building covered in *blue* concave fins like the slats of a Venetian blind—that is the Petroleum building.

We make our way to the central pool. In this plaza you are not merely drawn but actively, almost physically *tugged* in every direction at once. Between a waterfall to my left & a wall of fountains to my right? For some reason I close my eyes & give myself a big warm hug, & this turns out to be an excellent idea (though quite unintentionally), because Mark then suddenly smiles, *really* smiles, & although he hasn't figured out what to do the fog seems somehow to be lifting.

When you enter the Electric Utilities building you find yourself in a dark, gloomy, aggressively old-fashioned "Street of Yesterday." It is supposed to represent 1892, which was the tenth anniversary of the U.S. power industry. There are gaslights flickering, telegraph wires overhead, artificial breezes stirring the leaves—it's eery—considering it is all inside, a sort of movie set, very realistic and intriguing. There are actors in some of the store fronts. A lady in long skirts opens the door of a house, looks round blankly & closes it again. I suppose she is getting tired of emoting all day, or whatever she is supposed to do.

Now I've always been fascinated with the world my parents grew up in, I mean the actual *look & feel* of it, because the change between that time and this seems so uncannily large, as if five centuries had passed and not five decades, & the war makes a sort of opaque wall dividing that time from my own . . . My father would have been seven in 1892 & my mother two years old and I actually hear, as we stroll, an elderly lady repeating (did I imagine it?) *Yes, this was it, this was just the way it was* . . . (No! I remember her hideous goat-blue hat.)

I have always wanted so badly to *feel* what that time was like—because of a strange belief I suppose I was born with—that if, somehow, I could *feel* an era before I was born, the scales would fall from my eyes & I would then be able to feel *my own* life, grasp what it is really like, the way you can grasp time after the fact, when it is all over . . . well . . . you see a washing tub with scrub board in one house, a wooden Indian, an oil- and gaslamp store, a theater. In a hairdresser's store, there are life-like dummies showing a lady with the waist-length (longer?) hair of that era in the process of having it dried with a palm-leaf fan.

TECHNOLOGY: GOOD

I don't have to belabor the point, I expect, that the Avenue of Tomorrow is a good bit nicer. It's bright & ritzy-looking with modern shops, fancy streetlights, fancy cars poised at a perpetual red light & skyscrapers in the distance. You leave by way of the forty-foot waterfall.

Walking out through the glass tunnel is marvelous—a ton of water pounds down roaring & frothing-up around you, and you can't hear the voice of the person beside you; except you do feel slightly cheated that you can't *feel* anything—the glass tunnel deposits you well away from the falls onto a bridge over a shallow moat. Somehow it is too anti-septic (that is not the word)—one wants to be misted, at least a little. Or maybe I am merely trying to say, it is getting hot & I am getting tired & ever-more aware of *my feet*. My marriage and my feet are marked out henceforth as Predominant Themes, as Miss Acheson would say. There are beds of red begonias or something in the courtyard. The wonders of electricity point is well made, but it is the old-fashioned street that stays with you. It is one of the most evocative things at the Fair.

In 1939 technology, as I have mentioned, was not remote and esoteric. It was down to earth And its achievements were heroic.

In the factories of the pre-electrified age, lighting was dim and layout was dictated by the web of overhead shafts and leather belting that connected each machine to the central steam engine or water turbine. In 1939 middle-aged workers remembered that kind of factory. The routines of daily life had changed dramatically within living memory: In the late nineteenth century a bathroom was some-thing of a luxury. If you didn't have one, you'd set up a tub in the middle of the kitchen floor. Bathing was a traditional Saturday-night production number.

Housewives were the beneficiaries of the most important technological revolution of the century, a revolution that made it possible for wives who couldn't afford servants to devote themselves largely to a job or—more revolutionary still, because they had always *been* laborers—to their children. The Utilities' brochure documents the rise of electric appliances between 1923 and the fair: a roughly three-fold increase in vacuum cleaners, four-fold in washing machines, 250-fold in refrigerators. Any adult on the fairgrounds would have dealt with the iceboxes of the prerefrigerator age. A chunk of ice in a chest-high cabinet on top, a drip pan on the floor below, typically three narrow shelves in between. Forgetting to empty the drip pan was a classic kitchen accident. Refrigerators transformed the ways people shopped, cooked and spent their time.

"At every turn," writes a modern historian of the 1933 Century of Progress Exposition, "fairgoers were bombarded with pamphlets urging them to make use of the latest scientific research in industrial laboratories to modernize their kitchens."

It takes an intellectual to suggest that women had to be brainwashed into wanting electric kitchen appliances.

Fairgoers who trooped through the Electric Utilities exhibit were directly plugged into the dawn of the electricity age. It was no ancient saga to them. Gerald Wendt comments on a new power plant in Brooklyn. "The single units in this station produce 160,000 kilowatts as compared with a maximum of 50,000 in stations built in 1924, with 5,000 in a station dating from 1901, and with the sixty kilowatts in Edison's original installation at Pearl Street in New York in 1882." Nowadays technical-minded people over thirty get a certain feeling when they contemplate a computer. They can visualize the vastly weaker machines of the past; when they do they are apt to experience full force, like a faceful of sunshine, the flat-out marvelousness of modern technology. In the fair's age *anyone* over thirty might have experienced that same sensation whenever he looked at an electric outlet.

Many other technologies at the fair were as down-home and vital as electricity. Take automobiles. Technology had done it again: Within living memory it had changed all the rules, changed the world and made life tangibly better for vast numbers of people. Many 1939 fairgoers remembered 1911. In that year a Michigan county commissioner first conceived the idea of painting lines down the center of roads. The Lincoln Highway, connecting New York and San Francisco, was completed in 1927. It was the country's first continuous coast-to-coast roadway; it consisted mainly of existing roads patched together. Most 1939 fairgoers would have remembered the hoopla when the patching together was finally completed twelve years before. The Lincoln Highway was finished to specifications that called for cars to be driven at thirty-five miles per hour and trucks at ten. By 1939 it was absurdly outdated.

Between 1927 and 1939 cars had gotten better and more plentiful—and of course they'd made new problems in the process. But in 1939 technologists and designers seemed to regard those new problems—not only the safety problem but everyday down-to-earth issues like preventing traffic jams—as important and worthy of attention. In the 1930s, for example, Yale University had a Bureau for Street Traffic Research. (It no longer has one.) The Futurama, wrote Geddes, was exactly "a visual dramatization of a solution to the complex tangle of American roadways."

Today, relatively few technologists are intrigued by the question of how Mrs. Schwartz can shave half an hour off her weekly trip to the shopping mall. We have more significant things to worry about. We have goals that are more important than merely making people's lives easier in modest ways.

Our own characteristic technological marvel is the computer. The fair had no inkling of computers. It did foresee technologies that *depend* on computers, in their modern forms. Computers, no; robots, rocket ships and sophisticated highway-control systems, yes. H. G. Wells describes teleconferencing:

> Even the existence of business centers is no longer imperative. It is so close a Tomorrow it is almost Today when it will be possible for a dozen men or a score of men to sit in conference, seeing and hearing each other, by radio, television, telephone, when bodily they are hundreds of miles apart. All that this exhibition of the World's Fair will show plainly.

And the fair asked questions of the sort that computers induce *us* to ask: "Network of communications systems makes for speedy exchange of ideas; can we improve the spiritual side of life as we did the physical apparatus? Can serious breakdown be avoided in such a complex system?"

But computers would have been an astonishing novelty at the fair. Have they revolutionized everyday life to the extent electricity, cars, phones, movies, radio, kitchen appliances did in the thirties? I am inclined to say no. They have certainly revolutionized science, engineering and other specialized areas. Otherwise they are a big help, some of the time; but they have rarely changed the rules fundamentally.

Consider the production of text. Word processors and computer printers have made the logistics dramatically easier. On the other hand, technology pundits began in the early 1970s to forecast the demise of the book. And in the last few years, notebook computers have indeed given us the wherewithal to do away with books if we want—except, we don't want. It turns out that books are no mere stopgaps on the road to computers; they are ergonomic masterpieces, and they are here to stay. We have made some progress toward "paperless offices," but we are still adrift in a gale of paper that dogs us wherever we go, from birth certificates through owner's manuals, license renewal forms, deeds, titles, dollar bills and whatnot, not to mention a million drafts on paper of the typical word-processed, computer-printed book. Life in the text world goes on; the rules have changed, but not all that much. Not fundamentally.

One more example. Computers have changed the logistics of architecture. A computer-drawn picture of a building can be produced in far less time than a typical hand drawing—and is probably better to boot. If ever there were a clean victory for technology, this is it. *Except:* one glance at the work of a brilliant architectural draughtsman—a Benjamin Latrobe, Hugh Ferriss, Frank Lloyd Wright—will convince you that such drawings are in a fundamentally different class from anything a machine has ever produced or ever will. If computers make the average architectural rendering cheaper and better and the odd genius remains free to do as he likes, that is a big step forward. But if they cause peaks and valleys to be replaced by a featureless plateau of acceptable mediocrity—is that a victory?

Surveys suggest that more home computers are used for game playing than anything else. There's nothing wrong with toys. Recreation is important to our quality of life. Computers have brought us lots of ingenious new entertainments. But compare those new entertainments to the ones that were new or newish in the thirties: electric recordings, radio, talking pictures, television. The "newness" of computer games is real but trivial in comparison.

And meanwhile, computers have caused as well as solved big problems. Our institutions stagger under killing loads of complexity. Creating thousand-page bureaucratic rulebooks and million-line budgets is a lot easier when you have computers to help.

Computers are powerful and wonderful machines, and they

do have the *potential* to change everyday life radically. But for my money they haven't yet. An imagination deficit among software builders, complacency and low standards on the users' part have killed any chance of a real computer revolution so far. That conclusion is controversial (I have discussed it elsewhere); for now, I am content to leave it at this: In the high thirties, technology had accomplished breathtaking things.

That was the age of technology par excellence. Technology then dealt in the tangible and the everyday, not in strange stuff like software and silicon. Technology meant refrigerators and radios. It was about new ways to build bridges, dams and skyscrapers, not about space stations and supercolliders. It was about Lucite and Plexiglas, both on display at the fair. It was about nylon stockings—available as of December 1939—and rayon and cellophane. It was about *elevators:* Visiting from France, Le Corbusier, ordinarily a fierce critic of all things American, was enchanted by American elevators capable of powering big loads up and down thousand-foot buildings in a flash.

We sometimes think of ours as *the* technology age, but that's nonsense. Older people on the 1939 fairgrounds had lived through the most spectacular technology-driven world transformation in history. One late-thirties account lists achievements and discoveries of the previous forty-five years. It is a long list, but worth contemplating in full:

> Motion pictures, silent and sound; photo-electric cells; electron beams; radio direction beams; wire photos and electronic television; oil cracking; internal combustion engines, gas, gasoline and Diesel; automobiles; airplanes; X-rays, Gamma rays; radioactivity; the gyrocompass; turbine engines; steam boilers carrying pressures of over 2,000 pounds to the square inch; high-speed steel and a thousand new and

TECHNOLOGY: GOOD

marvelous alloys; vast improvement in the generation and distribution of electricity; synthetic rubber and silk.

Furthermore "the colloids and the vitamins have arrived," and "the atom is smashed." By the way, "many of these things will be shown at the New York World's Fair."

At the groundbreaking ceremony on Flushing Meadow, La Guardia turned up the first clump of earth with a rusty 150-year-old spade. "This is the way they did it 150 years ago," he couldn't help but remark; "over there," pointing to a steam shovel, "is what we use today." It's been a long time since we were capable of taking pride in a power shovel. We cannot understand the fair unless we grasp the extent to which 1939 technology had changed plain, everyday life for the better.

18

The Art
of the
Microcosm

"The Con Edison building," Miss Glassman's diary continues,

is across from Electric Utilities. First there is the line of
tall fountains against the gently concave facade. You enter
over a short bridge over a pool, under a sign that says
"The City of Light," & there is an extraordinary diorama
inside, huge—yes, *the largest diorama in the world*—along
the concave wall of a gigantic room where you stand &
watch the show. This diorama is unlike any other. It is
viewed not in the round but from the front—a sort
of mural in very-very-high relief, showing all of New
York City and centering, naturally, on the towers

of Manhattan. (What did you expect, Brooklyn?) It's lovely.

The buildings to the rear seem to be glued onto the wall; as they step outward they grow larger; the ones closest to the front are freestanding. [The free-standing Empire State Building is twenty-two feet high.] Within the small depth of the diorama there are maybe fifteen ranks of modelled skyscrapers stepping backwards, with the river & bridges & Queens beyond. The show lasts about ten minutes & takes you through a day. At the start it is dawn—"a penciled radiance etches a golden pattern on the mist," etc. etc., I could have done without the narration—but the model is gorgeous, the buildings in pinks, roses & grays against a pale blue background. The scene is impressionistic rather than true-to-life—buildings that don't belong together are set side-by-side; but it is incomparably dramatic because of the flattened perspective, the whole breathtaking jumble of the city *squished* into a depth of, maybe, a dozen feet, and the model's concave shape makes all the streets converge on you as you stand in the viewing well. As I look at this amazing model, which is packed with so much energy the whole room seems to fizz, that rolling floating swell of exaltation comes again.

There is so much complexity & detail & so much going on—trains are in constant motion, cars zip over bridges, elevators move up and down within the towers—& during the show there is a thunder storm with extraordinary light & sound effects; as it darkens all the *many* tiny lights come on & the buildings become deep blue—& when the storm is over, a peaceful evening falls & still more lights come on. In terms of sheer drama there is nothing like this show at the whole Fair, & it is overwhelmingly beautiful besides. *"Is there any-*

thing more beautiful in the world than the New York sky-line?" Mark asks rhetorically as we go out; & I have to agree.

(The Con Edison diorama was another masterpiece by Walter Dorwin Teague.)

The fair was enchanted with dioramas. The art of the microcosm reached its apex there. What does a fascination with dioramas say about the high thirties? Possibly nothing, beyond the fact (and it is worth underlining) that urban landscapes were gripping in themselves. People admired the towering modern city, especially at night when the lights came on. Some were awestruck. It is a sight we are used to, but we are still struck by it. How much more intriguing must it have been when it was brand new, technologically leading-edge and characteristically American? The fair's urban dioramas were a good way of presenting a favorite thirties spectacle.

But it is hard not to wonder whether there might not have been more to it. "Today we hold tomorrow in our hands," said Grover Whalen at the Theme Center groundbreaking. Having a grip, a sure and confident sense of *control* over space and time, is a characteristic high-thirties attitude. Dioramas are the art form of overview and control—of holding the world in your palm, seeing things from a gods'-eye view, *grasping the big picture.* Perhaps this fair represented the high point of the art of diorama because fair makers were content that they could see things whole and wanted fairgoers to share that heady sensation.

The Con Edison building and Electric Utilities also were designed by Harrison and Fouihloux. After dark the fountains along the Con Edison facade were lit in blue and performed a "Water Ballet." Alexander Calder choreographed the waterworks. Have I mentioned that the best artists in the country decorated the Fair?

19

Robot!

We engage in detailed planning of the rest of the afternoon & evening. It's twenty to three and Mark is not satisfied by our rate of progress. And I am starting to worry that in the back of his mind he is formulating some sort of tight unanswerable argument that will leap out and crush me. For the first time since I got proposed-to at Ford, I am starting to feel uneasy—

But the agenda is: we polish off several more Production and Distribution Zone buildings. Then we attack the International Zone, have dinner, make a swing through the Amusement Area (he wants to take me dancing), & come back for a final look at the main grounds all lit up. Perhaps we take in the nine o'clock fireworks over the Lagoon of Nations. Perhaps I collapse first.

We head for Westinghouse but can't resist ducking under the eaves of the Steel building first: it is across the plaza from Westinghouse. The bluish helmet-like structure is lifted off the ground on a sort of colonnade, supported on vast curving steel ribs with holes punched out. Strolling underneath is like walking under a gigantic crouching Martian space-vehicle or a much-too-large bug. Not altogether pleasant. Then we can't help just *peeking* behind Steel at the Du Pont building—now we are headed away from the Plaza of Light. Du Pont is a creamy salmon-pink with accents in vermillion and gray, with a colorful tower out front that suggests chemistry equipment, & curved round the tower is a glimmering gray-blue wall of steel framing.

(The wall "was arrested at this stage," Walter Teague explains, "because the steel was too interesting to hide beneath the stucco.")

The Carrier building is right next to Du Pont & it is one of the few really hideous things at the Fair. A tall peaked dome of painful proportions, too vertical, like—nothing, but it's ugly. It is supposed to be an igloo. Carrier makes air conditioning equipment.

("The actual control of the weather for an entire town," writes Gerald Wendt, "will by no means be impossible for air-conditioning engineers of the future.")

We are now right at the verge of the main Fairground—next to Carrier is a great arching bridge that heaves itself high in a great oceanic swell over a busy roadway into the Amusement Area. We retreat back to the Plaza & then walk across, around the Pool, & approach Westinghouse.

ROBOT!

I suppose I've seen more newspaper references to the Westinghouse time capsule than to anything else at the Fair. The building is reported to be shaped like an Omega, for no obvious reason. Mark steps in. "It's of course the symbol for ohms, electrical resistance. It's a curious sort of reference to church architecture, cruciform buildings, I guess." Then he smiles, in a determined way, because suddenly he realizes how somber his tone has been.

Out front you can peer into a deep hole where the time capsule is lodged, or look at a reproduction in a glass tube. But the area is thronged, & neither of us is interested enough to wait, so we go inside.

The time capsule was a seven-and-a-half foot tall narrow steel cylinder. In September of 1938 it was installed in its "Immortal Well," where it is supposed to stay until 6939. (Will any Queens resident who happens to be reading this book in 6939 please remember to go dig it up?) The time capsule included small articles of clothing, fabric, plastic and metal samples, many texts on microfilm, a newsreel together with instructions on how to make a newsreel projector and other odds and ends: a child's Mickey Mouse cup. A rhinestone clip from Woolworth's. A copy of the best-seller *Gone with the Wind*. The newsreel included scenes of Jesse Owens winning the 100-meter dash at the 1936 Berlin Olympics; of the veterans reunion on the seventy-fifth anniversary of the Battle of Gettysburg. One of the most telling snippets about the age that made it is the fact that, although the time capsule was designed for the express purpose of sitting in a hole in the ground for five thousand years, it is neatly streamlined at both ends.

(Of course in the 1930s, you could get streamlined coffins.)

Thousands of copies of *A Book of Record of the Time Capsule* were distributed to libraries, museums and convents throughout the world. The book included messages to the future from Albert Einstein, Thomas Mann and the American physicist Robert Millikan. In an age of authority, it was not hard to appoint ambassadors to the seventieth century. The *Book of Record* also contained the geodetic coordinates of the Immortal Well and instructions on building electromagnets so you could locate the capsule. "The human anxiety to die but never be forgotten is touching," *The New Yorker* comments, "but the notion that in five thousand years the period between 1920 and 1940 will appear as any more than a little breathing space between two great wars strikes us as an almost perfect comment on the vanity of a strange day."

"There are lots of exhibits inside," the diary continues,

> & a big mob. I can't conceive how it happened, but somehow *we do not miss* the three o'clock show put on by an object called Elektro, a "moto-man" & his dog (honest to God) "Sparko." This Elektro is a fairly abstract-looking metal man, seven feet high, designed to do tricks like walking, moving its fingers & so on—it is heavy & clunky, with all the charm of a vacuum cleaner.

("Ever since the invention of the radio tube and the photo-electric cell," *Newsweek* reports, "the robot has been a favorite toy of gadgeteers. Many of the mechanical men have been able to walk, talk [via a phonograph record], lift their arms at a command, and smoke pipes, but the search for bigger and better Frankensteins has gone forward." Elektro is covered in aluminum and "looks like a man from Mars.")

"Its keeper talks into a microphone," the diary continues,

> & the thing does stunts in response. I am taken aback, I confess, when the colors red & green are held in front of the

machine & it is able to speak the words "red" & "green" in response. But my inclination is to find the whole thing ridiculous. I am *much* more impressed with the automatic electric dishwasher in the Hall of Electrical Living.

General Electric fronts directly on the Plaza of Light & it was first on Mark's list of things to see, so of course after Westinghouse we have to go in. It has a lightning bolt out front. Relatively few buildings, I should think, can make that statement. The bolt emerges from (or actually, is supposed to be plunging *into*) a pool tiled in pale-blue. The bolt is covered in shiny stainless steel. It zigs up, zags down, zigs up more, zags, zigs, & has a something on top. Is that clear? Looking from the bottom, the thing on top is like a compass rose mounted on two intersecting rings. Sparks in the shape of gleaming miniature Trylons fly outward from the base of the bolt in its pool.

The building has two wings, & Steinmetz Hall is to the left. That is where they perform the artificial lightning demonstration that Mark is so keen on seeing. In the right wing there is a television demonstration & a "magic kitchen." But we walk straight into Steinmetz Hall. The next show is supposed to start soon. It is crowded, & we sit near the back. The seats are ranged in straight rows in a sort of balcony; the show itself takes place on the floor below & before you. The stage is dominated by bizarre things not a one of which I can identify. At the far ends are two groups of three tall black columns each, banded in silver. Mark points to spear-like gadgets on each side—"must be the electrodes," he says. "I guess the lightning will arc that gap, between the two of them." They are easily fifty feet apart. Men pace among the columns & electrodes and other *odes,* setting things in order.

Mark is about to say more, but the lights dim. An

announcer explains that G.E. needs artificial lightning in order to test its field equipment, to make sure thunder storms don't damage it. Big glass tubes begin to glow. There is a palpable drawing-in-of-breath all over the room. I have never been in an audience where attention is so intently fixed & has such a palpable air of *anxiety*. The tubes glow brighter. The men stroll around checking the odes. A few loud, casual bangs make everybody start, but you don't *see* anything—there is a bit of chattering—"Well, was that *it?*" And then—

A *tremendous* explosion: a gasp of purple flame sheer across the front of the room. It is impossible to tell which way it is travelling, it is just *there* & then it's gone & the effect is overwhelming & the bang deafening. You barely even have time to *see* it while it's happening—it is as if the sights & sounds are implanted directly in your head, & *then* you see & hear them. The whole room lit up violet; the thunder-clap ringing in your ears. That was *fifty thousand* volts, the announcer mentions, sort of in passing.

They do more lightning tricks. Bolts split logs, strike a shiny model of the Trylon & Perisphere & vaporize (I never knew that things actually *could* vaporize) a fine metal wire. The audience is remarkably silent as it files out.

Mark is shaking his head & half-smiling. Says nothing. So we we make off for the International Zone.

20

The
Landscape
and Its
Sanctity

In the American religious community of the high thirties, people had the remarkable idea that they could build the future: ponder it, design it, construct it. We feel differently today. We have little sense of control over the future. There are many reasons for the shift. One is that high-thirties society, which got lots of practice in behaving as it ought and was consequently very good at it, was also highly practiced and proficient when it came to building and controlling things.

The high thirties had a deep sense of control over the American landscape, and to a significant extent reshaped it. A sense of mastery and control, derived at least in part from throwing dams and bridges across rivers, digging tunnels and raising tall buildings, permeates high-thirties life. High-thirties society knows and *feels* that it is able to control and to reshape. Part of that feeling comes from the New Deal, which remade society. But part just as surely derives from the act of large-scale building. (Much of the large-scale building was paid for, of course, by the same New Deal.) And here again, the powerful alliance between art and technology imbued the work of controlling the landscape with a spiritual aura approaching sanctity.

Today we feel little sense of control over the landscape. It can hardly be surprising that we feel little control over the future either, little confidence in our capacity to build it: The act of building comes hard to us in general. Control comes hard. To build and control the future (or anything else) is just *unnatural* to us. In the 1930s things were different.

Let's listen again to the high thirties. What we hear is not vague optimism. It is concrete confidence.

"This is not a vague dream of a life that might be lived in the far future," says Robert Kohn about Democracity, "but one that could be lived tomorrow if we willed it so." "It is evident, first of all," writes Gerald Wendt, "that the tools for building the world of tomorrow are already in our hands." "The Motorway System as visualized in the Futurama," writes Norman Bel Geddes, "could be built today." The project for a new town of Radburn was "led by men who felt the responsibility of making a contribution toward improved living. They planned Radburn; they are building Radburn." The 1930s held a *literally* constructive view of the future. "Building the world of tomorrow" is the theme of the 1939 fair. BUILDERS OF THE WORLD OF TOMORROW is emblazoned on fair workers' uniforms. "Today," said Fair President Whalen at the Theme Center groundbreaking, "we hold tomorrow in our hands." The idea was to think, plan, then *do*.

The 1930s had a characteristic style. That style is substantially *our* style. "So revolutionary was this style" writes Martin Greif in his beautiful essay "Depression Modern," so all-pervasive, that in a period of only half a decade it changed the shape of virtually everything in the American home, including, finally, the home itself. So total was its success, so complete its acceptance (we live surrounded by its offspring today), that its origins in the 1930s and its innovative creators, if not completely forgotten, are now simply taken for granted.

He doesn't mean that we build streamlined modern structures today. Rather that our lives are furnished with high-thirties-style objects, from our gas ranges and refrigerators to our standard-issue office desks, storefronts and movie-theater seats. Clean, simple, utilitarian design is a thirties idea. The everyday life of the twenties, Greif notes, was full of objects that would seem strange to us. But in the thirties we would feel—not at home, but almost.

Let me add another proposition to Greif's claims. Not only did the thirties invent modern style, to a startling extent it built the modern world. Consider just New York City. The roads and bridges of those years shape New York City today. The Belt and Gowanus and Henry Hudson Parkways, The West Side Highway and East River Drive are products largely of the thirties (spilling over into the early forties). The city's first airport, North Beach—later La Guardia—was begun in 1937. The George Washington Bridge opened in 1931, followed by the monumental Triborough Bridge in 1936, the Henry Hudson in 1936, the Marine Parkway in 1937 and the Bronx-Whitestone in 1939. The Lincoln Tunnel opened in 1937 and the Queens-Midtown Tunnel in 1940.

Granted, New York was exceptional because of the nearly unstoppable juggernaut of its parks commissioner, Robert Moses. But all across the country the 1930s saw the American landscape transformed. On the opposite coast, both the Oakland–Bay Bridge and the Golden Gate were finished in 1937. Boulder Dam (called "Hoover" when it was begun, "Boulder" when it opened under a Democratic administration and "Hoover" again with the Republicans back in control of Congress in 1947) was the highest in the world when it opened in 1936. The Grand Coulee Dam, which opened in 1941, generated more power than any other. And so on.

The thirties defined *modern* and built a good deal of the landscape we inhabit today.

When we hear the word "landscape," we are apt to think first of nature. When Stuart Davis used the term (*Swing Landscape,* 1938) he meant a sprawling collection of chimneys and bridges and oil derricks rendered with electric sparkle in a lovely ensemble of greens, oranges, reds and lilacs. In the 1930s, a stretch of waterfront no longer in a state of nature was said to be "improved." The American environment we care about is the natural one; the thirties cared most for the man-made environment. That disagreement speaks to a profound difference in world view. And that difference is vital in turn to our differing views of the future, because our view of space matters to our view of time. The 1930s had a grip on space—and on time, too, on the future; and more than likely those two feelings are related.

Nineteen hundred thirty-nine didn't lack for nature lovers. Nature shouldered aside by the rude, burgeoning city is a familiar thirties lament. In the 1920s Georgia O'Keeffe scattered floral still lifes among the urban scenes at the Stieglitz Gallery, where she showed her work: "I will make even busy New Yorkers take time to see what I see of flowers." In 1939 the president had a long history of conservationist interests, and came from a notably conservationist family. The Roosevelt administration established new national parks and forests; the Civilian Conservation Corps tended forests and built wildlife shelters. The electrical engineer who designed the spectacular fountain-and-fireworks, music-and-gas-jets display on the Lagoon of Nations had to be called out of retirement on Nantucket, where he had been raising wind-adapted trees for coastal planting. We know, in other words, that at least one of the fair's crack technicians would have been puttering around his plants had he not been called upon to design one of the age's greatest high-tech extravaganzas.

But of course our own attitude toward nature differs radically from what was typical in the 1930s, regardless of the thirties' fond regard for flowers and forests. Ironic distance is our own very particular house specialty, yet it fails us utterly where nature is concerned. Perhaps that's good. I merely note that a change has taken place. "How can you disregard the Atlantic Ocean, the Grand Canyon, and Niagara Falls?" asks Delmore Schwartz on behalf of Randall Jarrell, attempting to summarize Jarrell's views. "Poetry," he answers, "has the overwhelming reality of these natural phenomena, and it is certainly far more interesting." The essay dates from 1953 but would have been perfectly at home in the high thirties, when Schwartz first made his mark. "He who claims that man cannot improve on nature," writes Gerald Wendt in 1939, ". . . forgets that steel, concrete and glass are all unnatural products." Case closed. In 1928 Yeats had expressed his famous preference, should he die and be re-embodied, for the enameled gold birds of Byzantium over any mere fluff-headed, natural-born specimen. The 1930s loved nature but approached it with a certain detachment.

There *is* an "environment" that obsessed the 1930s —the man-made environment, of course. It was a brisk, businesslike era. And yet it had a spiritual, almost a mystical belief—though it would never have acknowledged it as such—in the transcendent beauty and importance of the act of building. "Building the future" was a resonant phrase in 1939, in part because 1939 knew all about building and believed deeply in building. Building was beautiful, so *building the future* was too.

That belief in the beauty of building resounds (the way thirteenth-century Christianity might in a reliquary or an altarpiece) in Lewis Hine's photograph of an engineer sighting through a theodolite, perched high on an unfinished skyscraper: In shirtsleeves and a dusty fedora and the barest smile, he has the presence of a Sforza on horseback. It resounds in Margaret Bourke-White's famous photograph of Fort Peck Dam under construction in Montana, *Life* magazine's first cover: Concrete abutments loom like manmade mountains over two tiny figures in the foreground. It is there in Hugh Ferriss's drawing of the Perisphere under construction, thrust forward within rendered space so the top of the sphere and the left and right edges of the Helicline are clipped off, pressed flat as if viewed through a long telephoto lens, done in charcoal like most of his drawings but seeming to exude light as if it were of silver. It is there in a Federal Writers' Project description of Raymond Hood's RCA Building: of its "great knife-like prow and cliff-like side." "It may be said without contradiction," observes the *Atlantic* magazine in 1931, "that in America architecture is now regarded as the foremost of the arts." New York's tall buildings, says the *Times*, "are the expression of American daring and American contempt for limits." They are lifted skyward "by a demoniac energy" that is "characteristically American." Like any spiritual belief it is hard to account for rationally, but it is there and it is unmistakable.

Our modern obsession with nature's landscape, the 1930s with its *own* landscape, have radically different implications. No doubt they are psychological next-of-kin. But the building focus of the thirties aroused (and of course reflected) large-scale national *activity*. Our nature focus makes us passive. The man-made environment was in their power to create. As for us, we cannot make the slightest contribution to nature's achievements; we are mere fusspot curators. We are necessarily passive. And our passivity matters to

THE LANDSCAPE AND ITS SANCTITY

the future, because getting a grip on anything is no specialty of passive people.

The thirties viewed the landscape from the standpoint of the young Robert Moses—on a ferry to New Jersey, he laid out for Frances Perkins a vision of Manhattan's West Side transformed. He would hide the railroad tracks, build parks on the mudflats, run a highway alongside the river, build clubs, marinas, restaurants, bicycle paths, tennis courts. In August 1994 state and federal transportation officials approved a new plan for a highway along the same West Side of Manhattan, a bit farther south. The old highway collapsed in 1974. In the intervening two decades the government and the public had been ... well ... mulling things over. Environmental objections killed previous plans. Our view of the landscape makes us passive. I don't say our view is wrong; I don't say it is less noble (although it is not self-evidently more noble either) than 1939's. I merely assert that it makes us passive.

In the 1930s ownership of the landscape built confidence in the future. Today we diffidently back away from the landscape. We don't own it any longer. We have largely ceded our moral right to control it. Yet we still claim a desire to control time, to own the future and make the world better.

Having surrendered space, is it inevitable that we will eventually surrender time as well, and leave matters to take their course, and no longer even *claim* to believe (we may already have stopped believing) that we will make things right in the end? Is it possible for a nation in the process of surrendering all moral claims on space to retain its claims on time?

I doubt it.

Our passivity is, I think, one of our defining characteristics. It is displayed most prominently in our view of the landscape, but it crops up in many other ways besides. And the *character* of our passivity is important and telling. It is not, by and large, that we lounge in our hammocks and snooze. The society we have made is usually doing something or other; an outside observer might even think us hyperactive. It is just that all our activity doesn't amount to anything. Ours is a postutopian society, milling about *within,* not marching toward the promised land.

In New York City some public toilets were installed by a French company on a trial basis in July 1992. The public was duly grateful. Then they were hauled away again, and the city still hasn't figured out how to get them back—still hasn't divined the circumstances under which it will allow such public toilets to be reinstated. The problem has to do with access for people in wheelchairs. Do some toilets have to be accessible, or must they all? Of course, toilets are a special case. Again in New York, a mentally ill man was finally carted off to a psychiatric hospital after menacing residents in a certain Upper West Side neighborhood for years. He escaped, was arrested and brought back—soon after which a state judge ordered the hospital to release him three months after the original incarceration date, not hold him for six months as psychiatrists wished to. Of course, the mentally ill homeless are a special case. New York is a special case. I don't deny that special circumstances hold in each instance of passivity I have mentioned. Complex competing interests must be balanced in each. Nothing, here, is black and white. This (to our way of thinking) unblack-and-whiteness is exactly the point. However you choose to interpret the facts—of course, the Left and Right interpret them very differently, the Left as evidence that we are compassionate and the Right that we are stupid—the facts themselves are plain. We are a passive society. Not a little passive but very, very passive, unable to secure even our basic needs for

protection from the criminally insane and a place to go to the bathroom. In this respect, 1939 would have found us funny and pathetic.

"Action is our slogan," writes the fair's science director.
"Not for us, as for our ancestors, to bear adversity with fortitude, to
await our reward in the next world. If the world is awry we can
change it."

Thirties art struggled with technology, co-opted and tamed it. The
populace struggled with the physical landscape and built bridges,
towers, dams that transformed it. The thirties compulsion not to
stand back passively but to *engage* is ushered in by the writer and
critic Jane Heap's 1927 *Machine Age Exposition*. An effective artist,
Heap writes briskly, "must affiliate with the creative artist in the
other arts and with the constructive men of his epoch: engineers,
scientists, etc." Her exhibition displayed painting, sculpture and architectural drawings alongside naked machinery—a crankshaft, an
airplane engine, a time clock, a propeller. That thirties compulsion
to engage inspired a mural at the World's Fair. It shows "an electrician, gazing defiantly at bolts of lightning," the goal being to depict
"man's desire to control and direct nature."

"Control and direct indeed!" we say indignantly.

21

Sudden
Dark

"**A**fter Mark enlisted we knew that he would enter the army soon but we did not know when. They told us about two months, probably, & it turned out to be exactly that." This is the last entry of the three-volume diary.

The idea of his becoming a soldier made Mark positively snort with amusement. A typical ten-year-old would be a better soldier than I, he said. If only I don't disgrace myself . . . Yet there was never the slightest remorse that he had enlisted, or any thought whatever of his getting out of it. It's my duty, he said, & that was that. The topic was not open for discussion.

I didn't understand him at first. Obviously he is no fighter, but why shouldn't he turn into as good a soldier as anyone else? He explains: He is not strong, he is not athletic, he is physically undeveloped. He is squeamish, he lacks the killer instinct, he is physically unaggressive. He has no experience getting along with "the common man," he doesn't play cards, he barely drinks, he is an intellectual. He has no sense of direction. He can find no grounds for suspecting that he is capable of being courageous. If anyone was ever *not* cut out for anything, he says, I am not cut out for being a soldier.

And yet he says it not with self-pity, not asking to be reassured, but in a dry matter-of-fact way & with bitter amusement.

I say, what about the time you jumped back into the Packard. That wasn't courageous? He waves it away. I tell him truly that he is the best conversationalist I ever met, *a propos* getting along with people. But that's irrelevant to the common man, he says. I point out a lot of his other qualities. He smiles & shakes his head. And after a little bit I understand him perfectly. Of course "common man" is his way of saying *goyim*. Perhaps excepting intellectuals. When he is thrown in for the duration with Irishmen, southerners, mid-western farmers, yes I *can* imagine him for all his terrific powers at a loss. Personally I think, no I *know* he is an exceptionally brave *brave* man, but he is also so tortured by moral questions & he *is* an improbable soldier. I am positive he will acquit himself nobly & yet I perfectly understand him: he is terrified. He says so himself, plainly and straight out, the way he says everything. "I am terrified." He quotes Falstaff on the topic of pitiful army recruits—"Food for powder, food for powder; they'll fill a pit as well as better." It upset me so, he was chastened & promised not to repeat it. But it was said & he didn't have to repeat it. It hung over us like the white winter sky.

His smile is abstract & he gets lost in small objects, sitting with me at the Fifth Ave Automat & studying a quarter—spinning it on the table; when he has been sitting alone & I surprise him & he smiles at me—when I walk up he always smiles at me—it is the smile of a man in pain. I mean the mouth smiles but not the eyes. He is dry. Everything has an ironic flavor. He is dry ice. He describes the ritual of picking up the mail at the front door of his building in New Haven. He shares the upstairs with two other Yale graduate school men. One inspired by Mark went to enlist soon after Mark did, but was turned down on medical grounds he refuses to divulge. He is bitter & envies Mark. The other has decided to wait for the draft to find him. So Mark gets the mail. Every day he picks up the pile of envelopes, his hands are cold & numb, his breathing quickens. Every day he leafs through the pile & the official letter is not there.

There must be a place where we can see each other alone in the weeks remaining, he announces. It develops that Mr. Tierney has a second cousin who winters someplace in the South & owns a home in New Haven, near the Yale Bowl. I can't imagine what Mark has told him to elicit this information & the loan of the house. I never want to look Mr. Tierney in the face again. But unheedful grimness has overtaken us both; it is spiteful cold; Mark is resolved to do what he has to do and I to do the little I have to do. So this small cold house becomes our only remaining tie to Tierney.

A ritual develops. On Sundays we drive up there. We arrive in the early afternoon with food, phonograph records and logs for a fire. The house is unheated and evidently there is no way to turn on the furnace. Neither of us had any idea how to make a fire (although I had certain intuitions) & it took consultation of books on my part at the library and some experimentation on his part. Isn't it typical of us, he says grimly, that we figure out how to make a fire by researching the issue in a library. Some soldiers.

He would put on a record, Gershwin songs, and we would dance. He is a good dancer. When he puts his mind to something he is awkward, but when it is elsewhere he can be the picture of grace, & he whirls me round the mostly empty room—an armchair, a small sofa, the phonograph—musically & with elegance. It is very lucky for us that this lady kept a phonograph in her living room, in the first instance because we needed to move around to get warm (I use the term loosely).

Then would come a second period of an hour or even longer that I cannot detail. At the end of it, I am utterly drained, hopelessly cold, deathly sore from an hour spent on my back on a small faded rug before the fire or more often once he cooked this up on my knees & I was not allowed to kneel on the rug; then he would stagger off & do what he needed to do, there was never any act of consummation, & as for me it is impossible to convey the empty grim cold desperation. I was engaged & my part was to yield but he did not press nor even *suggest* it & I did not nor *do* not understand unless the question was, if I got pregnant & we married & he went off to war . . .? And? Well, he would go off & I would crawl over to the fireplace & crowd the fire as I got back into my clothes & attempted to reorganize my hair using the mother-of-pearl French compact my father had given me for my sixteenth birthday. Misery, a Yiddish muttering, *a Schande*. Then again on my knees, but now back on my haunches before the fire, hugging myself & shivering. And in my head I would hear over & over, nothing is comfortable . . . nothing is comfortable. My earliest memory. I am three & have scarlet fever & my mother & father sit at my bedside. Nothing is comfortable. He returns & the mood is completely different. Warmth & wistfulness. He mocks himself for his ferocity. As a soldier I would do OK, he says, if I were put up against an army of unarmed girls. But not too many.

We would not have survived without the late Beethoven quartets. At the end of the afternoon we would eat something & then he would lie with his head in my lap & we would listen to the Budapest Quartet. Particularly to the C-sharp minor quartet, & of that especially the first & last movements, the first—incomprehensible loneliness; the last—a shriek; a soldier in black, Mark says, in a driving blizzard, who reaches his destination & freezes to death at the same moment. (Thinking of Erlkönig?) Sometimes we follow the score. The measures starting 76 before the end, the fortissimo crux, the shriek, when we first opened the score & saw what we had been hearing, its utter stark simplicity—it reduced us both to tears. The fire smokes & trembles, my toes are numb as I lean over him & stroke his hair, & lean lower, & his hair tickles my neck—the music stops cold, the needle goes scuttering madly round the inner grooves & then lifts off & we hear the fire licking & steaming & then plonk, the next disk drops in the changer & the flow resumes. He rolls his head back to look at me upside down. I can't read his expression, but the eyes are deep and blank & the same worry spins round and round on their surfaces as if the phonograph were reflected there.

And then, although I would always offer to take the

train home, he would always drive me home to the city and then drive back to New Haven.

Into the cold cave of his automobile, the 1939 Ford he got for a great price when it was barely a year old because his roommate's father had just passed a gorgeous little Cord on to the roommate—and acquired for himself Lord knows what extraordinary vehicle—well, we love the Ford; it is identical but for color to the Fords revolving atop that mountain in the Ford building on the day we first toured the Fair together—the day that will guide & go before us till we emerge on the far side of this war. On that we are agreed. It would be such a comfort if the Fair still stood. Just to drive past & crane our necks & see the wild colorful buildings set down like oversize parrots, & see where all the flags were & all the flowers & all the beautiful fountains & where Mark asked me to marry him & where at last I said yes I would; to hear again, as I hear constantly in my mind, the weird and lovely music of the Perisphere that filled the grounds after dark . . . Invariably he is about to start the engine but cannot bring himself to do it; & each time we spend another five minutes holding each other in the cold cave. The smell of the rubbery insides & of our woolen coats, the wind that drives a few dead leaves & the gentle rock-and-groaning of the car as we shift inside—finally he starts the engine & we are off.

I ask him to design a house for us. I thought it was the only sort of thing that might absorb him a little.

The house is strange. It is a collection of boxes with pitched roofs clustered around an elevated central courtyard. All the boxes of different sizes and distinct—no two blending into a single larger one. Some touching cheek-to-cheek and some separated. They have deep-set windows and each is a slightly different color stucco, colors that occur naturally in slate—mainly blues and grays and one gray-red. Outdoor staircases emerging from between the boxes descend to the ground. A succession of outdoor squares and plazas as rich and elaborate as the rooms inside. You might take it for a sort of castle or tiny European village, except for the cleanliness and simplicity of each element. It is an improbable & beautiful & romantic house, unlike any other, & only he could have designed it.

In mid-February he received the inevitable letter, Official Business, If Undelivered within Five Days Return to . . . ; he was to report to a certain place in Penn Station ten days later. "I almost laughed when I finally saw it," he said. He made his preparations. He hadn't much space for personal effects. He packed a few books. Rather I did, I was packing for him. Among them a tiny Bible and smaller prayer book, both in Hebrew and given him by his father at his *bar mitzvah*. The Bible with a worn leather binding, gold title and marbeled green endpapers, I believe it had belonged to his grandfather. A lovely thing in its way. I asked him did he believe in God. Of course I would not for the world have quarreled with or upset him. But it was a simple question I had never asked & I truly wanted to know, did he believe in God; he said—No I don't believe in God. I believe in my parents. If I should ever God willing (what he said) have children, I expect I'll believe in them also. That's Jewish faith. You see—and he brought the fingers of his right hand together and paused, as if he were about to add an explanation. But for some reason I don't recall, he didn't. I wish he had. He left my parents' house on a late afternoon soon after & I went to the window to watch him emerge from the lobby four floors below. In New Haven it is so cold and in New

York every building is so steaming over-hot. It was getting dark & snowing gently: sifting. Delicate. Weightless. I see him push out the door & walk away with hands in his pockets. It used to be, he would walk fast & his eyes straight ahead—I watch him now go slowly with head bent, stooped against the cold, the overcoat narrow like a boy's. His elbows jutting out behind. I burst into tears.

The last afternoon. My parents were having a dinner for him but the plan was, he would arrive in mid-afternoon. He was saying good-bye to friends. He did not arrive at 3:00 when he was expected, nor at 3:30 nor 4:00 nor 4:30. I wait in my father's study, in the cracked leather armchair—I rise to stand at the window & fiddle with the fins of the Venetian blinds. I take the cord and send them clattering open & stare out at West End Avenue. It is insane of me to think as I *do* that these hours will bother me forever—the faces of those homely buildings that I know so well sinking into their complex purple shadows; I pick up the *Tractatus* & put it down & pick it up et cetera, the notebook with my commentary has flopped off the coffee table ages ago & slumps face-down & forgotten on the floor. The sky is lavender to the south, the round headlights coming uptown are yellow & questioning & I rest my forehead on the cool of the windowpane.

He arrives just in time for dinner, is not grim & resolved but seems detached, & when he smiles it is almost in a daze. I draw him aside. Were you with Sarah Abbot? It was only because I was beside myself that I asked him. Do I make myself clear? Beside myself. He says "among other people, yes," & gives me a kiss. *And did you.* I did nothing he says, takes my hand & leads me back to the dining room. I rode with him & his parents in the taxi to Penn Station. The huge echoing cold room & the nerves that hurt actively in the pit of my stomach: the whole place, it very distinctly feels like, is full of farewell tears. He hugs me. He hugs his mother & father together, one in each arm. I feel grimly unworthy as I realize that, in my own mind, I am contrasting my debonair father to the silent inarticulate limping man who hugs Mark & speaks finally in abrupt heavily-accented admonitions. You'll write, no? You won't be stupid and forget about your health. No high-minded sentiments. Then Mark hugs me again & whispers, it is like a *shouted* whisper because it is so clattering-echoey noisy in here, "Remember how much someone loves you"—& then with a smile almost like his old smile, he must have worked very hard on it, he is off into a throng of other somber-faced men as they stream down the stairs to the waiting train. & now, Lord have mercy. I only know it in Greek. *Kyrie eleison.* Is that good enough?

22

Obsession

At times Miss Glassman's diary is obsessed with Jews, but so are the thirties in general. There are two sides to the story; we tend to be familiar only with one. The tragic history of the fair's failed Freedom Pavilion is a good introduction to the strange reality of power and fear coexisting.

Germany and China were the only two large countries not to be represented at the fair. China had a Japanese invasion on its hands (but the Japanese were delighted to attend). Germany had been invited, planned to exhibit but then withdrew, possibly—some sources reported—under pressure from a fair administration that had rethought the suitability of a Nazi pavilion.

Back in 1937 La Guardia had urged the creation at the fair of a "Chamber of Horrors" dedicated to Nazi Germany. The Germans were furious and protested to the State Department. The Nazi press noted helpfully that La Guardia was "a dirty Talmud Jew" and a "well-poisoner" and "war profiteer" to boot. As opening day approached, a coalition of German expatriates and Americans took up an idea something like La Guardia's. They proposed a "Freedom Pavilion" that would exhibit the works of Germans exiled by the Nazis and represent the "true Germany."

Grover Whalen liked the idea at first. He offered a free site and the fair's support. But when the chips were down he withdrew the offer, and the pavilion was never built. It is tempting to accuse him—and through him the fair itself—of cowardice, of valuing good cheer and business-as-usual above truth. But the real story is more complicated.

The original planners formed a committee and prevailed on Herbert Bayard Swope to serve as its temporary chairman. When James Thurber was informed, once, that he had been drinking in Swope's company, he declared himself astonished, because he had been "under the impression that Herbert Bayard Swope was a legend." Swope was just the sort of man to build support for the Freedom Pavilion. But he sabotaged it instead. He organized a meeting to which a crowd of prominent potential supporters were invited. At the podium he recognized the eighty-two-year-old Monsignor Michael J. Lavelle, rector of Saint Patrick's Cathedral in New York City. "I beg of you not to do anything that would provoke or bring us into trouble," said Monsignor Lavelle. "Some of the smallest things have caused war between nations." "A very sound caution," Swope declared. Lavelle's comments made headlines, and thereafter the effort fell apart. Many of the prominent people who had supported it hedged or backed out, including Governor Lehman, Robert Moses, Harry Frank Guggenheim and Henry Morgenthau. In the end Whalen backed out too, and that was that.

Many others were involved, but I mention Lehman, Moses, Guggenheim and Morgenthau because they were all (in an ethnic sense) Jews, and Herbert Swope was too. It is hard to accuse Whalen of cowardice when prominent New York Jews were unwilling to speak up for the effort. Nor is it the easiest thing in the world to accuse the New York Jews of cowardice. They were among the most powerful men in the country, but the American Jewish community anguished over drawing an unwilling country into war and bringing down the wrath of the citizenry. Refusing to stand up for the Freedom Pavilion was ignoble—but easy, if not to excuse, at least to understand. (In academia especially we are experts today in exactly the same sort of timorousness in the face of vastly less-powerful ignorance and evil.)

The fair mirrored the country. If the citizens weren't brave enough to stage a Freedom Pavilion, Grover Whalen wasn't either. But the fair *did* speak in its fashion of the tragedy in Europe. After the murder of Czechoslovakia, as I have mentioned, Mayor La Guardia sponsored a committee to collect funds to finish and operate the pavilion. The Ministry of Public Works in Nazi-ruled Prague ordered the process halted and the unfinished building sold, but Whalen (following the State Department's lead) declined to recognize the Nazi government, and construction went ahead. The building "symbolizes the spirit of freedom," according to an official fair publication, and "reminds the visitor of what freedom means." On opening day the still-unfinished pavilion was thronged. (The Nazi press made the best of the situation by pointing to the incomplete building as evidence of democracy's intrinsic incompetence.) Edvard Beneš, the dead country's last president, came to the pavilion to announce that "Czecho-slovakia is still alive. It will continue to live. And here is the evidence of that fact." The fair was America on display—fretfulness, heartfelt sympathies and all.

We understand well enough that anti-Semitism was rife in the thirties and that the United States was by no means free of it. Writers like Philip Roth and E. L. Doctorow have told us what the casual bully-boy anti-Semitism of the urban streets meant to children. It was no dominating concern, but it shadowed Jewish childhood with an occasional dark patch of fear. The "Radio Priest" Father Coughlin reached millions with his trashy Jew-baiting. Jews were not welcome in the Ivy League universities (although some attended anyway), or in the fancy private clubs that dominated upper-class business and social life. When Vance Packard examined American society in the late fifties, it was still true that "one of the persistent puzzles of American life is the tendency in thousands of communities to erect barriers against Jews." In the 1930s Henry Ford was an especially prominent and powerful dispenser of anti-Semitic lies (although he retracted them before the Second World War). He was intrigued by the *Protocols of the Elders of Zion,* a forgery based on a nineteenth-century novel: "Ford made the *Protocols* internationally famous," notes one authority on American Jews. In 1939 a resort called Tabor Farm in Sodus, Michigan, is proud to advertise that it has been "catering to gentiles since 1893." "Moderate rates," boasts the New Prospect Hotel somewhere out on Long Island, "restricted clientele"; "restricted clientele" meaning "no Jews." There was nothing unusual about Tabor Farm or the New Prospect Hotel. The story of Jews in 1930s America typically ends there.

Few observers have been enthusiastic about exploring the other side. Given their minuscule numbers, the prominence of 1930s American Jews is so outsized and startling it almost seems as if there must be some mistake. The actual facts of Jewish dominance never appealed much to anti-Semites, who focused mainly on alleged Jewish influence in areas such as banking and finance that actually harbored very few Jews. (When they claimed that Jews dominated Hollywood, on the other hand, they were right.) Nor has the Jewish community itself been much interested in flaunting its achievements, given its ever-present fear of anti-Semitic backlash. The fear was acute in the 1930s. In 1939 the rabbi and scholar Philip Bernstein is eager to cite *Fortune* magazine's carefully researched discovery that "Jews do not dominate the American scene." "The great mass of Jews in the United States," Bernstein adds, "are poor people whose lot it is to share the poverty and insecurity of that third of the nation who are ill fed, ill clad, and ill housed."

Jewish influence in thirties America does not excuse anti-Semitism. Nor does it explain anti-Semitism, which thrived millennia before our period. It may well have something to do with the touch of hysteria that is a special attribute of 1930s Jew hatred. In any case the facts collectively say something of profound importance about thirties America.

To start at the fair: When discussion and planning began in 1934, the effort (according to Grover Whalen) was led by three people. One of them was a Jew, Percy Straus of Macy's department store. (When I say "Jew" I mean, again, ethnic Jew. I imply exactly nothing about the religious practices of these people.) Straus of the Board of Directors supervised the Design Board, including Robert Kohn; Kohn chaired the Theme Committee, and Henry Dreyfuss designed the ultimate expression of the theme. The General Motors and the Ford buildings were designed by the firm of Albert Kahn, several smaller buildings by Ely Jacques Kahn. The fair's theme song was the work of two Jews. Billy Rose staged the most popular show at the fair, the "Aquacade" in the amusement area. Philip Guston won a prize for his mural at the WPA building. William Zorach contributed sculpture. The main auditorium in the General Electric building was named after Charles Steinmetz, who had been GE's chief consulting engineer. The RCA Pavilion was dedicated by David Sarnoff, the company's president.

Governor of New York Herbert Lehman was a Jew. "La Guardia in the city, Lehman in the State," wrote Gardner Harding in *Harper's,* are "guarantors of as good government as any American community possesses." President Roosevelt had close Jewish advisers—Henry Morgenthau, for example, and Felix Frankfurter. Jews were prominent among younger New Dealers too (witness, for instance, Benjamin Cohen); Bernard Baruch and Justice Louis Brandeis were respected political eminences; Walter Lippmann was the era's leading political commentator and "probably the most admired American journalist of the twentieth century."

The centrality of Jews in classical music, medicine and science is too well-known to need elaborating. Jewish composers and performers dominated not only serious but popular music: the Gershwins, Irving Berlin, Jerome Kern, Al Jolson, Artie Shaw, Eddie Duchin; Benny Goodman, "King of Swing." (The Goodman Trio, by the way, was "probably the first Negro and white combination to fill important ballrooms." Blacks and Jews were allies, and blacks fascinated Jews: thus Gershwin's *Porgy and Bess,* Kern and Hammerstein's *Show Boat.*) Aaron Copland composed Hollywood scores as well as serious ones. Prominent Jews on screen in the thirties included Edward G. Robinson, Paulette Goddard, Paul Muni, Peter Lorre, of course the Marx brothers; Douglas Fairbanks Sr. was said to be half Jewish. But actors were the least of it. Jews ran almost all the big Hollywood studios—Lasky and Zukor's Paramount, Laemmle's Universal, Fox's Twentieth Century, Mayer's MGM, Cohn's Columbia, the Warner brothers' (well . . .) Warner Brothers. Goldwyn and Selznick were leading producers. Pandro Berman produced the Rogers-and-Astaire movies. Irving Thalberg, who died in 1936, was the *Wunderkind* production manager at MGM who served as model for Fitzgerald's hero in *The Last Tycoon.*

I have mentioned Walter Lippmann, but there is far more to the story of Jews in the press. The Sulzbergers' *New York Times* was the most respected paper in the country. A. J. Liebling, Walter Winchell, Ben Hecht and Rube Goldberg were Jews. So was Herbert Bayard Swope, as I have mentioned; among his other distinctions, he invented the terms "op-ed" and "Cold War" and, in 1932, picked the phrase "New Deal" out of an FDR speech and made it famous.

In photography and on the art scene, Alfred Stieglitz was influential. Lincoln Kirstein helped to create the modern American dance world. Samuel Gompers, Sidney Hillman and David Dubinsky were important labor leaders. Raphael Soyer and Ben Shahn were respected painters, Bernard Berenson, Erwin Panofsky and Meyer Schapiro (Schapiro just starting out) important art critics. Sarnoff founded NBC in 1926. William Paley created CBS in 1928. Harry Houdini died in 1926 but he was remembered in the thirties by the millions who had watched him perform. Sports were a Jewish nonspecialty, but the Tigers' slugging Hank Greenberg thrilled Jewish boys across the country.

Nothing better captures Jewish prominence in the thirties than the fact that in this era, a leading bullfighter might be Jewish and come from Brooklyn. Hemingway writes in *Death in the Afternoon* about his friend Sidney Franklin. He was, in his day, "brave with a cold, serene and intelligent valor but instead of being awkward and ignorant he is one of the most skillful, graceful and slow manipulators of the cape"; his style "puzzled and amazed Spaniards" at his debut, and they carried him cheering from the ring.

I could go on, but the point is made. It transcends Jews. Ours is the age of the victim—and Jews are, alas, history's favorite victims.

Ours is the age of American guilt (by courtesy, at least in part, of Jewish thinkers). We dwell on our cruel treatment of blacks and Indians. There is justice in doing so. But when we ignore the other side of the story we spurn the truth. We tend not to teach our schoolchildren a fact that every one of them, Jew and gentile, ought to know—that America's willingness to stand aside and let Jews go wild in the 1930s, to attend and even politely to applaud that dazzling fireworks display of pent-up genius, is an extraordinary achievement in the history of toleration. We are fools not to credit this country with an awe-inspiring feat—a feat that few nations in all history could even have contemplated, much less carried off. In the decade of Hitler's ranting, journalist and reform politician Nathan Straus turned down the importunings of New York's leading good-government citizens that he run for mayor of the country's first city because, he felt, there were already enough powerful Jews calling the shots in the United States.

There is a secondary point also. American Jewry today is quietly, peacefully dissolving before our eyes, like a delirium into dead dreamless sleep. More than half of American Jews marry Christians, fewer than half support a synagogue; to all appearances the jig is up. Before it is quite gone American Jewry might pause to honor and remember the explosive rolling boil of Jewish achievement in 1930s America. If it doesn't, who will?

23

At Last

"In the Government Zone, Mark wants to see France," the diary continues.

Actually his first choice was Jewish Palestine, but the building isn't open yet [It offered one of the Fair's less prepossessing exhibits when it finally did, but it was crowded anyway. Graphics and dioramas illustrated the rise of a modern nation out of sand dunes. "Café Tel Aviv," the Fair's only kosher restaurant, offered "Palestinian specials."]

From the Plaza of Light we walk up the Avenue of Labor towards Lincoln Square, the terminus of Rainbow Avenue and the Ave of Pioneers. First we pass Con Ed on our left & Steel to our right; then, the blue triangle of Petroleum to our left & Du Pont to our right; & then Swift to our left, which is a very odd-shaped building—like a gleaming abstract metal hot-dog. Inside they show pork-curing, or ham-curing or whatever they call it. *"Chazerei* Heaven," Mark announces. Straight ahead of us in the middle of Lincoln Square (Lincoln Square, perhaps I haven't mentioned, is a circle) is Schaeffer Center, & over to the right is Eastman Kodak.

Schaeffer is a big round building with a restaurant in it, evidently specializing in dishes made with beer. I draw an utter blank. *Beer?* "Cream of Beer Soup?" Mark suggests. "Jiffy Beer Mold a lá King on buttered toast? Turkey, beer & tomato on rye?" We head off down the arc of Rainbow Avenue towards my favorite spot, the Four Freedoms bridge where you get the best view down the mall. We pass Belgium to our right (surprisingly big building, considering that it is a pretty small country—"maybe there's a life-sized map inside!" says Mark); then, just to the other side of the Four Freedoms, France overlooks the Lagoon.

You enter on the Lagoon side, up a curving flight of stairs into a glass-fronted hall. We browse. There are shops near the entrance selling souvenirs & stamps; model rooms done up with antique furniture in various French provincial styles. Alsatian, etc. Evidently the most uncomfortable chairs in the world come from Alsace—but that's just a guess; they don't let you actually sit in them. A big model plane & a French Pullman Car, & elegant free-standing escalators to carry you to the mezzanine, where there are jewels, perfumes, silverware, lovely silks; beautiful Limoges and Sèvres china. I can't help becoming somewhat entranced.

"They ought to call this exhibit," Mark says, *"things you might as well forget about ever having, just in case you should be dumb enough to marry an architect."* Somewhat downheartedly. The fact is, he has a magnificent & perfectly unique sense of style, & by far & away the most unerring taste of anyone I have ever met—when he disagrees with me about my clothes, he turns out (upon reflection) to be right precisely one hundred percent of the time (although of course, I never intend to tell him so). He'd love to be able to buy me elegant French things. And I guess, although I haven't thought about it too much one way or the other, that we are not likely to have much money. At least, not in the beginning. Or maybe ever. So I give him a little hug, which is what I was supposed to do all along.

It is quiet & pleasant & not too crowded. The ambiance is like a super-deluxe department store where there is nothing for sale. Eventually we sit down in the plush seats of the elegant oval movie theater & watch a long series of travel pictures—mountaineers & farmers & fishermen, cathedrals & chateaux. When you are very tired & a little uncertain about life, a movie show like this is entrancing & hypnotic, & we sit for a long time.

Finally pick ourselves up & walk off to the other foreign pavilion Mark is determined to see, Soviet Russia. To the far side of the Lagoon, diagonally across from France. A stream flows out of the Lagoon & Russia fronts on the stream.

It is a U-shaped building faced in marble, with Big Joe Tower at the U's center. On the two halves of the facade are a Stalin profile (left) & Lenin (right) looking at each other, presumably in considerable satisfaction, given that theirs is pretty much the fanciest building on the grounds. To get inside you walk up into the U's courtyard. Just past the front door is a huge mosaic map of Russia. Then, there is an odd sort of gigantic *trompe l'oeil* painting of a staircase, merging into a real staircase. In the painting, eminent Soviets descend the steps. And there is a life-size reproduction of a section of a Moscow subway station, which looks like a palace & doesn't remotely resemble any real subway station I have ever been in. I wonder if they are serious.

("Having [unlike other nations] nothing to sell," *Time* magazine reports, "the U.S.S.R. concentrates on its social and industrial progress." One of my sources vividly remembers a beautiful and unsmiling Soviet lady in a red blouse, earnestly explaining everything.)

We weren't as attentive as we should have been in there. After perhaps three-quarters of an hour of mainly silent shuffling around, we go outside, stroll down to the green stream bank right in front of the building & sit down. Peaceful water before us, the T&P in the distance.

Mark lies flat on the gentle slope, cradling head in arms. I sit beside him. I'm very tired; my body is glowing & seems not a part of me—I contemplate it peacefully from a distance as my thinking spreads out wider & wider & slower & slower, until the child who is shouting a dozen feet away beside the water seems to be located inside my head. The lagoon is so big it is the rippling blue of a lake, not clear like a pool. There are groups of fountains in the center, some jetting straight up & others making coronets—circles of fountains each shooting outward at an angle: a dense cylinder of spray rises in the center & then gracefully broadens & arches over and comes to ground in a delicate broad mist. A lagoon one-tenth the size would have been impressive. But everything at this Fair is heartfelt. To have put up a thing like this for the few months of a Fair! It is so heartfelt.

(The Lagoon was four hundred feet by eight hundred. "Who cares what they do?" said Robert Kohn *a propos* the fair's artists and architects. "We're going to throw it all away in a couple of years, anyway. There never was such a chance. Let them experiment.")

The crowd's chatter to our rear & gentle lap of water & cool breeze . . . We sit quietly a long time. It must have been almost half an hour of near-silence before Mark says suddenly, "I feel like I want to hug the Perisphere." I don't pay much attention, but he continues—

"I think I do understand what you mean about children. Ordinarily you just have them. But these aren't ordinary times. Now *I* said, because the times aren't ordinary, we need to wait; the only prudent thing is to wait. But you said—or rather you didn't say, you *thought*—no, because these aren't ordinary times, that is exactly the reason to *have* children. Because we have the privilege of making the having of them *significant* & no mere ordinary, everyday inevitability. We have the privilege of making the having of children an act of courage & confidence & trust in the future, & so you're saying, in effect—having children at *this* time, at this & no other, is like going to the top of the Trylon and balancing delicately on the tip & shouting at the top of our lungs *the future, YES!*"

(Carl Sandburg's *The People, Yes* was popular at the time.)

"Is that why you said I was a coward if I didn't do it?"

I stroke his hair—"Must I be honest? I don't know, actually. But I like your way of putting it." " 'Her voice was ever soft, gentle & low,' " he repeats, " 'an excellent thing in woman.' " I have a feeling that now he has made this connection, I am apt to hear it twice a day forever.

He continues: "So I say, you're right. Let's have children. The future, *yes*." He leans back & looks into my face upside down & clenches a fist &, with a smile, decisively punches the air. "Now will you marry me?" I lean over & kiss him. "Shall I take that as a yes?" I kiss him again. "What does this impulse mean," he says, *"I feel like hugging the Perisphere."* He sits up, gathers his legs before him, plucks a blade of grass & absently chews it. "Here's what. No actually it means two things. That I am the ship & you're the sea so I *have* to marry you, not because you make me happy, though you do, but merely because I'm a useless design without you." I lean my head on his shoulder. "But then also, the deep philosophical truth it all comes down to—it seems to me; you want me to tell you, or should I not get into deep, ultimate causes?" Go ahead I say—"I must marry you. I must. On the deepest philosophical plane I must. Whatever the spiritual cost, whatever the lasting philosophical consequences I must, because *damn,* I can't *wait* to get you into bed!" Pins me briefly to the grass & kisses me & lets me up—"even if I have to have kids!" "You lug," I say as he springs to his feet & extends his hand. "Future Mrs. Handler . . . ?"

I take it & stand, & we set off for the Amusement Area. I called it the Amusement *Zone* but Mark corrects me. "It's not a Zone. It is a mere *area,* because it has no focal exhibit. Understand? You see, that's why a girl needs a husband, to explain things to her"—& I give him a stiff elbow in the ribs & we walk off, only to run into a clutch of people, evidently two groups exclaiming over having run into each other. Mark says (*actually* says) in a low fog-hornish voice "Make way! Make way! Newly engaged couple coming through!" And they look at us with surprised smiles & they *do* make way &

several applaud. So I have to bury my face in my hands. But it is hard not to smile. A moment later there is a little girl running after us, shouting *Miss! Miss!* momentously—I turn & her mother is striding behind the child, smiling the *epitome* of a sweet apple-cheeked smile. "I thought perhaps I might mention," she says, "that another couple became engaged at the Fair today also. Outside the Futurama, right after the ride was finished. We overheard, quite accidentally! Quite." Unsure how she is supposed to finish up. She looks embarrassed. "I thought perhaps you might be interested." "Thank you very much for telling us," I say, "It was sweet of you, I appreciate it." Mark takes her hand in both his & smiles at her in a way that she will always remember. The little girl is staring up at us as if we were creatures from the moon—as if being engaged were the strangest, most palpably remarkable of states . . . as I suppose it is.

I tell Mark how I have worried all day since Borden's about running into that German in his black jacket. Now I can look forward to encountering the other engaged couple instead. I realize it doesn't make sense, but for some reason it is a load off my mind. He understands, as I knew he would. "A good omen," he says. And we walk off hand-in-hand, just as engaged couples are supposed to.

24

Parachute Jump

"The way to the Amusement Area leads through the Court of States," the diary continues.

We are now heading roughly parallel to the Parkway, but at quite a distance from it. We walk towards the towering Parachute Jump, through an underpass beneath a road called World's Fair Boulevard that leads away from the Parkway at right angles—& we are in the Amusement Area. We head towards the Billy Rose Aquacade, which takes us back again in the general direction of the T&P, but on the Amusement Area side of the Boulevard.

("Instead of a two-way midway," writes the fair's research director, the Amusement Area is based on "a great loop, two miles in length. Within the loop there will be found open-air rides, spectacles, and spectator-participation sports—all spaced by trees, shrubs and flowers to produce a park-like effect.")

> Mark had gotten the idea that the Aquacade show went on at 5:30, but it turns out it's not until 8:30 & we want to see the fireworks at 9:00, so we skip it. We had planned on seeing the show mainly just to sit and relax. So instead we'll have dinner, stroll around the Amusements and return to the main grounds.

Billy Rose's Aquacade was the hit of the Amusement Area. It was housed in an amphitheater constructed by New York State on the near shore of Fountain Lake, at the other side of the pedestrian bridge leading from the Plaza of Light to the Amusement Area. The ten-thousand seat theater was leased to Rose for the run of the fair.

You bought a ticket for forty cents (the best seats cost a dollar, and the program was fifteen cents), filed into the amphitheater and faced a stage at the far side of an arc-shaped tank of water in swimming-pool turquoise. Screening the stage from the tank was one of the show's best-known features, the 260-foot-long, 40-foot-high "water curtain"—a line of fountains, spectacularly lit up at evening performances. At the start of the show the fountains were turned off, the water wall dropped and you could see the stage.

The Aquacade was a variety show starring Eleanor Holm and Johnny Weissmuller. Holm was an Olympic backstroke champion and the future Mrs. Billy Rose. Weissmuller was an Olympic free-style champion and played Tarzan in the movies. There were singers, dancers and comedians, too, and a large supporting cast of "aquabelles" and "aquabeaux." ("JOHNNY WEISSMULLER, ELEANOR HOLM, MORTON DOWNEY," the ad said, "plus 500 GIRLS.") There were three episodes set at beaches in Florida, Coney Island and the Lido, and a finale centering on a parade of American flags. The episodes featured precision swimming: neat ranks of bobbing white swimming caps—girls in lines, girls in formed ranks, girls in circles and starbursts. "Miss Holm and Mr. Weissmuller are beautiful swimmers," Brooks Atkinson reported in the *Times,* "taking to the water without much fuss and cutting through it with the greatest of ease." There were high towers on each side of the pool so that diving stunts could be incorporated in the show, and even some dry-land comedy sketches thrown in as a bonus. "Good summer entertainment in any man's town," was Atkinson's verdict. In 1940 Buster Crabbe replaced Weissmuller (whose 400-meter free-style record he had broken in 1932), but Holm stayed. After the fair closed, *The New Yorker* pondered what it would remember best; "perhaps the goose flesh on a pretty swimmer's thigh." The Aquacade made five million dollars. Evidently you had to be there.

"We stroll from the Aquacade theater," the diary resumes, "past the big music hall." (The Music Hall was intended for serious concerts—"the most distinguished entertainment on the Fair grounds. Symphonic concerts, dances, drama . . ." On opening night La Guardia took the podium to conduct a specially composed fanfare by one Arcady Dubinsky, and "The Star-Spangled Banner." Reports claimed that he was an "energetic and professional" conductor who "even succeeded in making that standard and sugary orchestration of 'The Star Spangled Banner' acquire force." During the 1939 season the great black dancer Bill "Bojangles" Robinson starred with an all-black cast in the *Hot Mikado* at the Music Hall; during 1940 Abbott and Costello and Gypsy Rose Lee appeared in the *Streets of Paris.* One of my sources remembers seeing Robinson at the fair; thinks of him still as the most elegant and graceful dancer he has ever seen.)

"Then we turn right," the diary continues,

> & stroll down a path that, at the far end, loops round the Parachute Jump, then heads back along the shore of the lake. We pass girlie shows ("Living Magazine Covers"), freak shows ("Nature's Mistakes"), rides ("Silver Streak"—you ride a car round the outside of a spinning disk) & so forth, nothing to write home about. I'm hungry. Frank Buck's Jungle Land. Hungry. *Amazon Warriors!* I don't know what's inside but I can guess. ["The proper classical setting," according to the 1939 *Guide*, "for these young athletic women whose sole purpose is to display the harmony and beauty of the perfect feminine physique."]
>
> Across from the Warriors is a restaurant, & so we have dinner at Caruso's—which is famous (well, you know, *sort* of famous) for its big plate-glass windows giving out on the kitchen. [Caruso's ran a chain of six restaurants in mid- and downtown Manhattan.] Only, who wants to watch sweating chefs boil vats of water for spaghetti and put chickens into ovens? Furthermore neither of us much likes either chicken or spaghetti, and it is a large room & noisy & crowded. We both order a chicken-and-vegetables dish that arrives with a ton of tomato paste on top, but tastes OK.
>
> As soon as we sit down, Mark starts badgering me about going up on the Parachute Jump. But of course he is just like the Fair: he doesn't do anything in the ordinary way. "I'm afraid this will set a pattern for our whole marriage," he announces gravely, "me *nudnicking* you to do things that are against your better judgment—you've got to put your foot

down, I'm telling you, baby—I can call you 'baby' now that we're engaged, right?—I mean, of course I would really *like* to go on the Parachute Jump. I sort of think you'd enjoy it too. As a matter of fact I'm *sure* you would. But that doesn't change the fact that we darn well *shouldn't* enjoy it, &"—so on. "I don't want to go," I tell him. Rhetorically ingenious as ever. "It's too high."

We set off to do some Amusements. Sun Valley is farther down the path we've been strolling. A block-long group of Swiss-style buildings glued together—you can't look between them into Sun Valley itself; you enter under an arch. It costs a quarter. We go in. There's a small round pool in the center covered with real ice (they have all sorts of special plumbing in here). Far off to the left is a waterfall, & to the right is a ski slope with real snow on it. There are heaps of real snow everywhere—it's surprising & funny, & the artificial Swiss buildings (they house shops & restaurants) that surround the "valley" on every side are carefully, elaborately constructed & quite charming. It's hard to resist the impression that Switzerland is pretty much the cutest country on earth. Will you take me to Switzerland? I ask Mark. He says "but of course," exactly as he ought! There is a show going on as we walk in: girls in short skirts on the little ice-rink. We watch for a while & then stroll. Soon after we come upon a band & couples dancing. Mark looks at me hopefully. We dance. In the middle of a bouncy bright passage during the first number we hear *yodelling* in a definitely different key. The musicians don't bat an eyelash. Evidently they are used to yodelling. The yodellers stand around on an artificial mountain and let me tell you, *yodelling really carries.*

After dancing for longer than I had thought we would, we get dessert at one of the food shops. Dark chocolate cake. Very good. "So, you'll bake me cake like this?" Mark asks. I smile. "The young lady who can conduct an entire conversation in nuanced smiles" he says, & I smile again.

After a few more amusements we arrive at the inevitable Parachute Jump, on which I have of course consented to accompany him. It's all the way at the far end of the Amusement Area; only the Cavalcade of Centaurs is farther from the main fairgrounds. The Cavalcade is a fancy horse-riding exhibition staged by someone from the Ringling-Brothers-Barnum-etc. Circus. I don't suppose there is anything I hate worse than circuses, except for Parachute Jumps.

I honestly think *anybody* would find the sight of this machine alarming. The shaft is red & it seems like a million wires are hanging from the white crown. Looking at the top gives me the unpleasant sensation of being underwater and peering upward at a boat dangling fishing lines that are trying to snag me. There is a big Lifesaver in front—Lifesaver candies is staging this operation. I will make a point of remembering that the next time I go into a candy store. Each parachute runs on its own schedule. They all bob up & down independently like yo-yo's, & if I didn't have to ride on one it would actually be funny. Each parachute has its own special fenced-off cove round the base of the thing. There is an office in the base, but ordinary people don't go in. It costs forty cents (more than we spent on anything else except admission), & there is a long line at that. Unbelievable.

Here is what happens, the awful truth. When it comes your turn, you are directed to one of the coves. We get the one immediately to the left of the entrance. There are two seats beneath each parachute—the parachutes remain puffed out all the time, going up & coming down. Attendants in white, looking exactly like the rescue workers who ride in ambulances, and smirking, strap you tightly into the seats. Mark looks at me in a way that is supposed to be comforting, but I can't help but think that there is just a touch of nervousness at the lower-left corner of *his* smile, and that makes me smile—*but not for long* because, with a slight jolt, we are rising. They pull you up on cables; it's very much as if you are riding upward in an elevator, but the cab is eliminated & you are connected directly to the lift-cables & *there is no building around you.* It rises 250 feet. Which is to say *it is high,* & although it occurs to you somewhere deep inside your mind (in an inner office somewhere) that there is probably a great view of the Fair from up here & you ought to be taking it in, *you don't take anything in whatsoever* except as the vaguest sort of blur, because your body consists exclusively of a stomach & a pounding heart. When you are at the top you pause for the barest instant & then whoosh down at enormous speed & bounce on some sort of spring at the bottom. Cables guide you as you descend so you go straight down with no swaying, as if you were a fireman sliding down a pole. Actually it is a lot worse going up than coming down, because it takes longer & the anxiety is more acute.

The Parachute Jump was based on a training device for aviators. The Soviets had used contraptions of the same general type since 1932. By 1939 the U.S. Army was using a parachute jump more or less like the one at the fair as step one ("captive drop with seat") in parachute training for aviators. Step two was "captive drop with harness"; thereafter, free drops with no safety cables.

The jump was the number-two hit of the amusement area, after the Aquacade. Sun Valley was number three; then came Frank

Buck's Jungle Land and the *Hot Mikado*. During the 1939 season more than half a million visitors took the plunge. For the 1940 season the whole thing was taken apart, moved to the other side of the amusement area, where it would be closer to the main grounds, and reassembled with an added parachute.

"As we climb out," the diary continues,

> Mark (consulting his watch) announces "That took less than a minute." [Forty-two seconds to reach the top, ten seconds for the descent.] "Maybe we should go again?" But he's smiling. "I suppose I should chalk that up as my first wifely duty?" I say after I have collected myself. "In fact," he says, "I'm awarding you a battle ribbon. You're going to be the most decorated wife in Manhattan!" "So long as I don't have to go on any more parachute jumps." "Never!" We stroll back toward the main grounds to see the lights & the fireworks & go home.

When the fair closed, the Parachute Jump was carted off to Coney Island. It hasn't operated for many years, but you can still see it there today, strange shape against the pale blue ocean sky as you drive past on Robert Moses' Belt Parkway.

25

Late Afternoon

█ face Mrs. Levine again across the table before the window. It is late afternoon, and she looks worn and pale. I hesitate before asking her to continue the story, though she invited me for that purpose. I ask if she feels like it. She nods but then remains silent for several minutes. It is a clear, cool late-summer day, but the whole room has an edge of weariness. I ask if she is feeling well. "Thank you, no" she says. But insists that she is willing to talk, and eventually begins.

"They sent Mark first to a camp in Texas. Then they were all shipped out again to a place in upstate New York on Lake Champlain, to a camp specially designed for training engineers. He went through complex training of all sorts, infantry as well as engineering—training on machine guns and rocket launchers and flamethrowers. Some of the exercises they undertook were simply impossible for me to comprehend. I didn't see how people could do it, just could not picture it, couldn't fathom how Mark could do it; but he did. On a freezing black night with three feet of snow on the ground they hacked out a roadway through a forest to a ravine, and built a bridge over the ravine, and then disassembled the bridge and neatly stacked all the pieces on the bank and drove back to the barracks. They did that more than once.

"In an engineering regiment there was such a thing as a platoon of about fifty men, made up of three squads, I think they called them. A platoon was led by a staff sergeant and a lieutenant. To his unending amazement Mark was chosen for training as a lieutenant, because of all the engineering he knew. It just shows how desperate we are, he wrote. Many of the men arrived with some kind of crafts training, and some were very knowledgeable, Mark said, far more than he. But he sold himself short. Not only had he learned a great deal in several years of intense study, but there was a lot riding on a person's ability to sit down with a complex manual and read it through and grasp the point, and sheer intelligence was very useful there, and Mark had that. So, after extensive training in upstate New York, basic and advanced, they sent him off to a place in Maryland for officer training. When he was done with that, there was an interlude that is a sort of bizarre dream. It doesn't fit. But they gave him a two-week break, it was midsummer, and he came home in his lieutenant uniform, and I can tell you we were very proud of him. He refused to be proud of himself. Refused, period. 'If I'm a lieutenant,' he said, 'can you imagine what passes for a private?' But, well—we were very proud.

"He presented me with all sorts of elaborate lists. Henceforth he was only going to write to me and to his mother. He always hated to write. But there was a list of friends to whom I was supposed to write in turn, to pass on news. He wanted his friends kept informed. And then there was a list of people I was supposed to write *him* about. I was supposed to call Charlotte once a week and write him about Benny, call Marty, and so on; I was supposed to call his parents—I think—once a week, and visit them once every three weeks or if possible every two weeks, or something like that. Everything specified exactly. I was to follow three architecture magazines and clip every item about topics on another list, and mail certain ones and file certain others. And so on. I can't *begin* to tell you how totally uncharacteristic it was, all that neatness and organization. Not Mark's style, in the very least. But he told me he'd wake up sometimes at two or three A.M. and lie awake, and to pass the time, he'd composed and refined all these lists. And then this strange two-week dream was over and he returned upstate.

"He spent a long time at various camps in the States, undergoing more training and teaching new people. Then in late spring 1943, he was shipped overseas to North Africa. Rommel and the Nazis and Italians had only recently been cleared out. You know," she says suddenly and turns abruptly to the window, "this story is almost over."

Silence.

"His—I'm not even sure any more what sort of grouping it was, but his platoon was included; they were part of the Allied invasion of Sicily that began in July 1943. Part of Patton's Seventh Army. In the drive from Palermo to Messina he was badly wounded. He was shot in the stomach. He'd been engaged in no specially heroic activity, he said, but he had been advancing with his men under fire. Can such a thing possibly *not* be heroic? It gave him very great satisfaction that he had been carrying out, without shrinking or failing—though 'with no special distinction'—what was required of him. But I've always thought, he could easily have been acting with special distinction. He was in a field hospital in Sicily for a week; then he was taken on a hospital ship to Bizerte, in Tunisia. Although by that point Sicily was mostly Allied territory, and I guess most of the wounded were cared for there. Bizerte was actually in British hands, I think.

"So. All the status and connections at my father's disposal finally had a reason for being. *Connections.* Well. All through the war—; I hate the word. I hate the *sound* of the word. But if one didn't, it seems to me, or it seemed then, there is a certain—is it ethics or vanity, ultimately, that determines . . . I don't know. I just don't know. Just don't." Her tone is suddenly wistful, and her eyes so abstract it almost seems as if she is not hearing her own voice. I say something about its being natural to use all the connections at your disposal, under the circumstances. She looks at me with probing curiosity. "Yes." And looks away. "Excuse my incoherence." Another long pause. "I remember the woman from Smith College who visited when I was a high school student. She was going to admit me by fiat. Or, whatever— some arrangement. Such elegant, delicate condescension, like the neat little pink roses on the side of a hand-painted teacup. And yet she fidgeted constantly, kept smoothing her skirt and adjusting her hat—and my father said afterwards, *you* made *her* nervous! He thought that was marvelous. All I'd done was just look at her."

At length she continues. "Well they admitted me all right, but I was proud to go to Hunter. Which was fine with my father. He didn't want to neglect his duty, is all. He was always conservative about his connections." An incongruous note of pleading. "All his marvelous connections. He was no artist in that medium. But. I've never blamed him for it. Never. He did exactly what was right. Exactly. Well . . ."

And sighs.

"Through the intercession of Governor Lehman—that's what we believed, anyway—I was allowed to travel as a nurse to Bizerte; Mark being in no shape to come home. The whole plan was based on a complicated lie—it made me sick with nerves to think about it, I mean literally sick, not that I hesitated, but I was sure I would be found out and then God knows what; of course, I was not a nurse, but I was to act like one stateside; once I was in Tunisia someone would meet me and I could stop pretending; though it was also understood that I'd make myself useful, somehow, in the hospital over there. I went to Charlotte and after her exhausting days or nights on the wards—they worked longer shifts during the war— and I was tired myself, I'd taken a job in a factory in Brooklyn that made small metal parts for military gadgets, mainly mine-detonators—she'd teach me a little bit of nursing. You see I was the practical one, not Mark. 'Practical' is a relative thing of course, but what I mean is, I was pretty decent with my hands and I enjoyed the factory. And obviously, it made me feel a bit useful. The sense of uselessness would have been crushing, otherwise. Mark, you see—he was the purest artist I ever met, or ever heard of. He was able to do mathematics but it bored him, and he actively hated machines. *Hated* machines. The fact that he was able to become an engineer—it was by dint of sheer intelligence and willpower. An amazing feat. Becoming a soldier was the same thing again, only more so.

Well, we would sit with nursing textbooks at the kitchen table in the apartment Charlotte was sharing with three other girls. It was her apartment and Benny's, but with him gone she'd invited the others in. The radio playing music in the living room. I can see her sitting there motionless with exhaustion, in a red-checked blouse with the sleeves rolled up. Her cigarette held beside her at the level of her temples. Eyes closed. Motionless. The benign domestic smell of meatloaf and jello. The girls were all very kind to me, but they avoided my eyes. They were afraid to look me in the face. I was the nightmare. The textbooks made me shudder.

"During the last week I quit my job and went with her every

day to the Israel Zion Hospital in Brooklyn where she worked, and stuck by her side and she showed me a great deal about what one had to do. She was very patient with me and it was a blessing, also, just to talk to her, because she had gone through so much in her life so cheerfully, and so steadfastly. The exhaustion itself was good for me. I could sleep nights.

"Charlotte passed away only last year. Benny and I had much to talk over at the funeral.

"It was a frightening multileg flight to Bizerte. Mostly at night, and one had to sit in the rear of the plane in complete darkness—we weren't allowed even the smallest flashlight; the motors roared and it was freezing and the plane bumped and gyrated and of course, the possibility existed of being shot down at any moment; I had never been so terrified. But when we arrived finally in Tunisia it was hot, the air smelled strange to me—like curried dust; I was in a daze of exhaustion and anticipation and fright. I was indeed met at the base by the Lieutenant Gardiner I had been told to look for, and as we set out in a jeep for the hospital—it was a long ride, and my own state was so abnormal; I think I dozed—there was an element of relief in just being on the ground in the sunshine; but at the same time I was intensely frightened.

"Mark was in poor shape. But he was able to talk to me, and he smiled when he saw me. There was a small American flag on his bedstand. I'd hoped to find a phonograph at the hospital, and there was none, but my resourceful Lieutenant Gardiner found one at a British camp and hauled it out for me. I had brought some phonograph records." She smiles. "In galvanized steel shelves. I'd asked one of the men at the factory back in Brooklyn to make them for me. I can still see him cutting the steel sheet with those heavy shears, forming the thing in a sort of bending device . . . Records we had danced to in New Haven. Gershwin. I remember particularly a song for solo piano called *Do, Do, Do*. It was a scratchy old record, of a performance by Gershwin himself, I think. I sat beside Mark, sprawled with my head close to his on the pillow, and we listened to that song many times and imagined that we were back in our '39 Ford driving down to Queens from New Haven, over the Whitestone Bridge, and that somehow or other the fair had been magically resurrected. They still have the plans after all, Mark said. They could do it, as a sort of coming-home surprise for all us homesick people. He talked softly but smiled in the old, warm way he used to; with my head beside him on the pillow, I could hear him clearly. And we imagined approaching the fair and driving up and parking there; walking round it; we reminisced in great detail. We played the song over and over.

"Inevitably he set to work designing a building. He couldn't sit up. I would hold a pad above him, and he would draw, or later on I would hold it before him and he would tell me what to do, how to change it. I couldn't draw, of course, but neither could I tell him, 'No, I can't draw.' I'd work with absolutely *fantastic* concentration to produce with decent accuracy the shapes he painstakingly described to me. I would try again and again until I had drawn what he had in mind. And the building—I thought it was very interesting."

She is remarkably consistent about the brisk, objective tone she adopts when she is commenting on his work.

"It was a parliament building for an independent Jewish Palestine, which he assumed would come about after the war. 'Just in case they never get around to asking me,' he said, 'I'd better award myself my dream commission.' The building was in the shape of a gigantic seven-branched *menorah*. It was intended for a hill overlooking Jerusalem. It was faced in stone. The vertical segments had offices and windows; they didn't line up—some were moved forward and others back from the plane—windows on the sides of the vertical segments wouldn't look right at each other; it was a sort of abstract, sculptural menorah, but plainly a menorah. The middle branch, the central tower, thickened at the top into a tall glass-walled box that held the parliament chamber—Mark had the idea that from miles around you could look up and see your parliamentarians at work. 'No place for them to hide,' he said, and smiled. On top of that was a smaller glass-walled drum that held a synagogue.

"This synagogue was formed by two circular, concentric walls of glass. Between the two walls were four staircases that led upward from the Parliament chamber to the war memorial atop the roof of the central branch—the highest spot on the building was the memorial. There was a staircase, then a gap, and a staircase and a gap; in the gaps the walls were of clear glass, but the walls that fronted the staircases were frosted, translucent, and Mark's idea was that, inside the synagogue, you would indistinctly see people passing up and down the stairs, and it would be like the angels in Jacob's dream moving up and down the ladder between earth and heaven. And then on top would be the memorial, and it would consist of a rock set in the center with water running down it, and visitors to the war memorial would be in the position of Moses looking out at the promised land, and the rock was symbolic of Moses' never having set foot there because he had struck and not spoken to the rock, to make it yield water; and you were supposed to look out at the countryside and think of the dead who had not reached the promised land. After that he started another design; for a 'folly,' he called it, set in an oval pool where he would row me in a boat; very like a playground he had once designed, a structure of grottoes with stained glass. He weakened, and it was not finished. Well. He died toward dawn on the nineteenth of September. I sat with him a long time, as one does; and it was a priest, finally, who spoke no English, who took me out of there. He put his arm around me, which I hadn't known that priests were allowed to do. Perhaps they aren't. I've always been grateful to that priest and remembered him.

"He was buried over there but flown back after the war and reburied near here on Long Island. All the families of war dead were offered reburial after the war. Many of them accepted, I think. I'd written a piece of philosophy for him that I'd brought with me, my only opus, saying what he himself had tried to say—'On the Transcendent Beauty of Building,' I called it; he liked it, and it gave him a bit of pleasure, and it was buried with him. Childish gesture, I guess that was, on my part. More than a bit histrionic. I wasn't in a normal state of mind. But I can't say I regret the gesture, really.

"And that is the end of the story? No it is not. Nothing is that simple."

26

Unfinished
Business

"**I**t was the year after the war ended," Hattie Levine continues, "when I finally sought out Sarah Abbot. It was early spring 1946. She named a small restaurant on Fifth Avenue and we met there."

I ask her if she doesn't want me to come back another time, or at least to rest for a while before continuing. She looks pale to the point of ashen. The maid has materialized twice so far with pills and a glass of juice on a tray. "Thank you, but what I'd prefer to do is go on till the end," she says.

"What a time to meet. Sadness of early spring. I'd take long walks in Central Park. The snow was gone except for a few black crusted patches, and the fields were sodden mud, of course: dead matted grass where brown leaves tumbled. Endless gritty trickle into the sewers, the dirty streets. The few sparse, windy clouds. I'd see young mothers pushing prams, at least a few, with the same face I had, and our eyes would meet. It is over—you know, when you hear the wind and the leaves and all—it's over. The emptiness of spring. There were new cars in the city; new, snazzy, voluptuous, curvy models that Mark had never seen. You see, during the war time stood still, sort of. Well. I sought out Sarah Abbot.

"I sought her out because I was convinced that she had slept with Mark that last afternoon before he left. I had the idea they'd slept together and that she might perhaps have conceived a child. I had no basis for believing that; but if Mark had a child, I couldn't very well go through life without knowing it. I *had* to know it. And, besides, I had the strangest thought: that Sarah Abbot had somehow exercised some sort of bizarre right-of-the-first night, in the feminine—Mark had slept with other women, but somehow I had the notion that she'd connived it so that he couldn't sleep with me until after he had slept with her. As I repeat it, it sounds mad.

"And so, although my intention was to be absolutely polite and correct, I had gotten myself in a rage at Sarah Abbot—well, to be honest, I had been in a perpetual rage at her for years; and I guess I approached her with the haughtiness of the self-pitying wounded who believe they have paid their debt and don't need to defer to anyone. So we faced each other coldly across the table, and she was beautiful as ever, more beautiful, and she raised her eyebrows and just looked at me.

"And I had at her in a low, controlled voice. I wasn't looking at her but my voice was seething—I was confronting her with a plain, blunt question about that last afternoon, but she interrupted me with a simple statement: '*I read about Mark's death in the newspaper.*'

"It brought me to a halt. 'Before I finally got that letter of yours,' she said, 'I had read of it *in the newspaper.*'

" 'You were to keep me informed of his whereabouts and

condition,' she said. 'You promised him that, when he went overseas, hadn't you?' Yes, I had promised him that; but I had been
grudging in carrying out the promise, and my letters had been sparse,
brief and late.

" 'When my father spoke in Washington to one of General
Marshall's aides, Mark was not where I had claimed he was, and that
was that. My father wangled a meeting with the president. Do you
know what that meant in 1943? Do you think it was easy? But the
meeting never took place. It ought never to have been scheduled.
Because even before it was scheduled, unbeknownst to me, Mark
was dead.'

" 'I don't know what this means,' I said, 'but Mark would
never have allowed *connections* to take him away from his duty as he
saw it. *Never!*'

" 'He would never have known,' she said. 'That was part of
it: Listen, you. Forget what *he thought* was his duty. He was so often
deluded about his duty. I ask you what his duty *was*. To die in Sicily,
or live, to live, as a—' but she stopped in tears. I think there was a
waiter watching us from a discrete distance." She smiles slightly.
"He seemed utterly at a loss as to when and how to approach us. I
sort of felt for him, even then.

" 'Why should I believe your father had a meeting with the
president?' I said. It was an utterly stupid thing to say, but what
could I say? And she looked fiercely right at me. 'There is very little
you do know, isn't there?'—in sudden, real surprise; with sarcasm
and bitterness.

" 'Do you know Art Tierney has been a friend of my family
our whole lives? That he and I were introduced when I was a
week old?'

"I am looking down at the table. Suddenly I see everything
coming together and can't believe my denseness at not having understood it earlier.

" 'Where do you think he conceived his sudden interest in constructing a school and hiring a visionary young architect to do it? Do you think it just flew into his head one morning while he was shaving? Are the wealthy, do you think, ordinarily prone to hire young unknowns to carry out massive projects?'

"I am looking at the table and want to say something to make her stop, but am too slow on the draw.

" 'Do you think leading art museums, for that matter, are so eager to show the unbuilt work of unknown architects? Obviously it was Mark himself who made the show succeed, but can you honestly be so naive, even *you,* as to believe that it could ever conceivably have *happened* had not *two* close friends of my family been major contributors and held seats on the board?'

"Softly, and I think in a controlled manner, I say 'I assume he knew all this?' Phrasing it that way to protect myself; believing she would say no. 'Of course he knew,' she said scornfully. 'Of course he knew, and he was grateful. There was nothing secret about it. With the tiniest bit of curiosity, you could have found out yourself. You clearly chose *not* to know. You don't even know,' she said, 'do you: You don't even know why, though Mark and I were in love, he wound up courting *you. You!* Didn't that seem *odd* to you? Did you detect nothing the slightest bit *strange* in that? Or were you so wrapped up in yourself that you noticed nothing whatsoever? Is there *anything* you understand? You don't even understand, do you, why he should have wound up courting *you* if he loved me!'

"I am looking at my hands on the table.

" 'Because his *father'*—barely above a whisper—'would not countenance his marrying a non-Jew.' Her cameo locket trembling up and down: She is panting with hate and rage, and turns away.

"And for a minute or two, finally, she shut up. And then turned back to pounce once more, because this victim had been too easy to kill and there was no satisfaction in it—not enough, anyway, for all the misery she had borne; 'Why was the wedding put off for so long? *Why did he keep putting it off?'*

"And after about two years of silence I managed to say 'Well, he loved me!' I suppose I was crying. Felt as if I were staggering about overcome with dizziness. One of those states where you are oblivious of the world, and green stars pour down around your head. 'Yes, *he took his duties seriously,'* she said. She rose. She started to leave. Started to walk out. Then turned and sat again, swept her hand coolly over her hair in back and addressed me in a judge's death-sentence voice: intense precision.

" 'I have a little theory Just a little theory of mine. Look inside the Hebrew Bible he carried with him. If you have the honesty and the nerve.' Most intense, most quiet precision, each syllable perfect. 'I have a little theory that, inside that Bible, marking the one passage that meant more to him than any other, you will find three strands of my hair. Three strands he carried with him'—dismissing the prisoner with the softest, driest, most contemptuous precision: May God have mercy on your soul—*'always.'* And she rose. And she left. I never did ask my question. And," smiling again, "the waiter never did approach.

"I have the Bible. I've never had the nerve to look in it. No. No, I mean, I *chose not* to look in it. Though I've gone sometimes for months or maybe years without thinking about it, that unopened Bible has always been the basic fact of my life, ever since.

"In years after, she wanted to pay for the erection of one of the playgrounds he had designed, as a memorial. But she insisted that she have complete control over the project, that I turn over all the drawings to her. And I thought it was unfair and not right. We quarrelled. Again and again. It never came about, no playground was ever built, and it's time I admitted, I mean to myself, that I and my crushed pride are largely to blame.

"You see, I had to conclude—Mark must have decided that

Sarah Abbot's patronage ought to be kept a secret from me. And why would he have made that decision unless he were having an affair with her? I had to conclude they'd never really broken up. Well, it's just a guess of course. I could be wrong." She is bent over the table stubbornly scratching at a flaw in the finish. The late-afternoon sun catches the gauzy upper reaches of her hair. Dust specks tumble in the sun shaft and the noise of the street penetrates as she works with her fingernail. "I had to picture him seeing her at her place in New York—I assume she had her own place; or at odd moments in New Haven; or, for all I know, the house in New Haven that was said to belong to Tierney's cousin actually belonged to Sarah Abbot's cousin or, who knows, to Sarah Abbot herself. I picture her up on one arm above him, spilling her famous raven tresses on his chest."

Frowning as she scratches at the flaw. It is an orange mahogany gate-leg table, glowing as sunlight pours down upon it; a handsome table. I had asked her about it, but she hadn't seemed interested in tables. "I was never willing to pursue my hypothesis with Sarah Abbot. The small uncertainty I still have is precious. My dearest possession. He had a dominating personality and it must have given him great satisfaction to dominate such an indomitable person. Sleek, beautiful and indomitable." It occurs to me that she might never have told these things before.

"I picture her confronting him with argument after argument about why they ought to be married despite his father. Despite everything." The silver brushings of her hair in the light as her head moves slightly up and down are part of the silence when she pauses. "Great waves battering great rocks. And I picture him rejecting each argument, but not absolutely, and so the affair goes on." I couldn't imagine that she would impart this whole thought without once looking up, and now finally she looks right at me: "And for all I know, on those terrible Sunday afternoons in New Haven he was showing me his version of the deepest, most uncompromising fidelity—of course, fidelity to her." Beautiful eyes of the twenty-one-year-old girl.

"But you have no real *grounds* for believing any of this?"

She shrugs.

"I don't believe it."

At length she continues. Her look is hardening again into the brilliance that is typical of her. You suspect there are endless depths but can't see them because of the ice-cold glare.

"There were other valid reasons why the memorial was never built. The subject of Mark pained my kind husband deeply, and Lord knows I was enough of a trial to him without pressing on with the memorial. The air at large grew steadily more different and wrong. Mark would not have erected his thirties designs in the completely different era that was coming on faster and faster—I felt like a skier plummeting out of control, faster and faster; he'd have looked round him and seen—yes, as you say, a utopia, in people's relative wealth and comfort and their fair-mindedness; but he would also have sensed instantaneously that the future is gone, like smoke. It would have mattered to him greatly, and I don't know what he would have done about it, but he would have done something. He would have spent every ounce of energy trying to get it back.

"It's all true, but ultimately it's my pride. I'm very close to regretting my life, in large part. Though how can I in the end? There are the times we spent together."

She closes her eyes and smiles the relaxed, peaceful, exhausted smile of someone who has gotten through a hard physical trial.

"Even if he were struggling with some kind of choice between two women," I say, "we know whom he chose."

"Perhaps, but—" her eyes still closed. "If he had chosen the future and not the past, he would have lived."

"But there's another perfectly consistent reading of the facts in which none of this ever happened—and he cared only for you. To the extent we believe in him, isn't that the only *possible* reading?"

" 'I call heaven and earth to witness before you this day,' " she says, " 'that I have set before thee life and death, the blessing and the curse. Therefore, choose life.' " Without opening her eyes. "For all my years, the only piece of wisdom I've acquired is that time doesn't have to move forward. The noblest achievement of the imagination is to make it run some other way, and terminate in beauty and forgiveness." Still faintly smiling with her eyebrows gathered to a quizzical point—asking herself an endless question; shaking her head slowly.

I called her twice over the next few weeks, but we talked only about the fair, never Handler. Then I visited her again, and we talked at length about Democracity and some old photographs of the fair. When I called her after that, the phone rang. It happened again for almost a week. Then an Express Mail package arrived from Houston:

Hortense passed away on September thirtieth, very nearly the day on which Mark Handler died. [In a vigorous, sprawling hand.] You know she observed his *yahrzeit* every year and said *kaddish* as if he had been her husband.

She was much the smartest person I ever knew and in some ways it pains me to say the most unhappy. She had the burden of knowing so much and not the means to express it—her Mark Handler always urged her to write and I can't think why she never did, except that the very act might have reminded her painfully of him, or very possibly it was her perpetual and to me ever-puzzling lack of self-assurance. You should know that the process of unburdening herself to you left her, it seemed to me, in her last months more content than ever I can recall her for many years. We old people do have a thing or two to say for ourselves, I imagine, but who can judge of its value in the end? I should like you to keep the diaries and any other memorabilia she may have given you, and am sending you one thing more it occurs to me you may gwant to have—if there is anything else you would like, I'm not making any promises, but please do not hesitate to ask. Yours affectionately, Frances Glassman Lasker."

Should I have asked Frances Lasker for the Bible and looked in it myself? I am content to believe that had I turned to that passage in Deuteronomy, *I call heaven and earth to witness before you this day that I have set before thee life and death, the blessing and the curse. Therefore, choose life*—that I would have found three strands of no one's hair; or of Hattie Levine's.

I slid a small unsealed envelope out of the larger one and emptied it into my palm. A white button with neat dark blue lettering. *I have seen the future.*

27

The Voice
of the
Perisphere

"The mall at night is weird and beautiful," the entry concludes.

The grounds have emptied out a good deal & it is more relaxed & serene. The fountains are white, & the trees are lit from below so it is as if the sun is shining on them upside down—their bottoms are rich green, their tops dark. Red airplane-warning signals climb the Trylon, four on each face and a single one on top. And most remarkable, the Perisphere is beautiful blue, with clouds appearing to revolve. We gaze hand-in-hand & Mark says *the blue is the light.* It is an utterance, evidently, of Viollet-le-Duc, quoted by Adams in his *Mont-Saint-Michel and Chartres,* a book Mark is very attached to though he says Adams is an anti-Semite. Viollet-le-Duc is commenting on the special significance of blue in medieval glass. Mark's love & knowledge of medieval architecture are deep, & very unusual, I think, for his generation of architect. But the most remarkable thing about the Trylon and Perisphere at night is the music—it is unearthly—tuneless but beautiful, the music of the spheres, indescribable—a ringing of bells, but the bells are somehow harplike; the whole mall is filled with the strange music.

(The Voice of the Perisphere is one of the fair's most unusual but least documented features. It filled the grounds nightly with ethereal music. One of my sources, who visited often as a teenager, comes to a dead stop in trying to describe it; then says that it was fascinating, like "space music."

The Perisphere's voice was the amplified sound of a piano wire in a wooden box. The speaker was hidden in a well beneath the sphere.)

And then we simply wander with no goal in mind, very tired—we lean against each other & stroll slowly like two drunks, or swing hands, but we are both in a daze of delight at the colors. Big Joe's star is (surprise!) red, his pedestal is lit in red & spotlights pick out the red flags on either side.

The lightning bolt outside of General Electric is a series of yellow-white zigzags. The singing tower outside Westinghouse is brilliant red but still not singing. The oranges, reds and blues are aglow in the tower outside the Du Pont building. The Petroleum building (who would have thought *Petroleum?*) is the most gorgeous on the grounds, its broad fins lit the brightest, deepest blue; the whole building *exhales* blue; it is breathtaking. *The blue is the light,* Mark says again.

When it is almost nine we walk (just as everyone else is walking) towards the Lagoon of Nations & the display there is indescribable. The oval pool seems still larger in the dark. The fountains are lit in yellow-golden white, but a few minutes before the show proper they are turned off & their waters fall as if startled back into the pool & all is still, except (of course) for the crowds gathered everywhere. And then the show begins. The waters of the pool start to glow, brighter & brighter. Then a dense mysterious mist rises from the surface. Suddenly a cloud of blue steam hisses round the edges—people are startled & step back. And then fountains rise in the center, & grow higher & higher & a dense mist rises around them, changing colors, rose & amber & blue—& then huge pillars of flame rear up enormous (the crowd gasps) on either side of the fountain. It is all happening in time with the music, which seems to be coming *from inside* the Lagoon. As the music bumps up the fountains ride higher. Searchlights make a roof like an arch of swords overhead. More fire & mist & colored steam, & then the fireworks start, reds blues & golds; they are almost noiseless. They glide up over the pool &, because of their strange quiet, seem not to explode but rather to open like flowers. At the climax, everything is turned off at once, lights, fountains, flame & music—the waters crash back into the pool with the roar of a breaker driving into a cliff, & the sudden black is immense & a little frightening & incomparably dramatic. For a few moments no-one moves. The show is amazing. And it recalls many others things at this Fair in being simply *unlike anything* you have ever seen before.

The Lagoon show drew on a thousand water nozzles, capable of throwing twenty tons of water into the air at a time. There were 400 gas jets, 350 fireworks guns, 3 million watts of light. A band performed in a studio at a distance, and the music was broadcast—in stereo, no less!—from great speakers that poked up above the Lagoon's surface. Three technicians masterminded each night's performance from inside the United States building. They sat at a console something like an organ's, facing a mass of switches and buttons that controlled the nozzles and gas jets. The "score" unscrolled before them under glass, like the roll of a player piano. It instructed them symbolically which switches to throw and buttons to push.

An electrical engineer named Bassett Jones had been hired out of retirement to design the show. He went in search of John Craig, who had staged a memorable fireworks display at Queen Victoria's jubilee. Craig was traced to a Long Island potato field, where he was allegedly in the habit of fertilizing his crops with gunpowder. He developed noiseless fireworks for the Lagoon extravaganza. Joseph Jarrus was an expert gas engineer; at an abandoned gas plant in Brooklyn, Jarrus and Jones developed gas nozzles and colored flame displays.

The critics raved. Fountain displays like the ones at the Lagoon of Nations and San Francisco's 1939 fair "deserve to be called examples of a new art," wrote Talbot Hamlin. "The best of them are as emotionally compelling as they are visually exciting." The show at the Lagoon gave the New York fair "its most unique and perhaps its most artistically memorable element." "Dramatic and indescribable beauty" wrote Gardner Harding.

On clear nights, a young boy in Queens who went often to the fair could see the highest-rising fireworks from his bedroom window.

"You think that was good?" says Mark. "The one at mid-night in the Amusement Area is supposed to be even bigger. Though not as sophisticated." "Next time," I say. We are walking down Rainbow Avenue towards Bowling Green and the Long Island Rail Road Station where we began. In Bowling Green the two lower drums of the Fountain of the Atom are lit a soft yellow-white from inside, and flame shoots from the narrow taller drum on top. Down Petticoat Lane to the station. It was mobbed in the morning and is mobbed now—many touring chairs, both hand-pushed & the kind with motors like little tractors, clustered round to pick people up in the morning & are dropping off now. The station is one of the prettiest things at the Fair, Mark says, & I agree—a horizontal column, in profile a smoothly rounded triangle, winging its way over the tracks & sending graceful staircases like tendrils down to the temporary wooden-plank platforms, like boardwalks. We don't have long to wait. I slump my head against his shoulder as we ride. The concourse of Penn Station is always exciting when one arrives. As you mount the stairs & come into the great room, it is as if you are an underwater explorer surfacing in a vast unknown king-dom—anyway *I* imagine it that way, & have since a child. It gives you energy.

"We can't go home. We have to drink a champagne toast," Mark announces & I say *what?*—I am *so* tired—but here we are walking briskly crosstown & up Fifth Avenue & we are headed to the Rainbow Grill which, Mark believes, has as good a view as the Rainbow Room but is not so formal. & yes that is *us* rising to the sixty-fifth floor of the RCA building & I cannot even record the amount of money he spent on a bottle of champagne. *Do you honestly think we can finish a bottle of champagne??* I demand, but it is not up for discussion, evidently, & when he says, *How many times does a fellow get engaged?* well I have to concede the point—not that it matters whether or not I concede it. But we *do* finish the bottle! It is so lovely up there, you can see over the top of Central Park all the way up to the Bronx, & the champagne on top of exhaustion on top of intemperate happiness makes a mood like a dream awake—I fold my hands on the table & lay my head down & close my eyes & am literally asleep—& then open them & I am awake again & Mark is smiling. In front of the RCA building on Fifth he hands me into a cab & then climbs in himself to ride me home. I make him promise to take the cab home afterward & not climb out & go to the subway. He is tired too. We pull up out front. "Thank you for saying you'll marry me," he says in his plainest, sweetest way; & I say, "any time!"

It could only have happened at this Fair—I could only have become engaged there—because? Because of its smile. Can all that magnificence be reduced to a mere *smile?* The whole wall-of-water hedge-of-fountains Fair, monkey-goddess cow-carousel Fair, aquamarine glowing-golden demented-red & deep deep blue Fair, Constitution Mall and Rainbow Avenue and ten-cent-hot-dog Fair? Yes, to a smile. Only the Perisphere & never I could have convinced Mark that beyond what is awful there is bound to be at least the possibility of joy. *Weeping may tarry for the night,* the psalm & the Fair say, together, *but joy cometh in the morning.* Faced with evil we dreamed up this lovely future & *we smiled.* I say they will always remember us for that, whatever our fate may be.

And here it is almost dawn. My father's study where I love the books & sweet solemn photographs that seem so knowing in the silence & comfortable chair & sea of cool paper clips in the heavy glass ashtray that I run my fingers through, the dark faces of the buildings across West End Avenue & smell of leather & phonograph records. The city beats reassuringly like a clock in my weightless deeper-than-exhaustion. The light coming on slowly. The building stretching & creaking. A far-off siren. The traffic down below never-ending, bundled-up shoeboxes pointing with their lights. They make their appearances, move furtively left or right & are gone. To the east beyond the tall buildings I cannot see but I feel the Trylon and Perisphere, as I used to feel my childhood bedroom without opening my eyes when I awoke. I asked Mark *& can we tell everyone?* & he said of course, why not? Why not indeed. I will tell my father first. Perhaps I will wire Aunt Fran or is there something vulgar in that. It doesn't trouble me too much. I think it is light enough to wake him. Is there not much to be said for perfect happiness?

28

Epilogue:
Here
in
Utopia

I. HISTORY

The fair's origins go back to 1934 and a small group of New York businessmen. The depression was on and New York City was hurting. Business was bad. The group decided to hold regular meetings to figure out how to make things better, "to work out," in particular, "some form of promotion to attract new business and bring visitors to New York."

The group was led by three presidents, Grover Whalen of Shenley Distilleries, George McAneny of the Title Guarantee and Trust Company and Percy Straus of R. H. Macy's. Four other prominent businessmen joined them: Harvey Gibson of Manufacturer's Trust; Mortimer Buckner of New York Trust; Bayard

Pope of Marine Midland Trust, Thomas McInnerney of National Dairy.

Chicago's 1933 World's Fair caught the group's attention. The Century of Progress Exhibition brought much business to Chicago and even earned a minuscule profit (seven hundred thousand dollars on an investment of forty-seven million, to be precise). The group figured that a New York fair would do even better—New York was a bigger city, after all.

Or maybe not: That is Grover Whalen's version of the birth of the fair. There is an alternative story in which Joseph Shadgen and Edward Roosevelt burst into the *Herald Tribune's* editorial offices in May, 1935. Edward Roosevelt was FDR's distant cousin; Joseph Shadgen was a Belgian engineer and a naturalized American citizen. They present a full-fledged plan for a New York's World Fair to another Roosevelt cousin, who is a *Tribune* editorial writer, and are given a letter of introduction to George McAneny. McAneny convenes an informal group. Percy Straus is the only point of overlap between this alleged group and Whalen's; in this version, McAneny invites Whalen to join later on.

The two accounts come together on September 17, 1935, the first undisputed date in the fair's history. The proposal that New York host a world's fair is presented on that date to an assembly of notables, including La Guardia and Governor Lehman, at a Manhattan dinner. The notables are duly enthused and a few days later, on September 23, the World's Fair project is announced to the public for the first time. In October one hundred some-odd "distinguished leaders" form the non-profit World's Fair of 1939 Corporation, with McAneny as president. In May 1936 McAneny is named chairman of the board and Grover Whalen takes over as president. The operation moves into the Empire State Building, where it soon occupies five full floors.

As far as the two conflicting creation stories go, each originates with a well-informed and self-interested source—for the latter story, the *Herald Tribune*. It seems clear that Joseph Shadgen did in fact dream up the idea of linking the fair to the 150th anniversary of Washington's inauguration. Other sources concur on that point. It seems, also, that the idea of locating the fair on the famous Flushing Meadow ash heap came from McAneny, and it is at least plausible that—as the *Tribune* alleges—the site, too, was suggested originally by Shadgen. Shadgen's is a strange story. He worked for the Fair Corporation for around a year starting in mid-1936, but he was fired on grounds that "he did not fit at all." He went on to sue the Fair Corporation over his claim to be the unrecognized and unrewarded originator of the whole idea. The corporation settled with him out of court. Newspapers called him the "Father of the Fair," but he was too angry or sulky ever to set foot in it. (Whalen's account, for its part, is fascinating and authoritative but spotty. He leaves out Shadgen altogether. He also leaves out all of 1940. He does reveal that the reason King George VI of England behaved so strangely on his visit to the fair, among other things outright refusing to review the troops as he had been scheduled to, was that he had to go to the bathroom. On this particular there is no reason to doubt him.)

McAneny was head of the Regional Planning Association; he was a respected New York elder statesman with a background as a reformer. But it was Whalen who by all accounts made the fair.

He had been born on Grover Cleveland's wedding day, June 2, 1886. He was charming, wealthy, handsome and a nonstop talker. He had developed a career as New York's "official greeter"—a welcomer of celebrities on behalf of the city and its mayor. The Grover Whalen of the photos and newsreels has dark shining hair, a clipped mustache, splendiferous shoes, inconceivably elegant clothing. He is suave. He is self-assured. He favors a blue cornflower for his immaculate lapel. His presence and his smile are nearly Clark Gable-ish. The smile informs us that this man has many important

things to do, is accustomed to being in charge, is inevitably the center of attention—and is truly gracious and genial for all that. You
like him despite yourself. He was an institution in New York, and
when he died in 1962 the city's flags flew at half-staff.

He had been New York City Police Commissioner under
Mayor James Walker. After his police stint he returned as manager
of Wanamaker's Department Store (where he had worked before),
and he served, also, as head of the National Recovery Administration for New York City during the early New Deal. In 1937 he considered seeking the Democratic nomination to challenge La Guardia
when the Mayor ran for reelection, but thought better of it—a decision on which La Guardia publicly complimented him.

Whalen was thought to be vain. He was thought to be a tool
of the city's powerful business interests (he never made any bones
about the fact). Before his work with the fair he was believed to be
an intellectual lightweight, a mere fancy figurehead. When Harvey
Gibson took over toward the end of the fair's money-losing first
season, he was assumed to be a rotten businessman.

But in retrospect—and his fans said as much while the fair
was still under way—Whalen was recognized not only as a magnificent salesman ("fair claim to the title of greatest salesman alive,"
said *Time* magazine) but a regular mini-Moses, with a striking ability
to get things done. And whatever else good or bad you might say
about him, he was a visionary; there was no question about that.

The Fair Corporation's first problem was to develop some
idea of what the event would be like. A Board of Design was appointed to draw up plans. It was headed by the architect Stephen
Voorhees ("an excellent administrator," according to an architectural journal, which sounds like a distinctly guarded endorsement),
and reported to Percy Straus, who was now serving on the Board of
Directors. Robert Kohn's Theme Committee was a subcommittee of
the design board, which also included the distinguished designer

Walter Dorwin Teague; Richard Shreve of Shreve, Lamb and Harmon, the Empire State Building firm; Jay Downer, who had supervised the construction of a Westchester amusement park called Playland. Playland was famous (still is) for its deco classiness. Whalen invented the phrase "The World of Tomorrow" and set out his goals:

> The Fair will exhibit the most promising developments of ideas, products, services and social factors of the present day in such a fashion that the visitor may get a vision of what he could obtain for himself, and for his community, by intelligent, co-operative planning toward the better life of the future.

> It will demonstrate the vital interdependence of communities, peoples, and nations. Thus in submitting to the world of today a new layout for life, we are engaged in building a world of tomorrow. The New York World's Fair will predict, may even dictate, the shape of things to come.

The next problem was to get money. Sixteen Manhattan banks advanced $1,600,000 between them to get the ball rolling. Then the Board of Directors set to work hawking a $28,000,000 bond issue. By February 1937 $20,000,000 had been sold, but sales were slowing. So Whalen invented the "Terrace Club," an exclusive site at the fair to be open only to big bondholders. Sales picked up again, but not enough to sell out the issue; the banks stepped in and bought up the leftovers. Another $12,000,000 materialized in "pre-fair revenues" from prospective concessionaires. The Board of Design had estimated $40,000,000 as the cost to be borne by the corporation itself. With forty-some-odd million dollars under its belt, the fair was in business.

Good relations with the city, state and federal governments were crucial to get the fair off the ground. La Guardia was enthusiastic. He was a hard-nosed do-gooder and tightfisted administrator, but he was also a builder, a civic improver, a devotee of great engineering; a lover of beauty. He was delighted with the idea of a world's fair. "While other nations of the world are wondering what the spring will bring," La Guardia said, "we will be dedicating a fair to the hope of the people of the world. The contrast must be striking to everyone. While other countries are in the twilight of an unhappy age, we are approaching the dawn of a new day."

Robert Moses was enthusiastic. ("By God, that *is* a great idea.") He had extended his Grand Central Parkway so that it would link up with his Triborough Bridge, but unfortunately the new stretch of parkway ran through a grotesque ash heap—hardly the setting for a *Robert Moses* parkway. Try as he might, Moses couldn't pry loose the money to clean up or even plant over the ash mountains. So a world's fair in Flushing Meadow was a godsend, because that was the site of the ash dump. The fair would provide the money Moses needed to clean up the site and turn it into a park. He negotiated an arrangement whereby the first two million dollars of any fair profits would be set aside for park building. Moses was never a man to beat around the bush. "As park enthusiasts," he told Grover Whalen at a ceremony during the first season, "we are more interested in the park that is to be here than in the Fair that is here today."

Of course the fair's profits amounted to zero; the grounds became a park—never as grand a one as Moses had imagined—only gradually during the years following the Second World War. In 1964 another world's fair occupied the same site. Robert Moses himself ran the second (and to date the last) New York World's Fair. Until his death Grover Whalen was honorary chairman.

Franklin Roosevelt was far removed from the details of local planning. But he was sufficiently enthusiastic about the world's fair to sign formal invitations for delivery by American ambassadors all over the world.

Groundbreaking took place on June 29, 1936. Whalen himself still doubted that the project would come to pass. Signing exhibitors was the hard part, and that effort hadn't even begun. But at least the locals were enthusiastic. There is a photograph showing La Guardia and Whalen side-by-side at the groundbreaking. Whalen wields the spade (La Guardia's turn had been earlier), and he wears a fine dark business suit. La Guardia's suit is rumpled. The jacket is closed with two buttons— standard practice at the time, which accentuates the rumple; he hooks a thumb in his pocket and grins down boyishly at the spade. Whalen stooped to his task and the mayor upright are the same height. Robert Moses announced that he would have the site cleaned up and prepared on schedule if he and his people had to work twenty-four hour days to do it.

"This fair is as official," La Guardia said emphatically, "as *government* can make *anything* official."

Moses' men set to work. "Dust clouds sweeping over Flushing Meadow by day, the glare of arc lights by night and the constant rumble of trucks attested to the speed with which the work of grading the site progressed," wrote the fair's research director. "Eight giant steam shovels and four drag-line derricks kept one hundred trucks occupied day and night . . . By the end of March, 1937—far ahead of schedule—the contractors had completed the filling and grading of the site." What Moses promised, Moses delivered. The Administration building was the first at the fair to be completed. In August 1937 the staff moved in.

The city invested around twenty-seven million dollars in clearing the site and erecting the New York City building. The state invested $6,200,000, some in improvements to the site, the rest in the New York State Amphitheater and associated exhibit hall. The federal government came up with $3,500,000, of which $3,000,000 went for the United States Pavilion. Any remaining profits after Moses' $2,000,000 for parks were to go to the city and state for "charitable and scientific purposes."

In the fall of 1936 Whalen set out to sell the fair. The International Bureau of Expositions was the governing body of world's fairs. It recognized expositions in two categories, a "restricted" or small-scale category and an unrestricted fair, at which exhibitors could spend as freely and build as grandly as they chose. The bureau decided initially that New York's was to be a small-scale fair. Whalen said thank you very much and retreated to think things over. The Soviet Union was not a member of the International Bureau, and would not be bound by its restrictive decisions. (The United States was not a member either.) Working through the Russian ambassador to Washington, Whalen persuaded Stalin to build a pavilion—in fact, to build a great big one. When it was announced that Soviet Russia would sink four million into the fair, other nations rose to the challenge.

Whalen signed up every large nation in the world except China and Germany. He signed up thirty-three U.S. states as well, and Puerto Rico. News reports claimed that 90 percent of the world's population would be represented.

American exhibitors followed one of two paths. Some formed groups to split the costs: railroads, aviation, glass, electric utilities, petroleum. The others went it alone. General Motors'

$5,000,000 building would be the most expensive on the grounds.

Contracts with exhibitors were all written for one season, but a second season was anticipated from the start, if things worked out all right in 1939. Whalen presided over a management council consisting of the fair's chief engineer, John Philip Hogan; its chief architect, Stephen Voorhees; and the vice president in charge of commercial exhibits, concessions and the amusement area, Howard Flanigan. Flanigan was said to be the number two man.

But Whalen ran the whole operation in every detail, and he was an overwhelming presence. He personally negotiated and signed the major contracts and hired the key people. He rose early, exercised for an hour and regularly beat his three secretaries to work. "Barrel-chested and haughty," writes *Time* magazine, "he pads about his swank offices in the Empire State Building or another set of offices at the fair with regal pomp (stenographers greet him: 'Good morning, Mr. President') " He was said to earn a formidable hundred thousand high-thirties dollars a year. Not bad, especially considering that the fair was a nonprofit venture.

But Whalen was surely worth the $100,000. All told he rounded up $157,000,000 worth of fair. As opening day approached, the publicity buildup was monumental. Back in April 1938, a year before opening day, the fair had staged "probably the greatest and most ambitious promotional project ever attempted," a big parade that started in Lower Manhattan and drove all the way out to the fair site. There was also a music festival and a "brilliant Junior League Ball," and "automotive couriers" were dispatched to spread the word to the governors of all forty-eight states.

"Even now," *The New Yorker* reported, "before the Fair is actually open, we feel we know more about it than we have ever known, or ever wanted to know, about any other subject in our life. Month after month Mr. Whalen's publicity men labored."

The week before opening day Whalen was bedridden with

fatigue and a bad cold. The fatigue was understandable. "Mr. Whalen," *The New Yorker* commented that week, "has been working twelve to fourteen hours a day, sometimes including Sundays, since the beginning of 1938. That adds up, roughly, to 5,460 Whalen hours." The time was well spent. "The complete picture of the Fair," La Guardia proclaimed on opening day, "the layout of its attractions and the manner of its presentation surpass anything ever presented any place, anywhere in the world."

The opening-day ceremonials were elaborate. The gates opened at eleven. At quarter to one a parade of thirty thousand people got under way. It marched from the Theme Center down the mall, around the Lagoon and into the Court of Peace. The marchers were uniformed soldiers, sailors and marines, veterans' groups, foreigners from the exhibiting nations in the most colorful and elaborate "native costume" they could dig up; a contingent of workmen who had built the place, in white caps and overalls. There was also an official World's Fair contingent, led by Grover Whalen. This was Whalen's show and, as he marched down the magnificent thronged avenue through the heart of the greatest exhibition the world had ever seen, it would have been a proud moment for the man who had been dismissed as a mere pretty-boy figurehead.

At 3:12 P.M. President Roosevelt officially dedicated the fair. Governor Lehman, Mayor La Guardia, Grover Whalen and several others spoke as well, including the Englishman Sir Louis Beale on behalf of the foreign commissioners general.

There were many other special events on opening day, of which the strangest was the ceremony in which Albert Einstein turned on the dramatic nighttime lighting. He had been asked to explain cosmic rays to the audience in a few hundred words; he gamely complied. Unfortunately his thick German accent channeled through multiple reverberating speakers made it impossible for the crowds to hear anything past his opening words—"Science must enter into the consciousness of the people." After the speech he was supposed to activate a mechanism, set up at the Hayden Planetarium, designed to meter the arrival of ten cosmic rays. On the arrival of the tenth, the nighttime lights would come on. (A similar stunt had figured in the 1935 dedication of the Hayden Planetarium itself.) The arrival of each ray was to be signaled by the flashing of a belt of lights toward the top of the Trylon, and the sounding of the "great bellwire at the base of the Perisphere." Unfortunately the climax fizzled, because "something happened to the electrical system," as the *Times* astutely reported; the grand illumination never took place. Luckily, spectacular fireworks over the Lagoon kicked in shortly afterward and the crowd was adequately entertained.

The "great bellwire" refers, of course, to the Voice of the Perisphere.

On opening day, the wire services sold prepackaged telegrams home. Most popular model: FAIR WONDERFUL, CLIMATE GORGEOUS, HAVING SWELL TIME, WISH YOU WERE HERE.

The fair was optimistic—about the future of America; about its own future. On the topic of its own future, in fact, it journeyed past optimism into outright craziness. Whalen predicted an opening day gate of a million visitors. Roughly 400,000 materialized. (The fair administration claimed 600,000, but was revealed to have been inflating the gate in various ingenious ways—for example, counting fair staffers in the total. And staffers would sometimes leave the grounds, re-enter and be counted several times a day.) At that, the opening-day throngs were enormously larger than those of any other fair in recent memory. Opening day in San Francisco had drawn 138,000 earlier in 1939. Some 170,000 had attended the Chicago Exposition's first day. If Whalen's estimate had been less demented, 400,000 visitors would have been stupendous instead of a figure to apologize for—and explain away in terms of late-afternoon bad weather.

During the first year, predictions were, a minimum of 40,000,000 people would visit the fair, and more likely 50,000,000 would. 26,000,000 did. Once again it would have seemed like a handsome total had Whalen's predictions been less crazy. But those crazy predictions were the basis of the Fair Corporation's undertakings to its bondholders. On August 31, dourly responsible Harvey Dow Gibson became chairman of the Fair Corporation board, replacing George McAneny, who had wished for some time to step down. Whalen remained president, but responsibility for running the fair was handed unambiguously to Gibson, in hopes he would turn the financial picture around.

Banker Gibson had thinning silver hair, wire-rimmed spectacles, conservative suits and a pained smile. He had been a banking prodigy, assuming control of Liberty National Bank at age thirty-four: New York's youngest bank president. He was fifty-seven when he took over the fair, but still possessed in spades the steady-as-she goes, what's-so-funny? characteristics that banking prodigyhood no doubt requires. "They presented a contrast," the *Times* reporter could not help but notice at the news conference where the leadership change was announced. "Mr. Whalen in a blue suit, with maroon boutonniere, natty dark blue shirt and homburg hat to match, and the stranger," Gibson that is, "conservatively clad in a neat brown suit."

The new administration's first big move was to announce a second season. A 1940 season had been widely rumored, but there had been no official decision until Gibson's announcement. Then, on September 27, admission was cut to fifty cents, effective October 1. "More Fair for less money," said banker Gibson. The fifty-cent admission was intended originally just for October, but was extended throughout 1940. On October 31, the 1939 season drew to a cold, wet, miserable close. "Buses, touring almost empty through the grounds, sent sprays of water dashing ten feet away. A strange spectacle in the middle of the afternoon deluge was the sight of the fair's fountains, spraying more water upward into the rain." The fair was $23,000,000 in debt.

It reopened on May 11, 1940. (La Guardia had argued that the most popular exhibits should stay open over the winter, but the board said no.) "The Fair this year is within reach of every pocketbook," Gibson assured the masses in his introduction to the new and completely rewritten *Official Guide*. Other changes were in line with his observation for the newspapers' benefit that, during its first season, the fair had "awed country boys like myself." In later years he elaborated:

> The Fair opened with overpowering ceremony . . . So much so, that the common run of people, especially those from small places throughout the country, which were counted upon to comprise the backbone of attendance, seemed to become sort of frightened in a way by it all and were ill at ease rubbing elbows or at the prospect of doing so, with what had unfortunately become known throughout the country as the high silk hat group which seemed to them as predominating.

Do not underestimate (in that age of well-understood *oughts*) the significance of the top hat *itself* in creating a mood that some people found intimidating. Gibson meant what he said. On opening day, the *Times* had reported, "one band of out-of-town visitors seemed fascinated by the number of toppers on the grounds . . . 'Who might they be?' one raw-boned stranger wondered . . ."

In its second year the fair strove for folksiness. It was just one "super country fair," Gibson explained. A few weeks before the 1940 opening, a character named Elmer was introduced as the star of a nationwide advertising campaign: The fair, proclaimed Elmer, "makes you proud of your country." Elmer was "a beaming, portly, average American," about fifty years old. A New York actor who had previously posed as Stalin played the part. He appeared on posters, toured the country and wandered the reopened fairgrounds greeting people like an intimation of Mickey Mouse at Disneyland. The fact that the *Times* described him as "more or less the Fair's official greeter" must have struck Grover Whalen as a low blow, but the contrast between Grover the gorgeous and Elmer the average perfectly reflected Harvey Gibson's new strategy.

"Zones" were dropped from the fair's literature. "For Peace and Freedom" became the new slogan. The amusement area became the "Great White Way." The Consumers building became the "World of Fashion." ("Into this fresh-as-paint, gay awninged building, the fashion capital of America has moved bag and baggage for the summer . . . The 'World of Fashion' is out to prove that American styles for American women have come into their own to stay.") Two new model houses were added to the Town of Tomorrow, each intended to be home for a week to a series of American families. Each lucky family would get an all-expenses-paid vacation at the fair in exchange for becoming one of the exhibits. "The families will be selected by newspapers in various parts of the country, and will consist of a father American, a mother American, and two little Americans, preferably a boy and a girl." But no canine Americans, evidently.

Every exhibiting nation had been invited to remain for the 1940 season. Of the ten that declined, the Soviets were the most

prominent. Their withdrawal was announced only days after the Soviet invasion of Finland, and there was little love lost between host
and withdrawing guest. The Fair Corporation made no expression
of regret. The Finns stayed. (In November the New York City government had voted a resolution of thanks to foreign participants at
the fair—the Soviet Union included, but over vociferous objections.
After the Hitler-Stalin pact, Russia's American defenders were few
and far between.) The Soviet building was taken down and replaced
by the "American Common"—"a two-and-a-half acre square dedicated to the perpetuation of a democratic idea," under Robert
Kohn's chairmanship.

The 1940 fair mounted a musical show called *American
Jubilee* in the Great White Way, "upon the largest revolving stage
ever constructed—a gigantic circular platform, two hundred and
seventy feet in diameter and built upon rollers." "A huge and rather
heavy-handed historical pageant," according to *The New Yorker*.
And there were many smaller changes. Westinghouse demonstrated
the sterilizing effect of a flash of light on a drop of water; the show
was called "Microblitzkrieg." The aviation exhibit displayed "up-
to-the-minute fighting planes." Britain showed a captured German
mine-laying parachute. (July 4 saw the only conspicuous tragedy at
the fair: A bomb was planted in the British pavilion and two detectives were killed carting it away.) Despite these changes and many
others, the backbone of the 1940 fair was exactly what it had been—
Democracity and the Futurama, the mall and Rainbow Avenue, the
Time Capsule, the Rotolactor, the Road of Tomorrow.

Did Gibson's changes work? Was the revamped fair a bigger
draw than the old one? There is no way to tell; a fair would ordinarily
do less business in its second season than its first, and so it was at the
New York fair. Roughly 26,000,000 people came the first season and
19,000,000 the second. In other words, the second year's attendance
was around 73 percent of the first. I mention the fact only because at

Chicago's Century of Progress, 22,000,000 came the first year and, after no special retooling and no Elmer, 16,000,000 came the second. That is to say, 73 percent. It proves nothing, but is worth pondering.

"Blaze of Old Glory Week" was the fair's last. La Guardia ordered a great flag flown from the Trylon, and gigantic crowds turned out to say farewell. The fair closed forever on October 27, 1940. 45,000,385 people had come altogether. The second season made money, but not enough. Profits were zero. The fair's backers were repaid something under forty cents on the dollar.

Closing day saw the biggest gate of all—"typical of this incomparable and perverse Fair," said the *Herald Tribune*. It was the only day on which attendance exceeded half a million. The fair "opened with happy hopes of the World of Tomorrow," *Life* magazine wrote, "and closed amid war and crisis." The closing day crowds "were torn between a carnival and melancholy mood. They ripped out signs, picked flowers, sang *Auld Lang Syne*."

On that last day, "Addressing themselves to Japanese officials from the Japanese pavilion across the way, Church of God representatives expressed hope there would be no war between the United States and Japan."

The last-day crowds "seemed awkwardly conscious that they were making melancholy history. You sensed this in the tense words of the broad woman who swung a grave-eyed little blond boy around to face the refreshment booths at the foot of the Long Island Rail Road Ramp. 'Look at that frozen custard stand, Herman. That's the frozen custard stand where your daddy worked at the World's Fair.' " "I think we're stopping at just the right time," a fair administrator said, "but I've cried more than once, just thinking about it."

EPILOGUE: HERE IN UTOPIA

Bob Murray, who was in charge of daily operations at the Futurama, "fought back the tears when his show went dark." Murray and his men were the last passengers on the Futurama. "They left with bridges and trees in their pockets for souvenirs."

Last-day visitors grabbed whatever mementos they could lay their hands on—plants, signs;

> but in many gentler ways—by plucking a chilled yellow flower from the Court of Communications Lawn, by writing initials for the last time at the foot of George Washington's statue, by hoisting a final cup at favorite bars—the last visitors demonstrated acute melancholia at the thought of the great World's Fair being ploughed under.

The fair was supposed to close with taps ringing out from the Helicline at midnight. But the bugler bugled an hour early, after the hundred some-odd employees of the Perisphere had taken a final ride round Democracity and the great sphere was emptied of people and shut down. Toward midnight a writer from *The New Yorker*, a photographer from the *Daily News* and a few others gathered beneath the *Astronomer* at the foot of the Helicline and waited for taps. They held out until quarter to one, and went home.

What did it all amount to, in the end?

The New Yorker wrote the fair's epitaph at the very start of its run. It lodged some good-humored objections to the World of Tomorrow and promised more. And then it casually added, "Life will probably always be like that—the men of vision creating, the little men carping, with terror and amazement in their hearts." It is a sentence to treasure.

Many complaints have been raised against the fair. The objections of modern historians are usually matched in substance by those lodged by the fair's contemporaries.

Some are clearly valid. If the fair's spirit overall was a good and accurate distillation of America's spirit, much nonetheless was left out. Gardner Harding quoted a fair administrator:

> To be fully representative of community interests, the Fair should have included the cooperative movement, the granges and farmer's groups, the many useful and important social organizations that make up life in every American community. But you can't sell space to those folks. They haven't any money.

Harding criticizes the Town of Tomorrow as "a definite breach of faith," because most of the houses it shows are far too expensive for the average fairgoer. Only six of the fifteen "meet the absolute minimum requirement of social usefulness in costing less than $10,000 apiece." He finds the whole 1939 fair too expensive.

The fair has been rightly criticized for mirroring and not repudiating America's antiblack prejudice. World's fairs like Chicago's in 1933 and New York's in 1939 "were cast out of the same racist mold as their Victorian antecedents," according to Robert Rydell, "and continued to lend legitimacy to prevailing white supremacist values and practices." Again, the same criticism was heard at the time. "There have been complaints of discrimination against Negroes," *Time* magazine notes during opening week. There were none in any important position on the fair staff. Those objecting included the Harlem Community Cultural Conference; Louise Johnson, who presided, declared that the "position allotted" at the fair "to the Negro gives a false picture of his place in the World of Tomorrow." But there is more to this story. The full story will not make us conclude that the charges of bigotry are false. It will merely show us once again that the fair mirrored America, and America was a complicated place.

For example, there is the fact that *The Harp*, by the black sculptress Augusta Savage, stood near one of the entrances—black figures within "the hand of God" form the harp strings. Black visitors seem often to have posed before *The Harp* for photographs. *Hot Mikado* was a hit in the amusement area. The *Democracity* hymn was the work of a black composer, William Grant Still. (No one lost any sleep worrying about whether he owed the distinction to affirmative action.) Back in 1937 Grover Whalen had promised that blacks would not be discriminated against "in any way" at the fair. He broke that promise, but it is noteworthy that he felt compelled to make it in the first place. A panel discussion on racial prejudice, sponsored by the American Committee for Democracy and Intellectual Freedom, was conducted toward the close of the fair's first season in the Hall of Science and Education.

The 1940 Guide extols the "American citizens of different racial backgrounds" who perform at the fair on the American Common; "it was a fusing of bloodstreams that begot the Union and continues to keep it a working reality nowhere else achieved." The American Common was the scene of the fair's observance of "Negro Week" in July 1940. Harvey Gibson, Mayor La Guardia, A. Philip Randolph and W. E. B. Du Bois were among the participants. The point was "to help many to a more complete understanding and a more solemn appreciation of the tremendous debt American culture owes to the Negro." (Capitalizing the term "Negro" was an innovation, by the way, of Herbert Bayard Swope.) "One of the most flagrant of the omissions from the usual History of the United States is the part the Negro has played in the making of the nation," the *Souvenir Program* reports. An end to bigotry was not a prominent part of the fair's utopian vision, but it was a part. "The struggle of the ages," writes Harry Emerson Fosdick, "has been to persuade men to get their heads up above the prejudicial lines of race, nation and class and to see men as children of God."

None of this means that the fair was unbigoted. It *was* bigoted, and its bigotry mirrored America's, to America's lasting disgrace. But our final verdict must be more complicated than "good" or "evil," because the fair was Distilled Essence of U.S.A., and if there was much evil in the country, there was also much serious struggling toward an honorable utopia for the community of the faithful.

The most common and persistent charge against the fair is commercialism. A New York City councilman called it a "great con game," designed to line corporate pockets. The prominent chemist Harold Urey claimed that "the World of Tomorrow will be built by ideas and not by meaningless symbols such as a sphere with a long shaft beside it . . . It seems to me that the New York Fair will be very severely criticized, and very justly so, for managing its affairs entirely on a commercial basis and not from the standpoint of an educational program." "Most of the things which have hurt the New York World's Fair, artistically and from the point of view of its educational possibilities," Talbot Hamlin writes, "have been the result of over-commercialization." (Though we ought not forget Hamlin's final verdict: "a confused melting pot, enormous, impersonal, but withal dynamic, exciting and magnificent.")

Modern historians concur. "All forms of artistic activity were exploited at the Fair to promote a merchant's vision of a profitable future," Francis O'Connor writes. Peter Kuznick comments on some scientists' unhappiness with the fair: "The nascent consumer culture—already suffused with advertising irrationality and awash in a flood of fragmented, decontextualized information—found little use for either scientists' social vision or science's presumed rationality." Warren Susman dwells on "the contradictions between the planners' ideology and the demands of consumer capitalism." Robert Rydell notes that business leaders spent "extravagant sums" in order to "convince Americans to modernize by consuming the products of American industry." He files the fair under "revelries of corporate capitalism."

In many modern accounts a common theme emerges: The typical American fairgoer exposed to propaganda reacted with the vigor, discernment and critical perspicacity of a sponge in water. He absorbed every last drop and the experience transformed him. "The Fair was a carefully contrived conditioning experiment (Germany was another, at the time)," Francis O'Connor explains, "and few among the multitudes entering its gates were ready in 1939–40—or subsequently—to 'psyche out' the reasons they suddenly yearned for television sets, superhighways, foreign foods, and a streamlined life . . ." "The great car companies," writes Thomas Kessner, "put on the best exhibits and captured the heart of the fair, convincing Americans that the auto meant comfort and freedom." And so on.

The sour complaints about commercialism are all true; and they are all wrong. The fair was indeed a consumerist extravaganza. Getting Americans to buy their products was every commercial exhibitor's goal. (Obviously.) The whole *point* of the thing had been "to attract new business and bring visitors to New York," and Whalen, Gibson, the whole fair administration were unambiguously *pro*-buying, *pro*-selling, *pro*-business—had they not been, they would not have bothered. But there are two points to bear in mind as we assess these charges of overcommercialism.

Gardner Harding brings up Democracity and the focal exhibits. They are the fair's "major defense against the overcommercialism of its original purposes." Harding "testifies unhesitatingly" of the fair "that it is a more nearly honest performance, on a more comprehensive and beautiful scale, than any event of its kind."

The Fair Corporation's own exhibits were the heart of the show, and gave out the gospel according to the Theme Committee. Management might easily have dispensed with the lot; in most cases it put them in the hands of leading designers instead. And those exhibits weren't merely for the committee's edification. People were supposed to *come see* them. They were to be lured inside at all costs. How could "a social message be brought home to 60,000,000 sightseers intent on making whoopee?" a Publicity Department document impatiently demands. "How make them stop, look and listen?" (Using the language that the old railway grade crossings made famous: It was urgent that people stop, look and listen, so they wouldn't get flattened by a locomotive.) The answer was Democracity in the Perisphere, "a drama so new, so forceful it would shine out as the climax of a day at the Fair." "Fair visitors do not read signs," reports Gilbert Rhode in his script for the fair's Community Interests exhibit—so he tells the story in animated, lit-up tableaux and narration instead. The focal exhibits were of uneven quality—science was particularly weak; transportation was unconnected to the social themes the committee wanted to push. Some critics at the time (Joseph Wood Krutch in the *Nation,* for example) urged fairgoers to skip the whole lot and seek out pure entertainment instead. But Democracity at least was a huge hit with the public, more popular than any commercial exhibit except General Motors, and there can be no question that the fair's own exhibits—the intellectual and (in Democracity's case) physical heart of the show—were strikingly *non*commercial.

If the fair was "a carefully contrived conditioning experiment," the goal must have been at least in part to make Americans value community and the spiritual side of life, and wish fervently for a broader distribution of wealth, the elimination of slums and the triumph of planned towns. Those were the messages that the theme exhibits were retailing.

Turning, now, to the commercial exhibits: One of their most striking aspects was their noncommercialness.

Kessner on the Futurama is representative of a whole school of thought. "General Motors' futuristic paean to the automobile in modern life, not Democracity, was the fair's most popular exhibit— rank commercialism dressed up in the shiny idiom of 'American progress.'" But then again, *The New Yorker* was moved to observe at the time that

> automobile manufacturers seem to take the same attitude towards their exhibitions that they do toward their radio programs. In both cases they remind the public from time to time that they are in the business of making motorcars, but the emphasis is on entertainment and not, as it is so frankly at the annual Automobile Show, on the product. This is probably all for the best.

Should General Motors have been barred from the grounds? Or forbidden to mention cars, or to stage a fancy show? Should the public have been sternly warned not to be so damned *enthusiastic* about those corporate exhibits? In the event, large corporations sank millions into free entertainment for the public, and the public was duly entertained. "Since G.M. will sell nothing on the premises," *Time* magazine observed, "it is investing only in advertising and good will. Whether this huge expenditure . . . will pan out is General Motors' worry." "A ride through Mr. Geddes' Futurama," says *The New Yorker,* "covers a third of a mile and lasts fifteen minutes. It should be twice as long."

The point applies more broadly. The fair "gets away from the immediate job of selling goods," Gardner Harding writes:

General Motors, Westinghouse, General Electric, the utilities, the other automobile companies, the railroads, and the great food companies, to mention but a few, have all sponsored exhibits of a significance far beyond the limits of even their great businesses. Ten great industries—notably aviation, oil production, glass manufacturing, pottery making, the gas industries, the railroads, and the distillers—have pioneered with exhibits which play down trade names and emphasize the social contributions of their professional calling to the average man and woman.

How then to understand those persistent charges of crass commercialism? The right way, I suspect, is in light of a comment by Rydell. "Obscene is not quite the right word, but the discrepancies between the wealth and power, not to mention the streamlined glamor, manifest in exposition buildings and the grim economic conditions of the depression can still jar the senses a full half century after the New York World's Fair closed its gates." This is a moral judgment with which we can agree or not. But might it not be a tad disingenuous? We might possibly wonder whether there has *ever* been an American decade during which the poor did well enough to justify, in Rydell's mind, a "revelry of corporate capitalism" like the Futurama.

A final point respecting the commercial aspects of the fair— and it is, I think, the most important one. Listen to the earnest and devoted chroniclers of the planned town of Radburn, writing in 1934. They wish to deal wisely with the motor vehicle, "not forgetting that it may be a menace," but also "remembering the happiness it brings."

How's that again, the happiness? *Happiness?* Automobiles *bring happiness?* Oh yes, happiness. Plain old fragmented, decontextualized happiness. You see, many Americans *liked* their cars.

EPILOGUE: HERE IN UTOPIA

Ah!—certain things become clearer. Could it possibly be that Americans "yearned for television sets, superhighways, foreign foods, and a streamlined life" because they *wanted* television sets, superhighways, foreign foods and a streamlined life? To hypothesize as much is not to deny that advertising is a powerful influence on how people behave. But the fair hardly concocted American consumerism out of whole cloth.

The modern fair historian's all-time favorite citation is by Walter Lippmann on the Futurama. (I know of at least five accounts that quote it, and I am about to make it six.) "GM has spent a small fortune to convince the American public that if it wishes to enjoy the full benefit of private enterprise in motor manufacturing, it will have to rebuild its cities and highways by public enterprise." Lippmann "noticed the irony of GM's extraordinary success with the Futurama," Susman writes. "Did the people, from their comfortable seats at a fascinating show, notice the contradiction?" Robert Stern, Gregory Gillmartin and Thomas Mellins refer to the "ironies and contradictions of the Futurama." Kuznick introduces the quote as follows: "Walter Lippmann accused GM's Futurama of another form if deceit."

Out of fairness to Lippmann we ought to note, first, that it was not at all his intention to criticize GM for propagandizing or foisting off "contradictions." He had been touring the exhibits of statist and totalitarian nations. When he came upon GM, his first impression was that "this is what private enterprise can do, and the best the Italians or the Russians have to show is no more than a feeble approximation of it." But upon reflection, "one comes away" from the Futurama "feeling that men are right when they affirm the value of private enterprises and when they affirm the necessity of public enterprises: where they go wrong is in denying that both are necessary." Lippmann's intent is not to bury the "ironic contradiction" between private and public enterprise but to praise it.

That said, it is of course true that GM stood to gain enormously by a nationwide road-building project, and after the Second World War it pumped lots of money and effort into accomplishing one. But I read it as the intention of some modern historians to suggest, by citing Lippmann, that the Futurama was the launchpad of an evil GM scheme to foist highways on an unwilling public—and that is absurd. Highways were a hotly debated topic in the high thirties. Nineteen thirty-nine's leading highway builder was Robert Moses. No one ever suggested that Moses was the auto companies' or anyone else's paid shill. To the contrary, politicians fought for his services because of his reputation for integrity and for building projects the public wanted and liked. Geddes's ideas about *transcontinental* superhighways were admittedly radical. Robert Moses liked some aspects of the Futurama but denounced this element as "plain bunk." Highways should feed cities, he said. (If a third city cropped up on the path between two others, by the way, the highway needn't bypass it on a ring road; it could barrel right through, boring through buildings in insulated tunnels at the second- or third-story level.) Geddes blasted back at Moses' "short-range viewpoint"— not an accusation Moses was accustomed to. The army was in favor of transcontinental superhighways. The *New York Times* was against them, because they would cost too much—and hardly anyone wanted to drive cross-country anyway. But in *Magic Motorways* Geddes emphasized that his roads were for trucks and industry, not just for cars: "To operate profitably on long-distance hauling, truck drivers must maintain 40 or more miles an hour." In any event the *Times* was forced to concede the existence of "the widespread belief that we need transcontinental highways."

GM's was one voice in a wide-ranging national discussion. A loud one, granted. But Robert Moses and the *New York Times* were no shrinking violets either.

The commercialism critics make an important point. My goal

is not to argue it down, merely to set it in the right context. Yes, the commercial tide ran strong at the fair. But when critics complain about the fair, what really pains them, it seems to me, is the character of American society itself. In the high thirties we were a brash, loud and obsessed nation. "Most men lead business lives of such concentration that only a fraction of their faculties seem to become developed to any great extent." Fancy consumer goods excited us, new technology excited us, flashy engineering and great public works excited us, the prospect of a comfortable life and a home in the suburbs excited us. Perhaps those were unworthy aspirations, but that is how it was. The fair was no conspiracy. Warts and bigotry and brashness and brilliance and high hopes and all, the fair was us.

One last thing that certain modern historians overlook. Whalen's extravaganza drew forty-five million people all told. Many of them loved the fair.

They loved it because it was brave, bold, colorful and, most important, made them feel as if they could achieve great things. You don't get that feeling from an event that has no connection to your life. The fair divined something about the character of its visitors. It made a wild guess that it could find a point of connection with those people—locate the other half of a handshake, find a frequency that would resonate. It found one. The resonant frequency said "You are masters of a good, bold, brilliant future" and the resonating echo came back, "We are masters of a good, bold, brilliant future," and the fair hummed louder, bolder, brasher and the echo came back louder and bolder and brasher, and the fireworks unfurled over the Lagoon of Nations, and a sort of calm ecstasy resulted. "We are masters of a good, bold, brilliant future." People loved the fair, and on its last day, they plucked chilled yellow flowers from the Court of Communications to remember it by.

It cannot be measured and has left little tangible evidence, the love people felt for this fair. The fair was a mass event. The patrons felt whatever they did among crowds. But the emotions the fair generated were not crowd emotions. If fairgoers were affected emotionally, it was not because they had merged their strengths or identities into the crowd's. The fair spoke to each visitor privately. Visitors did not lose but rather found themselves there, in the act of being inspired. One by one they filed up to the mountaintop, gazed outward and felt happy, and filed down. How do we know? We know because, if we listen carefully to those people who were there and can't help but smile when we mention the topic, we can still hear today the resonant roar of a good, bold, brilliant future just over the edge of time in Flushing Meadow. The fair reverberates in the persons of the many thousands still alive who were there and loved it. In future generations that roar will go dead, will become as irretrievable as the Voice of the Perisphere. So we had better listen now, faint as the sound has become; we are the last generation that will have the privilege. There is little concrete to which I can point to prove that the roar is there. You will have to listen for yourself. But seeing as I have the piles of meticulously preserved fair memorabilia that survive today all over the country, I am willing to bet that somewhere pressed in a scrapbook there is a yellow flower that tells us something about love and the fair.

II. RELIGION

Nineteen thirty-nine's optimism is surprising and profoundly moving. But when I argue that we tend nowadays to be pessimistic about the future, there is nothing surprising about that. Our pessimism is well-known, and as a society we have discussed it at length. We associate our deep change in national mood with the late sixties. It started well before then, it seems to me, and yet in the late sixties something *did* change, dramatically. It was the Vietnam War, we say;

also rock music and drugs and things like that. Or maybe it was the Great Society. But a change as deep as the one we experienced ought not to happen merely on the basis of external events. The "asteroid theory"—Vietnam, rock music et al. just cropped up suddenly and smashed into us—is too shallow and easy. One has to be prepared internally for changes as big as the ones we experienced. We forget that the late sixties was also the period in which we entered utopia. As 1939 saw it: a world in which, for vast numbers of people, life all in all was pretty good.

The fair predicted that Americans would move out of the cities into the suburbs, and we did. It claimed that the automobile would remake the landscape and it did remake the landscape. It foresaw working and middle classes that were rich enough to live "the good life," and in the fair's terms that is exactly what we have done. We have vigorously addressed the social aspect of the fair's vision, its desire that we understand and do justice to "American citizens of different racial backgrounds." And all sorts of gadgets and wonder-stuff the fair ballyhooed or introduced, from TV to Lucite, fax machines to fuel-efficient cars and fluorescent lighting and robots and rockets and nylon stockings—they have all taken root and are flourishing.

The fair's predictions were bold but rarely startling. They accorded with the anticipations of most forward thinkers at the time. What is remarkable is not that the fair hit the nail on the head but *which* nail it hit. Because the fair wasn't envisioning the future of hemlines or pork belly prices. When you envision the future of pork bellies and you are right, you make a lot of money, but when you foretell an eventual entry into the promised land and you are right— the consequences are profound. We have achieved utopia, *our* utopia, a utopia not of perfection but of comfort; and so the future disappeared. It simply vanished. It *had* to.

Of course there has been real degradation since the late sixties in our quality of life. Frighteningly real. The economy is worse, crime is worse, the schools are worse, morale is worse. Doesn't that make it absurd to claim that we live in utopia? And isn't it more logical to argue that all this real degradation, not post-utopian angst, is the cause of our numb pessimism? *But why did the degradation happen?* Where did it come from? Liberals are at a loss, and conservatives who point to the triumph of the Great Society and the "counterculture" still haven't answered the question. If these were in fact diseases, we'd fended off lots of other diseases before. Why did we catch these? The thirties were bumper years for crackpot, dangerous or plain silly mass movements. You could be an unrepentant Prohibitionist or a Townsendite. (The Townsendites proposed extravagant monthly payments from the federal government to each citizen over sixty; recipients would promise, in return, to retire and to spend each month's check before the next arrived.) You could be a follower of Coughlin or Father Divine or Huey Long or communism or fascism. Lots of people were. But the social fabric held fast, and life overall continued to get better. What happened at the end of the sixties to change all that?

I can't accept an asteroid theory that makes us hapless, passive victims. I am more disposed to believe the truism that there is almost nothing more dispiriting than getting exactly what you have always longed for. It is a commonplace (which doesn't make it false) that human beings are apt to measure happiness by progress toward a goal. Not having but hoping seems to be the big thing with us; not so much *being* well off as getting better. Once you have everything you have dreamed of, it's awfully hard to sustain the tautness of will to hold on to it—much less to get more.

Pondering religion gives us a clue to one final mystery as well.

I have argued that our future is darker than 1939's, but in a sense that statement is misleading. It is more accurate to say that for us, the future no longer exists.

EPILOGUE: HERE IN UTOPIA

We can talk about it when we are asked to. We conjure it into being, examine it and then it slips away. But in 1939 it was ever present. Like the Trylon and Perisphere—merely raise your eyes and you couldn't miss the future. "The promise of the future is still greater than all the glories of the past," "I am optimistic for the future," "I am a great believer in a wonderful future," "that is.why America still has a future," *"All eyes to the future."* The future was a tangible, tasteable, nearly corporeal presence in your life. So we are faced in the end not with an intellectual question (Why do we suppose this, whereas 1939 supposed that?), but with a question about *seeing.* Nineteen thirty-nine sees a lake in the desert, a radiant host of angels, what have you; and as for us, we don't see a thing and it seems to us if 1939 must be drunk or crazy. It is easy to miss this subtlety because, as I say, we *can* imagine the future when we need to. But if we pay attention to the subtlety, we learn something important about the thirties versus our own age.

Religion helps explain this phenomenon, because religion makes you see things differently. It affects not merely what you believe but how the world looks. When a person loses his religious faith, it is not that God's character seems to change; God disappears. Religion is above all a matter of *seeing.* In the American civic religion at its height, the future was an article of faith and the faithful saw and felt its presence. Today, by dint of achieving the utopian future, we have lost our faith and see nothing.

Should we ever wish to change things and return to a world view more like the high thirties', to imagine the future in rosier tones will not be our biggest task. Our biggest task will be to see something where today we see nothing; to imagine the future, period.

We will succeed at that task. The successful effort will start, my guess is, within some sort of movement whose aims aren't grandiose political ones; whose only goal is to educate children—perhaps in modest Sunday-school fashion, for a few hours a week. But the topic won't be religion. It will be honest history. If I'm wrong about that, here is one prediction that is guaranteed to come true: eventually, if we are patient, there *will* be a new American future.

◢●

Let's slip back one last time into high-thirties New York on the evening of May 18, 1939. You stand on Fifth Avenue and look up at the RCA Building, where Hattie Glassman and Mark Handler are drinking champagne in the Rainbow Grill; then you stroll slowly uptown to say good-bye.

Good-bye to this city of heavy wooden paintbrushes, of crammed hardware shops displaying birdcages and potbelly stoves, saws, hatchets and doormats, desk fans, rubber hot-water bottles and assorted light bulbs at six cents each. Of two East River, ten Hudson and three Staten Island ferries, and men in long white aprons hawking roast corn and baked sweet potatoes from push-carts at curbside. Of Jack Benny on the radio at 7:00 on Sunday evenings, Edgar Bergen at 8:00, Walter Winchell at 9:30. Benny and Bergen on WEAF and Winchell on WJZ—those two (both head-quartered in the RCA Building) being the anchor stations of NBC's *two* national networks, the "Red" and the "Blue," respectively. Good-bye to a city of exactly one television station, W2XBS—video frequency 45.25, audio frequency 49.75—broadcasting this and that every now and then. If you were lucky, you might catch *Gunga Din.* A city of Bromo-Seltzer and Brioschi the *Delicious* Anti-Acid, where you could spend all day at a beauty parlor if you wanted the full treatment or have a drink, gender permitting, at the occasional all-male bar ("probably pretty dull," says guidebook author Marjorie Hills)—Pap's at the Ritz-Carlton, or McSorley's Ale House. City of the *Trib's* celebrated book editor Irita van Doren and her famously discreet affair with presidential contender Wendell Willkie; of Mary

McCarthy, the Tantalizing Trotskyist ("among Stalinist males, I heard the Trotskyists were believed to have a monopoly of 'all the beautiful girls' ") and her indiscreet carryings-on with the fire-breathing *intensely* bear-like intellectual-about-town who chose his own surname, Philip ("my last name means Rabbi") Rahv (who got his higher education at the Forty-second Street Library).

City of *Life* and *Pic* magazines, of *Click, Look* and *See,* and of La Guardia and Moses screaming at each other full blast as their flacks and assistants follow the blow-by-blow just outside the mayor's door. City of "Deb Doings" that are front-page news in Section Two of the *Sunday Times*: BUSY FALL AND WINTER SEASON ABSORBS DEBUTANTES' ATTENTION—COMING-OUT PARTIES INTERMINGLE WITH THEIR ACTIVITIES IN PHILANTHROPIC ENTERPRISES; and when the deb season is over, there are always breaking developments like YOUNGER SET AT PALM BEACH TURNS TO TENNIS COURTS FOR RECREATION to supply material for those Sunday banner headlines. City of Harlem newsstands that display the *Amsterdam News* ("Project Tenants Charge 'Bossing' "), The *Afro American* ("Joe Louis No Heavy Lover But Grand Guy in New Film"), the *Pittsburgh Courier* ("Judge Denies Request of White Convict That Colored Spectators Be Kept Out of Courtroom"), the *Chicago Defender* ("Dewey Says Harlem Is New York's Cleanest Section"), the *Journal and Guide* (START FINAL DRIVE AGAINST LYNCHING). City of union-run radio stations that are intellectual hotbeds, and socialist newspapers in Yiddish. City of Times Square lights: "PLANTER'S PEANUTS A Bag a Day for More Pep," "CAMELS never get on your nerves," "AUTOMAT." City of baseball, at the Polo Grounds, Yankee Stadium and Ebbets Field. Of boxing and six-day bicycle races (the contestants napping occasionally in trackside tents) at Madison Square Garden (which "belongs to the nineteenth century, a subject for an early Bellows painting").

Good-bye to that city: On Fifth Avenue you hail a cab. "The taxi plunges forward fiercely into the stream of fast-moving cars.

Everything is dynamic. You are excited," writes a foreign visitor, "even by the driver's easy insolence as he spits, talks, puffs a cigar, sounds his klaxon to indicate he is overtaking—" Good-bye to that plainspoken city. "When I make a mistake," said La Guardia, "it's a beaut." Good-bye to *which* city? An English visitor explains: To the "greatest city the world has ever seen." That one. You are on your way home. But you've missed one last thing. A thing you must see in order to understand the taut, serious society you are leaving: you must see the dancing.

Because in this city, people are *always* dancing. They dance so insistently, you can't help but wonder whether all the dancing might not be connected, somehow, to the city's very essence. This society's joy and passion don't spill out unconstrained as ours do, wine from a burst barrel running out on the sidewalk; they are *forced* out through the narrow fissure of society's *oughts,* and emerge jet-powered. If this city is roaring forward (it is!), joy and passion are the fuel and the engine is dance.

Of course I mean *serious* dancing as 1939 understood it: in time to the music, the right steps in the right sequence, with due regard to the social conventions and wherever possible, cheek to cheek. And 1939 favored serious dances: the occasional waltz or fox trot, yes, but also the hectic jitterbug, the complex rhumba and still more complicated samba. "By 1940 there must have been close to two hundred dance orchestras" in the United States; every last one of them wanted to play Manhattan.

All over this serious city, people dance. They dance at the Rainbow Room, "where society, celebrities and men of affairs entertain." They dance at the Stork Club: "plenty popular, plenty atmosphere, plenty expensive." They dance at Roseland and El Morocco. They dance at Leon & Eddie's ("most famous cabaret nightclub in the country") and the Savoy Ballroom in the center of Harlem and at

EPILOGUE: HERE IN UTOPIA

"200 Beautiful Dancing Partners 25¢ Admission 25¢" on Broadway and at the Arcadia, where tickets are ten cents a dance with one of the "professional hostesses"—seven cents to the lady and three to the house. They dance at dinner, cocktail hour and even (in a few hotels) at *lunch*. They dance to Eddie Duchin at the Plaza, Guy Lombardo at the Roosevelt, "high-class music" at the Iridium Room and (on a lucky night) to Benny Goodman at the Pennsylvania. "Even the hotels which have no pretension to smartness have wonderful bands." They dance at the beach. They dance in the schools. They dance in their living rooms. On the *Daily News* radio page there is a separate box just for dance music. On a typical night you can tune in dance bands at 5:00, 5:30, 6:00, 6:30, 7:00, 7:30, 8:00, 9:30, 11, 11:30 and midnight. When you rocket home at night on the Third Avenue El, you will see couples dancing as you roar lurch-and-clattering past their lit-up windows.

And of course, they dance at the fair. High school students "came in groups at night for the free swing dances." Free dancing every night. On opening night they stayed late to dance; on closing night they danced to a song called "Man and his Dreams." In the amusement area "dancers may match their moods to the tunes of top-flight name bands." "There is a place in the spotlight for dance devotees whether your dish is the rhumba, conga, jitterbug capers or some yet unnamed step." "In this scintillating center children are not forgotten. For them there are matinee dansants . . ."

And back on top of the town at the Rainbow Grill ("informal relative of the haughty Rainbow Room") I happen to know that, after they had finished their champagne and just before they caught the elevator down, Mark Handler and Hattie Laura Glassman lingered for a last dance. And that is the way we ought to leave them: dancing.

On impulse you tell the driver to turn around. You get out at

Rockefeller Center: You can't leave before you see the dancing. You sprint down the Channel Gardens toward the RCA Building. Its austere, majestic face lit up. Prometheus aglow beneath the base. The heroic figure might be doing a loose-jointed sidestroke—in typical Manship fashion it appears not to soar but rather to be suspended by prop wires from the heavens—and yet its vigor and directness are appealing, and the downturned face seems thoughtful in the shadows as you hurry past. You walk up some stairs and stride down the sidewalk along RCA's right flank, under the bright marquee and into the elevator lobby; with a casual push forward on the control level, the operator sends you whirring upward for a last look at the dancing.

You sit in a plain leather-covered dining chair at a round table, and listen and watch and breathe cigarette air amid the fluff-and-crinkle of a dozen conversations with silver sounds tangled up in them. The ring of a glass. Clink of a fork. Laughter. The band of four saxophones, three trumpets, two trombones, piano, guitar, bass and drums start to play. Backscrape of a chair behind you. Prominent jazz beat, the trumpets' acid scream, and then ironic backchatting saxophones. Tall windows run up the sides of the room: your city stretched out taut and glistening to the horizon. The cigarette girl is murmuring (scrape of chairs as the couple to your right gets up to dance) to a customer, bending over (burst of noise from the kitchen as the door bats open and swings shut). On the floor before you couples dance. They swing apart and grope together. Across the room you see intermittently between dancers the bandleader's black satin lapels. He has turned away from his musicians, is facing the microphone in his black tie and gleaming hair, waves his long baton in time, is preparing to sing; taps the microphone absently; brass gleam of the trombone behind his left ear. The manager off to one side taking a loud thoughtful pull on his cigarette. *Gardens*—drifting in from the conversations around you—*Eddie—commu-*

nism—La Guardia. Laughter. The couple in the center of the floor moving slowly, her arm on his shoulder, his arm on her waist—that one, where the man is leaning down, now, to rest his forehead on the girl's auburn hair: That is Mark Handler dancing with his fiancée. I don't know the name of the band but they're good, aren't they? What *is* that song?

It's just on the tip of my tongue.

Notes

ABBREVIATIONS USED IN NOTES AND BIBLIOGRAPHY

Gallup = George H. Gallup, *The Gallup Poll: Public Opinion, 1935–1971,* vol. 1, *1935–1948* (New York: Random House, 1972)

NY Advancing = Rebecca B. Rankin, ed., *New York Advancing: World's Fair Edition* (New York: Publisher's Printing Co., 1939)

NYHT = *New York Herald Tribune*

NYT = *New York Times*

NYWF = New York World's Fair

Survey = Market Analysts, Inc., "Third Attendance Survey of the New York World's Fair 1939" (Nov. 13, 1939), YCOP.

WPA *Guide* = Committee for Federal Writers' Publications, *New York City Guide* (New York: Random House, 1939)

WPA *Panorama* = Committee for Federal Writers' Publications, *New York Panorama* (New York: Random House, 1938)

YCOP = Century of Progress—New York World's Fair Collection, Manuscripts and Archives, Yale University Library (Yale Century of Progress Collection).

1. PROLOGUE: THE CENTER OF TIME

If that doesn't make you catch your breath: Hillis (1939), p. 57. **the splendid example:** Monahan (1937), unpaginated. **a color organ:** WPA *Guide,* p. 337.

dumb bunnies, playboys: Moses (1943), p. 18. **To the victor:** *NY Advancing.* **I shall not rest:** cited in Kessner (1989), p. 271. **Our Mayor is the most appealing:** cited in Kessner (1992), p. 321.

Crucifying a market inspector: Moses (1957), pp. 14–15. **like Toscanini:** Cuneo (1955), p. 198. **When she sees uncollected:** Liebling (1938), p. 155. **a great deal for your money:** Harding (1939) pp. 197–198. **under the direction:** Hillis (1939), p. 71. **kept spick-and-span:** ibid, p. 103.

best policed city: Lait and Mortimer (1948), p. 153. This particular assessment dates from ten years later, but it would have been perfectly at home in the late 1930s. La Guardia took a particular interest in the police; see chapter 15, "Technology: Frightening."

One may walk the streets: Fay (1936), p. 121. **A dark blotch:** WPA *Guide,* p. 29. **The City is ever vigilant:** *NY Advancing,* p. 36. **a name that is world famous:** Monaghan (1937), unpaginated. **Maybe real Communists:** McCarthy (1992), p. 15. **Don't go to Harlem:** Hillis (1939), p. 92.

They feel that the white world: Liebling (1938), p. 154. **people maintain:** ibid., p. 151.

Stop Japanese Aggression: See Beaton (1938), p. 161. **certainly not of restaurants.** There were a few Japanese restaurants in Manhattan, but the WPA *Guide* lists more Armenian restaurants than Japanese. **Beigels:** this is the spelling used in (for example) Monaghan (1937), unpaginated.

"major" daily newspapers: WPA *Panorama,* p. 304.

their triumph at the Paris: Monaghan (1937), unpaginated.

the literary genius of Aurora High School: WPA *Guide,* p. 49. **visitors sometimes wonder:** Monaghan (1937), unpaginated. **the popular music business:** see Taylor (1992), p. 33. **an incredible scene in the movies:** Hillis (1939) p. 136. **neighborhood movie houses:** Liebling (1938), p. 157.

A 1939 photo: in Riesenberg and Alland (1939), following p. 54. **to spread the agreeable shade:** White (1984), p. 213.

Roger Starr presents: Starr (1985), pp. 9–14.

(not *the* **Brooklyn) Bridge:** readers of Hart Crane's "To Brooklyn Bridge" knew this already.

We seek to present: *NY Advancing,* p. xv. **No matter the year:** *Life,* Dec. 9, 1940, p. 26. **the Army exhibited the layout:** see "America Begins Training First Conscript Army in Its Peacetime History," *Life,* Dec. 9, 1940, p. 29. **Throughout the land:** This and the following quote are from the *March of Time* newsreel segment "America's Youth" (1940). **some of you are communists:** ibid. **were always so** *strict:* McCarthy (1939), p. 83.

muses James Thurber moodily: "Unfamiliar Misquotations," *The New Yorker,* June 3, 1939, p. 18.

were taller than you: see Diehl (1985), pp. 105 ff. **Already in 1938, an out-of-towner's:** White (1990), p. 199. **is so stupendous, gigantic;** Hillis (1939), p. 187.

greatest show: "Curtains," *Time,* Nov. 4, 1940, p. 72. **the biggest, costliest:** *NYT,* Oct. 28, 1940, p. 1. **surprising beauty:** *NYT* May 1, 1939, p. 1.

the miracle wrought: *NYT,* May 1, 1939. **the most stupendous exposition:** From a newsreel clip included in the documentary film *The World of Tomorrow,* a production of Media Study, Lance Bird, Tom Johnson and the Television Laboratory at WNET / Thirteen, 1984.

revolutionary in its contrast: Harding (1939), p. 200; **in a world swept by terror and hysteria:** ibid. **a constructive world concept:** NYHT, NYWF section, Apr. 30, 1939, p. 6.

an entirely new degree of fluidity: Haskell (1940), p. 65. **adventure in pigments:** "Adventure in Pigments," *NYHT,* NYWF section, Apr. 30, 1939, p. 39. **a thing so fantastic:** John O'Reilly: "A new, mighty instrument of entertainment, *NYHT,* NYWF section, Apr. 30, 1939, p. 39. **used superlatives:** *Survey,* p. 49.

New York cannot get away: Fay (1936), p. 65. **His Italian vigour tends:** ibid., p. 64. **a fabulous history:** *NYT,* Oct. 28, 1940, p. 1.

There was never another Fair: Melvin Halbert, personal communication. **a new view of the world:** John Ekizian, with reference to his father, personal communication.

a late-August survey: *Gallup* (Aug. 21, 1939), p. 176. **October 1939:** *Survey,* p. 49. **One sixteen-year-old:** John Ekizian, with reference to his father, personal communication.

a coin no one recognizes: *Harding (1939), p. 197.* **according to** *Life*

magazine: Jan. 9, 1939, p. 28. **At the ground breaking:** *NYT,* June 30, 1936, p. 21.

long shuffling lines: See, for example, Kazin (1989), p. 77.

according to a Gallup poll: *Gallup* (May 14, 1939), p. 154. **Roughly sixteen million:** *NYT,* Oct. 28, 1940, p. 1. **an almost perfect illusion:** *The New Yorker,* May 13, 1939, p. 85. **How will the little boy climb it?:** White (1944), p. 75. **Les Américains:** "L'exposition de New York," *L'Illustration,* July 1939, unpaginated.

four-fifths of the people: *Survey,* p. 52. This is something of an over-estimate; roughly five of twenty-six million visitors saw the Futurama during its first year, but of those twenty-six million many were repeat customers.

The Fair designers could not divide it: Robert D. Kohn: "Social Ideals in a World's Fair," *The North American Review,* 247 (March 1939), reprinted in Susman (1973), pp. 297–300; p. 298.

Peering through the haze: Geddes (1940), p. 8. **The promise of the future:** David Sarnoff, "Might of the Speeding Word," *NYT,* NYWF section, Mar. 5, 1939, p. 64.

I am optimistic for the future: Harry Hopkins, "Government and Business to Cooperate for Better World," *NYHT,* NYWF section, Apr. 30, 1939, p. 5. **There are big changes ahead:** Charles F. Kettering, "Wheels, Keels and Wings," *NYT,* NYWF section, Mar. 5, 1939, p. 46.

typical American boy: " 'Typical Boy' Wins Title at Fair," *NYT,* Sept. 30, 1940, p. 36. **The Fair's Science Director:** Wendt (1939), p. 101. **there have been hit shows:** Geddes (1940), p. 3. **In January 1938 a majority expected:** *Gallup* (Jan. 2, 1938), p. 83.

a still larger majority: *Gallup* (Aug. 28, 1939), p. 177.

Roper poll from the middle of the Fair's second season: "What the U.S.A. Thinks," *Life,* July 29, 1940, p. 20.

historian Sydney Ahlstrom wrote: Ahlstrom (1972), p. 2. **author and editor Ellis Cose:** *NYT Book Review,* Mar. 17, 1994, p. 11. **one the Right's most learned and distinguished:** Himmelfarb (1994).

Pride and conscience: H. G. Wells, "World of Tomorrow," *NYT,* NYWF section, Mar. 5, 1939, p. 61. **clouded by the electric storms of today:** Anne O'Hare McCormick, "World of Undying Hope," *NYT,* NYWF section, Mar. 5, 1939, p. 18.

because we are simply more sophisticated: thus, for example, Peter L. Rothholz writes from the standpoint of 1980 about the era of the 1939 World's

Fair: "Characteristic of the naiveté of that time was America's confidence in herself and her ability to forge a better tomorrow." Foreword to Helen A. Harrison, ed., *Dawn of a New Day: The New York World's Fair, 1939/40.* New York: New York University Press, 1980, p. vi. This book will argue that the confidence was neither naive nor misplaced.

The World Grows Smaller: Wendt (1939), p. 38.

To hell with Europe: cited in Leuchtenburg (1963), p. 216. **Wines made "dry":** *Life,* Nov. 11, 1939. **a distinguished volunteer faculty:** WPA *Panorama,* p. 298.

the Sandwich of Tomorrow ... Sentence of Tomorrow: *The New Yorker,* Apr. 29, 1939, pp. 16, 17.

Because most pictures of starlets: *Life,* July 3, 1939, p. 7; **What congress most wanted:** ibid., p. 14.

the dances are perfect: Mueller (1985) has a superb discussion of Astaire's dances. **When Irving Berlin escorted:** Barrett (1994), p. 142.

The narration marches double-time: Strictly speaking, this is the style of the popular *March of Time* newsreels. They were produced by Time [magazine] Inc., and echo *Time's* own distinctively choppy thirties style.

cars will be smaller: Geddes (1940), p. 55. **to make automobile collisions impossible:** ibid., p. 6. **it costs too much:** ibid., p. 146. **In 1927, 44%:** see Flink (1988), p. 131. **The pictures are unreeled:** The *Times* was commenting on a preliminary test. "Test of television started in secret," *NYT,* June 30, 1936, p. 21.

Wow idea of the Fair: "Specialties in Flushing," *Time,* June 12, 1939, p. 11. **Perhaps no other display on the grounds:** Haskell (1940), p. 68. **New York's four greatest problems:** Franklin (1937), p. 112. **a virtuoso, a political Heifetz:** Franklin (1937), p. 122. **A successful Polish businessman:** Susan Arellano, personal communication.

I am here entrusted: This statement and the subsequent one by William King are cited in "Spotlight at Fair Swings to Dedication of the Palestine Pavilion," *NYT,* May 29, 1939, p. 7. See also (for example) "Life on the Newsfronts of the World," *Life,* June 12, 1939, p. 18: "In his long exploration of the mysteries of the universe, Albert Einstein has not forgotten the arid patch of earth on which Jerusalem stands."

Suddenly you see the first intimation: White (1944), p. 72.

the end of the book of Deuteronomy: author's translation.

our creed of liberty and democracy: from a 1943 speech, cited by Schlesinger (1991), p. 37.

In the late thirties it was an intense and heartfelt faith: This argument must not be misunderstood as implying that late-thirties morale was uniformally high and the country gung-ho about every aspect of national business. The combined effects of depression and the evident vigor of European fascism made some people wonder whether democracy might not be doomed. Fringe political and social movements blossomed in the 1930s; I will discuss some of them later. The fitness and morale of American youth were questioned. The popularity of the "Veterans of Future Wars" society gave evidence of at least a degree of cynicism. In the summer of 1940, the *Time* magazine company's newsreel division released a film called *The Ramparts We Watch* that was intended, at least in part, to combat cynicism among the young and to clarify for them the fact that there *was* "something worth fighting for." (See Herzstein 1994, p. 156.) 1939 was full of dissenters. What is important is that in 1939, there was a church from which to dissent. Nowadays the Left still likes to think of itself as a band of anti-establishment anti-establishmentarians, the Right sees itself as progressive or "revolutionary," and the church is gone.

It emerged in modern form: on this and the rest of this paragraph, see Paul Johnson's brilliant essay "God and the Americans" (1995); also Schlesinger (1991), particularly pp. 30–37, Ahlstrom (1972) pp. 640–642, Williams (1969) pp. 472–492.

On every hand there is symbolized: "Texts of addresses delivered yesterday," *NYT,* May 1, 1939, p. 5. **to the future of the American people:** "La Guardia Runs a Steam Shovel As Work Starts on World's Fair," *NYT,* June 30, 1936, p. 21. **we are most unselfish about it:** "Texts of addresses delivered yesterday," *NYT,* May 1, 1939, p. 5. **the George Washington Bridge and the nave of Chartres:** Teague (1940), plate 74. Norman Bel Geddes had included juxtapositions between modern machines and medieval structures in *Horizons* (1932); on the relationship between those and the "visual analogies" Le Corbusier introduced in the 1920s, see Kihlstedt (1986), p. 117, n. 40.

a religion that has seen its promises *realized:* the opposite holds for a religion that has made promises and seen them broken—in many cases, it will see an upsurge of believers. See, for example, Nisbet (1982), p. 183.

forward-looking young architects: NYWF (1939), Dept. of Feature Publicity, "The Theme of the New York World's Fair of 1939" (undated press release), p. 1, YCOP.

2. INTO THE FAIR

voices had risen in lively controversy: McCarthy (1939), p. 146

proved insufficiently water-tight: *Architectural Review,* vol. 86, Aug. 1939, cited in Kihlstedt (1986), p. 116 n. 33.

a kind word for the man-eating shark: *NYT,* Nov. 11, 1936, cited in Leuchtenburg (1963), p. 196.

Roosevelt's personal popularity remained high: Soon after the election, a Gallup poll showed 55.5% of the public approving of Roosevelt's performance. *Gallup* (Dec. 4, 1938), p. 127.

If these boys continue: cited in Heims (1980), p. 166.

skyscraper skeleton: WPA *Panorama,* p. 497.

Paris's ugliest landmark: "Paris, War Darkens the Beautiful and Happy 'City of Light,' " *Life,* June 3, 1940, p. 63.

the man who started it all: Simon (1967), p. 3.

There is something in this observation: Moses (1943), p. 3.

it's curious: Dos Passos (1937), pp. 63 and 65.

pick out fluorescent paint in the model: The *NYT* published a short "science news" note on the fluorescent paint, July 2, 1939, section 2, p. 4.

the interdependence of all people: *NYHT,* NYWF Section, Apr. 30, 1939, p. 6.

an acre and a quarter large: see Harrison, "The Fair Perceived" (1980), p. 50.

planless jumble of slum and chimney: cited in Cusker (1980), p. 14.

a film called *The City:* the documentary film was itself a fairly new idea at the time: "U.S. movies in the last decade have made impressive headway in a new direction—the documentary film." "The City," *Life,* June 5, 1939, pp. 64–65. **a hectoring documentary film:** Stern, Gilmartin and Mellins (1987), p. 731.

an ordinary exhibit of city planning: NYWF (1939), Dept. of Feature Publicity, "City of Tomorrow" (undated press release), p. 3, YCOP.

newspaper piece about Democracity: "Theme Center of the Fair—Democracity," *NYHT,* NYFW Section, Apr. 30, 1939, p. 6.

insured mortgages and favored suburbs: see, for example, Jackson (1985), pp. 203 ff.

Robert Moses felt obliged to assert: Moses (1956), p. 88.

by explicit contractual stipulation: see Wattel (1958), p. 303.

a perfectly integrated garden city of tomorrow: NYWF (1939), Information Manual Entry (June 30, 1939), YCOP.

Town and country must be married: cited in Mumford (1938), p. 396.

The motor highway surrounding: Hudson (1934), p. 3.

The City of Tomorrow will be inspired: NYWF (1939), Dept of Feature Publicity, "City of Tomorrow." (undated press release), p. 4, YCOP; **so as not to utilize:** ibid., p. 2; **Intoxicated drivers will be rare:** ibid., p. 5.

when I finally presented myself: White (1944), p. 72.

3. COLOR CODED

As a teenager he went often: Ernest Schwartz, personal communication.

during the 1930's, Robert Moses: Caro (1974), p. 508.

the most visible fruits: Moley (1940), pp. 193–194. **the question which posterity will ask:** Moses (1943), p. 17. **Moley quotes Moss:** Moley (1940), p. 194. **We must employ ingenious means** Moses (1956), p. 210.

He has vision: Swope's forward to Moses (1956), p. vii. **The New York Parks Department:** Teague (1940), caption, plate 127.

You know, I said to an official there: this quote and the subsequent one about Bathgate, Fay (1936), pp. 178, 179.

a second class intellect: cited in Ward (1989), p. xiii. **a pleasant man:** cited in Friedel (1990), p. 168. **moving slowly towards the podium:** Ward (1989), pp. 693–694.

In this quarrel: Churchill (1948), p. 214.

For those who had expected: "Roosevelt Speaks," *NYT,* May 1, 1939, p. 1. **as a polite but pointed lecture:** "Roosevelt Pledges Peace Policy To Continue Gains of Democracy," *NYHT,* May 1, 1939, p. 1. **I have predicted:** *NYT,* Oct. 27, 1940, p. 42.

like all my friends, I distrusted: Kazin (1962), p. 85. **Silone, Malraux, Hemingway:** ibid. **Mr. Folger is a socialist!:** Trilling (1947), p. 58.

superior to liberal capitalism: Wreszin (1994), p. 48. The quotation itself comes from the book that Macdonald was reviewing, *The Coming American Fascism* by Lawrence Dennis. Macdonald endorsed Dennis's claim.

looked at the blank wall: Schlesinger (1988), p. 12.

the key inspiration was Peixotto's: "Adventure in Pigments," *NYHT,* NYWF Section, Apr. 30, 1939, p. 39; see also Harrison, "The Fair Perceived" (1980).

writes Gardner Harding: Harding (1939), p. 193.

tossed its hat in the air: "Adventure in Pigments," *NYHT*, NYWF Section, Apr. 30, 1939, p. 39.

frankly enclosures for rentable space: Hamlin (1938), pp. 675. **interesting and beautiful:** ibid., p. 677; **form a group of great interest:** ibid., p. 678. **a magnificent conception:** Hamlin (1939), p. 645; **daring and dynamic:** ibid., 647. Robert M. Coates in *The New Yorker* agreed with Hamlin, up to a point. "Though most of the sculpture along the mall is distinguished mainly by its awfulness, I thought the big statue of George Washington, by James Earle Fraser, had a simplicity of mass and a dignity of treatment that quite justify its size and importance." May 27, 1939, p. 55.

They drop you twenty floors: "The World's Fair," *The New Yorker*, Oct. 26, 1940, p. 11.

4. THE NECKTIE

the perspiration from the encasement: *NYT*, May 1, 1939, p. 6.

a certain class of people: cited in Schwartz (1973), p. 278. **white shoes or sports clothes:** see Hillis (1939), p. 43. **even though he perform this office:** Post (1937), p. 732.

Lucinda Franks catalogs: Franks (1993), pp. 32, 32, 34. **some students are simply in a better environment:** cited in *Wall Street Journal*, Oct. 10, 1994, p. A20. **news reports told of a mother:** *National Review*, Jan. 8, 1994, p. 12. Evidently the story was reported on CBS's *Sixty Minutes* as well.

Gerald Wendt commented: Wendt (1939), cited in Cusker (1980), p. 12. **spoke the word** *syphilis:* see Leuchtenburg (1963), p. 176.

F. Scott Fitzgerald's lovely unfinished novel: Fitzgerald (1941), p. 117.

Harrison reports that the Perisphere's shape: Newhouse, (1989), p. 82. **greatest urban complex of the twentieth century:** White and Willensky (1978), p. 169. **carried that idea to the obvious extreme:** see Santomasso's discussion of *architecture parlante* at the fair, Santomasso (1980), pp. 35–36.

financial constraints forced a reduction: Newhouse (1989), p. 89.

the Statue of Liberty connection: see Kent (1936), p. 612. **another, stranger coincidence:** "L'Exposition de New York," *L'Illustration,* July 1939, unpaginated.

supposed to have been finished in concrete: see Newhouse (1989),

p. 89. **"In many ways," Harrison reflected:** cited in Harrison, "Catalogue of the Exhibit" (1980), p. 79.

5. THE MONKEY GODDESS

Talbot Hamlin disliked all the pylons: Hamlin (1938), p. 678.

the "Four Freedoms": The idea for a Four Freedoms plaza came from *NYT* publisher Arthur Hays Sulzberger. FDR subsequently made a variation on the freedoms famous in his State of the Union address on January 6, 1941: "We look forward to a world founded upon four essential human freedoms . . . ," cited in Friedel (1990), p. 360.

Mrs. Modern orders a house: Gilbert Rhode, "Description and Script of the Community Interests Focal Exhibit at the New York World's Fair 1939, Inc.," (Sept. 22, 1938), p. 10, YCOP.

CLEAN as a whistle: cited in Hirschorn and Izenour's exceptionally interesting *White Towers*, p. 64.

6. DOUGHNUTS

the fraction of attendees per month: *Survey,* p. 4. **One hundred and fifty years ago:** cited in Cusker (1980), p. 10.

in 1935, the typical middle-class family: see Phillips (1969), p. 414.

The average 1939 income: these are figures as of 1989: see Derks (1994), pp. 258 ff.

the theme permeates the chief features: Monaghan (1939), p. 29. **a change from relative independence:** these and subsequent quotes in this paragraph from Gilbert Rhode, "Description and Script of the Community Interests Focal Exhibit at the New York World's Fair 1939, Inc.," p. 2 ("electric phonograph"), p. 5 ("1789"), p. 7 ("1939"), p. 12 ("feeling of uplift") p. 5 (Sept. 22, 1938), YCOP.

nearly empty shell: Harding (1939), p. 196.

The Future, holding her distaff: WPA *Panorama,* p. 490.

The doughnut apparently: *NYT,* Oct. 28, 1940, p. 11.

7. HAVEN'T WE MET SOMEWHERE BEFORE?

a pair of lovers in a 1936 novel: Dos Passos (1937), p. 70.
The Amusement Area was eclipsed: *Survey,* p. 28.
sporting a G-string labeled: Rydell (1993), p. 142. **the exhibitors did not dilly-Dali:** "Pay as You Enter," *Time,* June 26, 1939, p. 10. **He stalked off to Europe:** see Stern, Gilmartin and Mellins (1987), p. 755. **he had smashed a display window:** see *Time,* June 26, 1939, p. 10.
Americans today consider the display: "Betty Kuzmeck Lies in Bed of Venus at New York World's Fair," *Life,* July 29, 1940, pp. 50–53. *Life* covered other amusement area attractions too: for example, "Midway's Latest Stunt Is Bouncing Pretty Girl Out of Bed at the De-Bunk-Her," June 24, 1940. "The utterly primitive satisfaction of hitting a target with a baseball and thereby knocking a pretty girl out of bed is available at the New York World's Fair to any man or boy with two bits and a steady aim," p. 80.
A minister from Brooklyn inveighed: for this citation and the "Mandatory Bras and Net Coverings order," Rydell (1993), pp. 141, 142. **"insufficient clothing":** "Two Fair Show Girls Arrested For Nudity," *NYT,* June 13, 1939, p. 20. **Does the city want this:** "Decision Is Reserved in Nudity Show Case," *NYT,* June 20, 1939, p. 16. **dramatizing women as sexual:** Rydell (1993), p. 11.
78 percent of a Gallup survey: *Gallup* (Dec. 25, 1938), p. 131.
Women's participation was a first thought: NYWF (1939), "Cultural and Social Aspects of the New York World's Fair of 1939," p. 10. On opening day *NYT* reporter Kathleen McLaughlin wrote: "Unconditionally and instantly, women loved the Fair. They told their admiration and enthusiasm endlessly, in widely varying accents and phrases. But the sum of their comments was the same, whether voiced from a seat on the Presidential platform, twittered gaily in the sacrosanct precincts of the National Advisory Committee's building, or yelled with college girl vivacity from a perch on a stool at a hamburger stand." "Many feminine touches revealed as women analyze attractions," *NYT,* May 1, 1939, p. 3.
comments a 1937 biography: Franklin (1937), p. 125.
in this modern day: Post (1937) p. 365, p. 365; **Many a man has asked:** ibid., p. 713. **The Handy Woman About the House:** cited in Stilgoe (1988), p. 266. **Girls Favorite Play Things:** *Wall Street Journal,* Sept 23, 1994, p. B1.
In a 1939 survey: *Gallup* (July 9, 1939), p. 164.

Miss Nude of 1939: "Fair nude show promoters held guilty by Mayor," *NYHT,* June 6, 1939, p. 12.

He fires sixty of them: see Kessner (1989), p. 296. **political whiners:** "Mayor Opens Whitestone Bridge to Fair," *NHYT,* Apr. 30, 1939, p. 36. **writes University of Chicago president:** Robert M. Hutchins, Vital Education," *NYT,* NYWF section, Mar. 5, 1939, p. 34.

The New Deal era is over: Al From, cited in M. Kelly, "You say you want a revolution," *The New Yorker,* Nov. 21, 1994, p. 58. **Government relief payments:** cited in Limpus and Leyson (1938), p. 416. **a narcotic, a subtle destroyer:** cited in Leuchtenburg (1963), p. 124.

WPA officials used exactly the same word: Leuchtenburg (1963), p. 254. **the "discovery" of the New World:** NYWF (1940), "Negro Week on the American Common, World's Fair of 1940 in New York, July 23-28" ("souvenir program"), p. 4, YCOP. **social causes, environment, education:** Lionel Trilling (1947), p. 298. **Political correctness is not an innovation:** Diana Trilling (1993), p. 197.

in the World of Tomorrow: Arthur Krock, "Foundations of the Nation," *NYT,* NYWF section, Mar. 5, 1939, p. 32.

8. PARTY

known as "plastics": Wendt (1939), pp. 164-165.

9. CHOOSING FORD

One of my sources: Melvin Halbert, personal communication.

the machine with the human voice: "The World's Fair," *The New Yorker,* June 3, 1939, p. 10. **that was** *Business Week's* **theory:** "What Shows Pulled at the Fair." *Business Week,* Nov. 4, 1939, p. 22. **No listener can resist:** Wendt (1939), p. 119.

La Guardia did as a matter of fact: see, for example, Cuneo (1955), p. 191.

essential that we give some attention: cited in Harrison, "Catalogue of the Exhibit," p. 100. **There's nothing fancy about it:** "Motors and Motoring," *The New Yorker,* May 13, 1939, pp. 85-88.

In the entire history of art exhibitions: "Guide and Picture Book," published by the *Art News* for Masterpieces of Art (1939), p. 5; **It cannot be denied:** ibid., p. 6.

Rocket flight is at present: Wendt (1939) pp. 110–111.

ranked fourth-best: *Gallup* (May 17, 1939), p. 154.

10. TECHNOLOGY: GORGEOUS

What particularly baffled: *Time,* Feb. 20, 1939, cited in Harrison, "Catalogue of the Exhibit," p. 109.

the most popular compositions: liner notes, "Gershwin Gold 1," RPO/Impact Records. (The best current recordings of Gershwin are the three volumes of pianist Jack Gibbons's extraordinary Authentic Gershwin series, on the English ASV Digital label.) **earned the unspoken tribute:** WPA *Panorama,* p. 264. **Fred Astaire recalls that:** Mueller (1985), p. 15. **Ira assembled it:** see Schwartz (1973), p. 287.

beyond that they know nothing: "Television," *Life,* Feb. 20, 1939, p. 45. **Gerald Wendt presents:** Wendt (1939), pp. 145, 148–149. **last week, of course:** "Notes and Comments," *The New Yorker,* May 13, 1939, p. 13. **one of the pioneer owners:** "Television in the Home," *The New Yorker,* June 3, 1939.

with a feeling of humbleness: "World's Fair R.C.A. Building Dedicated; Ceremony Televised," *NYHT,* Apr. 21, 1939, p. 9.

the end of the world as we know it: *The Economist,* Oct. 16, 1993, pp. 15–16; also see, in the same issue, "Multimedia", pp. 21–24; "Roll Over, Gutenberg," pp 195–196.

This is going to forever change our lives: cited in John Markoff, "A Phone-Cable Vehicle for the Data Superhighway," *NYT* Oct. 14, 1993, p. C24. **A Revolution in home entertainment:** *Business Week,* Oct. 25, 1993, p. 34.

The workshop is the closest: cited in O'Connor (1980), p. 65.

The New York skyline: Elmer Davis, "Too Stately Mansions," *New Republic,* July 1, 1932, cited in Stern, Gilmartin and Mellins (1987), p. 603.

which has replaced the plodding horse: Geddes (1940), p. 10. **When engineers are given:** John O'Reilly, "A new, mighty instrument of entertainment." *NYHT,* NYWF section, Apr. 30, 1939, p. 39. **engineers fascinated him:** see Caro (1974), p. 359. **should be possible to convince:** cited in Leuchtenburg (1963), p. 341.

For sheer originality of invention: the *NYT* delivered this verdict in a

cryptic piece by science editor Waldemar Kaempffert, "Magic Carpet in Futurama," Sept. 10, 1939, Section II, p. 8.

11. FLIGHT IN SPACE

Mysteriously the crowd moved: Haskell (1940), p. 68.
    one of the oddest buildings: WPA *Panorama,* p. 492.
    there will then be no reason: Wendt (1939), p.106. **a 1939 poll:** *Gallup*
(May 29, 1939), p. 156.
    listening to the rumble: Dos Passos (1937), p. 117.
    We learn something about him: "Symbols of Tomorrow," *The New
Yorker,* June 3, 1939, pp. 12–13.
    Jeweled plumes of spray: NYWF Information Manual Entry (June 17,
1939), YCOP. **New York's most typical:** Haskell (1940), p. 66.

12. PLAYGROUNDS

I am the I.: Liebling (1938), p. 69; **When the checks bounced:** ibid. p. 75.

13. HIS OWN WORDS

Daniel Patrick Moynihan wrote: "Toward a Post-Industrial Social Policy,"
Public Interest 96 (Summer 1989) pp. 16–27. **A girl whom I have in mind:** cited
in Riesenberg and Alland (1939), p. 47; **I am a girl in my late twenties:** ibid.
p. 48; **publishes a menu submitted:** cited in Lingeman (1970), pp. 14–15.

14. DYNAMITE, MANHATTAN, 1939

Portrait of America 1939: *Life,* June 5, 1939, p. 52.
    a construction site with pedestrians: in Riesenberg and Alland (1939),
before p. 63.
    a gentleman of course removes: Post (1937), p. 25; **He lifts his hat:** ibid.
p. 28; **a maneuver half-way between:** ibid. p. 28; **reply to an introduction:** ibid.

p. 10; **When the need arises:** ibid. p. 26; **an old gentleman of great distinction:** ibid. p. 4.

Robert Moses installed playgrounds: see Caro (1974), p. 488.

general rules of behavior: Beaton (1938), p. 34. **Take off your hat:** Limpus and Leyson (1938), pp. 383-384.

your stick should be: Post (1937), p. 726. **the 1992** *Emily Post:* Post (1992), p. 496. **For maybe ten years:** "The Four-in-Hand Outrage," in Benchley (1928), p. 185. (But those unfamiliar with Benchley are cautioned not to misclassify him as some kind of fashion reporter. He is one of the funniest American writers of the twentieth century.)

just under two-thirds: *Gallup* (July 3, 1939), p. 163. **the best of all time:** except for the opening moments of a quiet Rogers-and-Astaire dance with no stunning virtuoso passages at all—the *Carefree* sequence in which psychiatrist Fred conjures languid dance steps out of hypnotized Ginger to Irving Berlin's lovely and haunting "Won't you change partners and dance?" The dancers stand apart but she is born up by his aura and, although ostensibly he is manipulating her by hypnotic remote control, he does it with touching sweetness. Neither Astaire's greatness as a dancer nor as a choreographer depends on mere technical virtuosity.

Take off that collar and tie: Orwell (1952), p. 228.

In a 1941 survey: *Gallup* (Jan. 3, 1942), p. 315. **divorce-bound, train-traveling narrator:** McCarthy (1939), p. 21.

Contraceptives were widely available: see Green (1992), pp. 131-132. **by sheer dint:** cited in Morris (1979), p. 794 n. 71. **They sweat into their:** *NYT,* July 15, 1994, p. 1.

15. TECHNOLOGY: FRIGHTENING

Was not the finest element: Haskell (1940), p. 68. **we now see 10,000 trees:** "Gardens Display Pledged for Park," *NYT,* May 19, 1939, p. 18. **just a sprinkling:** *NYT,* Oct. 28, 1939, p. 11.

He quit the FBI: see Phillips (1969), p. 321. **La Guardia had them delivered:** Cuneo (1955), p. 195

Quick! The bombers: Wendt (1939), p. 83. **used her air power:** Churchill (1948), p. 214.

not inspiring but horrific: see Daix (1993), p. 252. **a battle scene from**

a pediment: cited in, for example, Hilton (1985), p. 245. **Franco's Dream and Lie:** see Daix (1993), p. 247.

16. WHEN LIFE TURNS OUT TO BE A SANDCASTLE

the decline of the sheet music: WPA *Panorama,* p. 244. **It furnishes a jazz undertone:** Fay (1936), p. 218. **"Of course,"** writes another: Beaton (1938), p. 27.

    covers fifty acres: WPA *Guide,* pp. 474–475. **Luna Park was intended:** see Silver (1967), pp. 190–191. **couples usually went together:** *Survey,* p. 32. **no meal was complete:** *NYT,* Oct. 28, 1940, p. 11.

17. TECHNOLOGY: GOOD

"At every turn," writes a modern historian: Rydell (1993), p. 124. **The single units in this station:** Wendt (1939), p. 37. **a Michigan County Commissioner:** see Geddes (1940), p. 66.

    a visual dramatization of a solution: Geddes (1940), p. 4.

    even the existence of business centers: H. G. Wells, "World of Tomorrow," *NYT,* NYWF section, Mar. 5, 1939, p. 5. **can we improve the spiritual:** cited in Cusker (1980), p. 10.

    I have discussed it elsewhere: for example, in "The Cyber-Road Not Taken," *Washington Post,* April 3, 1994, pp. C1–C2.

    It was about nylon stockings: see, for example, "Nylon Stockings May Ruin Japan's Silk Trade," *Life,* June 5, 1939, p. 68.

    Motion pictures, silent and sound: Riesenberg and Alland (1939), p. 52. **This is the way:** cited in *NYT,* June 30, 1936, p. 21.

19. ROBOT!

was arrested at this stage: Teague (1940), caption, plate 39. **actual control of the weather:** Wendt (1939), p. 172.

    streamlined coffins: see Beaton (1938), p. 165. **Thousands of copies:** On the *Book of Record,* see Kihlstedt (1986), p. 112. **The human anxiety to die:** *The New Yorker,* May 24, 1939.

Ever since the invention: "Finger-Counting Robot," *Newsweek,* Apr. 24, 1939, p. 28.

20. THE LANDSCAPE AND ITS SANCTITY

This is not a vague dream: cited in Cusker (1980), p. 14. **The Motorway System as visualized:** Geddes (1940), p. 10. **led by men who felt the responsibility:** Hudson (1934), p. 1. **we hold tomorrow** cited in *NYHT,* " 'Theme Center' Site Dedicated for World's Fair," Aug. 17, 1937, p. 17.

So revolutionary was this style: Greif (1975), p. 17.

I will make even busy New Yorkers: cited in Wilson, Pilgrim and Tashjian (1986), p. 215.

How can you disregard: Schwartz (1953), p. 190. **He who claims:** Wendt (1939), p. 157.

great knife-like prow: WPA *Panorama,* p. 229. **It may be said without contradiction:** Chester Henry Jones, "Architecture Astray," *Atlantic,* Jan. 1931, pp. 64–74; cited in Stern, Gilmartin and Mellins (1987), p. 603. **the expression of American daring:** Simeon: Strunsky, "Soul of the City." *NYT, NYWF* section, March 5, 1939.

on the ferry to New Jersey: see Caro (1974), p. 67. **the City still hasn't figured out; a state judge ordered the hospital:** both of the incidents are referred to as of August, 1994.

Action is our slogan: Wendt (1939), p. 83.

must affiliate with the creative artist: cited in Wilson, Pilgrim and Tashjian (1986), p. 231.

22. OBSESSION

some sources reported: *Time,* "Mr. Whalen's Image," May 1, 1939, pp. 72 ff.

La Guardia had urged: "Religious Center at Fair Proposed," *NYT,* Mar. 4, 1937, p. 25. **The Nazi press noted:** Kessner (1989), p. 403.

They proposed a "Freedom Pavilion": on the story related in the following paragraphs, see Hobson (1939). **I beg of you:** Hobson (1939), p. 496. **under the impression that Herbert Bayard Swope:** cited in Whitfield (1988), p. 137.

Ministry of Public Works in Nazi-ruled Prague: "Fair Defies Nazis on Czech Pavilion," *NYT*, Apr. 14, 1939, p. 1. symbolizes the spirit of freedom: Bernback and Jaffe (1939), p. 49. The German press pointed: "Europe Divided on World's Fair," *NYT*, May 7, 1939, section IV, p. 10. Czecho-slovakia is still alive: "Benes, at Czech pavilion, Says Show Goes On," *NYHT*, Apr. 30, 1939, p. 10.

one of the persistent puzzles: Packard (1959), p. 264. Ford made the *Protocols:* Whitfield (1988), p. 131. catering to gentiles: *Highway Traveler,* April–May 1939. Moderate rates: *The New Yorker,* June 3, 1939.

Jews do not dominate: Bernstein (1939), p. 502.

La Guardia in the city: Harding (1939), p. 198. probably the most admired: Whitfield (1988), p. 136.

probably the first Negro: WPA *Panorama,* p. 260. he invented the terms: see Whitfield (1988), p. 136. brave with a cold, serene: Hemingway (1932), p. 473; puzzled and amazed Spaniards: ibid. p. 199. Nathan Straus turned down: see Caro (1974), p. 353.

23. AT LAST

The Lagoon was four hundred feet by eight hundred: *The New Yorker* ran a cartoon by Helen Hokinson showing an irate lady on the telephone: "*I* was beside the Lagoon of Nations. Where were *you?*" May 13, 1939, p. 29. Who cares what they do?: cited in *NYHT*, NYFW Section, Apr. 30, 1939, p. 6.

24. PARACHUTE JUMP

Instead of a two-way midway: Monaghan (1939), p. 45. Miss Holm and Mr. Weissmuller: Brooks Atkinson, "Billy Rose's Aquacade Opens With a Splash," *NYT*, May 5, 1939, p. 28. perhaps the goose flesh: *The New Yorker,* Oct. 26, 1940, p. 13.

an "energetic and professional" conductor: *The New Yorker,* Apr. 29, 1939.

27. THE VOICE OF THE PERISPHERE

its most unique: Hamlin (1939); see also Harrison's discussion, "The Fair Perceived." Dramatic and indescribable beauty: Harding (1939), p. 199. a young boy in Queens: Melvin Halbert.

28. EPILOGUE: HERE IN UTOPIA

"to work out," in particular: Whalen (1955), p. 174. There is an alternative story: Emmit Crozier: "Five-year history of an idea and a Fair," *NYHT*, NYFW Section, April 30, 1939, p. 2. one hundred some-odd "distinguished leaders": Monaghan (1939), p. 27.

he did not fit at all: "World's Fair Ousts One of its Planners," *NYT*, June 6, 1937, p. 41. Newspapers called him: for example, " 'Father' of Fair never visited it," *NYT*, Oct. 27, 1940, p. 43. a decision on which La Guardia: "World's Fair Space Is 85% 'Spoken For'," *NYT*, Aug. 17, 1937, p. 17.

fair claim to the title: "Mr. Whalen's Image," *Time*, May 1, 1939, p. 72. an excellent administrator: Kent (1936), p. 616.

The Fair will exhibit: quoted in " 'Theme Center' Site Dedicated for World's Fair," *NYHT*, Aug. 17, 1937, p. 17. While other nations of the world: cited in Kessner (1989), p. 437. By God, that is: Caro (1974), p. 654.

the first two million dollars of any Fair profits: Caro (1974), p. 1085, reports that the figure was four million. He may well be right, but all the contemporary sources I can locate say two million. As park enthusiasts: quoted in "Gardens Display Pledged for Park," *NYT*, May 19, 1939, p. 18.

Dust clouds sweeping over Flushing Meadow: Monaghan (1939), p. 34. charitable and scientific purposes: NYWF, Information Manual Entry (Feb. 25, 1939), YCOP.

News reports claimed that ninety percent: *Newsweek*, May 1, 1939, pp. 46ff. Those calculations would have ceded Chinese Manchuria to Japan. Flanigan was said to be: "Mr. Whalen's Image," *Time*, May 1, 1939, pp. 72ff.

probably the greatest and most ambitious: Monaghan (1939), p. 41. "Even now," The *New Yorker* reported; twelve to fourteen hours a day: The *New Yorker*, Apr. 29, 1939, pp. 15-17. The complete picture of the Fair: "La Guardia Sees Success Assured," *NYT*, May 1, 1939. great bellwire; something happened to the electrical system: *NYT*, May 1, 1939, p. 6.

They presented a contrast: "New Economy Moves at Fair Seen in Choice of Banker as Chairman," *NYT* Sept. 1, 1939, p. 12. Buses, touring almost empty: "Fair Closes: Seen by 26,000,000," *NYT*, Nov. 1, 1939, p. 1.

awed country boys like myself: "Synthetic Elmer 1940 Fair Greeter," *NYT*, Apr. 13, 1940, p. 21. The Fair opened with overpowering ceremony: cited in Susman (1980), p. 24. one band of out-of-town visitors: *NYT*, May 1, 1939, p. 6. a beaming, portly, average American: "Synthetic Elmer 1940 Fair

Greeter," *NYT,* Apr. 13, 1940, p. 21. **The families will be selected:** cited in Susman (1980), p. 26.

no expression of regret: "Russia Quits Fair; Finns to Stay," *NYT,* Dec. 2, 1939, p. 1. **over vociferous objections:** "Thanks To Soviets Voted After Row," *NYT,* Nov. 1, 1939, p. 17. **A huge and rather heavy-handed:** "The World's Fair," *The New Yorker,* Oct. 26, 1940, p. 11.

typical of this incomparable: *NYHT,* Oct. 28, 1940, p. 1. **opened with happy hopes:** "Radio Reporters Run Riot on Last Day of N.Y. Fair," *Life,* Nov. 11, 1940, p. 42. **Addressing themselves to Japanese officials; seemed awkwardly conscious: I think we're stopping; Bob Murray, who was in charge; but in many gentler ways:** "Rush as Fair Ends Brings Out 527,839," *NYT,* Oct. 28, 1940, p. 1. **They held out until quarter:** *The New Yorker,* Nov. 2, 1940.

Life will probably always be like that: *The New Yorker,* April 29, 1939, p. 15. **Gardner Harding quoted; a definite breach of faith:** Harding (1939), pp. 196–197. **were cast out of the same racist:** Rydell (1993), p. 157.

There have been complaints: "Mr. Whalen's Image," *Time,* May 1, 1939, p. 72. **Louise Johnson, who presided, declared:** cited in "Harlem Conference Sees 'Discrimination'," *NYT,* May 7, 1939, p. 39.

Back in 1937 Grover Whalen: "World's Fair Bans Bias Against Negroes," *NYT,* Jan. 25, 1937, p. 17. **A panel discussion:** see Kuznick (1994), p. 364.

to help many to a more complete understanding: "Negro Week on the American Common, World's Fair of 1940 in New York," July 23–28 ("souvenir program"), back cover, YCOP. **Capitalizing the term** *Negro:* see Whitfield (1988), p. 136. **The struggle of the ages:** Harry Emerson Fosdick, "Faith for Groping Man," *NYT,* NYWF section, Mar. 5, 1939, p. 31. **great con game:** cited in Kessner (1989), p. 437. **The prominent chemist Harold Urey:** cited in Kuznick (1994), p. 357. **Most of the things which have hurt:** Hamlin (1939), p. 641.

All forms of artistic activity: O'Connor (1980), p. 58. **the nascent consumer culture:** Kuznick (1994), p. 343. **extravagant sums; revelries of corporate capitalism:** Rydell (1993), pp. 116, 118.

The Fair was a carefully contrived: O'Connor (1980), p. 61. **The great car companies:** Kessner (1989), p. 438.

Gardner Harding brings up: Harding (1939), p. 194. **a social message be brought home:** NYWF 1939, Dept of Feature Publicity, "The Theme of the

New York World's Fair of 1939" (undated press release), YCOP, p. 4. **Fair visitors do not read signs:** Gilbert Rhode, "Description and Script of the Community Interests Focal Exhibit at the New York World's Fair 1939, Inc." (Sept. 22, 1938), p. 3, YCOP. **Joseph Wood Krutch:** "Report of the Fair." *The Nation,* June 24, 1939, p. 722.

    General Motors' futuristic paean: Kessner (1989), p. 438. **automobile manufacturers seem to take:** "Motors and Motoring," *The New Yorker,* May 13, 1939, pp. 85–88.

    Since G.M. will sell nothing: "Mr. Whalen's Image," *Time,* May 1, 1939, p. 72.

    A ride through Mr. Geddes' Futurama: *The New Yorker,* May 13, 1939, p. 86.

    gets away from the immediate job: Harding (1939), p. 194 **Obscene is not quite the right word:** Rydell (1993), p. 118. (I agree. It's not quite the right word.)

    not forgetting that: Hudson (1934), p. 3.

    Walter Lippmann on the Futurama: Lippmann, "A Day at the World's Fair" *NYHT,* June 6, 1939, p. 25. **I know of at least five accounts:** Rydell (1993), pp. 115 and 134, Kessner (1989) p. 439, Stern, Gilmartin and Mellins (1987), p. 751, Susman (1980), p. 25, Kuznick (1994) p. 364.

    Robert Moses liked some aspects: "Moses Envisages Future Highways," *NYT* Jan. 21, 1940. **Geddes blasted back:** "Fair's Theme Song Has Its Premiere . . . Geddes Assails Moses," *NYT,* Feb. 3, 1940, p. 9. **to operate profitably:** Geddes (1940), p. 144. **the *Times* was forced:** *NYT* editorial, Jan. 28, 1940, section IV, p. 8.

    Most men lead business lives: Beaton (1938), p. 27.

    probably pretty dull: Hillis (1939), p. 89. **among Stalinist males, I heard:** McCarthy (1992), p. 74.

    belongs to the nineteenth century: Beaton (1938), p. 196.

    The taxi plunges forward: Beaton (1938), p. 9. **greatest city the world has ever seen:** Fay (1936), p. 227.

    By 1940 there must have been: Simon (1981), p. 15. **where society, celebrities; plenty popular, plenty atmosphere:** *New York Day & Night,* 1939 ed., pp. 187, 188. **most famous cabaret nightclub:** Lait and Mortimer (1948), p. 44. **Even the hotels which have no pretension:** Beaton (1938), p. 194. **came in groups at night:** *Survey,* p. iii.

    informal relative: Seaton (1940), p. 95

Bibliography

I list here only those books, scholarly articles and longer magazine articles that are cited explicitly in the text. References to newspaper articles, short magazine articles and New York World's Fair publications, publicity and archival material appear in the notes.

Rarely cited in the text, but underpinning the entire discussion, are the brochures and booklets produced by individual exhibitors. For access to this invaluable material I have relied on the collections of Melvin Halbert, Walter Chestnut and Yale University (the Century of Progress Collection), and on my own material.

Please consult the preface for a brief big-picture discussion of the bibliography of the fair.

AHLSTROM, SYDNEY E. *A Religious History of the American People.* New Haven, Conn.: Yale University Press, 1972.

BARRETT, MARY ELLIN. *Irving Berlin: A Daughter's Memoir.* New York: Simon and Schuster, 1994.

BEATON, CECIL. *Cecil Beaton's New York.* Philadelphia: Lippincott, 1938.

BENCHLEY, ROBERT. 20,000 Leagues Under the Sea or David Copperfield. New York: Blue Ribbon Books, 1928.

BERNBACH, WILLIAM, AND HERMAN JAFFE. *Book of Nations* (Auspices of Foreign Government Commissioners [NYWF 1939]; New York: Winkler and Kelmans, 1939.

BERNSTEIN, PHILIP S. "Some Facts About Jews." *Harper's,* vol. 178 (Dec. 1938–May 1939), pp. 501–506.

CARO, ROBERT A. *The Power Broker: Robert Moses and the Fall of New York.* New York: Alfred Knopf, 1974; Vintage Books ed., 1975.

CHURCHILL, WINSTON S. *The Gathering Storm.* Boston: Houghton Mifflin, 1948.

COMMITTEE FOR FEDERAL WRITERS' PUBLICATIONS, *New York Panorama,* New York: Random House, 1938.

COMMITTEE FOR FEDERAL WRITERS' PUBLICATIONS, *New York City Guide.* New York: Random House, 1939.

CORN, JOSEPH J., ed. *Imagining Tomorrrow: History, Technology, and the American Future.* Cambridge, Mass.: MIT Press, 1986.

CUNEO, ERNEST. *Life with Fiorello.* New York: Macmillan, 1955.

CUSKER, JOSEPH P. "The World of Tomorrow: Science, Culture and Community at the New York World's Fair." In Helen A. Harrison, ed., *Dawn of a New Day.* New York: New York University Press, 1980.

DAIX, PIERRE. *Picasso: Life and Art.* New York: HarperCollins, 1993.

DERKS, SCOTT. *The Value of a Dollar: Prices and Incomes in the United States, 1860–1989.* Detroit: Gale Research, 1994.

DIEHL, LORRAINE B. *The Late, Great Pennsylvania Station.* New York: American Heritage Press, 1985.

DOBRINER, WILLIAM M., ed. *The Suburban Community.* New York: G.P. Putnam's, 1958.

DOS PASSOS, JOHN. *The Big Money.* New York: Random House/Modern Library, 1937.

FAY, E. STEWART. *Londoner's New York.* London: Methuen, 1936.

FITZGERALD, F. SCOTT. *The Last Tycoon.* New York: Charles Scribner's Sons, 1941.

FLINK, JAMES J. *The Automobile Age.* Cambridge, Mass.: MIT Press, 1988.

FRANKLIN, JAY. *La Guardia: A Biography.* New York: Modern Age Books, 1937.

FRANKS, LUCINDA. "Little Big People." *NYT Sunday Magazine,* Oct. 10, 1993, pp. 28–34.

BIBLIOGRAPHY

FRIEDEL, FRANK. *Franklin D. Roosevelt: A Rendezvous with Destiny* New York: Little, Brown, 1990.

GALLUP, GEORGE H. The Gallup Poll: Public Opinion, 1935–1971. Vol 1, *1935–1948*. New York: Random House, 1972.

GEDDES, NORMAN BEL. *Magic Motorways.* New York: Random House, 1940.

GREEN, HARVEY. *The Uncertainty of Everyday Life, 1915–1945.* New York: HarperCollins, 1992.

GREIF, MARTIN. *Depression Modern: The Thirties Style in America.* New York: Universe Books, 1975.

HAMLIN, TALBOT. "World's Fairs, 1939 Model." *Pencil Points,* Nov. 1938, pp. 673–685.

———. "Some Fair Comparisons." *Pencil Points,* Oct. 1939, pp. 641–648.

HARDING, GARDNER. *"World's Fair, New York." Harper's,* vol. 179 (June–Nov. 1939), pp. 193–200.

HARRISON, HELEN A., ed. *Dawn of a New Day: The New York World's Fair, 1939/40.* New York: New York University Press, 1980.

———. "The Fair Perceived: Color and Light as Elements in Design and Planning." In Helen A. Harrison, ed. *Dawn of a New Day: New York World's Fair, 1939/40.* New York: New York University Press, 1980, pp. 43–56.

———. *"Catalogue of the Exhibit."* In Helen A. Harrison, ed. *Dawn of a New Day: New York World's Fair, 1939/40.* New York: New York University Press, 1980, pp. 73–120.

HASKELL, DOUGLAS. "To-morrow and the World's Fair." *Architectural Record,* Aug. 1940.

HEIMS, STEVE J. *John von Neumann and Norbert Wiener: From Mathematics to the Technologies of Life and Death.* Cambridge, Mass.: MIT Press, 1980; paperback ed. 1982.

HEMINGWAY, ERNEST. *Death in the Afternoon.* New York: Charles Scribner's Sons, 1932; Reprint, 1960.

HERZSTEIN, ROBERT E. *Henry R. Luce, A Political Portrait of The Man Who Created The American Century.* New York: Macmillan, 1994.

HILLIS, MARJORIE. *New York: Fair or No Fair.* New York: Bobbs-Merrill, 1939.

HILTON, TIMOTHY. *Picasso.* New York: Thames and Hudson, 1985.

HIMMELFARB, GERTRUDE. *On Looking into the Abyss.* New York: Alfred A. Knopf, 1994.

HIRSCHORN, PAUL, and STEVEN IZENOUR. *White Towers.* Cambridge, Mass.: MIT Press; paperback ed., 1981.

HOBSON, LAURA Z. "The Freedom Pavilion." *The Nation,* Apr. 29, 1939, pp. 492–498.

HUDSON, ROBERT B. *Radburn: A Plan of Living.* New York: American Association of Adult Education by Little and Ives Co., 1934.

JACKSON, KENNETH T. *Crabgrass Frontier: The Suburbanization of the United States.* New York: Oxford University Press, 1985.

JOHNSON, PAUL. "God and the Americans." *Commentary,* vol. 99 (Jan. 1995), pp. 25–45.

KAZIN, ALFRED. *Starting Out in the Thirties.* Ithaca, N.Y.: Cornell Paperbacks ed. 1989.

KENT, RICHARD. "World's Fair at New York: Its Theme and Its Designers." *Pencil Points,* Nov. 1936, pp. 609–617.

KESSNER, THOMAS. *Fiorello H. La Guardia and the Making of Modern New York.* New York: McGraw-Hill, 1989.

———. "Fiorello H. La Guardia and the Challenge of Democratic Planning." In David Ward and Olivier Zunz, eds. *The Landscape of Modernity: Essays on New York City, 1900–1940.* New York: Russell Sage Foundation, 1992, pp. 315–330.

KIHLSTEDT, FOLKE T. "Utopia Realized: The World's Fairs in the 1930's." In Joseph J. Corn, ed., *Imagining Tomorrow: History, Technology, and the American Future,* Cambridge, Mass.: MIT Press, 1986, pp. 97–116.

KUZNICK, PETER J. "Losing the World of Tomorrow: The Battle over the Presentation of Science at the 1939 New York World's Fair." *American Quarterly,* 46, no. 3 (Sept. 1994), pp. 341–373.

LAIT, JACK, and LEE MORTIMER. *New York: Confidential!* Chicago: Ziff-Davis, 1948.

LEUCHTENBURG, WILLIAM E. *Franklin D. Roosevelt and the New Deal.* New York: Harper Torchbooks ed., 1963.

LIEBLING, A. J. *Back Where I Came From.* Sheridan House, 1938. Reprint, San Francisco: North Point Press, 1990.

LIMPUS, LOWELL M., and BURR W. LEYSON. *This Man La Guardia.* New York: E.P. Dutton, 1938.

LINGEMAN, R. R. *Don't You Know There's a War On?* New York: G.P. Putnam's, 1970.

MCCARTHY, MARY. *The Company She Keeps.* 1939. Reprint, New York: Harvest, 1970.

BIBLIOGRAPHY

——. *Intellectual Memoirs: New York 1936–1938.* New York: Harcourt Brace, 1992. Harvest Ed., 1993.

MOLEY, RAYMOND. *27 Masters of Politics.* New York: Funk and Wagnalls, 1940.

MONAGHAN, FRANK, ed. *New York: The World's Fair City.* Garden City, NY: Garden City Publishing Co., 1937.

——. *New York World's Fair 1939.* Rev. ed. Chicago: Encylopaedia Britannica, 1939.

MORRIS, EDMUND. *The Rise of Theodore Roosevelt.* New York: Coward, McCann & Geoghegan, 1979.

MOSES, ROBERT. *What's the Matter with New York?* New York: N.P., 1943.

——. *Working for the People.* New York: Harper, 1956.

——. *La Guardia, A Salute and A Memoir.* New York: Simon & Schuster, 1957.

MUELLER, JOHN. *Astaire Dancing: The Musical Films.* New York: Wings Books, 1985.

MUMFORD, LEWIS. *The Culture of Cities.* New York: Harcourt Brace, 1938.

NEWHOUSE, VICTORIA. *Wallace K. Harrison, Architect.* New York: Rizzoli, 1989.

NISBET, ROBERT. *Prejudices: A Philosophical Dictionary.* Cambridge, Mass.: Harvard University Press, 1982.

O'CONNOR, FRANCIS V. "The Usable Future: The Role of Fantasy in the Promotion of a Consumer Society for Art." In Helen A. Harrison, ed. *Dawn of a New Day: The New York World's Fair, 1939/40.* New York: New York University Press, 1980, pp. 57–72.

PACKARD, VANCE: *The Status Seekers.* New York: David McKay, 1959.

PHILLIPS, CABELL. *From the Crash to the Blitz, 1929–1939.* New York: Macmillan, 1969.

POST, EMILY. *Etiquette.* New York: Funk and Wagnalls, 1937.

POST, ELIZABETH L. *Emily Post's Etiquette.* New York: HarperCollins, 1992.

RANKIN, REBECCA B., ed. *New York Advancing: World's Fair Edition.* New York: Publisher's Printing Co., 1939.

RIESENBERG, FELIX, and ALEXANDER ALLAND. *Portrait of New York.* New York: Macmillan, 1939.

RYDELL, ROBERT W. *World of Fairs: The Century-of-Progress Expositions.* Chicago: University of Chicago Press, 1993.

SANTOMASSO, EUGENE A. "The Design of Reason: Architecture and Planning at the 1939/40 New York World's Fair." In Helen A. Harrison, ed., *Dawn of a New Day: The New York World's Fair, 1939/40.* New York: New York University Press, 1980, pp. 29–42.

SCHLESINGER, ARTHUR M. *The Coming of the New Deal.* Boston: Houghton Mifflin, 1958; American Heritage Library ed., NY, 1988.

——. *The Disuniting of America: Reflections of a Multicultural Society.* New York: Norton paperback ed., 1993.

SCHWARTZ, CHARLES. *Gershwin, His Life and Music.* New York: Bobbs-Merrill, 1973. Reprint, New York: Da Capo Press, 1979.

SCHWARTZ, DELMORE. "On Poetry in the Age." In Robert Lowell, Peter Taylor, and Robert Penn Warren (eds.), *Randall Jarrell, 1914–1965.* New York: Noonday Press, 1968, pp. 188–192.

SEATON, GEORGE W. *Cue's Guide to New York City.* New York: Prentice-Hall, 1940.

SILVER, NATHAN. *Lost New York.* Boston: Houghton Mifflin, 1967.

SIMON, GEORGE T. *The Big Bands.* 4th ed. New York: Schirmer, 1981.

STARR, ROGER. *The Rise and Fall of New York City.* New York: Basic Books, 1985.

STERN, ROBERT A. M., GREGORY GILMARTIN and THOMAS MELLINS. *New York 1930: Architecture and Urbanism between the Two World Wars.* New York: Rizzoli, 1987.

STILGOE, JOHN R. *Borderland: Origins of the American Suburb, 1820–1939.* New Haven, Conn.: Yale University Press, 1988.

SUSMAN, WARREN I., ed. *Culture and Commitment 1929–1945.* New York: Braziller, 1973.

——. "The People's Fair: Cultural Contradictions of a Consumer Society." In Helen A. Harrison, ed., *Dawn of a New Day: The New York World's Fair, 1939/40.* New York: New York University Press, 1980, pp. 17–28.

——. *Culture as History.* New York: Pantheon Books, 1984.

TAYLOR, WILLIAM R. *In Pursuit of Gotham: Culture and Commerce in New York.* New York: Oxford University Press, 1992.

TEAGUE, WALTER DORWIN. *Design This Day.* New York: Harcourt, Brace, 1940.

TRILLING, DIANA. *The Beginning of the Journey: The Marriage of Diana and Lionel Trilling.* New York: Harcourt Brace, 1993.

TRILLING, LIONEL. *The Middle of the Journey.* New York: Viking Press, 1947.

WARD, GEOFFREY C. *A First-Class Temperament: The Emergence of Franklin Roosevelt.* New York: Harper & Row, 1989.

BIBLIOGRAPHY

WATTEL, HAROLD. "Levittown: A Suburban Community." In William M. Dobriner, ed. *The Suburban Community*. New York: G.P. Putnam's, 1958, pp. 287–316.

WENDT, GERALD. *Science for the World of Tomorrow*. New York: Norton, 1939.

WHALEN, GROVER. *Mr. New York*. New York: G.P. Putnam's Sons, 1955.

WHITE, E. B. *One Man's Meat*. New York: Harper & Row, 1944.

———. *The Second Tree from the Corner*. New York: Harper & Row, 1984; Perennial Lib. ed., 1989.

———. *Writings from the New Yorker, 1927–1976*. New York: HarperCollins, 1990, Harper Perennial ed., 1991.

WHITE, NORVAL, and ELLIOT WILLENSKY, *AIA Guide to New York City*. Rev. ed., New York: Macmillan, 1978.

WHITFIELD, STEPHEN J. *American Space, Jewish Time*. Hamden, Conn.: Archon Books, 1988.

WILLIAMS, J. PAUL, *What Americans Believe and How They Worship*, 3d ed. New York: Harper and Row, 1969.

WILSON, RICHARD GUY, DIANNE H. PILGRIM and DICKRAN TASHJIAN, *The Machine Age*. New York: Brooklyn Museum in association with Harry N. Abrams, 1986.

WRESZIN, MICHAEL. *A Rebel in Defense of Tradition: The Life and Politics of Dwight Macdonald*. New York: Basic Books, 1994.

Index

Note: Only strictly non-fictional parts of the text are indexed.